PLA INFLUENCE ON CHINA'S NATIONAL SECURITY POLICYMAKING

PLA INFLUENCE ON CHINA'S NATIONAL SECURITY POLICYMAKING

Edited by Phillip C. Saunders
and Andrew Scobell

Stanford Security Studies
An Imprint of Stanford University Press
Stanford, California

Stanford University Press
Stanford, California

Printed in the United States of America on acid-free, archival-quality paper

Library of Congress Cataloging-in-Publication Data

PLA influence on China's national security policy-making / edited by Phillip C.
Saunders and Andrew Scobell.
    pages cm
    Includes bibliographical references and index.
    ISBN 978-0-8047-9462-6 (cloth : alk. paper)
    ISBN 978-0-8047-9625-5 (pbk. : alk. paper)
    1. China. Zhongguo ren min jie fang jun—Political activity. 2. National security—
China. 3. China—Military policy. 4. Civil-military relations—China. 5. China—
Foreign relations—21st century. 6. China—Politics and government—21st century.
I. Saunders, Phillip C. (Phillip Charles), 1966– editor. II. Scobell, Andrew, editor.
UA837.P57 2015
355'.033551—dc23

                                                                    2015005332

ISBN 978-0-8047-9628-6 (electronic)

The editors dedicate this book to our mothers (Loni Saunders and Myrtle Scobell), wives (Julie Hayne and Michele Bulatovic), and daughters (Linnea Claire Saunders and Sophia Scobell), with love and thanks for all they have taught us.

Contents

Acknowledgments

THE BOOK GREW OUT OF A CONFERENCE ON "THE PLA's Role in National Security Policy-Making" co-sponsored by Taiwan's Council of Advanced Policy Studies (CAPS), RAND, the Carnegie Endowment for International Peace (CEIP), and National Defense University (NDU). The editors gratefully acknowledge the intellectual contributions of co-organizers Arthur Shu-fan Ding (then at CAPS, now at Chengchi University's Institute of International Relations) and Michael Swaine (CEIP) in shaping the agenda and recruiting paper writers, discussants, and panelists, and securing the financial support of the four sponsoring organizations.

Conference participants Ken Allen, Jean-Pierre Cabestan, Chia-sheng Chen, Roger Cliff, Bernard Cole, Cortez Cooper, Scott Harold, Alexander Huang, Brian Lafferty, Chong-pin Lin, Kim Taeho, Ma Chengkun, Cheng-ting Tsai, Shinji Yamaguchi, and Suisheng Zhao all provided comments or participated in discussions that improved the chapters in this book. Andrew Nien-Dzu Yang, Yi-su Yang, and Polly Shen (CAPS), Cortez Cooper, Scott Harold, and Lyle Morris (RAND), and Michael Glosny, Isaac Kardon, Deborah Jefferson, and Don Mosser (NDU) all provided support in organizing the original conference.

The editors thank the two anonymous reviewers who provided much useful advice in shaping the book and updating the individual chapters. Molly Murphy and Deborah Jefferson provided assistance in the legal and administrative aspects of publishing this book. Joseph Kettel helped produce summaries of the chapters for the introduction. Drew Casey provided invaluable assistance in reformatting the chapters, tracking down stray references, and standardizing the English and Chinese language endnotes.

Geoffrey Burn and James Holt at Stanford University Press deserve special thanks for guiding the book through the approval and publication process.

PLA INFLUENCE ON CHINA'S NATIONAL SECURITY POLICYMAKING

Introduction: PLA Influence on China's National Security Policymaking

Phillip C. Saunders and Andrew Scobell

IN RECENT YEARS, THE MEDIA HAVE FREQUENTLY reported on actions purportedly taken by People's Liberation Army (PLA) units without civilian authorization and examples of senior Chinese Communist Party (CCP) civilian leaders seeking to curry favor with the military. Some analysts credit a nationalistic and increasingly influential PLA with pushing Chinese civilian leaders into more assertive policies on a range of military and sovereignty issues.[1] Retired officers such as Major General Luo Yuan and military academics such as Air Force Senior Colonel Dai Xu are prolific writers and frequent guests on Chinese television programs, often spewing hardline, nationalistic positions on military and foreign policy issues. These stories and activities give the impression of a Chinese military that is exerting increasing influence across a wide range of policy issues.[2]

Many China scholars and Chinese military specialists have a very different impression of PLA influence on Chinese policymaking. Applying a historical perspective, many note that CCP and PLA leaders fought together in the Chinese civil war, with civilian leaders such as Mao Zedong and Deng Xiaoping making important military contributions and military officers playing important roles in civilian positions after the founding of the People's Republic of China (PRC) in 1949. None of today's PLA leaders has the political stature of Marshal Peng Dehuai, who dared to criticize Mao's Great Leap Forward at the 1959 Lushan conference (for which he was purged), or Marshal Lin Biao, who edited Mao's Little Red Book and may have mounted a coup attempt in 1971.

The Chinese military clearly plays a much smaller role in politics today than it did in 1968 during the Cultural Revolution, when Mao called on the PLA to suppress the Red Guard movement and restore order.[3]

Moreover, numerous examples exist of supposedly weak CCP civilian leaders intruding in the military domain to impose decisions that go against the institutional interests of some or all of the PLA. These include major military personnel reductions in 1985, 1997, and 2003; Jiang Zemin's 1998 decision to force the PLA to divest most of its extensive business empire; requiring the PLA to participate in ideological campaigns against the Falungong movement and to study the "three represents" and the "scientific development concept"; curtailing privileges of PLA officers as part of General Secretary Xi Jinping's current austerity campaign; and corruption investigations of senior PLA officers, including the ongoing investigation into former Central Military Commission (CMC) Vice-Chairman Xu Caihou. Civilian leaders have reportedly rebuffed PLA efforts to regain a seat on the Politburo Standing Committee (PBSC), the highest CCP decisionmaking body, and rejected PLA Navy efforts to gain control of maritime paramilitary forces.[4] Although the membership and responsibilities of China's new National Security Commission are not yet clearly delineated, civilian leaders reportedly overrode long-standing PLA opposition to the creation of such a body.[5]

To most experienced PLA watchers (and to PLA officers), reports of the Chinese military acting on its own without orders from civilian party leaders bear no resemblance to reality.[6] Despite the existence of civil-military tensions, the PLA remains a "party-army" that is responsive to orders from the Communist Party (via the party's CMC) rather than from the Chinese state (e.g., the State Council and the National People's Congress). One veteran observer of Chinese military and foreign policy issues noted that during his long career he had never seen a case where civilian party leaders told the PLA to do something and the PLA did not do it or where civilian party leaders told the PLA not to do something and the PLA did it anyway.[7] This book seeks to move beyond speculation and newspaper headlines to an in-depth examination of the PLA's role in national security policymaking.

Civil-Military Relations

The military's role in policymaking is a subset of the broader field of civil-military relations.[8] The central challenge in civil-military relations is for civilian leaders to build a capable, effective military that can defend the state against external enemies and internal rebellions, while simultaneously ensuring that the military remains responsive to civilian orders and does not use its control of the means of violence to threaten the civil order. Political scientist Samuel Huntington distinguished between *subjective control* and *objective control*.[9] Subjective control involves a military that is integrated with society and an active participant in the political system. Civilian control is accomplished by shared values and beliefs, which reduce tensions between civilian and military leaders. In the Chinese case, this involves shared belief in Marxist-Leninist ideology, including Mao's dictum that "the party must always control the gun." Objective control involves military and civilian leaders with differentiated responsibilities and expertise. Because professional military leaders have different experiences, values, and perspectives than their civilian masters, civilian leaders must develop effective oversight and control mechanisms to ensure that the military remains responsive to civilian orders.

Civil-military relations in China are different from those in Western countries because the PLA is a "party-army" that responds to orders from the CCP rather than a "state-army" that responds to orders from the head of the government. Although this arrangement closely resembles the one employed in the Soviet Union and other communist countries, it differs from Western models and affects the PLA's role in policymaking because the premier cannot directly order the PLA to obey government decisions. Traditionally, CCP leaders have employed a mix of objective and subjective mechanisms to control the PLA, with many of the control mechanisms operating through party channels (such as party committees within PLA organizations and uniformed political commissars throughout the military).[10] There is a historic tension between "red" (politically reliable) and "expert" (professionally capable), with the CCP insisting on a military that is "both red and expert."

Four trends have reshaped civil-military relations in China and affected the PLA's role in policymaking. The first is *gradual erosion of elite belief in Marxist ideology*. After the collapse of communism in the Soviet Union and thirty years of market-oriented reforms, Marx's writings are no longer seen as providing useful answers to concrete problems in China's governance and economic development.[11] Declining faith in Marxism reduces the shared values and beliefs that helped reinforce subjective control of the military. CCP leaders have cultivated nationalism as a partial substitute for Marxist-Leninist ideology. But nationalism provides independent criteria for judging the performance of civilian leaders (are they achieving nationalist goals?), not an automatic endorsement of their right to rule.

The second trend is *increased emphasis on professional expertise within the PLA*. This parallels broader developments in China, where professional knowledge and formal educational credentials are increasingly important. Emphasis on professional expertise is evident in the PLA's efforts to upgrade the technical skills of officers and soldiers in order to operate more sophisticated equipment and conduct more complicated operations.[12] Science and technology are stressed at Chinese military academies, coupled with efforts to recruit and retain graduates from civilian universities with specific technical skills. The PLA now endorses professional military education (PME) as a requirement for promotion and assignment to senior positions. Emphasis on improving the quality of personnel is coupled with revised doctrinal and training materials that delineate a body of specialized knowledge military officers must master and increased emphasis on military training to raise combat effectiveness.[13] Discussions with PLA officers and study of PLA writings indicate that a sense of the military's special responsibility for national security is widespread within the PLA. The extent to which PLA officers possess a strong sense of a separate, corporate identity is harder to assess, but contacts with senior and mid-level officers in a variety of settings certainly give the impression that they do. Military professionalism gives the PLA the basis for offering an independent institutional military perspective on many national security issues.

The third trend is the *bifurcation of civilian and military elites*. China's revolutionary leaders served as military commanders or political commissars or were civilian cadres who worked closely with military officers. Shared revolutionary experiences forged enduring bonds between civilian and military elites. Even as they took on more specialized roles in the postrevolutionary period, civilian leaders still intervened in military affairs when necessary and many military leaders retained independent political standing within the party. This "dual-role elite" obscured the line between civilian and military leaders.[14] However, the almost four decades since Mao's death in 1976 have witnessed a bifurcation of Chinese political and military elites.[15] China's current top civilian leaders have little military experience or knowledge and lack the extensive shared experiences and ties with military leaders that characterized the revolutionary generation. (Xi Jinping, who spent three years early in his career as personal secretary to then-Defense Minister Geng Biao, is a rare exception, and even Xi's experience pales in comparison to that of leaders from the founding generation of the People's Republic.)

Elite bifurcation is reinforced by increasingly separate civilian and military career paths. China's civilian leaders make their careers on the basis of educational credentials, technical knowledge, management experience, family and political connections, and/or political skills. Conversely, China's current top military leaders are educated almost exclusively in military institutions, spend their early careers within a single military region, and have limited opportunities to interact with top political leaders until they attain positions in Beijing or are elected to positions in the Central Committee.[16] Coupled with an increasing sense of professional responsibility and a corporate identity as military officers, the result is an increasing separation between civilian and military elites.

A fourth trend is *reduced PLA representation in core CCP decisionmaking bodies* over the past twenty-five years. Alice Miller notes in her chapter that the "reduction in military representation on the party's Politburo and its Standing Committee appears part of a deliberate effort engineered by Deng Xiaoping in the 1980s to establish an effective collective leadership system that builds in checks and balances among the leadership oligarchy against attempts by any individual member—and especially by the party general secretary—to assert dominating power over the others." As a result, the PLA has been locked out of the PBSC since 1997. Notably, the last uniformed member of the PBSC was Admiral Liu Huaqing, who was probably the most influential military figure in the post-Mao reform era. Since his retirement no single senior PLA leader has wielded anything close to that kind of power. PLA interests are represented on the PBSC by the CCP general secretary, who is usually also the CMC chairman. Miller argues that this arrangement is intended to channel and limit military influence, including by reducing the PLA's ability to play civilian PBSC members off against each other and by limiting the potential for top civilian leaders to use alliances with the military against each other.

Since 1992 the PLA has been represented on the twenty-five person Politburo by two military CMC vice-chairmen; currently these two seats are held by Army General Fan Changlong and Air Force General Xu Qiliang, selected at the Eighteenth CCP Congress held in November 2012. Forty-one of the 205 seats on the CCP Central Committee are filled by PLA officers. Uniformed personnel participate in the National Party Congress and plenums, and also serve as delegates in China's legislature, the National People's Congress. In addition, some active and retired officers serve on the Chinese People's Political Consultative Conference. PLA representation on these bodies has declined significantly since its peak in the 1970s but has held steady since the late 1980s; PLA officers now routinely make up about 9 percent of delegates. Military representatives occupied 268 of 2,986 seats at the Twelfth National People's Congress held in March 2013.

How the diverging backgrounds, experiences, and responsibilities of China's civilian and military leaders affect the PLA's role in national security policymaking is not clear-cut. The relatively limited exposure of civilian leaders to national security issues until the late stages of their careers and the military's increasing focus on technical and professional expertise suggest that the two groups may differ in priorities and perspectives on at least some issues. Relatively limited contact between Chinese civilian and military leaders (most of which occurs in formal settings) may also limit trust and mutual confidence. On the one hand this can present challenges because it produces a divide akin to the civil-military "gap" identified in the United States at the turn-of-the century between civilian political leaders and their military counterparts.[17] The resulting chasm in terms of an absence of civilian knowledge of and experience with military matters can produce contrasting values and mindsets. Indeed, one senior PLA academic has privately observed that the lack of military expertise and background among China's civilian leaders is a significant problem.[18] On the other hand, this "gap" can serve to enhance the influence and power of PLA leaders because they possess a monopoly of expert knowledge of national security policy and defense issues. China has yet to see the emergence of a critical mass of civilian defense intellectuals in think tanks and academia of the sort who have been a fixture in the United States since the 1950s. Other than the CMC chairman, no Chinese civilians hold high-level leadership positions in offices at the CMC or in China's Ministry of National Defense.[19]

Two Approaches to Assessing PLA Policy Influence

Existing studies of the PLA's influence on policymaking raise more questions than answers. Conclusions about the growing influence of the Chinese military are necessarily tentative given that they are invariably based on limited evidence and/or academic overviews. More in-depth work is needed, particularly scholarship with more attention to methodological rigor and a focus on case studies.[20] A combination of two approaches may prove useful to assessing how much influence the military is likely to have on a particular national security issue. The first focuses on the nature of the issue under consideration, which affects where decisions on that issue are made within the Chinese system and what role the PLA plays in advising on or participating in those decisions. The second considers the overall policy process, focusing on the PLA's ability to influence the various stages in the policy process. Each is considered in turn.

The Nature of the Issue

Different types of policy issues are decided in different places in the Chinese system. It is useful to think of a spectrum of policy issues ranging from the purely military (doctrine, training, operations) to the purely political (selection of party civilian leadership, ideological themes and campaigns). In between is a vast middle ground where neither professional military judgments nor ideological guidance from civilian CCP leaders dictate clear policy outcomes. On mixed issues that involve both civilian and military equities, the PLA is one of many PRC actors seeking to influence policy, either through formal participation in the policy process or by indirectly shaping the broader policy debate.

Formal PRC policymaking structures and processes give the PLA a privileged role on purely military issues, which are usually handled within the CMC or under its supervision. Tai Ming Cheung's chapter in this volume illuminates the CMC's structure and functions, which appear to combine the advisory and coordination roles of a leading small group (LSG) with decisionmaking authority on most military issues. The most important military decisions likely are elevated to the PBSC for collective decisions. However, the Third Plenum reform decisions announced in October 2013, which cover a wide range of political, economic, government, and military issues, were approved by the CCP Central Committee rather than the CMC. This may have been simply a matter of packaging military reforms prepared by the CMC with those in other areas, but shifting the decisionmaking venue from the military-dominated CMC to the Central Committee may also have reduced PLA influence on the content of the military reforms.

As a party-army, the PLA reports directly to the CCP general secretary in his role as CMC chairman. The CMC vice-chairmen, and to some extent other CMC members, therefore have direct access to the top CCP civilian leader.

This arrangement provides considerable institutional independence, since the PLA does not report to the premier (who is in charge of civilian ministries). Isaac Kardon and Phillip Saunders argue in their chapter that it is easiest for CCP civilian leaders to reach into the military domain on issues where the PLA is divided and there are military supporters for the desired action. For example, some senior PLA leaders have supported downsizing of the ground forces as a means of funding modernization and viewed divestment of PLA business interests as necessary to combat corruption and refocus the PLA on military concerns. Conversely, civilian leaders may have more difficulty intervening in military issues where the PLA is unified in supporting clear institutional interests, such as military budgets and respect for the PLA as an institution.

The PLA's professional expertise, monopoly on classified military information, and ability to develop military plans, doctrine, policy options, and draft-policy guidance give it considerable autonomy over purely military issues and a degree of influence on foreign policy issues with a significant military dimension. Military secrecy about PLA capabilities and operations makes it hard for outsiders (including civilian ministries) to influence decisions on military issues or even to know what the PLA is doing. China's modest, but slowly increasing levels of military transparency limit the availability and credibility of alternative civilian analysis of military issues.[21] In some cases, such as recent debates on military-to-military relations with the United States, CCP leaders have commissioned alternative reports from civilian think tanks to provide additional options and policy analysis beyond that provided by PLA experts.[22] These institutional advantages help explain long-standing PLA resistance to a national security commission structure, which would likely require sharing more information with civilians and reduce PLA autonomy and policy influence.[23]

Conversely, the decline in PLA representation in CCP core decisionmaking bodies and increased institutionalization of the political succession process appear to have significantly reduced the PLA's role in political issues such as the selection and promotion of China's top civilian leaders. PLA officers, acting in their capacities as Central Committee members, are involved in formally ratifying top civilian leaders who have been chosen beforehand in a top-down process where the military wields little influence.[24] PLA delegates to the National People's Congress used to issue proposals and suggestions on social and economic policy, but now focus their attention on security and military issues.²⁵ On ideological issues, the PLA (including its General Political Department, which supervises political commissars and evaluates officers for political reliability), takes guidance from civilian party officials and disseminates it throughout the military. Political campaigns such as current austerity and anticorruption efforts are implemented within the PLA, but do not originate there. The PLA's ideological role is limited to repeating political slogans, reiterating its loyalty to the party, and translating CCP political guidance into language understandable to troops.

When policy issues involve broader economic, foreign policy, or national security concerns, decisions are usually made in party, government, or PBSC settings where the PLA has fewer institutional advantages.²⁶ The PLA has ex officio representation in the LSGs for foreign affairs, Taiwan affairs, and national security affairs and is also represented in a variety of interagency groups and task forces that coordinate Chinese policy in various issue areas.²⁷ However, the PLA is only one of many government and party actors attempting to influence policy on these issues, and must compete for influence within a more pluralistic decisionmaking process.²⁸ Nevertheless, the PLA can bring significant assets to bear in these policy debates, especially on issues with a significant military dimension. The PLA enjoys formal channels of access to the senior CCP leader (in his capacity as CMC chair), control of classified military intelligence and information about Chinese military capabilities and operations, a near-monopoly of expertise on military issues, bureaucratic independence from the state structure, and representation in many formal policymaking and advisory bodies. The salience of these assets varies across issue areas, but is important when the PLA is competing with other actors to influence policy decisions. Mixed civil-military issues are increasingly important to the PLA given the geographic and functional expansion of Chinese national interests (which imply a corresponding expansion of PLA missions and responsibilities) and the fact that efforts to build a capable modern military require access to advanced technologies, expertise, and resources from the civilian sector. This produces incentives for the PLA to organize, lobby potential supporters, and seek to shape the broader debate in order to increase its policy influence.

The evolution of Chinese policymaking in a more pluralistic direction provides the PLA additional informal and indirect channels to influence policy, even when final decisions are made in closed-door settings.²⁹ The PLA can potentially play on the increased sensitivity of the CCP leadership to public opinion and nationalist criticism to indirectly shape policy via media appearances and publications.[30] These efforts to shape policy provide a window into PLA views, though the opinions of PLA academics and retired officers are not necessarily authoritative indicators of the views of senior PLA officers. Of course, CCP leaders can empower or restrict the PLA's role in policy debates. The PLA has the most authority to speak when it is offering advice on the best means of pursuing goals that CCP leaders have endorsed (such as defending China's maritime territorial claims or deterring Taiwan independence). This gives the PLA incentives to try to shape the articulation of those goals in ways that serve its interests. Sometimes, as after the accidental bombing of the Chinese embassy in 1999, the CCP leadership will allow a public debate to proceed and then shut it down once a policy decision has been reached.[31] CCP leaders can also rein in PLA experts who are offering unwanted views, either by ordering them to stop writing about an issue or by formally reiterating official policy in a way that closes off debate.[32]

Many Chinese analysts emphasize the potential impact of family, personal, and factional ties between senior PLA officers and the CMC chairman as important informal channels for PLA policy influence. Such ties do exist, though they are likely less significant than in the Mao and Deng era. On the other hand, as Nan Li shows in his chapter, Xi Jinping appears to have both more personal authority and stronger ties with the military than his predecessors Hu Jintao and Jiang Zemin.[33] Although CCP leaders are somewhat responsive to PLA institutional concerns, the ability of the CMC chairman to determine which officers are promoted to senior positions is a powerful tool of influence.

The Policy Process

A second approach emphasizes the PLA's role at different stages of the policy process, from broad definitions of the nature of the international security environment, to framing specific policy problems and potential options, to advocacy of specific policies at key decision points, and then implementing the party's decision and providing feedback on the results. The PLA exercises influence in different ways at various steps in the process, and its ability to exert influence may vary depending on the type of issue at play. It is helpful to think in terms of three phases of the policy process: a *pre-decision phase*, which involves assessing the international environment, building capabilities that expand policy options, and defining the specific policy problem; a *decision phase*, which involves formulating and assessing alternative options and choosing a policy response; and an *implementation phase*, where various actors implement the policy decision and assess the results. This broader conception of the policy process highlights different ways the PLA can exert policy influence.

Pre-Decision Phase   **Assessments of the International Security Environment**: Official assessments of the international security environment identify potential national security problems and highlight appropriate responses; they also set implicit policy priorities by offering authoritative judgments on issues such as whether war is likely or whether "peace and development" remains the "trend of the times." Such assessments matter because Chinese discourse on security issues stresses that China is "forced" to respond to hostile actions of others or to react to negative trends in the international security environment. For example, then-PLA Air Force Commander General Xu Qiliang argued in a November 2009 interview that deployment of space weapons was a "historical inevitability"; an official assessment to that effect makes it easier to argue that China must also deploy space weapons.[34] PLA academics and intelligence analysts have opportunities to shape official CCP assessments through their analytical writings and their participation in drafting sessions for documents such as the National Party Congress work report and defense white papers.

Intelligence Collection and Analysis: Chinese intelligence collection and analysis can shape both broad attitudes of Chinese policymakers and specific judgments about unfolding events. Chinese intelligence analysis sometimes includes specific policy recommendations, so intelligence reporting and analysis can have a policy impact that goes beyond the details in reports. Because China has lacked a centralized intelligence body or national security council to evaluate and prioritize reports to Chinese leaders, there is a competitive aspect to the Chinese intelligence system. The PLA devotes considerable resources to intelligence collection and analysis, which can potentially be a source of policy influence.[35] For example, an Academy of Military Sciences report that concluded the United States had deliberately bombed China's embassy in Belgrade reportedly influenced the views of senior CCP leaders.[36]

Building Capabilities That Expand PRC Options: Although not tied specifically to a particular policy issue, PLA efforts to build new military capabilities can expand the options open to PRC policymakers. Successful PLA modernization and development of power projection capabilities give today's Chinese leaders options to deal with Taiwan or South China Sea maritime disputes that did not exist in the mid-1990s. Building new capabilities can also enhance the PLA's capacity to make contributions to nontraditional security challenges such as piracy or natural disasters; to conduct military diplomacy activities such as ship visits or joint exercises; or to engage with retired Taiwan or U.S. military officers in unofficial settings.[37]

Framing the Policy Problem: Chinese propaganda and the self-image of Chinese people consistently emphasize China's status as a uniquely peaceful country that always acts based on ethical principles. Chinese national security decisions tend to be framed in terms of justified defensive responses to hostile acts by other countries. This is not simply propaganda and often represents deeply held beliefs about Chinese strategic culture and the strategic cultures of other states.[38] Moreover, this perspective shapes how policy issues are defined and debated internally by Chinese policymakers; it may also influence which offices have the lead in managing an issue. Framing a policy decision about a territorial dispute in terms of "how to respond to Country X's violation of Chinese sovereignty" clearly biases policy debate in particular directions.

Decision Phase   **Formulation of Alternative Policy Options and Plans**: The PLA is responsible for drawing up military plans for contingencies. Its near monopoly on relevant intelligence, information about Chinese military capabilities, and expertise in military planning allow the PLA to shape the military options under consideration.[39] In his memoirs, Liu Huaqing, then serving as the CMC vice-chairman, describes presenting Party General Secretary Zhao Ziyang with a single, pre-coordinated military course of action for responding to Vietnamese force deployments on the Spratly Islands in 1988.[40] The days when a civilian leader could dictate specific operational details for the employment of military force are almost certainly over with the passing of the generation of dual role elites. In 1979, Deng Xiaoping's guidance on how long the PLA could be engaged in combat operations in Vietnam directly shaped PLA operational plans for China's invasion.[41] The ability to shape military plans is an important institutional advantage when the use of force is one of the options under consideration. This also applies more generally to formulation of policy options and draft guidance for the PLA. For example, the "new historic missions" that Hu Jintao gave the PLA in 2004 were reportedly drafted by PLA officers in the CMC General Office.[42]

Shaping Public Opinion: Senior PLA officers, military academics, and Ministry of National Defense spokesmen can potentially shape Chinese public opinion about national security issues via public statements, television appearances, and published writings. As Andrew Scobell notes in his chapter, stern public pronouncements by PLA figures shaped public opinion and altered policy in mid-2010. Lieutenant General Ma Xiaotian, then a deputy chief of the General Staff, told a Hong Kong television station on July 1, 2010, that China was "extremely opposed" to rumored U.S.-South Korean naval exercises because the location was "too close to Chinese territorial waters." Ma's comment was followed by supportive op-eds from Chinese think-tank researchers; the Ministry of Foreign Affairs (MFA) spokesman also subsequently spoke out against the exercises.[43] China's media environment is censored and PLA officers are subject to discipline for violating security restrictions or criticizing CCP policy. Nevertheless, numerous retired PLA officers and military academics regularly appear on television or write in Chinese and English media to shape both domestic and international opinion.

Building Coalitions: On broader political-military issues, the PLA can potentially form coalitions with other Chinese policy actors to build support for its policy preferences. Coalition-building is important in issue areas where the PLA has only a limited formal policy role. Examples might include setting priorities in Chinese national technology development efforts (in cooperation with Chinese civilian research institutes, universities, and scientists working on militarily-relevant technologies) and working with other ministries and experts to raise "maritime consciousness" among the Chinese public.[44] One common tactic is to describe a policy initiative as supporting or advancing goals already endorsed by the top CCP leadership; this potentially broadens support for the initiative. PLA Navy participation in counter-piracy operations in the Gulf of Aden provided a concrete example of PLA support for Chinese national interests under Hu Jintao's "new historic missions," illustrated Chinese contributions to regional stability (useful for the Foreign Ministry in dealing with the United States and African countries), and delivered concrete benefits for Chinese shipping lines and state-owned enterprises. That the counter-piracy operations advanced the interests of such a broad coalition of Chinese actors facilitated rapid approval of the deployment.

Advocacy of Particular Policy Options: On issues where the PLA has an advisory or decisionmaking role, it can advocate or oppose particular options in policy debates. Given the fragmented nature of much Chinese decisionmaking, PLA opposition can sometimes block or delay the adoption of policies (examples include the ten-year lag between initial proposals for a Chinese national security council structure and the decision to proceed in 2013). Since Chinese policy is often the product of compromise, PLA involvement may shape the final policy even if its preferred policies are not adopted. Conversely, some PLA ideas such as the Air Force proposal for an air defense identification zone (ADIZ) over the East China Sea have been adopted as national policy.[45]

Implementation Phase **PLA Role in Carrying Out Policy Decisions**: Once a policy decision is made, the PLA may have a large or small role in implementation, depending on the nature of the issue. In some cases, such as the 2001 collision between a PLA Navy fighter and a U.S. Navy EP-3, aggressive PLA efforts to challenge U.S. reconnaissance flights triggered an international incident.[46] In other cases, such as the 2007 antisatellite (ASAT) test, neither Chinese leaders nor the PLA were prepared to respond to international criticism after the test scattered satellite debris into orbit. Some routine PLA activities, including testing of weapons in development, have the potential to generate international consequences even if they are not the product of an explicit decision by either civilian or military leaders.[47]

PLA Reporting on Operational Activities: Because PLA units are typically operating within a military chain of command, senior CCP leaders (and others in the government) are dependent on information reported by the PLA about what happened during an operation. There have been instances where the PLA reported inaccurate information (e.g., that the U.S. EP-3 turned into the Chinese fighter) to its civilian leadership. PLA reporting also provides feedback on current policies, and can thus shape leadership assessments of whether current policy is working or needs to be altered.

Taken together, these two analytical approaches provide a useful framework for thinking about how much influence the PLA is likely to have on any particular policy issue (see Table I.1). First, consider the nature of the issue (political, military, or mixed civil-military) and where decisions on that type of issue are made within the Chinese policymaking system. This should illuminate the PLA's formal role in the relevant advisory and decisionmaking bodies and the types of political assets the PLA brings to the policy debate. Second, consider the various steps in the policy process that help to frame that issue, provide and assess alternative policy options, produce a decision, and

TABLE I.1 PLA Policy Influence: Issues and Phases

Policy issues	PHASES		
	Pre-Decision	Decision	Implementation
Military issues	HIGH	HIGH	DOMINANT
(privileged)	Assessments of military threats and technology trends Contingency planning	Military modernization priorities (joint operations, informationization) Weapons programs (aircraft carrier, stealth fighters, ASAT)	Military exercises Interceptions of U.S. reconnaissance ships and aircraft Weapons testing Military diplomacy
Mixed issues	MODERATE	MODERATE/LOW	MODERATE/LOW
(lobby/coalitional)	Importance of maritime and sovereignty issues	Control of civilian maritime agencies	Anti-Japan propaganda
Political issues	LOW	LOW/NEGLIGIBLE	LOW/NEGLIGIBLE
(one of many actors)	Content of ideological campaigns	Selection of top civilian leaders	Implement austerity and anticorruption campaigns within PLA

implement that decision. How important and influential a role does the PLA play at each step?

China's policy toward Japan since the Japanese government purchased three of the disputed Diaoyu/Senkaku islands from a private owner in September 2012 illustrates the potential value of these approaches. The dispute over the islands touches on protection of Chinese sovereignty and territorial integrity, a core PLA military mission. Yet relations with Japan also involve important Chinese foreign policy and economic interests due to extensive Sino-Japanese trade and investment ties. In addition, China's suffering at the hands of Japanese imperialism in the 1895 Sino-Japanese War and after Japan's invasion in 1937 makes policy toward Japan an issue with broader political salience, especially given the nationalistic and anti-Japanese sentiments among Chinese elites and the general public.

The importance and sensitivity of the issue suggest that final decisions are made by the PBSC and that the Foreign Affairs Leading Small Group (FALSG), Maritime Security Leading Small Group (MSLSG), and CMC likely provide policy inputs and recommendations and help coordinate implementation of PBSC decisions. Although there are no PLA officers on the PBSC, the PLA has representatives on the FALSG and MSLSG and direct access to the

CCP general secretary through the CMC. In addition to these formal channels, PLA assessments of Japanese intentions and intelligence about Japanese military capabilities may provide additional informal channels of policy influence by shaping the views of other actors. Finally, the CCP leadership's concern about being seen to defend Chinese interests against Japan suggests that PLA efforts to shape public and elite opinion about appropriate policy responses may provide indirect opportunities to influence policy through the media.[48]

In the pre-decision stage, PLA actors sought to shape public and senior decisionmakers views on Japan. One means was via assessments of the international security environment. Although contemporaneous internal assessments are not available, assessments published shortly after the decision provide evidence of a tougher PLA view of Japan. For example, Hu Jintao's November 2012 work report does not mention Japan or emphasize threats to China's maritime claims.[49] Conversely the April 2013 Defense White Paper complains that "some country" has strengthened its Asia-Pacific military alliances, warns that "some neighboring countries" are taking actions that complicate China's territorial sovereignty and maritime rights and interests, and singles out Japan by name for "making trouble over the issue of the Diaoyu Islands."[50] PLA officers participated in drafting both assessments, but had more ability to shape the defense white paper.[51] Subsequent PLA assessments of Japan, and especially of the Shinzo Abe government that took power in December 2012, have expressed concerns about a revival of Japanese militarism, especially after Abe visited the Yasukuni Shrine in December 2013.[52] Direct information on PLA intelligence analysis of improvements in Japanese military capabilities is not available, but in dialogues with American counterparts PLA officers have cited the modest increases in Japan's defense budget in 2013 and 2014 and alleged unsafe Japanese air and naval activity near Chinese ships as signs of Japanese militarism.[53] PLA efforts to build more robust military capabilities, including more capable fighter aircraft, pilots with experience flying over water, and unmanned aerial surveillance vehicles have also expanded the military options available to Chinese decisionmakers. Although Japan's action was framed as a unilateral change to the status quo that required a response, it is unclear if the PLA played a major role in shaping this official Chinese position.[54]

China decided to respond to the Japanese nationalization of the islands with political, military, and economic measures to challenge Japan's administrative control of the Senkaku/Diaoyu islands. When these measures failed to force the Japanese government to acknowledge the existence of a sovereignty dispute, Beijing intensified pressure through an anti-Japan diplomatic and propaganda campaign and by establishing an air defense identification zone (ADIZ) that covered the disputed islands in November 2013. The PLA Navy had intensified air and naval operations in the East China Sea in response to a previous incident in 2010, and likely presented plans and advocated further increases in patrols and exercises in response to the Japanese action. Although Chinese challenges to Japanese administrative control over the islands relied primarily on civilian maritime law enforcement vessels, PLA Navy ships and fighters supported their actions with patrols, intelligence collection flights, and interceptions of Japanese aircraft.[55] Such coordinated civil-military operations may reflect PLA coalition-building efforts. Some have cited the statement of a Chinese Defense Ministry spokesman that China reserved the right to take "reciprocal measures" in response as evidence of the PLA pushing for a military response, but these remarks appear to be part of a coordinated Chinese response.[56] One clear example of PLA influence is the proposal to implement a Chinese ADIZ that covered the disputed islands. This proposal originated within the PLA Air Force Command College, and was reportedly proposed and rejected multiple times before being adopted as a means to bolster China's claim and increase pressure on Japan.[57]

In the implementation phase, PLA actors carried out orders to increase pressure on the Japanese military and to support the CCP anti-Japanese propaganda campaign via military diplomacy and writings.[58] The PLA Navy stepped up its patrols and exercises in the East China Sea, including aerial patrols by H-6 bombers through Japan's Miyako Strait and into the Western Pacific. Although PLA aircraft and ships were careful not to fly over the 12 nm territorial sea surrounding the Senkaku islands or into Japan's territorial sea, the Japanese Air Self-Defense Force typically scrambled fighters to intercept Chinese civilian and military aircraft operation in Japan's ADIZ.[59] Such operations increased pressure on Japan to compromise in the dispute, but also prompted Japanese complaints about unprofessional Chinese airmanship in conducting interceptions of Japanese surveillance aircraft.[60] In addition to the direct impact, inaccurate PLA reporting on its operations may have shaped Chinese policy responses. Two January 2013 incidents where Chinese frigates reportedly used their fire control radars to illuminate a Japanese helicopter and destroyer prompted public complaints by the Japanese Ministry of

Defense.[61] The Chinese Ministry of National Defense denied the accusations, but Chinese military officials later acknowledged privately that a frigate had made an unplanned, "emergency decision" to use its fire control radar.[62]

This example suggests that the PLA influenced Chinese policy responses to Japan's purchase of the islands by promoting more negative assessments of Japanese motives, building military capabilities that offered Chinese policy-makers more assertive response options, framing Japan's actions as a challenge that required a strong response, and generating and advocating specific responses such as increased military patrols and the establishment of a Chinese ADIZ. The PLA has also played an important role in implementing the Chinese decision to challenge Japanese administrative control of the disputed islands and increasing diplomatic and military pressure on Japan. How much influence these PLA actions actually had in shaping China's response is difficult to discern without inside information on Chinese decisionmaking and because Chinese civilian leaders including Xi Jinping appear to have also favored a tough response.

Overview of the Book

These two analytical approaches should be kept in mind when reading the theoretical and empirical chapters. The first section of the book, "The PLA and the Party-State," examines structural factors that shape PLA interactions with the party-state.

In "Reconsidering the PLA as an Interest Group," Isaac Kardon and Phillip Saunders examine the degree to which the PLA can be thought of as an interest group, finding that past factors that limited the PLA's ability to act as a coherent policy actor have diminished. Today's PLA demonstrates numerous characteristics suggestive of interest-group behavior, including professionalization, growing coherence of its corporate interests, an expanding monopoly on national security expertise and information, and enhanced capacity to articulate and defend institutional goals and equities in order to shape public debate and influence policy.

Alice Miller's chapter on "The PLA in the Party Leadership Decision-making System" explains the political logic behind the transformation of the Chinese leadership's decisionmaking system, emphasizing a deliberate effort by Deng Xiaoping in the 1980s to establish an effective collective leadership system with checks and balances to prevent attempts by any individual member—and especially by the party general secretary—to dominate the others. She argues that these reforms have transformed civil-military relations from "subjective civilian control" to "objective civilian control" as PLA influence on political decisions has narrowed into institutional mechanisms focused primarily on security issues. These structural changes limit the ability of PLA leaders to exert influence on political issues or to exploit potential splits among top civilian leaders.

Tai Ming Cheung's chapter, "The Riddle in the Middle: China's Central Military Commission in the Twenty-first Century," uses new sources to describe the inner workings of this secretive organization. He identifies key political and organizational principles guiding the CMC's development; describes its current structure, workings, and responsibilities; highlights the critical role played by the CMC vice-chairmen; evaluates Hu Jintao's role as CMC chairman and problems in civil-military relations during his tenure; and conducts an initial assessment of Xi Jinping's early tenure as CMC chairman. Cheung stresses Xi's emphasis on the role of military power in a "strong China dream," efforts to impose stricter political and fiscal discipline, and the decision to restructure the military command system to improve its ability to conduct joint operations.

Nan Li's "Top Leaders and the PLA: The Different Styles of Jiang, Hu, and Xi" assesses how Jiang Zemin and Hu Jintao exerted influence over the PLA, and analyzes why their methods were different. He distinguishes between two approaches: "currying favor" by catering to PLA interests and "imposing will" by forcing the PLA to do things it would not otherwise want to do. He argues that Jiang curried favor early in his leadership and then imposed his will, while Hu curried favor throughout his tenure. Nan Li suggests Xi Jinping is likely to curry favor initially to consolidate power, but then to impose his will by downsizing and reorganizing the military.

The second section uses case studies to explore the PLA's role in foreign policy crises generally and in China's policy on Taiwan, the Democratic People's Republic of Korea (DPRK), and military-to-military relations.

In "The PLA Role in China's Foreign Policy and Crisis Behavior," Michael Swaine assesses the limited reliable open-source information about the role of the PLA in China's foreign policy processes and in political-military crisis behavior with other countries. He begins by examining the changing relationship of the PLA to the overall PRC leadership system and political power structure and then reviews the PLA's organizational and procedural interactions in the foreign policy process, looking at both senior-level and operational-level interactions. He examines five aspects of the PLA's role in crisis decisionmaking and implementation: upper-level participants and processes, lower-level actors, intelligence and information flows and preexisting plans, research institutes, and unplanned or uncontrolled behavior. Swaine challenges the view of a PLA that wields decisive influence over Chinese foreign policy or crisis behavior, noting that the PLA's strongest avenue for exerting influence is through the CMC headed by the CCP general secretary. At the same time, Swaine notes that the lack of an effective NSC-like structure raises doubts about adequate coordination and oversight of PLA operational activities such as weapons testing and military actions outside China's borders.

Bonnie Glaser's chapter, "The PLA Role in China's Taiwan Policymaking," assesses the extent of PLA influence on the PRC's cross-Strait policy and what avenues the PLA uses to influence that policy. Acknowledging the difficulty in judging whether PLA attempts to exert influence are successful, Glaser identifies ten methods the PLA uses to shape Taiwan policy. These include using the PLA's institutional representation in the CMC and other policy bodies, intelligence and research, military procurement, military exercises, official statements, defense white papers and other official documents, media exposure, informal mechanisms, cultural and social exchanges, and military-to-military channels with third-party countries. Glaser suggests that the CMC is the PLA's most important and direct channel for influencing China's Taiwan policy, with intelligence and research and defense white papers being the next most effective methods. She concludes that China-Taiwan tensions tend to increase the PLA's influence on Taiwan policy, while recent improvements in cross-Strait relations may have reduced PLA influence somewhat.

In "PLA Role in China's DPRK Policy," Andrew Scobell analyzes two case studies: the 2002–2003 "second nuclear crisis" and the 2010 Republic of Korea (ROK) Navy *Cheonan* crisis. Scobell argues that Chinese leaders place a high priority on stability, view the DPRK as volatile, and believe policy changes might destabilize the relationship and the region. China is therefore likely to maintain its current DPRK policy unless a crisis arises. Scobell notes that China and the PLA struggle to influence the DPRK. Because the military largely agrees with the party's overall Korea policy and with keeping the DPRK as a buffer state, it is difficult to assess whether the PLA has much independent influence on China's DPRK policy. This chapter concludes that China is unlikely to change its North Korean policy and that "maintaining stability both inside China and on its periphery is the highest priority along with sustaining China's status as a responsible great power."

Eric Hagt's "The Rise of PLA Diplomacy" assesses the PLA's role in China's increasingly active military diplomacy. The chapter surveys the PLA's international activities and examines the institutions and individuals who carry out PLA diplomatic efforts. The three key elements governing PLA military diplomacy are the General Staff Department (GSD) Foreign Affairs Office, the senior PLA officers who supervise military diplomacy and military-to-military (M2M) activities, and the personalities and backgrounds of the PLA officers involved in military diplomacy. Hagt argues that the PLA tends to focus on Chinese strategic objectives rather than on building stable bilateral relations; as a result Chinese military diplomacy complicates overall Chinese diplomacy and can produce outcomes incongruent with the objectives sought by the foreign affairs system.

The third section focuses on the PLA's role in Chinese territorial disputes, considering its interactions with foreign actors, with CCP leaders, and with other policy actors such as China's various maritime actors.

M. Taylor Fravel, in his chapter "The PLA and National Security Decision-making: Insights from China's Territorial and Maritime Disputes," examines the PLA's policy influence on China's territorial disputes. He argues that PLA policy influence is limited to bureaucratic influence within existing policy-making structures and processes. PLA actions in contested waters reflect the consensus of top CCP leaders on how to best address territorial claims, not independent military decisions or actions. Fravel traces the PLA's relatively limited role in previous territorial disputes, including border consolidation following the Chinese civil war and Beijing's initial claim over the Senkakus. He then discusses the PLA's role in the current territorial debates in the East and South China Seas, noting that there is little evidence that the preferences of civilian leaders and the PLA differ and citing examples of Beijing utilizing diplomatic and political tools rather than military instruments to assert its territorial claims. Fravel concludes that the PLA has exercised limited bureaucratic influence in line with existing national policies and that more assertive behavior likely reflects the shared preferences of the PLA and top civilian leaders.

Christopher Yung's "The PLA Navy Lobby and Its Influence over China's Maritime Sovereignty Policies" uses three case studies to examine how individuals and organizations affiliated with the PLA Navy, which he refers to

as the PLA Navy lobby, have influenced China's maritime sovereignty policies. Although these policies are ultimately decided by the highest levels of the
CCP, the PLA Navy lobby sought to influence the 1988 decision to use force
against Vietnam in the Spratly Islands; the decision to acquire an aircraft carrier; and the 2013 decision on centralizing the functions, command and control, and management of China's "maritime sovereignty" activities. Yung finds
that in the first case, the PLA got what it wanted by presenting a unified PLA
opinion to CCP leaders without alternative options. The PLA's initial attempt
to acquire an aircraft carrier was rebuffed, but the PLA sought and eventually
received "friendly guidance" from the leadership to achieve this goal. In the
third case, the results were mixed as CCP leaders did not agree to centralize
enforcement activities under PLA Navy control, but did pay more attention to
maritime sovereignty issues and seek to improve coordination.

In "The PLA and Maritime Security Actors," Linda Jakobson examines
how the PLA works with the many civilian agencies involved in maritime
security. In addition to the military and the restructured and consolidated
maritime law enforcement agencies, a wide variety of government bodies associated with maritime law enforcement, maritime security, and maritime economic development seek to influence maritime security policy. Her research
reveals a noteworthy increase in interactions between the PLA and maritime
law enforcement agencies since the March 2013 restructuring, including
joint training, research, and drills. Jakobson also finds that the PLA Navy is
attempting to influence decisionmakers directly and shape public opinion on
maritime security issues by engaging with civilian law enforcement, government ministries and agencies, state-owned enterprises, and universities. She
concludes that there remains great uncertainty over how the restructuring of
the maritime law enforcement agencies will affect interactions with the PLA
due to the opacity of the PLA command structure and the difficulty of achieving "jointness" between military and civilian agencies.

Overall Findings

The substantive chapters suggest some overall findings about PLA influence
on national security policymaking and reinforce the value of the analytic
framework outlined above. Generally speaking, today's PLA appears to have
somewhat more influence on purely military issues than in the past, much less

influence on political issues, and to be more actively engaged in policy debates on mixed civil-military issues where military equities are at stake.[63]

First, China's top civilian party leaders make the major decisions on political, economic, strategic, foreign policy, and security issues. PLA sources cited in Tai Ming Cheung's chapter state explicitly that the CCP leadership has "final authority" on "major questions concerning war, armed force, and national defense building." The military provides strategic assessments, intelligence analysis, policy options, and advice to support decisionmaking by top party leaders, but the empirical record over the last fifteen years provides little evidence of a dominant military role in major strategic decisions. Cheung notes that the Politburo decided on China's response to the accidental bombing of the Chinese embassy in Belgrade in 1999; the CMC vice-chairman subsequently convened an emergency meeting to convey CCP instructions to the PLA.

Second, military efforts to exert policy influence are more legitimate when couched in terms of advancing objectives endorsed by top civilian party leaders, such as protecting China's sovereignty and territorial integrity. The PLA's monopoly on military information and limited civilian expertise provide opportunities to shape civilian guidance through strategic assessments and intelligence, formulation of policy options and contingency plans, and drafting policy documents for approval by the CMC chairman. Although Hu Jintao gave the PLA its "new historic missions" in 2004, they were based on concepts developed earlier and drafted by the CMC General Office. The charge "to protect China's expanding national interests" provided a rationale for the PLAN to press for (and receive) permission to acquire an aircraft carrier. Similarly, defining China's maritime territorial claims as "core interests" where compromise was impossible allowed the PLA to advocate tougher measures to defend China's claims.

Third, the CMC is the most important channel for PLA influence on military issues and on foreign policy issues with a significant military component. The PLA can exploit its privileged access to the CCP general secretary (in his capacity as CMC chairman) to get ideas and policy advice directly to the top of the CCP decisionmaking system. PLA representation in bodies such as the Foreign Affairs, Military Affairs, and Taiwan Affairs leading small groups (LSGs) and the new National Security Commission provides additional formal channels for PLA input and potential policy influence.

Fourth, the decline in PLA representation in CCP core decisionmaking bodies such as the PBSC and increased institutionalization of the political succession process have significantly reduced the PLA's role in political issues such as the selection and promotion of China's top civilian leaders.[64] This implies reduced PLA influence over civilian leaders.

Fifth, the expansion of PLA interests and equities has forced the PLA to become actively involved in policy debates on mixed civil-military issues where its formal policy role and influence are limited. This produces incentives for PLA officers and scholars to lobby, to build coalitions, and to seek to shape the broader public and policy debate in China through media appearances, published writings, and relationships with civilian actors.[65]

Sixth, civilian and military policy preferences appear to be closely aligned on many foreign policy and security issues, suggesting there are considerable areas of consensus despite the gap in expertise and experience between Chinese civilian and military leaders. The empirical chapters on Taiwan, Korea, and territorial disputes certainly bear this out. This produces a major analytic challenge in assessing PLA policy influence because it becomes very difficult to discern the degree to which the PLA is actually influencing civilian leaders (rather than simply implementing their wishes).

Seventh, even when differences in policy preferences and priorities between the PLA and civilian leaders are evident, civilian leaders can and do rebuke PLA critics and impose party discipline to close down debates when necessary. Bonnie Glaser cites the example of Major General Luo Yuan being reprimanded in 2009 after characterizing Taiwan President Ma Ying-jeou's policies as "peaceful separation," an implicit criticism of CCP policy toward Taiwan. The chapters contain numerous examples of PLA efforts to influence civilian policy decisions, but no examples of the PLA disobeying orders from CCP leaders.

Eighth, the PLA's responsibility for implementing policy (and the accuracy of the information about PLA operations that it provides to civilians) can play a significant role in determining the success or failure of Chinese policy. Examples include the 2001 EP-3 incident when a PLA Navy fighter creating a major crisis with the United States by colliding with a U.S. Navy reconnaissance aircraft, the international response to China's 2007 test of an antisatellite (ASAT) weapon, and more recently, PLA Navy exercises in the South China Sea and incursions across the disputed Sino-Indian border that raised tensions with foreign countries.

Ninth, the Chinese foreign policy and national security policymaking system suffers from limited information-sharing and an overall lack of coordination that sometimes produces suboptimal policy choices and poor implementation of decisions. These problems are acknowledged by Chinese analysts, but many proposed remedies could reduce PLA autonomy and policy influence. The new National Security Commission approved by the Third Plenum of the Eighteenth CCP Congress in November 2013 is intended to address these problems, but its effectiveness remains to be seen.

Tenth, some analysts suggest that the relationship between top civilian party leaders and the military involves bargaining, with the party providing concrete benefits (such as pay increases and higher defense budgets) and concessions on policy issues to ensure the PLA's continued loyalty. For example, Nan Li argues in his chapter that CMC chairmen have sometimes "curried favor" in order to win PLA support, especially when their own political standing was weak. However, there are many more examples where CCP leaders made decisions that went against PLA institutional interests (such as divestiture of the PLA's business empire) or disregarded PLA policy preferences (such as the navy's effort to gain control of the civilian maritime law enforcement agencies). CCP leaders appear to be able to intrude into the military domain when necessary, although Isaac Kardon and Phillip Saunders argue that this is easier when the PLA is divided and civilian leaders have the support of some senior military officers for their actions.

The PLA's influence on national security policymaking in China is a topic of great importance to policymakers and considerable interest to scholars of international security and international relations. This volume moves the field of Chinese security studies forward while at the same time also highlighting the need for further research. As readers turn to the substantive chapters, they may find it useful to keep in mind the two analytic approaches presented in this introduction. The first focuses on the nature of the issue under consideration, which affects where decisions on that issue are made within the Chinese system and what role the PLA plays in advising on or participating in those decisions. The second considers the overall policy process, focusing on the PLA's ability to influence decisions at various stages in the process.

Notes

The views expressed are those of the authors and do not necessarily reflect the policies of the National Defense University, the Department of Defense, or the United States government. The authors thank Ken Allen, Bernard Cole, Cortez Cooper, Scott

Harold, and Christopher Yung for comments on previous drafts, and Denise Der, Jessica Drun, Joseph Kettel, and Drew Casey for research assistance.

1. For a newspaper report emphasizing the increased policy influence of the PLA, see Jeremy Page, "For Xi, a 'China Dream' of Military Power," *Wall Street Journal*, March 13, 2013. For a research report, see Willy Lam, "Commander-in-Chief Xi Jinping Raises the Bar on PLA 'Combat Readiness,'" *China Brief* 13, no. 2 (January 18, 2013).

2. For an assessment of the evidence, see Andrew Scobell, "Is There a Civil-Military Gap in China's Peaceful Rise?" *Parameters* 34, no. 2 (Summer 2009): 4–22.

3. For two major studies, see David Shambaugh, *Modernizing China's Military: Progress, Problems, Prospects* (Berkeley: University of California Press, 2002); and Andrew Scobell, *China's Use of Military Force: Beyond the Great Wall and the Long March* (New York: Cambridge University Press, 2003).

4. See the chapters by Alice Miller and Christopher D. Yung in this volume.

5. Joel Wuthnow, "Decoding China's New 'National Security Commission,'" *CNA China Studies* (November 2013); and Saunders interviews, July 2013.

6. For a more nuanced view, see Minxin Pei, "Is the PLA Going Rogue?" *National Interest*, February 10, 2014.

7. Personal communication to the authors from retired U.S. analyst Christopher M. Clarke, 2011.

8. For a critical review of the literature on civil-military relations in China, see Michael Kiselycznyk and Phillip C. Saunders, *Civil-Military Relations in China: Assessing the PLA's Role in Elite Politics*, INSS China Strategic Perspectives 2 (Washington, DC: National Defense University, August 2010).

9. Samuel P. Huntington, *The Soldier and the State: The Theory and Politics of Civil-Military Relations* (Cambridge, MA: Belknap Press, 1957).

10. See David Shambaugh, "The Soldier and the State in China: The Political Work System in the People's Liberation Army," *China Quarterly*, no. 127 (September 1991): 527–568.

11. CCP civilian and military elites do appear to share a continued belief in the validity of Lenin's approach to managing a one-party state.

12. Roy Kamphausen, Andrew Scobell, and Travis Tanner, eds., *The "People" in the PLA: Recruitment, Training, and Education in China's Military* (Carlisle Barracks, PA: U.S. Army War College, 2007).

13. James Mulvenon and David Finkelstein, eds., *China's Revolution in Doctrinal Affairs: Emerging Trends in the Operational Art of the Chinese People's Liberation Army* (Alexandria, VA: CNA Corporation, 2005).

14. Amos Perlmutter and William M. LeoGrande, "The Party in Uniform: Towards a Theory of Civil-Military Relations in Communist Political Systems," *American Political Science Review* 76, no. 4 (December 1982): 778–789.

15. This bifurcation is highlighted in Shambaugh, *Modernizing China's Military*; and Scobell, *China's Use of Military Force*.

16. Military leaders have some opportunities to interact with local, and potentially provincial-level, civilian leaders during the middle of their careers while leading local

units or serving in staff positions in military regions. However, the civilian leaders they interact with will not necessarily ascend to national positions. Moreover, some analysis suggests that primary responsibility for liaison with civilian officials is ordinarily handled by officers with long experience in a particular military region. Such individuals are typically not "fast burners" marked for promotion to top positions. See Elizabeth Hague, "PLA Leadership in China's Military Regions," in *Civil-Military Change in China: Elites, Institutes, and Ideas After the 16th Party Congress,* eds. Andrew Scobell and Larry Wortzel (Carlisle Barracks, PA: U.S. Army War College, 2004), 220–221.

17. Richard Kohn and Peter Feaver, eds., *Soldiers and Civilians: The Civil-Military Gap and American National Security* (Cambridge, MA: MIT Press, 2001).

18. Saunders interview with PLA officer, November 2007.

19. Andrew J. Nathan and Andrew Scobell, *China's Search for Security* (New York: Columbia University Press, 2012), 58. The sole exception is when the next party general secretary designate serves as a CMC vice-chairman for one or two years to gain experience with military issues.

20. See, for example, the pioneering work of Michael D. Swaine, *The Role of the Chinese Military in National Security Policymaking* (Santa Monica, CA: RAND, 1996); and John W. Garver, "The PLA as an Interest Group in Chinese Foreign Policy," in *Chinese Military Modernization,* eds. C. Dennison Lane, Mark Weisenbloom, and Dimon Liu (New York and Washington, DC: Kegan Paul International and AEI Press, 1996), 246–281.

21. Phillip C. Saunders and Michael Kiselycznyk, *Assessing Chinese Military Transparency,* INSS China Strategic Perspectives 1 (Washington, DC: National Defense University, 2010), 35–36.

22. Saunders interviews with Chinese civilian think-tank researchers, 2013.

23. Jane Perlez, "New Chinese Panel Said to Oversee Domestic Security and Foreign Policy," *New York Times,* November 13, 2013.

24. See Li Cheng, "The Battle for China's Top Nine Leadership Posts," *Washington Quarterly* 35, no. 1 (Winter 2012): 133–135.

25. Andrew Scobell, "China's Evolving Civil-Military Relations: Creeping Guojiahua," *Armed Forces & Society* 31, no. 2 (Winter 2005): 234, 237; *NIDS China Security Report 2012* (Tokyo: National Institute for Defense Studies, 2012), 40–42.

26. Two essential works on PRC decisionmaking are Kenneth Lieberthal, *Governing China: From Revolution to Reform* (New York: W.W. Norton, 2005), 2nd edition, and David M. Lampton, ed., *The Making of Chinese Foreign and Security Policy in the Era of Reform, 1978–2000* (Stanford, CA: Stanford University Press, 2001).

27. See Alice Miller's chapter in this volume.

28. See You Ji, "The PLA and Diplomacy: Unraveling Myths about the Military Role in Foreign Policy Making," *Journal of Contemporary China* (October 2013): 1–19.

29. Linda Jakobson and Dean Knox, *New Foreign Policy Actors in China,* SIPRI Policy Paper no. 26 (Stockholm: SIPRI, 2010).

30. Ibid.; Willy Lam, "Hawks vs. Doves: Beijing Debates 'Core Interests' and Sino-U.S. Relations," *China Brief* 10, no. 17 (August 19, 2010); and Yawei Liu and Justine

Zheng Ren, "An Emerging Consensus on the US Threat: The United States According to PLA Officers," *Journal of Contemporary China* 23, issue 86 (2014). For a contrasting interpretation, see Andrew Chubb, "Propaganda, Not Policy: Explaining the PLA's 'Hawkish Faction' (Part One)," *China Brief* 13, no. 15 (July 25, 2013), and "Propaganda, Not Policy: Explaining the PLA's 'Hawkish Faction' (Part Two)," *China Brief* 13, no. 16 (August 9, 2013).

31. See David M. Finkelstein, *China Reconsiders Its National Security: 'The Great Peace and Development Debate of 1999'* (Alexandria, VA: CNA Corporation, December 2000).

32. This is what happened in late 2010. See Andrew Scobell and Scott W. Harold, "An 'Assertive' China? Insights from Interviews," *Asian Security* 9, no. 2 (May–August 2013): 123, 126.

33. Also see James Mulvenon and Leigh Ann Ragland, "Liu Yuan: Archetype of a 'Xi Jinping Man' in the PLA?" *China Leadership Monitor*, no. 36 (Winter 2012).

34. See "Flying with Force and Vigor in the Sky of the New Century—Central Military Commission Member and PLA Air Force Commander Xu Qiliang Answers Reporter's Questions in an Interview," *PLA Daily Online*, November 2, 2009, 1.

35. Nicholas Eftimiades, *Chinese Intelligence Operations* (Annapolis, MD: Naval Institute Press, 1994); and Mark A. Stokes, Jenny Lin, and L. C. Russell Hsiao, *The Chinese People's Liberation Army Signals Intelligence and Cyber Reconnaissance Infrastructure*, Project 2049 Institute (November 11, 2011).

36. Bonnie S. Glaser and Phillip C. Saunders, "Chinese Civilian Foreign Policy Research Institutes: Evolving Roles and Increasing Influence," *China Quarterly*, no. 171 (September 2002): 602.

37. See, for example, Andrew S. Erickson and Austin M. Strange, *No Substitute for Experience: Chinese Antipiracy Operations in the Gulf of Aden*, China Maritime Studies 10 (Newport, RI: U.S. Naval War College, 2013), 1–7. The PLA also established a new organization to engage in unofficial talks with retired Taiwan military officers.

38. Andrew Scobell, *China and Strategic Culture* (Carlisle Barracks, PA: U.S. Army War College, 2002), and Scobell, *China's Use of Military Force*, chap. 2.

39. Andrew Scobell, Arthur Shuh-fan Ding, Phillip C. Saunders, and Scott W. Harold, eds., *The PLA and Contingency Planning in China* (Washington, DC: National Defense University Press, 2015).

40. *Memoirs of Liu Huaqing* [刘华清回忆录] (Beijing: Liberation Army Press [解放军出版社], 2004) in translation, 101–104. Also see Christopher Yung's chapter in this volume.

41. Ezra F. Vogel, *Deng Xiaoping and the Transformation of China* (Cambridge, MA: Belknap Press of Harvard University Press, 2011), 523–535; Scobell, *China's Use of Military Force*, chap. 6; and Xiaoming Zhang, "Deng Xiaoping and China's Decision to Go to War with Vietnam," *Journal of Cold War Studies* 12, no. 3 (Summer 2010): 3–29.

42. Personal communication from a U.S. China scholar.

43. See Michael D. Swaine and M. Taylor Fravel, "China's Assertive Behavior Part Two: The Maritime Periphery," *China Leadership Monitor*, no. 35 (Summer 2011):

12–14; and Yoshikazu Shimizu, "PLA Takes Hard Line in East China Sea," *Asia Times Online*, December 17, 2010.

44. Daniel M. Hartnett and Frederic Vellucci, Jr., "Towards a Maritime Security Strategy: An Analysis of Chinese Views since the Early 1990s," in *The Chinese Navy: Expanding Capabilities, Evolving Roles*, eds. Phillip C. Saunders et al. (Washington, DC: National Defense University Press, 2011).

45. See Shinji Yamaguchi, "The Foreign Policy of the Xi Jinping Administration and the Establishment of China's Air Defense Identification Zone," Briefing Memo, National Institute for Defense Studies (September 2013), www.nids.go.jp/english/publication/briefing/pdf/2014/briefing_e190.pdf.

46. See John Keefe, *Anatomy of the EP-3 Incident, April 2001* (Alexandria, VA: CNA Corporation, January 2002).

47. See Andrew Scobell, *The J-20 Episode and Civil-Military Relations in China* (Santa Monica, CA: RAND, March 2011).

48. See James Reilly, *Strong Society, Smart State: The Rise of Public Opinion in China's Japan Policy* (New York: Columbia University Press, 2012).

49. "Full Text of Hu Jintao's Report at 18th Party Congress," Xinhua News Agency, November 17, 2012.

50. Information Office of the State Council, "The Diversified Employment of China's Armed Forces," April 2013.

51. Saunders interview, Beijing, China, October 2013.

52. Michael D. Swaine, "Chinese Views Regarding the Senkaku/Diaoyu Islands Dispute," *China Leadership Monitor*, no. 41 (Spring 2013).

53. Interactions with PLA officers by the authors, 2012–2014.

54. Chinese Defense Minister General Liang Guanglie's remark that "the current escalation of tension over this dispute is totally caused by the Japanese side" and that China reserves the right to take "further actions" are consistent with this framing of the issue. See transcript of joint news conference with U.S. Secretary of Defense Panetta, September 18, 2012, www.defense.gov/transcripts/transcript.aspx?transcriptid=5116.

55. See Eric Heginbotham, "China's ADIZ in the East China Sea," *Lawfare* (blog), August 24, 2014, www.lawfareblog.com/2014/08/the-foreign-policy-essay-chinas-adiz-in-the-east-china-sea.

56. The MND spokesman's remarks followed a tough statement by Premier Wen Jiabao and were consistent with MFA statements on the issue, suggesting a coordinated Chinese response. See "China Ups the Ante in Its Row with Japan over Senkaku Islands," *Asahi Shimbun*, September 12, 2012; and J. Michael Cole, "China and Japan Turn the Screw over Island Dispute," *China Brief* 12, no. 18 (September 21, 2012).

57. See Michael D. Swaine, "Chinese Views and Commentary on the East China Sea Air Defense Identification Zone," *China Leadership Monitor*, no. 43 (Fall 2013).

58. This was quickly evident in PLA coordinated messages during military engagements with U.S. and other foreign militaries in 2012; also see Swaine, "Chinese Views Regarding the Senkaku/Diaoyu Islands Dispute."

59. Heginbotham, "China's ADIZ in the East China Sea."

60. Interactions with Japanese air force officers and defense officials by the authors, 2013–2014.

61. Martin Fackler, "Japan Says China Aimed Military Radar at Ship," *New York Times*, February 5, 2013.

62. Jethro Mullen and Yoko Wakatsuki, "China Denies Putting Radar-Lock on Japanese Warship," CNN, February 9, 2013; and "Chinese Officials Admit to MSDF Radar Lock Allegations," *Japan Times*, March 18, 2013.

63. This confirms the findings of earlier studies. For example, James Mulvenon contends the PLA's policy interests have shifted from being "a mile wide and an inch deep" to being "an inch wide and a mile deep." See "China: Conditional Compliance," in *Coercion and Governance: The Declining Political Role of the Military in Asia*, ed. Muthiah Alagappa (Stanford, CA: Stanford University Press, 2001), 324.

64. Much has changed. For an assessment of the PLA role in political succession in the early 1990s, see Michael D. Swaine, *The Military and Political Succession in China: Leadership, Institutions, Beliefs* (Santa Monica, CA: RAND, 1992).

65. This conclusion is highlighted in other scholarship. See Scobell and Harold, "An 'Assertive' China?" 124–126; Garver, "The PLA as an Interest Group," 252–254; and Andrew Scobell, "Show of Force: Chinese Soldiers, Statesmen, and the 1995–96 Taiwan Strait Crisis," *Political Science Quarterly* 115 (Summer 2000): 227–247.

PART I
  THE PLA AND THE PARTY-STATE

1 Reconsidering the PLA as an Interest Group

Isaac B. Kardon and Phillip C. Saunders

MANY OBSERVERS ASSERT THAT THE INFLUENCE OF the People's Liberation Army (PLA) in the Chinese national security policymaking process has increased significantly in recent years. They argue that changes within the PLA, in civil-military relations, and in the broader policy environment in the People's Republic of China (PRC) have increased military influence across a range of policy issues.[1] In assessing this claim, it is important to identify where the PLA's interests and preferences may differ from those of civilian ministries and the Chinese Communist Party (CCP) leadership and to understand how PLA views are expressed and pursued in the policy arena. One useful approach is to consider to what extent and on which issues the PLA acts as a coherent interest group.

John Garver's essay "The PLA as an Interest Group in Chinese Foreign Policy" provides a good point of departure.[2] Writing in the mid-1990s, Garver argued that despite significant hurdles to effective political action, there was evidence that the PLA acts as an interest group on some issues and under some circumstances. He drew on policy, observed practice, and Hong Kong reporting on PLA activities to support his claim that "the PLA more or less as an institution, in a fairly unified fashion, intervened in the policy process" to chart a more assertive Chinese policy toward the United States and Taiwan. Twenty years later, the factors Garver identified as affecting PLA capacity to act as an interest group offer a good starting point for assessing PLA policy influence. In the context of rapid political and social change, the PLA has consolidated and expanded many of the institutional traits that allowed it to take concerted political action on behalf of military interests. Meanwhile, a number of internal and external obstacles to PLA influence on policy have diminished or ceased to be relevant.

Although the Chinese national security decisionmaking process remains opaque, the PLA demonstrates characteristics suggestive of interest group behavior: professionalization, growing coherence of its corporate interests, increasingly specified "scientific" features of its mission, a monopoly on functional expertise and information in the national security realm, and enhanced capacity to articulate and defend institutional goals and equities to shape public debate and influence policy. Within the Chinese national security policy-making arena, the PLA commands prestige and privileged access to formal and informal institutional channels through which its interests can be represented, defended, and pursued.

The PLA's relationship to the party (it reports directly to the CCP general secretary, in his capacity as chairman of the Central Military Commission) gives senior military leaders direct access to China's top civilian leader. However, the fact that senior PLA officers are all party members and the close relationship between the PLA and the party has historically made it difficult for the PLA to act as a discrete interest group in Chinese politics. In serving the party rather than the state, the PLA is embedded within the broader political apparatus and prone to "divisions and cross-cutting cleavages"[3] that preclude the development and expression of institutional interests. At the extremes, the PLA has sometimes taken action consistent with CCP direction *against* its own organizational interests.[4] If PLA actors are motivated to political action on the basis of other affiliations—party, regional, and/or factional— then there is little payoff in trying to identify PLA institutional interests and means of pursuing them. However, if PLA actors share certain institutional policy objectives and demonstrate the capacity to mobilize and make political demands on that basis, there is value in understanding those interests and how they are expressed in the policy process.

Conceptualizing the PLA as an "Interest Group" in Chinese Politics

An "interest group," in David Truman's authoritative formulation, refers to "a group that, on the basis of one or more shared attitudes, makes certain claims upon other groups in the society for the establishment, maintenance, or enhancement of forms of behavior that are implied as shared attitudes. . . . [They also] share attitudes towards what is needed or wanted in a given situation, observable as demands or claims upon other groups in society."[5] In his assessment of the PLA, Garver established two parallel criteria: 1) "when one or several organizational segments have distinct institutionally-derived interests that lead some of its members to political activity to defend and promote those interests against others who hold antithetical views," and 2) "when there is a pattern of political participation by soldiers designed to achieve an authoritative decision in favor of a particular policy."[6] Garver stressed the centrality of "*institutionally*-derived interests" (italics added), but cautioned that the organization need not be a "unitary, monolithic actor . . . [nor] always act as a group."[7] In other words, only some critical mass of PLA personnel acting in concert some of the time is necessary for the interest group label to be analytically useful.

The PLA in 1996 was an unlikely candidate to be labeled an "interest group." Given its allegiance to the CCP rather than the state, its uneven institutionalization, and its formal responsibilities within a restrictive Chinese political system, the Chinese military lacked the coherence, autonomy, and voice usually associated with an interest group. In its various incarnations—as an organization indistinguishable from the party during the pre-1949 era, as shock troops for intraparty factional battles during the Cultural Revolution, as a marginalized appendage with vast private commercial interests during the early reform period, and now as an increasingly modern and professional military organization—the PLA has seldom functioned like interest groups in the American political system or other liberal democracies. Even after several rounds of personnel reductions, the PLA remains large, functionally differentiated, and geographically dispersed—characteristics that dilute the concentrated interests that typically underpin an interest group.[8]

Moreover, powerful political and ideological currents in China restrict the formation and action of interest groups, even if they are in fact latent in society. The party claims to represent the people completely, and formally rejects the liberal idea of autonomous civil actors or groups expressing their interests within the party-state.[9] Nonetheless, such groups do exist in the form of party members who represent the interests of particular segments of Chinese society or pursue the organizational imperatives of particular bureaucratic systems (*xitong*) or organizations.[10] This phenomenon is viewed unfavorably by the party, which considers it damaging to social harmony.[11] Chinese scholars distinguish the groups prevalent in China from Western interest groups organized along social or economic lines that bring money and political pressure to bear in attempts to influence legislation or policy implementation.[12] In the Chinese case, the most meaningful "interest groups" are state-owned enterprises with monopoly power and strong ties to the regulatory or administrative bodies that affect their interests.[13] Such enterprises are widely viewed as significant obstacles to the CCP's goal of rebalancing the Chinese economy toward a more sustainable economic model, and have been a target of Xi Jinping's anticorrpution campaign. Western scholars have also noted the increased role of private business lobbying in China.[14]

Opportunities for political participation are a necessary condition for interest group formation and efforts to exert influence. These can be formal institutionalized channels (representation and participation in the formal decisionmaking process), informal channels (lobbying of civilian officials responsible for a particular policy or set of policies), or indirect efforts to shape the broader public and policy debate. Some analysts regard the PLA's formal access to institutional channels such as the Central Military Commission (CMC) and seats in the Politburo as problematic because "the embeddedness of the PLA in the dominant system disqualifies it from being called an interest group"[15] and favors an inside access strategy rather than external lobbying. Yet because the PLA is *not* represented in some decisionmaking bodies that affect its core mission of national defense (e.g., the Politburo Standing Committee), it has incentives to pursue its institutional interests through informal and indirect channels as well.

Can the PLA Have Coherent Institutional Interests?

Arguments that the PLA has been incapable of representing itself as a coherent interest group have focused on its internal dynamics. An overarching "military view" was elusive for much of the PLA's history because the diversity of its sub-units tended to organize military personnel around interests derived from factional, regional, or political imperatives rather than shared institutional goals.[16] However, the PLA's evolution from a heavily politicized revolutionary organization to a modern professional military with specialized missions has helped produce a "military view" evident in the statements, behavior, and institutional imperatives of today's PLA. Two broad trends in civil-military relations have increased the PLA's ability to form and pursue coherent institutional interests: increased military professionalism and bifurcation of PRC civilian and military elites.[17]

Professionalism is a dominant theme in reform-era studies of the PLA, and has sharpened the PLA's sense of its organizational interests and equities. Samuel Huntington describes professionalism in terms of expertise, responsibility, and corporateness.[18] Reflecting a broader trend in Chinese society, expertise is particularly valued in today's PLA. Military leaders are focused on the need to field an army capable of using more sophisticated equipment in the complex joint and informationized operations that characterize modern warfare. Emphasis on a specialized *military* body of knowledge has produced programs to upgrade the technical skills of soldiers through education and training in science and technology. A better-educated and credentialed officer corps—some recruited from civilian universities and others through military academies—lay claim to unique professional expertise in military affairs. Formal technical training and professional military education reinforce the importance of military expertise.

PLA doctrine and military attitudes convey a heightened sense of the military's special responsibility for national security and for defending China's sovereignty and territorial integrity. This is reinforced by the PLA's professional monopoly on information and knowledge about military affairs, which implies that only the PLA is competent to take responsibility for the military aspects of national security. A firmer sense of corporate identity among senior- and mid-level officers is also evident, contributing to expectations that the PLA will exercise significant autonomy in military affairs and should possess goals, prerogatives, and a culture unique to the organization. Overarching concern with "army-building," for example, is a function of an increasingly corporate view of PLA priorities.

Military professionalism interacts with a second important trend in civil-military relations: the bifurcation of civilian and military elites as the career pathways of military and civilian leaders have diverged in recent years.[19] The first generation of revolutionary leaders were all military men in some capacity, whether as combat commanders or political commissars—or at least as civilians interacting closely with the military during the Chinese civil war. These relationships between civilian and military elites endured well into the postrevolutionary period in the form of a "dual-role elite" whose relationship was characterized by interdependence and symbiotic behavior.[20] By virtue of close bonds and shared experiences, military and civilian leaders intervened freely in affairs outside their formal areas of responsibility. The PLA's central role in the Cultural Revolution is an example of the military's overt forays into civilian politics.

The current generation of Chinese civilian leaders lacks firsthand revolutionary experience and has matured professionally in a much more technocratic and civilian environment. Their education and substantive political experiences have occurred on a separate track from their military counterparts, leading to relatively little substantive interaction between the two groups. Civilian and military leadership have succeeded in their respective fields due to professional skills that do not overlap much. Typically, civilian officials have only limited substantive civil-military interaction until achieving high levels of seniority.[21] President and CCP General Secretary Xi Jinping may represent an important exception to this trend, given his status as the first party secretary since Deng Xiaoping with direct military experience. (Xi served in the PLA for three years, as personal secretary to then-Defense Minister Geng Biao from 1979 to 1982.) The perception that Xi has close military ties and will "augment the military establishment's already formidable clout in foreign policy and other arenas"[22] probably overstates the military's influence, especially given the CCP system of collective leadership. Some PLA officers regard Xi as sympathetic to military interests given his personal and family background, but this experience may instead give him more confidence and leverage in dealing with the PLA.[23]

PLA personnel are incubated in an almost exclusively military environment where emphasis on technical expertise and professional duties leads to distinctive military perspectives on national security policy. Lack of systematic interaction between civil and military people until later stages of their careers may also undermine mutual trust and decrease the PLA's confidence that civilians possess sufficient knowledge and experience in military affairs to craft effective national security policy. This is clearly evident in PLA attitudes toward Foreign Ministry officials. PLA officers consistently proclaim their loyalty to the Communist Party, but the authors' interactions with Chinese military officers reinforce the impression that they believe their special responsibility for China's national security distinguishes them from civilians. This sense of mission contributes to a strong sense of corporate identity that facilitates acting as a coherent interest group.

Writing in the mid-1990s, Garver could not have fully anticipated the developments noted above. His essay furnishes a useful set of criteria with which to evaluate those developments and reassess his conclusions. Garver detailed eight sources of competing or divergent interests within the PLA that limited its capacity to act as a coherent interest group:

- Combat-oriented group armies vs. commercially oriented garrison units
- Emergent blue-water navy vs. ground forces
- Military Regions (with close linkages with provincial elites and central authorities)
- Senior officers with differing old field army affiliations
- National Defense University (NDU) graduates vs. non-graduates
- Officers with higher education or academy training vs. non-educated officers
- Different patronage cliques
- Patron-client relations, factional alignments, and policy differences that create venues for PLA sub-group linkages with non-PLA/civilian groups

Only three of these factors (competition between the navy and ground forces, patronage ties within the PLA, and links between PLA sub-groups and civilian counterparts) remain clearly meaningful today. Tensions between combat-oriented group armies and commercially oriented garrison units are less divisive because of the general decline in PLA commercial activity following forced divestiture of PLA businesses in 1998.[24] Military Region (MR) leaders were thought to build close ties with provincial elites and to prize contacts with central authorities responsible for their welfare. Senior officers in MRs probably do cultivate ties with provincial leaders, but increased rotation of both civilian and military leaders who are candidates for top positions likely decreases the strength of these ties, as does the fact that military regions now receive more direct funding from the central government budget and are less dependent on financial support from provincial and local officials. MR and local-unit leaders do need support from civilian officials in the context of mobilization plans and exercises. This requirement promotes greater civil-military interaction, but is probably a source of tension as military leaders try to persuade civilian officials to devote resources to military support rather than economic development.

Revolutionary-era field army orientations, once a mainstay of PLA analysis, are defunct due to generational change and the deaths of revolutionary-era civilian and military leaders. Educational and professional backgrounds are now the key experiences underpinning whatever personalistic ties exist within the PLA.[25]

Military professionalism and the resulting emphasis on creation of a modern, technically proficient officer corps created two of the tensions Garver identified: disparities between NDU graduates and non-NDU military personnel and disunity due to an officer corps in which only some personnel receive higher education or advanced military academy training. The advent and rapid adoption of professional military education (PME) in the PLA initially exacerbated and then dissipated this source of tension as progress was made toward ambitious educational goals: by 2010, these included having 60 percent of regiment and higher-level officers earn a four-year college degree and 100 percent attend a command college for advanced training in science and technology; by 2020, all regiment and higher-level officers were meant to have a bachelor's degree, while half should possess a master's degree.[26] The PLA has instituted regulations that require study at NDU for all senior officers.[27]

Garver posited a struggle between an "emergent blue-water navy" and the ground forces, suggesting that the more technologically oriented, resource-hungry navy might compete with the traditional center of gravity within the PLA, the army. As in all militaries, service interests are likely to produce varied perspectives on the relative importance of threats and procurement priorities. Interservice tension has arguably increased since 1996 as PLA modernization has focused on Taiwan and maritime threats and the share of the military budget devoted to navy, air force, and Second Artillery modernization has increased.[28] The army's argument for mechanization of ground forces as a modernization priority and recent grumbling by army officers about the ground forces being neglected are evidence that this tension is real and growing.[29] Interservice tensions over budget shares have not been a major source of divisiveness because the overall military budget has been growing at a double-digit pace since the mid-1990s, but could become contentious in a more austere budget environment.

The informal, personalistic networks endemic to most Chinese institutions also exist within the PLA. However, patronage cliques are notoriously difficult to analyze from the outside and any conclusions about PLA group identity derived by this method rely as much on conjecture as on empirical analysis. Professionalization and the heightened importance of individual skills and performance as promotion criteria likely reduce the importance of these dynamics as significant divisive factors. The reported widespread role of corruption in PLA senior officer promotions may undercut the importance of performance, but paying for promotion is a transactional relationship unlikely to create deep ties.[30]

The last factor Garver identified—links between particular sub-groups within the PLA and civilian groups on the basis of patron-client relations, factional alignments, or policy preferences—is probably still relevant. The importance of civil-military patronage or factional relations has likely declined due to the bifurcation of civil and military elites. Links between PLA sub-groups and civilians based on common policy preferences do exist and have become more important in China's more pluralistic policy environment.[31] The Bo Xilai scandal revealed the existence of ties between certain senior military personnel and some civilian political leaders, but the obscurity of these connections makes any firm judgment impossible. Except where there are strong conflicts of interest between *different* PLA sub-groups, these connections are better understood as interests pursued by sub-groups within the PLA.

Contrasting Military and Civilian Roles in Chinese Politics

Civil-military relations are often conceptualized as separate civilian and military spheres with fundamentally different values, attitudes, rules, and norms. Founded as a revolutionary party-army, the PLA fits uneasily into this mold given the civilian and military "dual-elite" during the Chinese civil war and prereform era, as well as the party's ongoing efforts to dictate appropriate values and political attitudes to PLA soldiers and officers through political education. However, trends such as professionalization, bifurcation of Chinese civilian and military elites, a reduced PLA role in political decisions and reduced emphasis on political work have tended to reinforce separate civilian and military spheres.[32]

Although the concept of separate spheres has value, in analyzing PLA influence on national security policymaking it is more useful to think of a spectrum of policy issues ranging from the purely military (doctrine, training, operations) to the purely political (content and themes of political education, selection of party civilian leadership). In between lies a vast middle ground where neither professional military prerogatives nor political guidance from civilian leaders dictates clear policy outcomes. This is especially true in the context of the geographic and functional expansion of Chinese national interests (which implies a corresponding expansion of PLA missions) and military modernization that increasingly require access to technologies, expertise, and resources from the civilian sector.

At one end of the spectrum, the CCP's emphasis on education, professional credentials, and scientific decisionmaking tends to reinforce doctrine, training, and operations as areas where professional military judgments should be dominant. Although the relevant guidelines and regulations are formally approved and signed by a top civilian leader (Xi Jinping, acting in his capacity as CMC chairman), such documents are drafted and reviewed by military officers. The CMC chairman has the right to review, revise, or reject such documents, but does he routinely have the time or expertise necessary to do so? For example, the "new historic missions," the signature political guidance given to the PLA by Hu Jintao in 2004, were reportedly drafted by the CMC General Office.[33]

In principle, CCP civilian leaders should provide guidance about what political ends the development and employment of military power should seek to advance and set political constraints on how military power should be employed in pursuit of those ends. The PLA can then apply professional military judgment to identify and develop the most efficient and effective means to advance the political objectives it has been given. In a few military areas, such as nuclear doctrine, clear political guidance by authoritative Chinese civilian leaders has shaped PLA force structure, doctrine, and training for decades, despite concerns from some PLA officers that policies such as "no first use" will place China at a military disadvantage.[34] In other areas, such as potential employment of antisatellite weapons or cyber attacks, civilian leaders do not appear to have issued clear guidance and military writings and operational practice may be more influential in shaping policy.

Chinese secrecy about military capabilities and operations and the PLA's ability to tightly control information helps insulate many military issues from civilian scrutiny, even by government officials with security clearances. Few Chinese academics or civilian think-tank experts have the expertise or standing to write knowledgeably about military issues, and those who do are usually restricted to the very limited information available in the public domain.[35]

Information in technical military areas is jealously guarded by the PLA; for example, a senior MFA arms control official admitted that he did not know details on the number and locations of Chinese nuclear weapons.[36] This pattern holds with regard to detailed information about Chinese military operations, which is transmitted through military channels and may not always be reported in depth or accurately to civilian leaders.[37]

At the other end of the spectrum, increased institutionalization of the political succession process appears to have significantly reduced the PLA's role in purely political issues such as the selection and promotion of China's top civilian leaders. For example, civilian candidates for the Politburo Standing Committee must now satisfy criteria including service as leaders in two different provinces, assignments made by civilian party organs without military input. PLA officers, in their capacity as Central Committee members, are involved in formally ratifying top civilian leaders who have been chosen beforehand in a top-down process where the military wields little influence.[38] PLA delegates to the National People's Congress (who in theory have standing to address both political and military issues) used to issue proposals and suggestions on social and economic policy, but now focus their attention primarily on security and military issues.[39] In terms of ideology, the PLA is a consumer of slogans and campaigns developed by civilians rather than a contributor to their development. More mundanely, the PLA takes political and public relations cues directly from civilian authorities: for instance, the present austerity and anticorruption campaigns intended to promote a more frugal image for the party and state have produced tighter restrictions on PLA travel and general avoidance of ostentatious displays of elite privilege.[40]

The interesting area is in the middle, where a growing number of issues involve both civilian and military equities. Some issues, such as the size of defense budgets or the PLA's degree of influence over Chinese defense industries, have been long-standing sources of civil-military disagreement. China's rapid economic development has created new issues, such as the role of military considerations in the construction of highways and high-speed rail lines or in research and development priorities. The dramatic expansion of Chinese international trade and investment has also created regional and global economic interests that give rise to new PLA missions (rescue of PRC citizens, protection of maritime trade routes) and also to potential political constraints on PLA actions (due to the potential for military actions to damage important political and economic relationships or to prompt destabilizing responses from China's neighbors). Space- and cyber-warfare issues are especially troublesome in this regard, given the potential for the PLA's focus on the military utility of antisatellite weapons and cyber-espionage to create problems for Chinese civilian and commercial actors. International complaints about space debris created by China's 2007 antisatellite test and criticism of the PLA's role in cyber-espionage against foreign military and commercial targets highlight the overlapping and interactive nature of civilian and military interests in the space and cyber domains.[41]

Military equities are at stake in many of these issues, but the limited capacity of China's national security decisionmaking system to weigh the relative importance of military and other interests and make rational decisions has produced a series of mistakes and counterproductive actions (most notably in China's assertive behavior in pursuing its maritime claims in the South and East China Seas since 2009). Some civilian political guidance and rhetoric (e.g., about the importance of defending China's sovereignty and territorial integrity) empower military voices in policy debates by heightening the importance of national goals where the military has responsibilities.

These developments suggest that the PLA's influence over purely political issues has declined, that its autonomy and influence over purely military issues has increased, and that there is an expanding set of issues in the middle that involve both military and civilian equities. The latter provides motivation for the PLA as a collective entity (or for sub-groups within the PLA) to seek to influence policy debates and decisions. One way to assess this is to identify institutional interests widely shared across the PLA and contrast these with narrower (or sometimes conflicting) interests that only involve PLA sub-groups (e.g., individual military services or branches). Identifying and analyzing these interests can help guide assessments of where, when, and how the PLA is likely to assert itself as an interest group.

PLA-Wide Institutional Interests

The cumulative result of these trends is a PLA more likely to conceive of itself as a discrete group within the Chinese political system with institutional interests that do not necessarily align fully with those of the civilian political leadership or other parts of the Chinese state. In practice, the degree to which PLA interests are coherently formulated and acted upon varies and may not be observable in all cases. It is helpful to disaggregate interests that flow directly from the PLA's institutional role and are largely shared by other modern militaries and those that are the product of situational, historically specific factors unique to China. The former include a strong interest in the survival and efficacy of the military institution itself, which requires the maintenance of organizational hierarchy, discipline, and cohesiveness.[42] All military organizations also pursue interests such as increased resources, autonomy in making military decisions, and military prestige.[43]

Perhaps the clearest PLA institutional interest is ensuring adequate material resources. Like other militaries, the PLA seeks pay and benefits (including facilities and housing) that will attract and retain high-quality personnel and increased military budgets that will support training and modernization of military hardware. Despite pride in their special responsibility for national security, PLA officers make comparisons with the salaries and benefits earned by civilians with equivalent skills.[44] In the current context of rapid economic growth that expands available resources and a central leadership committed to modernizing the military, overt civil-military conflicts about military budgets may be muted. However, slower growth or fiscal hardship would place these demands in stark relief and provide a good test of the PLA's effectiveness as an interest group. Under any economic circumstances, we can assume that the PLA views maximizing its budget and off-budget expenses as a fundamental institutional interest.

Less concrete but equally important is the military's regard for its prestige and status within the party, government, and society. The PLA's role in winning the Chinese civil war and its status as a party-army provide a continuous basis for demanding prestige and respect from CCP leaders. Military leaders want respect for the importance of the PLA mission and expect deference to the officers and men responsible for carrying it out. This concern is not only symbolic, but substantive: the desire for respect extends into a desire for acknowledgment of the PLA's professional expertise and right to speak authoritatively on military matters, in both public and private settings. This shades into an institutional desire, common to most militaries, for autonomy on military issues such as development of weapons systems, military doctrine and strategy, the execution of military operations, and operational training. However, such military issues can have broader consequences that bleed into political territory (when military operations affect foreign or trade relations, or in the potential for military modernization and weapons tests to spark arms races). As issues move across the spectrum from purely military to a mix of civilian and military interests, the PLA, like other militaries, is obliged to define and defend its institutional interests.

Other PLA institutional interests arise in the context of specific Chinese economic and political conditions. Because the PLA is "swimming in a new sea" in which the institution may be maladapted to present power dynamics and operational demands,[45] some institutional interests may be defined on the basis of uncertainty in a dynamic environment. The lack of precedent or formal guidance on how new security demands should be managed creates a contested political arena in which the PLA actively seeks to define and pursue its missions.

The 1989 Tiananmen incident and its civil-military aftermath is perhaps the clearest instance of a highly contextual factor that informs the PLA's sense of its institutional interests.[46] Although PLA units ultimately intervened on behalf of the CCP to suppress the demonstrations, they did so at considerable cost to the PLA's image among the Chinese public (and in international society more broadly). The episode amplified the dissonance between the PLA's self-appointed role as professional security guarantor for the state—and by extension, its citizens—and its formal subservience to the party. Since 1989, the PLA has sought to avoid this potential conflict of interest by transferring primary responsibility for internal security to the paramilitary People's Armed Police (PAP). It could be argued that the PLA has succeeded in asserting and defending this institutional interest, given the PAP's almost exclusive responsibility in domestic affairs and the PLA's curtailed role. The new arrangement was reflected in the 1997 PRC Law on National Defense, which codified the dual command structure for the PAP shared by the PLA and the State Council; the August 2009 Law on the People's Armed Police Force further specified the circumstances under which the PAP would be deployed to suppress domestic unrest.[47] All militaries share the responsibility to defend the state against citizen rebellions or unrest, but Tiananmen made the issue especially salient for the PLA. Without renouncing formal responsibility to protect Chinese Communist Party rule, PLA officers have advocated and pursued measures to keep the PLA as far from the domestic fray as possible. This is consistent with the PLA's broader institutional interest in maintaining sufficient autonomy to define and fulfill its responsibilities as a professional military.

China's turbulent history in the nineteenth and twentieth centuries has produced a heightened concern about protection of sovereignty and territorial integrity, not least because China claims a number of territories (including Taiwan, the Diaoyu/Senkaku Islands in the East China Sea, and the Spratly Islands in the South China Sea) that it does not fully control. The CCP's assertion that sovereignty and territorial integrity are "core interests" where no compromise is possible and the PLA's functional role as guardian of China's sovereignty and territorial integrity give the Chinese military standing to speak out on these issues. Statements from current and retired PLA leaders and a general pattern of military assertiveness suggest that the PLA sometimes differs from civilian officials in its view of how China's sovereignty claims should be defended.[48] While civilian "security experts" are among the loudest and most bellicose voices in the Chinese public sphere on these issues, their views are legitimized by frequent commentary from retired PLA officers and military academics about China's readiness to defend its claims. Retired military officers like Luo Yuan and Yang Yi use the media to shape the contours of the public discussion. Luo's March 2012 comments about the efficacy of "military measures" to support China's legal and administrative presence in the South China Sea are illustrative in this regard.[49] PLA officers have been willing to lobby publicly and privately to ensure that China's sovereignty is not infringed. In taking a starker and more urgent view of the challenges to Chinese claims, the PLA elevates its importance relative to other organizations in defending a national "core interest"—and in the case of Taiwan, the centerpiece of Chinese nationalism. Consistent with the institutional drive for more resources, the PLA has used threats to Chinese sovereignty and the need to achieve reunification with Taiwan to demand enhanced capabilities. Such lobbying also presents the PLA in a patriotic/nationalistic light, leveraging a vocal, nationalist public to increase the PLA's policy influence on how best to defend Chinese sovereignty or prevent Taiwan independence.

Another area where context matters is the expansion of Chinese economic and political interests that has accompanied its growing international trade and investment. Rapid economic growth has multiplied Chinese national interests overseas and produced a wider range of potential contingencies that may involve military action, including counter-piracy, counter-terrorism, protection of Chinese nationals overseas, and protection of the international economic interests of Chinese companies and individuals.[50] President Hu Jintao's articulation of "new historic missions" for the PLA, which include safeguarding national development and national interests, effectively expanded the functional and geographic scope of PLA responsibilities—and by extension its institutional interests.[51] Such interests and missions are not unique to China, but clash with long-established PRC foreign policy principles such as equality, mutual benefit, and respect for sovereignty.[52] The rapid expansion of Chinese interests (and potential vulnerabilities) has outstripped the government's institutional capacity and the historic roles played by different bureaucratic actors within the Chinese system. There have been periodic proposals to reorganize China's foreign policy and national security decisionmaking apparatus to increase policy coordination and coherence. A number of Chinese academics have privately argued that the PLA opposes such reforms, which might bring the military under civilian government control on some security issues, thus diminishing its current autonomy.[53] Nevertheless, the CCP leadership endorsed formation of a new National Security Commission with responsibilities for both internal and external security.[54]

The PLA may also seek a greater voice in defining and managing issues involving these "new" national interests. PLA officers appear to take a harder-line posture in construing these interests (and potential threats to them), partly because PLA officers seem to perceive a somewhat more hostile international security environment than civilian leaders. Military research and intelligence sub-units (e.g., the General Staff Department's Second Departments, the Academy of Military Sciences, and the National Defense University's Institute for Strategic Studies) play an important role in defining the international security environment and articulating potential threats to China's interests. Military officers participated in drafting the assessment of the international and regional security environment in the Eighteenth Party Congress Work Report issued in 2012. One officer involved in this process noted that even though the assessment in the work report did not fully reflect PLA opinions, the PLA was bound to respect the party consensus and draw from it for the 2013 Defense White Paper.[55] China's self-perception as a peaceful country with a purely defensive strategy also influences Chinese assessments of the external environment. Since Chinese actions must always be portrayed as responses to international trends or the hostile actions of other states, official assessments of the security environment or of the origins of a crisis have a significant influence on what responses are deemed appropriate.

Another context-specific set of interests revolves around the PLA's representation at the highest levels of the Chinese decisionmaking structure. The CMC nominally stands as highest deliberative and decisionmaking body for major military and strategic decisions, and is also charged with determining the PLA's organizational structure, missions, and responsibilities. The CMC also coordinates the PLA's budget with the State Council.[56] In reality, final decisionmaking authority rests with the Politburo Standing Committee (PBSC) and the CMC (under the leadership of the CMC chairman) ratifies these decisions.[57] Expansion or contraction of the CMC's roles can be a means of corralling issues under the PLA banner or avoiding responsibility for potentially detrimental issues. The PBSC member serving as CMC chairman provides formal PLA access to top civilian leaders,[58] but the PLA has not had its own representative on the PBSC since Liu Huaqing departed in 1997. Such a representative would provide a direct military voice and vote on all major issues, not just military issues. Although some military officers have expressed a desire for military representation on the PBSC, Deng Xiaoping's reorganization of that body's composition appears to have been designed in part to limit military influence on nonmilitary issues.[59]

The interests discussed above are all PLA institutional interests, some common to all militaries and others peculiar to the Chinese context. Other institutional interests likely only matter to select sub-groups within the PLA. For example, the relative importance of Chinese maritime interests is a critical institutional interest to all of the PLA Navy and to those parts of the PLA Air Force (PLAAF) and Second Artillery with antiship missions, but of little salience to the ground forces. This does not necessarily prevent the PLA from having and expressing a policy preference, but if only some parts of the PLA seek to influence Chinese policy the PLA voice may be less influential. What Garver discussed as "PLA sub-group linkages with non-PLA/civilian groups" can also be conceptualized as lobbies that cross military and civilian lines; these may be channels for PLA (sub-group) influence rather than barriers. Ties between individual services and related defense industries are an obvious example, as is the existence of a Chinese "naval lobby" on the importance of Chinese maritime interests that includes the PLA Navy, civilian paramilitary forces with maritime missions (including the State Fisheries Administration and the State Oceanic Administration), and civilian academics.[60]

In other cases, the PLA's organizational complexity (compounded by the stovepiping inherent in Chinese bureaucracy) and the diversity of its missions may preclude it from formulating a coherent organizational interest. Growth in military missions and capabilities has likely proceeded faster than the organization can adapt, creating a range of circumstances in which the notion of a coherent military interest is premature. Specific roles and responsibilities for sub-units may be undefined, or the technological capabilities required for a new mission area may remain aspirational or incomplete. Interservice competition for ownership of particular missions may divide the PLA in ways that limit its overall influence. For example, the question of whether space should be an air force service mission (a view articulated by then PLAAF Air Force Commander Xu Qiliang in interviews for the PLAAF's sixtieth anniversary) is a divisive issue within the PLA.[61] The tension Garver identified between a blue-water navy and ground forces is even more pronounced in today's PLA, where services compete for modernization resources and control over space, nuclear deterrence, and conventional strike missions.

Disputes over priorities reflect differences within the PLA leadership and the services on the relative importance of particular national interests and related modernization programs. For example, the navy advocates a carrier-based force to project power into disputed maritime areas, the air force sees strategic airlift as essential for disaster relief operations, and the Second Artillery highlights the strategic value of antiship ballistic missiles. From this perspective, the institutionalization of CMC membership for the air force, navy, and Second Artillery Commanders can be viewed as a nod to the need to represent the interests of those services. Even in an era of rising budgets, there are opportunity costs to pursuing any particular weapons system or capability. Inevitably, these decisions leave some actors within the PLA relatively worse off and thus promote internal dissension, encouraging political coalitions with external organizations and groups to help pursue narrower interests. Steps to improve the performance of the Chinese defense industry by giving the individual services more budgetary autonomy and empowering the General Armaments Department and the service armaments departments have increased the ability of the different services to articulate and pursue their own modernization projects and may have exacerbated interservice competition and rivalry.[62] Although interservice competition may sometimes limit concerted PLA political action, the dominant trend is toward increased PLA corporate identity and activism on behalf of widely shared organizational interests.

Conclusion

Many of the factors John Garver identified in the mid-1990s as cleavages that limited the PLA's ability to act as a coherent interest group are no longer relevant. Trends such as bifurcation of China's civilian and military elites and military professionalism have increased the PLA's sense of corporate identity and awareness of its own institutional interests. The Chinese political system's emphasis on the importance of expertise, credentials, and "scientific laws" highlights the military realm as an area marked by a coherent body of knowledge that must be mastered in order to comment knowledgeably. Coupled with military secrecy and the ability to control operational information, the PLA has arguably increased its autonomy significantly within the military realm. Although PLA officers have ceded many of the political roles that their revolutionary predecessors played, the expanding range of Chinese interests where military power is relevant and the imperatives of building an "informationized" military give the PLA equities in an expanding range of civilian areas. Thus, the military has both an increased ability to act as a coherent interest group and increased motivation to express and pursue its interests on a wider range of issues.

Broader trends in Chinese politics and society over the course of the reform period have reshaped the policymaking environment in which the PLA operates, contributing to the judgment that there are now fewer and less potent external forces inhibiting concerted PLA action as an interest group on national security policy. Today's China is a more rationalized, technocratic political system with greater functional differentiation and a technical specialization ordered largely on bureaucratic, rather than factional, lines. Within this context, the PLA's functional expertise gives it influence and autonomy within the military domain that was not possible in a less institutionalized Chinese political system. Continued pluralization in the policymaking process, bolstered by more open public forums for policy debates, also creates conditions more favorable to the PLA acting as an interest group.

The decline in personal authority at the pinnacle of the Chinese system since Deng is also conducive to greater PLA influence on policy. The absence of a paramount leader with unquestioned authority and prestige sufficient to speak for PLA interests—or to act against those interests—is highlighted by the limited military experience and expertise among the fourth and fifth generation party leadership. Top PLA leaders may no longer enjoy a high degree of informal access to central leadership built upon intertwined career paths and close relationships forged in a period of revolutionary struggle. But CCP leaders are also less likely to intervene in the PLA's domain on purely military issues. This changed dynamic at the elite level creates a stronger incentive for the PLA to conceive of its interests as distinct from those of the party and government and to pursue those interests in the policy realm.

In liberal political systems, interest groups freely organize, lobby, fundraise, and articulate their policy goals while seeking to influence government policy directly via channels established by the state as well as indirectly through the broader, public arena. In the PRC, extensive party control limits the range of acceptable opinions that may be expressed in the media. Restrictions on this means of expressing and generating political support for group interests, which previously limited PLA commentary on military and security issues to preapproved talking points, appear to have eased significantly in recent years. The sometimes contrarian voices of senior PLA officers and military pundits have found outlets in the party-controlled media as well as popular press, TV, and newspapers. This phenomenon is the product of a PLA with better-defined institutional interests that is able to make use of new channels to rally public support for its goals. Greater access to public media affords the PLA with a potent source of leverage to promote its interests and perspectives into the decisionmaking arena: popular nationalism. Couching appeals in the language of nationalism and rehearsing key tropes like unification, protection of sovereignty, resistance to hegemony, and Chinese dignity, media-savvy active and retired military officers have become more vocal and potentially more effective advocates of PLA interests. The net result is a PLA better able to formulate and articulate its interests as a distinct interest group and better equipped to pursue those interests through formal, informal, direct, and indirect channels.

The ability to articulate collective PLA interests offers no guarantee of success in producing the outcomes the PLA wants. At the end of the day, China's top CCP civilian leaders make the major decisions. However the nature of the issue at stake (military, political, or mixed) and the degree to which the PLA is unified in supporting common institutional interests likely affect when CCP civilian leaders seek to impose their will on the military. CCP leaders are more likely to intrude in the military domain on issues where the PLA is divided and there are military supporters for the desired action. For example, some senior PLA leaders have supported downsizing of the ground forces as a means of funding modernization and viewed divestment of PLA business interests as necessary to combat corruption and refocus the PLA on military concerns. Conversely, civilian leaders may have more difficulty imposing their will on military issues where the PLA is unified in supporting clear institutional interests, such as on military budgets and respect for the PLA as an institution.

Notes

The views expressed are those of the authors and do not reflect the official policy or position of the National Defense University, the Department of Defense, or the U.S. government.

1. See, for example, Linda Jakobson and Dean Knox, *New Foreign Policy Actors in China*, SIPRI Policy Paper 26 (Stockholm: SIPRI, 2010); Andrew Scobell, "Is There a Civil-Military Gap in China's Peaceful Rise?," *Parameters* 34, no. 2 (Summer 2009): 4–22; James Mulvenon, "Rogue Warriors? A Puzzled Look at the Chinese ASAT Test," *China Leadership Monitor*, no. 20 (Winter 2007); Bates Gill and Martin Kleiber, "China's Space Odyssey: What the Anti-Satellite Test Reveals about Decision-Making in Beijing," *Foreign Affairs* 86 (May/June 2007): 2–3.

2. John Garver, "The PLA as an Interest Group in Chinese Foreign Policy," in *Chinese Military Modernization*, eds. C. Dennison Lane, Mark Weisenbloom, and Dimon Liu (Washington, DC: AEI Press, 1996), 246–280.

3. Ibid., 250.

4. You Ji, "China: From Revolutionary Tool to Professional Military," in *Military Professionalism in Asia: Conceptual and Empirical Perspectives*, ed. Muthiah Alagappa (Honolulu: East-West Center, 2001).

5. David B. Truman, *The Governmental Process: Political Interests and Public Opinion* (New York: Alfred A. Knopf, 1962), 34–35.

6. Garver, "The PLA as an Interest Group," 250.

7. Ibid.

8. Mancur Olsen, *The Logic of Collective Action: Public Goods and the Theory of Groups* (Cambridge, MA: Harvard University Press, 1965).

9. The CCP acknowledged the existence of different interest groups in its Report on the Second Plenary Session of the Thirteenth Central Committee in 1988: "There are conflicts among different groups of people under the Socialist regime." Subsequently, Zheng Bijian [郑必坚] published an article analyzing the interest groups that emerged as a result of economic transformation. See "Great Change, Reconsider It" [大变动, 再认识], *People's Daily* [人民日报], May 20, 1988.

10. Wang Changjiang [王长江], "Research on the Problem of Valuing the 'Party Interest'" [重视对 "党的利益"问题的研究], *Marxism and Reality* [马克思主义与现实] 4 (2004): 4–7.

11. Yu Fenghui [余丰慧], "'Special Interest Group' Is the Enemy of Social Harmony" ["特别利益集团" 是和谐社会的对头], Xinhua [新华], October 5, 2006.

12. Yang Guangbin and Miao Li, "Western Political Science Theories and the Development of Political Theories in China," *Journal of Chinese Political Science* 14 (2009): 287.

13. Yang Guangbin and Li Yuejun [杨光斌, 李月军], "The Interest Group and Its Governance in Chinese Politics" [中国政治过程中的利益集团及其治理], *Xuehai* [学海] 2 (2008): 55–57.

14. Scott Kennedy, *The Business of Lobbying China* (Cambridge, MA: Harvard University Press, 2008).

15. Yu-Wen Julie Chen, "China's Foreign Policy: Challenges and Players," testimony before the U.S.-China Economic and Security Review Commission, April 13, 2011.

16. Gerald Segal, "The Military as a Group in Chinese Politics," in *Groups and Politics in the People's Republic of China*, ed. David E. Goodman (Armonk, NY: M.E. Sharpe, 1984), 83.

17. The next paragraphs draw on Michael Kiselycznyk and Phillip C. Saunders, *Civil-Military Relations in China: Assessing the PLA's Role in Elite Politics*, INSS China Strategic Perspectives 2 (Washington, DC: National Defense University, August 2010), 4–11.

18. Samuel P. Huntington, *The Soldier and the State: The Theory and Politics of Civil-Military Relations* (Cambridge, MA: Harvard University Press, 1957).

19. David Shambaugh was the first to apply the concept of "bifurcation" to the China case.

20. Amos Perlmutter and William M. LeoGrande, "The Party in Uniform: Towards a Theory of Civil-Military Relations in Communist Political Systems," *American Political Science Review* 76, no. 4 (December 1982): 778–789. See also David Shambaugh, "The Soldier and the State in China: The Political Work System in the People's Liberation Army," *China Quarterly*, no. 127 (September 1991): 527–568.

21. Provincial party secretaries are typically dual-hatted as chair of the provincial party military committee, but this responsibility appears to involve only limited involvement in local military affairs. Thanks to Monte Bullard for pointing out that Hu Jintao's experience as party secretary of Tibet during martial law in 1989 is an exception to the rule of civilian leaders having limited experience working with the military.

22. Willy Wo-Lap Lam, "PLA Gains Clout: Xi Jinping Elevated to CMC Vice-Chairman," *China Brief* 10, Issue 21 (October 22, 2010).

23. See Nan Li's chapter in this volume and Saunders interviews in Beijing, 2012.

24. Tai Ming Cheung, *China's Entrepreneurial Army* (New York: Oxford University Press, 2001), 232–258; James Mulvenon, "PLA Divestiture and Civil-Military Relations: Implications for the Sixteenth Party Congress Leadership," *China Leadership Monitor*, no. 1 (2002).

25. Li Cheng and Lynn White, "The Army in the Succession to Deng Xiaoping: Familiar Fealties and Technocratic Trends," *Asian Survey* 33, no. 8 (August 1993): 757–786; June Teufel Dreyer, "The Military's Uncertain Politics," *Current History* 95, no. 602 (September 1996): 254–260.

26. *A Comprehensive History of Chinese Military Education* [中国军事教育通史], vol. 2 (Shenyang: Liaoning Press [辽宁出版社], 1997); Roy Kamphausen, Andrew

Scobell, and Travis Tanner, "Introduction," in *The "People" in the PLA: Recruitment, Training, and Education in China's Military*, eds. Roy Kamphausen, Andrew Scobell, and Travis Tanner (Carlisle Barracks, PA: U.S. Army War College, 2008), 14.

27. Saunders interviews, 2008–2013. In 2013, a PAP officer was required to attend the Chinese NDU strategy course even though he had already been promoted to lieutenant general, indicated that this requirement has been formalized.

28. The 2004 Defense White Paper states that "The PLA will . . . enhance the development of its operational strength with priority given to the Navy, Air Force and Second Artillery Force." PRC State Council Information Office, "China's National Defense in 2004" (December 27, 2004). The Third Plenum decision document adopted on November 12, 2013, reiterates this priority. "Decision of the Central Committee of the Communist Party of China on Some Major Issues Concerning Comprehensively Deepening the Reform," China.org.cn, January 16, 2014.

29. See the relative treatment of mechanization and informationization goals in defense white papers; comments by PLA ground force officer to Phillip Saunders, 2011.

30. Shannon Tiezzi, "Xi Aims His Anti-Corruption Campaign at the PLA," *The Diplomat*, July 2, 2014.

31. The emergence of a civilian and military "naval lobby" emphasizing the importance of China's maritime interests is an example. See Michael A. Glosny and Phillip C. Saunders, "Correspondence: Debating China's Naval Nationalism," *International Security* 35, no. 2 (Fall 2010); M. Taylor Fravel and Alexander Liebman, "Beyond the Moat: The PLAN's Evolving Interests and Potential Influence," and Daniel M. Hartnett and Frederic Vellucci, "Towards a Maritime Security Strategy: An Analysis of Chinese Views Since the Early 1990s," both in *The Chinese Navy: Expanding Capabilities, Evolving Roles*, eds. Phillip C. Saunders et al. (Washington, DC: National Defense University Press, 2011).

32. See Kiselycznyk and Saunders, *Civil-Military Relations in China*, 4–11.

33. Daniel M. Hartnett, *Towards a Globally Focused Chinese Military: The Historic Missions of the Chinese Armed Forces* (Alexandria, VA: CNA Corporation, June 2008). The CMC General Office role in drafting the guidelines is based on interviews of PLA officers by a U.S. academic.

34. M. Taylor Fravel and Evan S. Medeiros, "China's Search for Assured Retaliation: The Evolution of Chinese Nuclear Strategy and Force Structure," *International Security* 35, no. 2 (Fall 2010): 48–87.

35. Chinese scholars writing about PLA issues almost always base their analysis on Western estimates of Chinese military forces and capabilities. For a brief discussion of the potential costs of lack of military transparency and internal debate on Chinese military effectiveness, see Phillip C. Saunders and Michael Kiselycznyk, *Assessing Chinese Military Transparency*, INSS China Strategic Perspectives 1 (Washington, DC: National Defense University, 2010), 35–36.

36. Saunders conversation, 2013.

37. This was reportedly an issue in the April 2001 EP-3 incident; see Michael Swaine's chapter in this volume.

38. See Li Cheng, "The Battle for China's Top Nine Leadership Posts," *Washington Quarterly* 35, no. 1 (Winter 2012): 133–135.

39. *NIDS China Security Report 2012* (Tokyo: National Institute for Defense Studies, 2012), 40–42.

40. Saunders interviews in 2013 reveal anecdotes about PLA officers being reluctant to park vehicles with military plates in front of fancy restaurants for fear that cell phone photos might get them in political trouble.

41. See *APT1: Exposing One of China's Cyber Espionage Units* (Alexandria, VA: Mandiant, 2013), http://intelreport.mandiant.com/Mandiant_APT1_Report.pdf; and David C. Gompert and Phillip C. Saunders, *The Paradox of Power: Sino-American Strategic Restraint in an Era of Vulnerability* (Washington, DC: NDU Press, 2011).

42. Morris Janowitz, *The Professional Soldier: A Social and Political Portrait* (New York: Free Press, 1960); Samuel E. Finer, *State- and Nation-Building in Europe: The Role of the Military* (Princeton, NJ: Princeton University Press, 1975); Jacques Van Doorn, *Military Profession and Military Regimes: Commitments and Conflicts* (The Hague: Mouton, 1969).

43. Barry Posen, *The Sources of Military Doctrine: Britain, France, and Germany between the World Wars* (Ithaca, NY: Cornell University Press, 1984).

44. For example, a PLA flag officer noted privately in 2010 that despite a recent doubling of military salaries, civilians in comparable positions earned three times his annual salary.

45. David Finkelstein and Kristen Gunness, *Civil-Military Relations in Today's China: Swimming in a New Sea* (Armonk, NY: M.E. Sharpe, 2006).

46. Ellis Joffe, "The Chinese Army: Coping with the Consequences of Tiananmen," in *China Briefing, 1991*, ed. William A. Joseph (Boulder, CO: Westview, 1992), 37–55; and Michael Swaine, *The Military and Political Succession in China: Leadership, Institutions, Beliefs* (Santa Monica, CA: RAND, 1992).

47. Michael Wines, "China Approves Law Governing Police," *New York Times*, August 27, 2009.

48. Michael Swaine, "Perceptions of an Assertive China," *China Leadership Monitor*, no. 32 (Spring 2010); M. Taylor Fravel and Michael Swaine, "China's Assertive Behavior—Part Two: The Maritime Periphery," *China Leadership Monitor*, no. 35 (Summer 2011); and Andrew Scobell and Scott W. Harold, "An 'Assertive' China? Insights from Interviews," *Asian Security* 9, no. 2 (May–August 2013), 111–131.

49. *NIDS China Security Report 2012*, 32.

50. See Andrew Scobell, Arthur Shuh-fan Ding, Phillip C. Saunders, and Scott W. Harold, eds., *The PLA and Contingency Planning in China* (Washington, DC: National Defense University Press, 2015).

51. James Mulvenon, "Chairman Hu and the PLA's 'New Historic Missions,'" *China Leadership Monitor*, no. 27 (Winter 2009).

52. Mathieu Duchâtel, Oliver Bräuner, and Zhou Hang, *Protecting China's Overseas Interests: The Slow Shift away from Non-interference*, SIPRI Policy Paper 41 (Stockholm: SIPRI, June 2014).

53. Saunders interviews, 2011.

54. Jane Perlez, "New Chinese Panel Said to Oversee Domestic Security and Foreign Policy," *New York Times*, November 13, 2013.

55. Saunders interview, 2013.

56. Kenneth Allen, "Introduction to the PLA's Administrative and Operational Structure," in *The People's Liberation Army as an Organization*, eds. James Mulvenon and Andrew N. D. Yang, Reference vol. 1 (Santa Monica, CA: RAND, 2001), 7.

57. See Michael Swaine's chapter in this volume.

58. Sometimes there is also a civilian CMC vice-chairman preparing to take the top leadership position.

59. See Alice Miller's chapter in this volume.

60. Fravel and Liebman, "Beyond the Moat"; Hartnett and Vellucci, "Towards a Maritime Security Strategy." See also Christopher Yung's chapter in this volume.

61. See "Flying with Force and Vigor in the Sky of the New Century—Central Military Commission Member and PLA Air Force Commander Xu Qiliang Answers Reporter's Questions in an Interview," *PLA Daily Online*, November 2, 2009, 1.

62. See the Cole, Saunders and Wiseman, and Chase chapters in *The Chinese Defense Economy Takes Off: Sector-by-Sector Assessments and the Role of Military End Users*, ed. Tai Ming Cheung (San Diego, CA: UC Institute on Global Conflict and Cooperation, 2013).

2   The PLA in the Party Leadership Decisionmaking System

Alice Miller

THE MODES AND MECHANISMS OF PLA PARTICIPATION in the decisionmaking processes of the PRC's political leadership have undergone a profound change in the post-Mao period. PLA interests seem nowadays to be conveyed primarily through institutional rather than personalistic channels. In a stark departure from the century-long pattern of military strongmen—from Yuan Shikai to Deng Xiaoping—serving as China's top political leaders, men of very limited or no military background—Jiang Zemin, Hu Jintao, and Xi Jinping—have presided over the PRC since the early 1990s. From all appearances, PLA representation on the party's core decisionmaking bodies over the past twenty-five years has been sharply downgraded. This reduction in military representation on the party's Politburo and its Standing Committee appears part of a deliberate effort engineered by Deng Xiaoping in the 1980s to establish an effective collective leadership system that builds in checks and balances among the leadership oligarchy against attempts by any individual member—and especially by the party general secretary—to assert dominating power over the others. This chapter sketches the transformation of the place of the PLA in the decisionmaking processes of the Chinese Communist Party (CCP), explains the political logic that has shaped it, and suggests some of the implications that stem from it.

Transformation of Party and PLA Elites

Until the late 1980s, the PLA's participation in PRC leadership decisionmaking reflected the historical circumstance that most of the regime's political and military leaders were professional revolutionaries who founded their regime by building an army and by defeating their political adversaries on the field of battle. As a consequence, most of the Chinese Communist Party's leadership had extensive military experience from the revolutionary period, and many continued after 1949 in military roles. For example, among the twenty-five members of the CCP Politburo appointed at the Twelfth Party Congress in 1982, twenty-three had joined the party before the 1935–1936 Long March. Most therefore had direct experience in military affairs during the 1926–1928 Northern Expedition and the insurgencies in Nanchang, Changsha, and Guangzhou in late 1927, in the CCP's struggles against Chiang Kai-shek's suppression campaigns in the early 1930s, in the Sino-Japanese War, and in the civil war that overthrew the ROC (Republic of China) on the mainland and established the People's Republic. At the time of the 1982 party congress, seven of the twenty-two remained in military posts.

The members of what the PRC has called its first two "leadership gen-erations" were therefore simultaneously political and military leaders. This blurred boundary between civilian political and military leaders had fun-damental consequences for policymaking, not only with regard to military affairs but also with regard to policy across all sectors. The existential threat posed by one or both superpowers across the first three decades of the PRC meant that the foremost priority of the regime was security, a reality that reinforced the relevance of military expertise and experience in leadership decisionmaking on virtually all fronts. Consequently, the military role in leadership decisionmaking was intrinsic to the party leadership itself. Partici-pation of the PLA brass in the deliberations of the party leadership rested not simply on formal bureaucratic channels, but also on the extensive informal relationships among the party elite that had founded the PRC and governed it over its first four decades. PLA leaders who wanted to raise some issue with the party leadership could simply call on Mao Zedong—routinely celebrated as the PLA's cofounder—or in the early post-Mao period on "Old Deng" or "Uncle Ye" and expect a hearing, based on decades of close association.

By the early 1990s, this long-standing pattern of military participation in party leadership decisionmaking changed fundamentally. One reason was simply actuarial: by the early 1990s, most of the veteran leaders who helped found the PRC and who dominated its leadership politics down through the 1980s had retired or passed from the scene. Deng Xiaoping himself retired from formal participation in leadership politics in 1990, and his staff office closed in 1994, indicating the end of even informal involvement. He died in 1997.

A second factor in the emergence of a new pattern of military participation in leadership decisionmaking was complementary political reforms that Deng Xiaoping inaugurated in the 1980s that stressed substantive expertise in the selection and promotion in both the party and PLA elites. These reforms, which have received extensive attention among observers of China's politics and military, brought a simultaneous effort to restore professionalism in the PLA and to recast the CCP itself into a body attuned to the tasks of guiding China's rapid modernization rather than to Mao Zedong's priority on waging class warfare. The party reforms included steps to weed out party members who had been recruited in the past according to Mao's "revolutionary" criteria of adherence to his ideological doctrines and who possessed skills of political mobilization that suited his penchant for great campaigns. In their place, the party reforms sought to recruit party cadres who had a formal education in technical and managerial fields and long administrative experience in substantive policy sectors of China's bureaucratic hierarchy and who therefore would be competent to implement the modernization policies Deng espoused. The party reforms also imposed term limits and retirement norms that have generated routinized turnover of party leaders and rejuvenated the party from bottom to top. The PLA reforms included a restoration of officer ranks in 1988, the concurrent adoption of explicit promotion and retirement provisions for active duty officers in the same year, and the expansion of professional military education attuned to the needs of conducting modern, increasingly technology-driven warfare. What resulted from this emphasis on expertise among both political and military leaders has been a sharp bifurcation of the political and military arenas, with an almost completely civilian political leadership in the CCP presiding over what has become a thoroughly professional PLA brass.

As a consequence of these reforms, the relationship between China's political and military elites since the early 1990s approximates the optimal model of civilian-military leadership decisionmaking relationships described more than fifty years ago by Samuel Huntington in his 1957 classic study *The Soldier and the State*. Huntington contrasted what he called "objective civilian control" of the military, by which the civilian state recognized an autonomous professional military sector, from "subjective civilian control," which resulted from blurred boundaries between the civilian political and military sectors. Huntington argued:

> Civilian control in the objective sense is the maximizing of military professionalism. More precisely, it is that distribution of political power between military and civilian groups which is most conducive to the emergence of professional attitudes and behavior among the members of the officer corps. Objective civilian control is thus directly opposed to subjective civilian control. Subjective civilian control achieves its end by civilianizing the military, making them the mirror of the state. Objective civilian control achieves its end by militarizing the military, making them the tool of the state. . . . The essence of objective civilian control is the recognition of autonomous military professionalism; the essence of subjective civilian control is the denial of an independent military sphere.[1]

From this perspective, civil-military relations in China since the 1980s have undergone a transformation from subjective civilian control to objective civilian control. By virtue of that transformation, on one hand, the PLA's influence in the processes of political decisionmaking of the top party leadership has narrowed into predominantly institutional mechanisms and the CCP leadership has recognized the legitimacy and practical necessity of an autonomous professional military sphere. On the other hand, as the division of roles created by this transition consolidates itself, it may over time erect significant conceptual and behavioral barriers against deep intrusion into military operational decisionmaking by a thoroughly civilian political leadership.

Structural Reforms

Complementing the reconstitution of the party and PLA elites, Deng Xiaoping also introduced reforms to instill a new dynamic in party leadership politics and processes intended to institutionalize an oligarchic collective leadership at the top. These reforms have had fundamental consequences for PLA representation in the CCP's top decisionmaking bodies and for the mechanisms by which PLA interests and concerns are expressed in the party leadership.

Deng's reforms of party leadership processes trace their roots back to the mid-1950s, when Mao and his colleagues in the top leadership began to establish a party decisionmaking structure better suited to the tasks of stable governance and promoting China's national prosperity and power.[2] From the Yan'an period down to the Eighth CCP Congress in 1956, the party's top decisionmaking body had been the Party Secretariat. The Seventh Party Congress in 1945 had appointed a Politburo, but that body, according to authoritative party histories, rarely met. The CCP had had a Politburo Standing Committee since November 1924, but the Seventh Party Congress did not appoint a new one. This streamlined party structure led at the top by a Mao-dominated Secretariat facilitated efficient leadership decisionmaking on the eve of the civil war against the ROC led by Chiang Kai-shek.[3]

In the wake of the establishment of full-scale socialist political institutions at the First National People's Congress in September 1954, the leadership began planning a complementary revamping of the party's leadership institutions that were formally set down at the Eighth Party Congress in September 1956. The Eighth Central Committee's First Plenum after the party congress reinstituted a Politburo Standing Committee, appointing six members with Mao as chairman, as well as appointing a 20-member Politburo. It also appointed a Secretariat composed of twelve members and three alternates under the direction of Deng Xiaoping, who was given the restored post of general secretary.[4] In this new structure, the Politburo Standing Committee was to make all major political and policy decisions, while the role of the Secretariat was to coordinate and supervise implementation of decisions made by the Standing Committee. The link between the two bodies was Deng Xiaoping, who presided over the Secretariat but also served as the lowest-ranking member of the Standing Committee. Under this structure, the full Politburo met only occasionally. In June 1958, the leadership created five leading small groups (领导小组) under the Secretariat to facilitate and coordinate implementation of policy in the financial and economic, political-legal, foreign affairs, science and technology, and cultural and education sectors.[5]

Political leadership over the PLA was also altered among the 1954–1956 revisions of leading party and state organs. The state constitution adopted at the First National People's Congress (NPC) in 1954 stipulated that "the armed forces of the PRC belong to the people" (Article 20) and the "the President of the PRC shall command the armed forces" (Article 42). Also in 1954, the party leadership re-created a Central Military Commission (CMC) as the party's military policymaking body under Mao's leadership. The revised party constitution adopted at the Eighth CCP Congress did not mention the CMC or prescribe its role. It stated only that "the Party organizations in the Chinese

PLA carry on their work in accordance with the instructions of the Central Committee" and that "the General Political Department in the PLA, under the direction of the Central Committee, takes charge of the ideological and organizational work of the Party in the army" (Article 35).

The structure of leadership decisionmaking and policy supervision put in place in the 1954–1956 period prevailed over the subsequent decade. With the onset of the Cultural Revolution, however, the Secretariat was crippled with the purge of the "black gang" at a Politburo session in May 1966, and the Cultural Revolution Small Group at the same meeting effectively displaced the Politburo Standing Committee. With the demise of the Secretariat, the leading small groups ceased functioning.

In addition, for the first three years after the Eighth CCP Congress, this ambiguity of the party and state institutional role in guiding the PLA did not appear to affect Mao's leadership of the military, given his role as both CMC chairman and PRC president. It did, however, seem to unravel following Liu Shaoqi's appointment at the Second NPC in April 1959 and especially following the leadership clash at Lushan the following July and August. With the assistance of his left-hand man Lin Biao as CMC vice-chairman, Mao moved to re-politicize the PLA, both in service to the revamped "people's war" defense doctrine that emerged in the wake of the Soviet cut-off in military assistance and to consolidate control over the military as an asset in a developing leadership struggle. In the Cultural Revolution, the PLA served as a critical asset for Mao. Finally, in 1970, in a context of leadership debate over convening a Fourth NPC and after a major intraparty struggle that led to the purge of Chen Boda, consideration of restoration of the post of PRC president was rejected, eliminating the ambiguity created in the mid-1950s over who commanded the military. The party constitutions adopted at the 1969 Ninth, 1973 Tenth, and 1977 Eleventh Party Congresses and the PRC constitutions adopted at the 1975 Fourth and 1978 Fifth NPCs all stated that the party guides the PLA. The 1978 PRC constitution stated flatly that the chairman of the CCP Central Committee (by that time, Hua Guofeng) "commands the armed forces."

After establishing himself as the PRC's paramount leader at the December 1978 Third Plenum, Deng Xiaoping moved to restore the 1956 leadership system to make policy decisions and supervise their implementation. The Eleventh Central Committee's Fifth Plenum in February 1980 restored the Secretariat and appointed ten secretaries under the direction of Deng's right-hand man,

Hu Yaobang, who was given the resurrected post of general secretary. In addition, the leading small groups were gradually reestablished, beginning with the Central Finance and Economy Leading Small Group (*Zhongyang caizheng jingji lingdao xiaozu*) on 17 March 1980. The Twelfth Central Committee's First Plenum, convened the day after the close of the Twelfth Party Congress in September 1982, appointed as the decisionmaking core of the leadership a six-member Politburo Standing Committee, composed, as in 1956, of the top leaders of the major hierarchies in the PRC's political order: Party General Secretary Hu Yaobang, NPC Chairman Ye Jianying, CMC Chairman Deng Xiaoping, Premier Zhao Ziyang, soon-to-be PRC President Li Xiannian, and Party Central Discipline Inspection Commission Secretary Chen Yun. The plenum also appointed a Politburo of nineteen regular members (excluding the six Standing Committee members) and a Secretariat of ten members under Hu Yaobang. As in the 1956 system, the Politburo Standing Committee was to serve as the key decisionmaking core of the leadership, while the Secretariat would coordinate and supervise implementation of Standing Committee decisions. The link between the two bodies was Hu Yaobang who, as general secretary and with the abolition of the post of party chairman at the Twelfth Congress, now was the party's top-ranked leader. In the years following the 1982 Party congress, as in the 1956–1966 period, the broader Politburo met only occasionally.

Finally, in 1982 both the party and PRC constitutions were revised to restore and clarify the ambiguity in the 1954–1956 system in the division of responsibility between party and state authority in guiding the PLA. The party constitution adopted at the Twelfth Party Congress stipulated that:

> Party organizations in the Chinese PLA carry on their work in accordance with the instructions of the Central Committee. The political work organ of the Central Military Commission of the Central Committee is the General Political Department of the PLA; the GPD directs party and political work in the army. The organizational system and organs of the party in the armed forces are prescribed by the Military Commission of the Central Committee. (Article 23)

The revised PRC constitution promulgated by the Fifth NPC's Fifth Session in December 1982 established a new PRC CMC alongside the CCP's. It specified that PRC CMC "directs the armed forces of the country" and that "the chairman of the [PRC] CMC is responsible to the National People's Congress and its Standing Committee" (Articles 93 and 94).

Deng's restoration of the 1956 system served two purposes. One was, as in the mid-1950s, to create a leadership decisionmaking system suited to the task of effective policymaking in governing a country undergoing rapid modernization. This required representation of all of the major institutional hierarchies and political constituencies that had a stake in all major sectors of national policy. A leadership collective—government by committee—served that purpose best. Second, Deng and his reform colleagues sought to inhibit the potential for any leader—and especially the general secretary—to assert the dictatorial leadership that Mao had attained after the late 1950s and, before him, Stalin had in Soviet politics after the late 1920s, with disastrous consequences in both countries. In his landmark speech "On the Reform of the System of Party and State Leadership" in August 1980, Deng advised:

> Even so great a man as Comrade Mao Zedong was influenced to a serious degree by certain unsound systems and institutions, which resulted in grave misfortunes for the Party, state, and himself. . . . Stalin gravely damaged socialist legality, doing things which Comrade Mao Zedong once said would have been impossible in Western countries like Britain, France, and the United States. Yet although Comrade Mao was aware of this, he did not in practice solve the problems in our system of leadership. Together with other factors, this led to the decade of catastrophe known as the "Cultural Revolution." There is a most profound lesson to learn from this.[6]

Because of that concern, the collective leadership system required balances and constraints to sustain relative equality in standing among its members.

The restored 1956 system, however, ultimately failed. Hu Yaobang was demoted as general secretary in January 1987 for a variety of sins, but the underlying reason was his abuse of the Secretariat at the expense of the Politburo Standing Committee. The Thirteenth CCP Congress in October 1987 therefore revised the leadership system accordingly. The Secretariat was reduced to only four members and one alternate under the direction of General Secretary Zhao Ziyang. In addition, while the Politburo Standing Committee continued to serve as the core decisionmaking body in the leadership, the full Politburo began to meet more regularly—roughly once a month—and began the practice of hearing reports by Zhao on the work of the Standing Committee.[7]

The Thirteenth Party Congress also introduced new steps to reinforce collective leadership. The first steps toward balancing institutional constituencies on the Politburo emerged at this time. For example, for the first time since

1958, the Politburo began to include regional members—from Beijing, Shanghai, Tianjin, and Sichuan—creating a new representational bloc in the central decisionmaking arena. In the opposite direction—presumably in an effort to blunt the use of the PLA as a base of power either by the general secretary or on its own—the new Politburo also counted only a single PLA leader—CMC member and Minister of National Defense Qin Jiwei—among its members. The 1982 Politburo had included eight members of the CMC and PLA. In addition, Deng Xiaoping, who retained his positions as chairman of both CMCs, retired from the Politburo and its Standing Committee, while General Secretary Zhao Ziyang was added as CMC vice-chairman, preparing for the way for Zhao to succeed Deng as chairman when Deng retired two years later.

Finally, at its first meeting after the party congress, the Politburo adopted "work rules" (*gongzuo guize*) for the Politburo, its Standing Committee, and the Secretariat. Although these rules have never been publicized, their purpose was to reinforce consensus decisionmaking by reducing the prerogatives of the general secretary, to enforce the responsibility of the Standing Committee to the full Politburo and, in turn, of the Politburo to the Central Committee by regular reporting procedures, and to make the Secretariat simply a working body (*banshi jigou*) of the Politburo.[8]

The alterations introduced in 1987 established the structure of party leadership decisionmaking that prevailed for the remainder of Zhao Ziyang's brief tenure as general secretary and, with small modifications, through the thirteen years of Jiang Zemin's leadership. Under Jiang, the Secretariat grew somewhat in size—to five following the Fourteenth CCP Congress in 1992 and to seven following the Fifteenth CCP Congress in 1997. PLA representation on the Politburo, however, continued to be limited—to two during Jiang's tenure.

The Party Leadership System under Hu Jintao and Xi Jinping

The leadership decisionmaking structure that prevailed across Hu Jintao's tenure as party general secretary and now exists under Xi Jinping is a refinement of the structure set down in 1987. First, the Politburo Standing Committee appointed at the Sixteenth Central Committee's First Plenum in November 2002—at the beginning of Hu's first term—was expanded from seven to nine members. Table 2.1 shows that this expansion made the 2002 Politburo Standing Committee the largest in the post-Mao period.

TABLE 2.1 Size of the CCP Politburo and Standing Committee, 1956–2012

Central Committee	Chairman	General secretary	Standing Committee	Full Politburo
8th (1956)	Mao Zedong	Deng Xiaoping	6	19 + 6 alts.
8th (1958)	Mao Zedong	Deng Xiaoping	7	20 + 6 alts.
8th (1966)	Mao Zedong	Deng Xiaoping	11	21 + 5 alts.
9th (1969)	Mao Zedong	none	5	21 + 4 alts.
10th (1973)	Mao Zedong	none	10	22 + 4 alts.
11th (1977)	Hua Guofeng	none	6	28 + 3 alts
12th (1982)	none	Hu Yaobang	6	25 + 3 alts.
13th (1987)	none	Zhao Ziyang	5	17 + 1 alt.
14th (1992)	none	Jiang Zemin	7	20 + 2 alts.
15th (1997)	none	Jiang Zemin	7	22 + 2 alts.
16th (2002)	none	Hu Jintao	9	24 + 1 alt.
17th (2007)	none	Hu Jintao	9	25
18th (2012)	none	Xi Jinping	7	25

NOTE: Hua Guofeng was replaced as party chairman by Hu Yaobang at the Eleventh Central Committee's Sixth Plenum in June 1981. The post of chairman was abolished the following year at the Twelfth CCP Congress.

Rumors and speculation at the time attributed this expansion to Jiang Zemin's effort to stack the Standing Committee with his own supporters and so to hem Hu Jintao in from altering the direction of policies that Jiang favored. The ability of Hu and Premier Wen Jiabao to institute new policy departures immediately out of the gate, however, raises doubt about the validity of this line of interpretation.[9] Moreover, the retention of a nine-member Standing Committee by the 2007 Seventeenth Party Congress—at which Jiang's "Shanghai gang" clique was dismantled and at which Hu's power was consolidated—also casts doubt on this conventional wisdom.

A better explanation is that the expansion of the Politburo Standing Committee reflected an attempt to enhance collective leadership decisionmaking. The expanded Politburo Standing Committee appointed in 2002, as before, brought together the heads of all of the major institutional hierarchies in China's political order. But it also now included representatives of the other key policy sectors that had not been included in the 1997 Fifteenth Central Committee Politburo Standing Committee around Jiang Zemin. Specifically, the 2002 Standing Committee included the head of the internal security sector (Luo Gan) and the head of the ideology-propaganda system (Li Changchun).

In addition, beginning in 2002, the members of the Standing Committee also served concurrently as directors of the Central Committee's seven leading small groups that coordinated and supervised policy. This had not been the case previously. In the Politburo Standing Committee appointed in 1997, for example, Jiang Zemin served concurrently as director of both the Central Foreign Affairs (*Zhongyang waishi gongzuo lingdao xiaozu*) and Central Taiwan Affairs (*Zhongyang duitai gongzuo lingdao xiaozu*) Leading Small Groups and Premier Zhu Rongji served as director of the Central Finance and Economy Leading Small Groups. However, Luo Gan, the director of the Central Politics and Law Committee, and Ding Guan'gen, director of the Central Ideology and Propaganda Leading Small Group (*Zhongyang xuanchuan sixing xiaozu*), served only on the Politburo, not on its Standing Committee. The resulting division of combined policy sector representation and supervision among the members of the 2002 Sixteenth and 2007 Seventeenth Politburo Standing Committees is as shown in Tables 2.2 and 2.3.

The significance of these changes in the size and division of policy sector representation and supervision on the Politburo Standing Committee has been to make it concurrently the decisionmaking and policy coordination and supervision core in the PRC's political system. Encompassing the heads of all of the major institutional hierarchies—the party, its Discipline Inspection Commission, the NPC, the State Council, the military, and the Chinese People's Political Consultative Conference—as well as representatives of all of the major policy sectors—foreign relations, party affairs, legislative, government administration, economic policy, united front affairs, propaganda, internal security, and military affairs—the Politburo Standing Committee under Hu Jintao was organized to address and decide in a balanced and comprehensive way all major issues that the CCP's central leadership might encounter.

The 8–14 November 2012 Eighteenth CCP Congress and the 15 November Eighteenth Central Committee's First Plenum reduced the size of the Politburo Standing Committee under new General Secretary Xi Jinping but preserved the logic of policy sector representation and supervision. In the reduction, representation of two policy sectors (management of the party apparatus and ideology and propaganda) that were previously supervised by separate Standing Committee members was placed under a single leader, Liu Yunshan, and one policy sector (internal security) was dropped altogether.[10] Table 2.4 lays out the revised Standing Committee structure under Xi Jinping.

TABLE 2.2 Sixteenth CC Politburo Standing Committee's Division of Policy Work, 2002

Member	Other posts	Policy sector	Leading small group
Hu Jintao	CCP general secretary, PRC president, CMC chairman	Foreign relations; military affairs	Director, Foreign Affairs LSG, Taiwan Affairs LSG, and Finance & Economy LSG
Wu Bangguo	Chairman, National People's Congress	Legislative affairs	
Wen Jiabao	Premier, State Council	Government administration	
Jia Qinglin	Chairman, Chinese People's Political Consultative Conference	United front affairs	
Zeng Qinghong	Executive secretary, CC Secretariat; president, Central Party School; PRC vice president	Party apparatus; Hong Kong & Macao affairs	Party-building LSG; Hong Kong & Macao Affairs LSG
Huang Ju	Executive vice-premier, State Council	Finance and economy	Deputy director, Finance & Economy LSG
Wu Guanzheng	Chairman, Central Discipline Inspection Commission	Party discipline	
Li Changchun		Ideology and propaganda affairs	Ideology & Propaganda LSG
Luo Gan		Internal security	Politics & Law Committee

TABLE 2.3 Seventeenth CC Politburo Standing Committee's Division of Policy Work, 2007

Member	Other posts	Policy sector	Leading small group
Hu Jintao	CCP general secretary, PRC president, CMC chairman	Foreign relations; military affairs	Director, Foreign Affairs LSG, Taiwan Affairs LSG, and Finance & Economy LSG
Wu Bangguo	Chairman, National People's Congress	Legislative affairs	
Wen Jiabao	Premier, State Council	Government administration	
Jia Qinglin	Chairman, Chinese People's Political Consultative Conference	United front affairs	
Li Changchun		Ideology & propaganda affairs	
Xi Jinping	Executive secretary, CC Secretariat; president, Central Party School; PRC vice president	Party apparatus; Hong & Macao affairs	Party-building LSG; Hong Kong & Macao Affairs LSG
Li Keqiang	Executive vice-premier, State Council	Finance & economy	Deputy director, Finance & Economy LSG
He Guoqiang	Chairman, Central Discipline Inspection Commission	Party discipline	
Zhou Yongkang		Internal security	Politics & Law Committee

TABLE 2.4 Eighteenth CC Politburo Standing Committee's Division of Policy Work, 2012

Member	Other posts	Policy sector	Leading small group
Xi Jinping	CCP general secretary, PRC president, CMC chairman	Foreign relations, military affairs	Director, Foreign Affairs LSG, Taiwan Affairs LSG, and Finance & Economy LSG
Li Keqiang	Premier, State Council	Government administration	
Zhang Dejiang	Chairman, National People's Congress	Legislative affairs	
Yu Zhengsheng	Chairman, Chinese People's Political Consultative Conference	United front affairs	
Liu Yunshan	Executive secretary, CC Secretariat; president, Central Party School	Party apparatus; Hong & Macao affairs; ideology & propaganda affairs	Party-building LSG; Hong Kong & Macao Affairs LSG; Ideology & Propaganda LSG
Wang Qishan	Chairman, Central Discipline Inspection Commission	Party discipline	
Zhang Gaoli	Executive vice-premier, State Council	Finance & economy	Deputy director, Finance & Economy LSG

One major casualty in the focusing of both decisionmaking and policy supervision in the Standing Committee has been the Secretariat. The various Central Committee leading small groups were originally created in 1958 to enable the Secretariat to coordinate implementation of decisions made by the Politburo and its Standing Committee. In their reincarnation in the post-Mao era, their leadership has gradually migrated into the hands of members of the Standing Committee, to the point that by 2002, the directors of all seven were focused there. Over the Hu period, in fact, the Secretariat was successively downgraded to the point that, since 2007, it became effectively the body for coordinating Politburo Standing Committee decisions affecting the party apparatus only, and it no longer included representatives from other sectors, including the military. Tables 2.5 and 2.6 show the policy areas represented on the Fifteenth and Seventeenth Central Committee Secretariats.

Along with the alterations to make the Politburo Standing Committee the core arena for balanced and effective policy deliberation and coordination,

TABLE 2.5 Fifteenth Central Committee Secretariat, 1997

Member	Other posts
Hu Jintao	Politburo Standing Committee; Executive secretary, Secretariat
Wei Jianxing	Politburo Standing Committee; Dep. secretary Central Discipline Inspection Commission
Ding Guan'gen	Politburo; Director, CC Propaganda Department
Zhang Wannian	Politburo; Vice-chairman, Central Military Commission
Luo Gan	Politburo; State councilor, internal security
Wen Jiabao	Politburo; Vice-premier, finance & economy
Zeng Qinghong	Politburo alternate; Director, CC General Office

TABLE 2.6 Seventeenth Central Committee Secretariat, 2007

Member	Other posts
Xi Jinping	Politburo Standing Committee; Executive secretary, Secretariat
Liu Yunshan	Politburo; Director, CC Propaganda Department
Li Yuanchao	Politburo; Director, CC Organization Department
He Yong	Dep. secretary, Central Discipline Inspection Commission
Ling Jihua	Director, CC General Office
Wang Huning	Director, CC Policy Research Office

steps were undertaken to reinforce the Standing Committee, and the full Politburo, as a consensus-driven oligarchy. Oligarchies are inherently unstable, suffering from two countervailing tendencies—one centripetal and the other centrifugal. On one hand, the oligarchy must inhibit its foremost leader or any bloc within the leadership collective from acquiring overwhelming dictatorial power, as Mao did after 1957 and as Stalin did in the USSR after the late 1920s. On the other hand, the oligarchy must inhibit any group of leaders in the oligarchy from destabilizing the collective by reaching out to outside constituencies to enhance its power and split the leadership, as Zhao Ziyang attempted to do in May 1989 by visiting the demonstrators in Tiananmen Square and as Boris Yeltsin did in CPSU politics in 1991.

With regard to the first concern, there was a clear-cut effort across Hu Jintao's tenure as general secretary to treat him simply as first among equals. Hu was not designated the "core" of the PRC's "fourth generation" leadership, as Deng designated Jiang Zemin "core" of the "third generation" leadership and himself as "core" of the "second."[11] Deng introduced these designations in the immediate wake of the 1989 Tiananmen crisis in an evident attempt to shore up the standing of Jiang Zemin as the new, unexpected party general secretary. And across the entire Jiang era from 1989 to 2002, PRC media fastidiously referred to "the Central Committee leadership collective with Comrade Jiang Zemin as the core." It is striking, therefore, that this elevated stature was not attached to Hu Jintao. Instead, PRC media routinely referred to "the Central Committee leadership collective with Comrade Hu Jintao as general secretary." During Hu's first term as general secretary, this omission might have been explained as a reflection of Hu's relative weakness and his not having consolidated power. However, the failure to designate Hu as "core" leader continued after the 2007 Seventeenth Party Congress, at which Hu clearly consolidated his power, and so that explanation is not persuasive. So far, Xi Jinping has been treated similarly as first among equals in the Politburo since his appointment as general secretary in November 2012.

In addition, Hu Jintao was not credited with any major ideological or policy initiative. Several major departures emerged during his tenure as general secretary—the focus on "people-centered" governance that began in 2002, the "scientific development concept" launched in 2003, the effort to build a "new socialist countryside" begun in 2005, and the goal of a "socialist harmonious society" raised in 2004 and endorsed in a long Central Committee resolution at the Sixteenth Central Committee's Sixth Plenum in October 2006. None of these departures was credited to the leadership genius of Hu Jintao or as his distinctive intellectual property. They were instead described as reflecting the initiative of "the Sixteenth Central Committee leadership collective." Similarly, two years into his tenure as party general secretary, Xi Jinping has not been praised as the innovator of any new ideological departures. By contrast, Jiang Zemin was personally credited with several new political and policy initiatives, such as the "three represents" in 2000.

In that regard, it is interesting that this leveling of Hu's stature in the party leadership did not extend to his leadership over the PLA. As Jiang was during his tenure as CMC chairman, Hu was routinely described in PRC media as imparting "important thinking" and new initiatives in the military arena. This disparity in treatment of Hu's leadership in the party and over the PLA was likely due to a concern to underscore his authority in presiding over the PLA, consonant with the ongoing sensitivity since 1989 on the PLA maintaining "absolute loyalty" to the party. Thus far, treatment in the official media of Xi Jinping's speeches and instructions to the PLA has paralleled that accorded to Hu Jintao's.

Why in this context the civilian party leadership has not sought to strengthen control over the PLA by increasing its representation on the CMC is not clear. One reason may simply derive from the logic of professionalization and a strict division of policy labor. That is, the CMC is intended as the locus of decisionmaking in purely military affairs. Broader questions of the implications of military decisions—for the economy, for politics, etc.—are allocated to the Politburo, where the CMC's two professional military vice chairmen sit, and, through the general secretary, its Standing Committee. Another reason may be that seating more civilian party leaders on the CMC enhances the prospects for politicization of military policymaking and for injecting the military into leadership politics. On one hand, multiple civilian party leaders on the CMC affords competing interests in the PLA and interservice rivalries opportunities to play to civilian party leaders beside the general secretary and so complicate CMC decisionmaking. On the other, more civilian leaders serving on the CMC affords more channels of potential PLA influence into Politburo policymaking. Finally, the negative lesson of expanded civilian party membership on the CMC during the highly politicized Mao era remains fresh in the minds of the successive post-Mao leaderships and so both reinforces the logic of professionalization and constrains any new impulse to expand civilian representation on the CMC.

Stabilization of the leadership oligarchy has also been reflected in efforts to balance institutional blocs on the broader Politburo. Such steps emerged first at the Thirteenth CCP Congress in 1987 and continued across the Jiang years, but appear to have reached maturity during the Hu era. Table 2.7 shows the representation among the members of the full Seventeenth Central Committee Politburo (excepting the heads of the four major institutional hierarchies—Hu Jintao, Wu Bangguo, Wen Jiabao, and Jia Qinglin) of the party apparatus, the state institutions, the provinces, and the military and security sector. PLA representatives are listed in bold.

The object of this balancing appears to be to inhibit any institutional bloc from asserting dominance over the rest of the leadership collective. In particular, the limitation of PLA representation to two members—a quota that has been sustained since 1992—appears to reflect a concern to inhibit the use of the military as a base of power by the general secretary, as Mao did as party chairman, and as Deng Xiaoping did in some measure, and to prevent the military from establishing itself as a dominating bloc in the collective leadership in its own right.

This careful balancing of institutional blocs on the Politburo continues in the Xi Jinping Politburo, as shown in Table 2.8.

TABLE 2.7 Representation of Institutional Constituencies on the Seventeenth Central Committee Politburo, 2007

Party apparatus	State institutions	Provinces	Military/Security
Li Changchun	Li Keqiang	Wang Lequan	Zhou Yongkang
Xi Jinping	Wang Zhaoguo	Liu Qi	
He Guoqiang	Wang Qishan	Wang Yang	**Xu Caihou**
Wang Gang	Hui Liangyu	Zhang Gaoli	**Guo Boxiong**
Liu Yunshan	Liu Yandong	Yu Zhengsheng	
Li Yuanchao	Zhang Dejiang	Bo Xilai	

TABLE 2.8 Representation of Institutional Constituencies on the Eighteenth Central Committee Politburo, 2012

Party apparatus	State institutions	Provinces	Military/Security
Liu Yunshan	Li Yuanchao	Sun Chunlan	Meng Jianzhu
Wang Qishan	Zhang Gaoli	Sun Zhengcai	
Liu Qibao	Ma Kai	Zhang Chunxian	**Fan Changlong**
Zhao Leji	Liu Yandong	Hu Chunhua	**Xu Qiliang**
Li Zhanshu	Li Jianguo	Guo Jinlong	
Wang Huning	Wang Yang	Han Zheng	

The PLA in the Party Leadership System

The upshot of all of these steps at establishing and stabilizing a collective leadership at the top of the party has been transformative with regard to the PLA's participation in party leadership decisionmaking. First, the effort to shape the Politburo Standing Committee as an arena for comprehensive, balanced, and effective policymaking has narrowed PLA representation as one among several major constituencies represented on the body. The PLA's sole representatives in the Hu Jintao period were Hu, serving concurrently as CMC chairman, and (since October 2010) Xi Jinping, serving as CMC vice-chairman and as Hu's intended successor as CMC chairman. On the Politburo Standing Committee led by Xi Jinping, only Xi himself represents the PLA.

In that regard, the CMC in some sense resembles the role of the Central Committee leading small groups. It, of course, ranks much higher—it is appointed by the Central Committee itself, while the leading small groups are informal task forces appointed by the Politburo. But from the perspective of the Politburo Standing Committee's division of policy sector representation and supervision, it is in effect the leading small group for military affairs.

PLA participation in the other leading small groups is also shaped by considerations of policy relevance and of ex officio representation. As Tables 2.9–2.11 show, PLA representatives sit on the Foreign Affairs and Taiwan Affairs Leading Small Groups and on the Politics and Law Committee.[12] PLA representatives are listed in bold in each case. The consistency of the PLA representatives in their concurrent posts in the military across periodic reshuffles of the leading small groups indicates that they participate ex officio. The membership of these leading small groups under the new Xi leadership is not yet available from official sources, though they may be guessed at using an ex officio logic.

The four remaining Central Committee leading small groups—Finance and Economy, Ideology and Propaganda, Party-Building, and Hong Kong–Macao Work—have no PLA representatives among their membership.

In most cases, in the Xi Jinping era the membership of the three major Central Committee leading small groups has not been made public. Presuming that appointments to these groups are made mainly on the basis of ex officio representation, the respective members of each group may be inferred (see Tables 2.12 and 2.13).

The Central Committee Politics and Law Committee still operates in the Xi era and presumably selects its membership on the same ex officio considerations that determined appointment in the Hu Jintao era. But it has been subsumed under a new State Security Committee, mandated at the Eighteenth CCP Congress and established in 2013. The role of the new committee has been described vaguely in Chinese media, which state that it will focus on strategic decisionmaking as well as security issues that transcend the domestic and foreign security realms and affect domestic stability, such as terrorism and separatist movements. The State Security Committee's importance is underscored by Xi Jinping's serving as its director. It replaces the former Central Committee National Security Leading Small Group, which was established in 2000 and under first Jiang Zemin and then Hu Jintao was coterminous with the Central Committee Foreign Affairs Leading Small Group. The foreign affairs group still exists, but the nature of its relationship with the new State Security Committee is not clear. Official media have not revealed the membership of the new State Security Committee, apart from Xi's appointment as director and NPC Chairman Zhang Dejiang's and Premier Li Keqiang's as

TABLE 2.9 Members of the Central Committee Foreign Affairs Leading Small Group, 2011

Director: Hu Jintao (CCP general secretary; CMC chairman)

Dep. director: Xi Jinping (PBSC; Secretariat)

Members:

    Liu Yunshan (Politburo; director, CC Propaganda Dept.)

    Liang Guanglie (CMC member; minister of national defense

    Meng Jianzhu (State councilor for internal security)

    Dai Bingguo (State councilor for foreign affairs)

    Liao Hui (Director, State Council Hong Kong-Macao Affairs Office)

    Yang Jiechi (Foreign minister)

    Qiao Zonghuai (MFA Party Group; CCP Hong Kong–Macao Affairs Office)

    Wang Jiarui (Director, CCP International Liaison Department)

    Wang Chen (Director, State Council Information Office)

    Geng Huichang (Minister of state security)

    Chen Deming (Minister of commerce)

    Li Haifeng (Director, State Council Overseas Chinese Affairs Office)

    Ma Xiaotian (Deputy director for intelligence and foreign affairs, General Staff Department)

TABLE 2.10 Members of the Taiwan Affairs Leading Small Group, 2011

Director: Hu Jintao (CCP general secretary; CMC chairman)

Dep. director: Jia Qinglin (PBSC; CPPCC chairman)

Members:

    Wang Qishan (Politburo; vice-premier, finance and economy)

    Liu Yunshan (Politburo; director, CC Propaganda Department)

    Guo Boxiong (Politburo; vice-chairman, Central Military Commission)

    Wang Gang (Politburo; vice-chairman, CPPCC)

    Liu Yandong (Politburo; state councilor for S&T, education)

    Dai Bingguo (State councilor for foreign affairs)

    Du Qinglin (Director, CC United Front Work Department)

    Wang Yi (Director, State Council Taiwan Affairs Office)

    Chen Yunlin (Director, CC Taiwan Affairs Office)

    Geng Huichang (Minister of state security)

    Ma Xiaotian (Deputy director for intelligence, General Staff Department)

    Chen Deming (Minister of commerce)

    Ling Jihua (Director, CC General Office; Secretariat)

SOURCE: PRC-owned Hong Kong newspaper *Ta Kung Pao*, February 20, 2013.

TABLE 2.11 Members of the Central Committee Politics and Law Committee, 2011

Director: Zhou Yongkang (PBSC)

Dep. director: Meng Jianzhu (State councilor for internal security)

Members:

    Wang Shengjun (President, Supreme People's Court)

    Cao Jianming (President, Supreme People's Procuratorate)

    Zhou Benshun (Secretary-general, CC Politics and Law Committee)

    Geng Huichang (Minister of state security)

    Wu Aiying (Minister of justice)

    Sun Zhongtong (Deputy director, PLA General Political Dept.)

    Wu Shuangzhan (Commander, People's Armed Police)

    Chen Jiping (Dep. director, CC Comprehensive Management of Social Security Committee)

TABLE 2.12 Members of the Central Committee Foreign Affairs Leading Small Group, 2014

Director: Xi Jinping (CCP general secretary; CMC chairman; PRC president)

Dep. director: Li Yuanchao (Politburo; PRC vice president)

Members:

    Liu Qibao (Politburo; director, CC Propaganda Dept.)

    Chang Wanquan (CMC member; minister of national defense)

    Guo Shengkun (State councilor for internal security)

    Yang Jiechi (State councilor for foreign affairs)

    Wang Guangya (Director, State Council Hong Kong–Macao Affairs Office)

    Wang Yi (Foreign minister)

    Zhang Yesui (MFA Party Group; CCP Hong Kong–Macao Affairs Office)

    Wang Jiarui (Director, CCP International Liaison Department)

    Wang Chen (Director, State Council Information Office)

    Geng Huichang (Minister of state security)

    Gao Hucheng (Minister of commerce)

    Qu Yuanping (Director, State Council Overseas Chinese Affairs Office)

    Sun Jianguo (Deputy director for intelligence, General Staff Department)

NOTE: All members inferred; none confirmed by official media.

TABLE 2.13 Members of the Central Committee Taiwan Work Leading Small Group, 2014

Director: Xi Jinping (CCP general secretary; CMC chairman; PRC president)

Dep. director: Yu Zhengsheng (PBSC; CPPCC chairman)

Members:

  Wang Yang (Politburo; vice premier, finance and economy)

  Liu Qibao (Politburo; director, CC Propaganda Department)

  Fan Changlong (Politburo; vice chairman, Central Military Commission)

  Du Qinglin (Vice chairman, CPPCC)

  Liu Yandong (Politburo; vice premier for S&T, education)

  Yang Jiechi (State councilor for foreign affairs)

  Ling Jihua (Director, CC United Front Work Department)

  Zhang Zhijun (Director, CC & State Council Taiwan Affairs Office)

  Geng Huichang (Minister of state security)

  Sun Jianguo (Deputy director for intelligence, General Staff Department)

  Gao Hucheng (Minister of commerce)

  Li Zhanshu (Director, CC General Office; Secretariat)

NOTE: All members inferred; none confirmed by official media.

Xi's deputies. Nevertheless it is certain to include significant PLA and internal security representation, given the sensitivity and importance of its functions.

On the full Politburo, PLA representation appears to be driven foremost and consistently since 1987 by the political priorities of limiting the potential for the general secretary to use the PLA as a base of power and to limit the PLA from asserting itself as a power bloc in its own right, as described above, through institutional balancing. Finally, in the State Council, CMC member Liang Guanglie, a professional military officer, served as one of five state councilors on the ten-member State Council Executive Committee in his capacity as minister of national defense. On the new State Council Executive Committee under Premier Li Keqiang in March 2013, Liang was replaced in both roles by Gen. Chang Wanquan.

Implications

The preceding examination of the evolution of the party leadership decisionmaking system and the place of the PLA in it suggests several conclusions. First, from its restoration by Deng Xiaoping and his colleagues at the beginning of the reform era down through its current configuration under Hu Jintao, the party leadership system now has a track record of thirty years. New leaders may tinker with it, as Hu Jintao evidently did in 2002 and as Xi did in 2012, but as time goes by it becomes increasingly difficult to alter it fundamentally. In that respect, to paraphrase Engel's Second Law of the dialectics of nature (quantitative change over time becomes qualitative change), the growing weight of precedent amounts over time to institutionalization. If so, prospects for consolidation of the PRC leadership's "objective civilian control" of China's military would seem to be enhanced.

Second, proposals to upgrade PLA representation in the party leadership system, for whatever policy rationale, would trigger immediate concerns about the expansion of PLA power in what has become a thoroughly civilian leadership. Most recently, amid the run-up to the Eighteenth Party Congress in November 2012, rumors circulated that the PLA had been agitating for a seat on the Politburo Standing Committee. From the perspective of the leadership decisionmaking structure sketched above, such a proposal would raise two immediate concerns. On one hand, granting the PLA a designated seat on the Standing Committee would amount to an implicit criticism of the general secretary and his effectiveness in representing the military in the party's decisionmaking core. On the other hand, if the general secretary and the proposed PLA representative were perceived as having close personal connections, other leaders would fear an attempt by the general secretary to assert dominating power and so destabilize the collective leadership. In the end, the number of PLA officers on the Politburo remained limited to two. On balance, PLA representation in the Xi leadership has followed the precedents set down in the Jiang and Hu eras.

Third, it is worth pondering how this carefully balanced collective leadership structure affects decisionmaking in both the Politburo and the CMC. Decisionmaking in an oligarchy depends critically on the ability of the leadership collective to establish a working consensus on the issues they deliberate. Across Hu Jintao's first term, the system appears to have worked well. The Hu leadership got off to a fast start after the Sixteenth CCP Congress in 2002. In their first month in power, they enunciated the overarching theme— "people-centered" policies—that framed the major initiatives that followed in steady succession over Hu's first term as general secretary. Thus the Hu leadership announced the "scientific development concept" in 2003, the concept of "socialist harmonious society" in 2004, and the "new socialist countryside" initiative in 2005. Despite Hu having perceptibly consolidated his power at the Seventeenth CCP Congress in 2007, however, no new policy departures of this scale were proclaimed during his entire second term. Instead, there seemed to be symptoms of a top leadership unable to make major decisions, despite mounting problems. For example, economic reform appeared to drift while a trend of creeping dominance of state-owned enterprises over the economy developed. Since 2007, Premier Wen Jiabao's complaints about the need for political reform persisted with increasing bluntness, but little action. The leadership seemed uncertain about how to deal with rising dissatisfaction and activism among an increasingly restive and wired society.

With regard to military decisionmaking, much depends on the effective leadership of the party general secretary in presiding over the CMC and his ability to establish personal relationships with the military brass. Nan Li and Tai Ming Cheung argue elsewhere in this volume that Hu Jintao's "indecisive and hands-off management style" may have hampered CMC policymaking and weakened civil-military relations in leadership politics. Early in Hu's tenure as CMC chairman it was clear that he was not making the concerted effort to build up personal ties in the PLA that Jiang Zemin had made before him.[13]

Nevertheless, evidence of stagnation in military policymaking is thinner. Immediately after assuming the post of CMC chairman in September 2004, at the annual CMC meeting the following December, Hu Jintao enunciated the PLA's "new historic missions." No new major departures in defense doctrine or military affairs on that scale emerged over the remainder of Hu's tenure as CMC chairman, but neither were there evident controversies or major gaps in military affairs that hint at a failure of CMC policymaking. One arguable exception is an apparent reduction, beginning in 2009, in Beijing's ability to coordinate the actions of its foreign and security apparatus, allowing a burgeoning array of old and new actors with competing and conflicting interests—including those in the PLA—to clutter and complicate China's international relations. This, however, points to a larger breakdown in the Politburo Standing Committee, perhaps aggravated by a lapse in CMC leadership effectiveness, rather than exclusively a problem in civil-military coordination.

From the perspective of 2014, it seems clear that the Xi Jinping leadership is working to overcome the apparent stagnation that stymied Hu's second term as party leader. The reduction in Politburo Standing Committee members from nine to seven at the Eighteenth Party Congress may reflect an effort to facilitate high-level consensus building. The establishment of the State Security Committee seems intended to streamline security decisionmaking at the top. The Eighteenth Party Congress bestowed on the Xi leadership a strong mandate to press ahead with new reforms across the board, registered in the 60-point "comprehensive reform" package laid out at the November 2013 Third Plenum of the Eighteenth Central Committee and the creation of a new super-LSG to coordinate its implementation until 2020. The Third Plenum reform package also authorized new reforms in the organization and command of the PLA, and a new leading small group under the CMC and directed by Xi Jinping has been established to oversee them. The party congress also authorized a powerful campaign against official corruption to break down "vested interests" that have heretofore impeded new reform.

Many observers have attributed these changes to the political power of the new general secretary, Xi Jinping, whom some see as a "new Deng Xiaoping" or a "new Mao." This impression derives in part from Xi's more engaging and confident public persona in contrast to the gray bureaucratic mien of his predecessor. But most of the changes and new reforms that have emerged under Xi's leadership—organizational, economic, military, and otherwise—were long debated before he came to power, and most were endorsed at the Eighteenth Party Congress. The decisive force with which they have been pressed since the congress underscores the strength of the mandate the Xi leadership received there, not Xi's personal power over the rest of the leadership. Xi has enjoyed an enhanced spotlight in official media since the congress, but this appears intended not to build a new cult of personality around him to accentuate his personal power, but rather to depict him as foremost in a unified collective leadership mandated to launch a second era of reform in China. All of the trappings of collective leadership that framed the Hu leadership remain in place with Xi at the helm. Nor has official media coverage of Xi's interactions with the PLA differed from the treatment of his predecessors Hu Jintao and Jiang Zemin.

The party leadership decisionmaking system has endured considerable stress and strain over the last thirty years, a fact that inspires confidence in its durability. The most severe stress was the breakdown of leadership unity in the 1989 Tiananmen crisis. Yet that strain on the system did not produce visible changes or stop Deng Xiaoping from his decision, most likely planned in 1987, to retire later that year. In the Hu Jintao era, despite apparently stagnant decisionmaking capacity in Hu's second term, the leadership nevertheless sustained its façade of consensus in the face of a serious crisis—the 2008 economic downturn—formulating a large and effective (initially, at least) economic stimulus in a matter of weeks.[14]

Nevertheless, it is not hard to imagine crises and stresses that provoke doubts among the leadership about the system's effectiveness or that provide opportunities for members of the oligarchy to subvert it. The subordination of the PLA to the party's civilian leadership, in particular, has not faced a severe test since 1989. It is remarkable how many observers of China's economy see trouble ahead and project a looming end to the extraordinary growth the PRC has enjoyed over the past three decades. If China's economy slows, then intensifying competition for allocations from a more slowly growing national budget among the PLA and other constituencies may provide a more difficult test for the leadership system. More acutely, were China to go to war, the strength of party leadership over the PLA may be sorely tested, whether by impulses on the part of the PLA brass to intervene more assertively in the party leadership's councils or, conversely, on the part of the party's civilian leaders to insert themselves deeply into PLA operational decisions, as Mao did routinely in the past.

Notes

1. Samuel P. Huntington, *The Soldier and the State: The Theory and Politics of Civil-Military Relations* (Cambridge, MA: Harvard University Press, 1957), 83. Huntington's thesis that "objective civilian control" is the optimal model of civil-military relations has recently been qualified by his student Eliot Cohen, who argues that the examples of Lincoln, Clemenceau, Churchill and Ben-Gurion demonstrate that deep intervention in military decisionmaking by top civilian leaders is desirable and critical to military success. Eliot A. Cohen, *Supreme Command: Soldiers, Statesmen, and Leadership in Wartime* (New York: Free Press, 2002).

2. I have sketched the evolution of the CCP's leadership structure previously in Alice Miller, "Institutionalization and the Changing Dynamics of Chinese Leadership Politics," in *China's Changing Political Landscape*, ed. Cheng Li (Washington, DC: Brookings Institution Press, 2008), 61–79.

3. On the evolution of the CCP's central decisionmaking institutions through 1956, see Central Committee Organization Department, Central Committee Party History Research Office, and Central Archive [中共中央组织部, 中共中央党史研究室, 中央档案馆], eds., *Materials on the Organizational History of the Chinese Communist Party* [中国共产党组织史资料] (Beijing: CCP History Press [中共党史出版社], 2000), vols. 1–5.

4. The post of general secretary had been abolished in 1937.

5. "Central Committee Notice Concerning the Establishment of Finance-Economy, Political-Legal, Foreign Affairs, Science, and Culture and Education Small Groups" [中共中央关于成立财政,政法,外事,科学,文教各小组的通知], June 10, 1958, in *Materials on the Organizational History of the Chinese Communist Party*, vol. 9, 611–612. On the evolution of party leading small groups, see Alice Miller, "The Central Committee's Leading Small Groups," *China Leadership Monitor*, no. 26 (September 2008), and Shao Tsung-hai and Su hou-yu [邵宗海, 蘇厚宇], *Chinese Communist Policy Mechanisms with Chinese Characteristics: The Central Committee Leading Work Small Groups* [具有中國特色的中共決策機制:中共中央工作領導小組] (Taipei: Weber Culture [韋伯文化], 2007), 63–122.

6. *Selected Works of Deng Xiaoping (1975–1982)* (Beijing: Foreign Languages Press, 1984), 316.

7. The meeting schedule of the full Politburo could be judged from Xinhua's practice—new after the Thirteenth Party Congress—of transmitting brief reports on a current basis of Politburo meetings in numbered sequence.

8. Xinhua, November 14, 1987, in Foreign Broadcast Information Service, *China Daily Report*, November 16, 1987, 19. On the purposes of these work rules, see Wu Guoyou [武国友], *History of the People's Republic of China* [中华人民共和国史] 4: 1977–1991 (Beijing: People's Press [人民出版社], 2010), 376–377. For a rendition of the Politburo's new decisionmaking procedures by Hu Qiaomu, a former Politburo member, see Alice Miller, "Hu Jintao and the Party Politburo," *China Leadership Monitor*, no. 9 (Winter 2004).

9. On the new policy directions of the Hu-Wen leadership, see Roderick MacFarquhar, ed., *The Politics of China: Sixty Years of the People's Republic of China* (New York: Cambridge University Press, 2011), 579ff.

10. There are at least two blooming and contending explanations for the reduction in Politburo Standing Committee membership from nine to seven. See Alice Miller, "The New Party Leadership," *China Leadership Monitor*, no. 40 (Winter 2013).

11. Deng Xiaoping, "Urgent Tasks of China's Third Generation Collective Leadership," recorded as a talk with "leading members" of the Central Committee on June 16, 1989, in *Selected Works of Deng Xiaoping* 3: 1982–1992 (Beijing: Foreign Languages Press, 1994), 300–301.

12. The 2011 membership list for each of the leading small groups in Tables 2.9 and 2.11 should be taken as provisional. Their listings derive from Chinese Internet sources and have not been confirmed by authoritative PRC media references. The members listed in Table 2.10 for the Central Taiwan Affairs Leading Small Group have been confirmed authoritatively by the PRC-owned Hong Kong newspaper *Ta Kung Pao* on February 20, 2013.

13. See Alice Miller, "Hu Jintao and the PLA Brass," *China Leadership Monitor*, no. 21 (Summer 2007).

14. On this point, see Alice Miller, "Leadership Sustains Public Unity amid Stress," *China Leadership Monitor*, no. 29 (Summer 2009).

3 The Riddle in the Middle: China's Central Military Commission in the Twenty-first Century

Tai Ming Cheung

IN THE HIGH POLITICS OF CIVIL-MILITARY RELATIONS and defense policymaking in China, all roads lead from or to the Central Military Commission (CMC—*Zhongyang junshi weiyuanhui*). Through its control of the People's Liberation Army (PLA), this diminutive and opaque organization is a core institutional pillar on which the power, authority, and rule of the Chinese Communist Party (CCP) rest. Understanding how the CMC operates and interacts within the Chinese political and defense systems offers important institutional perspectives into the nature and dynamics of the CCP's relationship with the PLA.

The CMC, however, is among the most impenetrable and poorly understood organizations in one of the world's least transparent political systems. To adapt Winston Churchill's definition of the Soviet Union, the CMC is a riddle, wrapped in a fortune cookie, inside an enigma. Official disclosures offer little more than a skeletal outline of the organization: its leadership lineup, occasional references to meetings, promulgation of rules and regulations, and the location of its headquarters. Its internal structure, decisionmaking process, coordination with CCP, state, and military bureaucracies, and roles and responsibilities remain a black box.

This chapter builds upon earlier academic research that examined the CMC in the late 1990s and early 2000s.[1] More detailed information has appeared since then on the inner workings of this institution, especially from firsthand accounts of senior CMC officials. Of particular importance are the memoirs of Gen. Liu Huaqing, who worked in the upper echelons of the military high command for much of his career, including as a CMC vice-chairman between 1987 and 1997, and his successor, Gen. Zhang Wannian, who served as a vice-chairman from 1995 to 2003. Bo Xuezheng has also provided a useful account of his forty-year career working in the CMC General Office from its establishment in 1950 until the late 1980s.[2]

This chapter explores a number of aspects key to understanding the nature, place, and role of the CMC: 1) the political and organizational principles that have guided the development of the CMC; 2) an organizational description of the structure, workings, and responsibilities of the CMC; 3) the role and responsibilities of the CMC vice-chairmen; 4) Hu Jintao's role as CMC chairman and problems in civil-military relations during his tenure; 5) the CMC's role in military strategy, weapons development, and the modernization of the defense science, technology and industrial base; and 6) Xi Jinping's early tenure as CMC chairman.

The Political and Organizational Principles Shaping the Evolution of the CMC

The CMC was established in the mid-1920s, although it did not become an important center of power within the CCP until the early 1930s. Many of the core principles that have shaped the organization, responsibilities, and leadership style of the CMC were drawn up during the first few formative decades of its development:

- **Personalistic control:** An unspoken but cardinal principle is that the country's top leader should also serve concurrently as CMC chairman. Only the chairman can have full authority over the military establishment because "the particularity of military struggles requires . . . the practice of the system of personal responsibility for the chairman, so as to execute highly concentrated command of the armed forces."[3] This became a de facto leadership principle after Mao Zedong became CMC chairman in 1935 and held onto this position until his death in 1975. Although Hua Guofeng subsequently assumed the title, he survived only a few years because of his lack of strong military leadership authority. Deng Xiaoping took charge of the CMC in 1978 and although he relinquished the title in 1989, he continued to exert widespread influence over this institution until his final few years.

- **CCP dominance:** The CMC is the organizational embodiment of Mao's dictum that power comes from the barrel of a gun and the Communist Party must always control this instrument of coercion. The CMC's overriding duty is to carry out the instructions of the CCP leadership, and more specifically the requirements of the paramount leader, at least during the rule of Mao and Deng.

- **Centralized top-down control:** The CMC has exercised strong top-down control over the military. This was a legacy of the Civil War and Anti-Japanese War years in which the CMC was in operational charge of the Red Army.[4] The army's headquarters command reported directly to the CMC. After Liberation in 1949, the CMC relinquished daily operational management to the PLA headquarters departments, but still maintained intensive and intrusive oversight of military affairs.

The political and organizational imperatives that shaped the CMC's development between the 1920s and 1980s are not unique to China. Other single-party authoritarian regimes have responded in a similar institutional fashion to the problem of how to maintain tight control over their own military establishments. The Soviet Union, for example, had a Higher Military Council in the 1950s and 1960s. North Korea has both a Central Military Commission and a National Defense Commission, although only the latter is active.[5]

One of the major challenges the Chinese leadership has faced since the 1990s is how to adapt these legacy principles to a changing political landscape, especially in an era of collective leadership and weakened legitimacy of the CCP. Efforts have been made to find and implement new rules of the game, although with mixed success so far:

- **Institutionalized control:** The model of the CMC as a personalistic fiefdom is gradually being replaced by a more institutionalized approach. While the CMC chairmanship continues to be held by the country's top leader, recent chairmen no longer exert the same degree of dominant personal control as Mao or Deng. A key goal has been to institutionalize the CMC leadership succession process. This has been a very difficult endeavor with mixed results so far. In the handover from Deng Xiaoping to Jiang Zemin, there was an early political challenge from the Yang brothers. In the succession from Jiang to Hu Jintao, the transfer of power was marred by a two-year delay in Jiang's relinquishing of his CMC title. This led to concerns of two rival power centers. When Jiang did finally resign in 2004, he argued in his farewell letter that he was asked to stay on by the CCP Central Committee because of the "complicated and ever-changing international situation and heavy tasks of national defense and army building." His decision to finally step down was because it would be "good for the development of the undertakings of the Party, the State and the armed forces." [6] Hu's decision to relinquish his CMC chairmanship at the same time that he retired as Communist Party general secretary and state president at the Eighteenth Party Congress in 2012 was an important signal of a return to a smooth and orderly transfer of power at the top of the military leadership.

- **CCP dominance, but with an expanding role for the state:** While the CMC remains firmly under the CCP's control, there has been a willingness in a few select areas to allow state organizations, primarily the State Council, to have a joint role in decisionmaking with the CMC. In 1989, for example, a Central Special Committee (CSC) responsible for approving major strategic technology programs was jointly set up under the CMC and State Council. The CSC is similar in nature to a leading affairs small group and is headed by the premier. A CMC vice-chairman is a member of this body, whose administrative functions are carried out by the State Administration for Science, Technology, and Industry for National Defense. [7]

- **Promoting coordination:** The CMC is gradually shifting from its vertical top-down governance model to more horizontal coordination with the PLA high command. In his efforts to reform the CMC in the 1980s, Deng complained that it held excessive control over military affairs and instructed that the PLA general departments should be allowed more decisionmaking powers. He noted that, "the Military Commission and the various general departments should be streamlined. It is not yet completely clear how that should be done. But the present system, method of leadership and organization of work in the army are not very satisfactory; they are too complicated. We have the Military Commission, its Standing Committee, its regular working conferences and then the several general departments. The fact is, we should increase the responsibilities of the General Staff Headquarters, the General Political Department and the General Logistics Department, and have only a small coordinating organization above them. With too many leaders, not only do the comrades at lower levels find it hard to get things done, but we ourselves have trouble circulating papers for approval."[8] This devolution of policymaking and oversight authority to the military high command continued in the 1990s and 2000s.

A useful methodological approach in examining the CMC's place in the broader context of the PLA's relationship with the CCP is through the principal-agent framework. The essence of civil-military relations, according to Peter Feaver, is a "strategic interaction between civilian principals and military agents" in which civilian leaders delegate power and authority to their uniformed subordinates but seek to carefully and intrusively monitor their behavior.[9] Communist and other authoritarian regimes have established over a long time a comprehensive, centralized, and highly intrusive internal monitoring system for the military. In principal-agent terminology, this is called "police patrol" oversight and refers to constant, institutionalized oversight of the agent by the principal.

In Communist regimes, this is known as "parallel rule," in which the government and military bureaucracies are overlaid by a parallel hierarchy of party structures that enables the ruling party to supervise their work.[10] The CMC sits at the apex of this parallel party structure and one of its chief roles is to closely monitor the political and military activities of the PLA general departments and other key service commands.

The Structure, Workings, and Responsibilities of the CMC

The CMC is a compact entity that operates above and outside the military high command, although with close and direct channels of coordination with the PLA. Some observers have argued that the CMC is comparable to high-level party leading groups as it is a forum for "facilitating coordination, communications, supervision and consultation" among leading military organs.[11] But the CMC wields far more decisionmaking authority and responsibilities than these coordinating bodies.

A CCP CMC and a state CMC coexist, but in reality they are the same organization with the same membership. This is known as the "one organization, two nameplates" (*yige jigou, liangge paizi*) phenomenon.[12] There are short periods during major leadership changes when the memberships of these two CMCs are out of alignment. The CCP National Congress meets once every five years, usually in October or November, to reshuffle the leadership of key CCP organs, including the party CMC. The corresponding changes to the state CMC only take place when the National People's Congress (NPC) convenes the following spring. While changes in the party CMC leadership line-up that are announced at the CCP congress have been identically mirrored in the new state CMC that is rubber-stamped at the NPC, this does raise the what-if question should the CMC be called upon to make major strategic decisions during this period when the two commissions have different line-ups. The new party CMC would very likely have superseding authority over its state counterpart.

As the supreme national organ in charge of military and defense affairs, the CMC includes among its functions the formulation of military strategy; timely handling of contingencies and key issues concerning defense building; comprehensive coordination of military, economic, political and diplomatic strategies; and formulation of guidelines and polices. In the event of war, the CMC "can take command of the whole army and quickly set up a wartime establishment while, at the same time, organize the soldiers of the whole country to make a quick and effective response."[13] While the CMC would assume control of the military establishment in the event of war, some PLA sources suggest that the CCP leadership through the Politburo has the final authority on "major questions concerning war, armed force, and national defense building."[14] Although the Politburo has "final authority," the lack of military expertise among its members and the principle that only the CCP general secretary and CMC chairman are allowed to have any decisionmaking power in military affairs means that the CMC has actual authority in the running of the military establishment.

How the CMC interacts with the CCP, especially at the functional level, is far from clear. At the senior leadership level, the CMC is represented on the full Politburo by at least one vice-chairman, although under Hu both of the CMC vice-chairmen were appointed to this body. Uniformed military representation on the Politburo Standing Committee ended in 1997 with the retirement of Liu Huaqing. This means that the PLA has to rely on the CMC chairman to represent its institutional interests. CMC representatives also served concurrently on the CCP Secretariat between the late 1990s and late 2000s, but there have been no military officers on this body since the Seventeenth Party Congress.

The most active and direct lines of coordination and cooperation between the CMC and the CCP and state are likely to be between their general offices.[15]

The structure of the CMC can be divided into two parts: its permanent administrative structure and the plethora of different types of meetings and leading groups that are convened under its authority. The CMC's main bureaucratic structure is its General Office, which Bo Xuezheng estimated had a staff of more than 1,000, of which between 700 and 800 were service personnel.[16] Other estimates put the General Office administrative staff at between 200 and 300.[17] This is modest compared to the CCP General Office, which according to some unconfirmed accounts has authorized personnel strength of around 2,400 employees.[18]

The CMC's Administrative Structure

The CMC General Office undertakes a number of key functions:[19]

- Provide advice, assistance, and administrative support to the CMC leadership;
- Maintain coordination and communication channels between the CMC and general departments and other leading organs of the defense establishment;
- Manage the drafting, distribution, and collection of key CMC documents;
- Archive all CMC communications.

The General Office wields considerable influence through its management of the flow of information and documents and the organization of routine and key CMC meetings and the setting of their agendas. Mao Zedong pointed to the unseen but influential role played by the CMC General Office when he commented in 1952 that, "in my understanding of the army's situation, no small part goes to comrade [CMC General Office Director] Xiao Xiangrong who delivered the materials."[20] The General Office collates reports from PLA organs and passes them on to CMC leaders in the form of reading material summaries, commentaries, and bulletins.[21] The General Office also liaises frequently with its counterparts in the CCP and state apparatuses. Xiao offered a more modest description of the role of the CMC General Office by saying that it was the *buguan bu*, which can be defined as the ministry responsible for undertaking tasks that are neglected or are too difficult or sensitive for the PLA to carry out.[22]

TABLE 3.1 CMC General Office Directors, 1950–2015

Name	Dates in office	Length of service (years)
Luo Guibo	1950–1952	2
Zhang Jingwu	1950–1952	2
Xiao Xiangrong	1952–1965	13
Yang Chengwu	1965–1967	2
Lu Yang	1967–1968	1
Xiao Jianfei	1969–1971	2
Vacant due to aftermath of Lin Biao affair	1971–1974	3
Hu Wei	1974–1977	3
Xiao Hongda	1977–1985	8
Liu Kai	1987–1990	3
Li Jijun	1991–1992	1
Cheng Jianning	1993–1996	3
Dong Liangju	1996–1999	3
Tan Yuexin	1999–2003	4
Jia Tingan	2003–2007	4
Wang Guanzhong	2007–2012	6
Qin Shengxiang	2012–present	

SOURCES: Various postings on bbs.tiexue.net [铁血网], and Bo Xuezheng, "Daily Work in the CMC General Office," *World Party History* [党史天地], January 2006, 8–16.

The General Office is headed by a lieutenant general and has several affiliated and subordinate entities that include a discipline inspection commission, policy research section, audit department, military trade bureau, legal affairs bureau, and communications war readiness office.[23] Moreover, General Office directors have occasionally been included within the inner circles of CMC decisionmaking, especially during periods of major reform. In the late 1980s and 1990s, directors such as Liu Kai and Li Jijun were often called upon for their policy input in the formulation of new strategies and personnel reform.

When Li Jijun headed the General Office's policy research section during the late 1980s, he wrote several policy papers that advocated a new local war strategy as part of a general shift that was taking place in the PLA's strategic posture at that time. These proposals were well received by his superiors, including Yang Shangkun and Zhao Ziyang, who served as CMC first vice-chairman between 1987 and 1989, although there was strong bureaucratic opposition from other parts of the PLA apparatus. Although Li's initiative was shelved after Zhao was ousted from power in the Tiananmen Square crackdown, it eventually played a major role in shaping the PLA's new operational strategy in the early 1990s.[24]

The personnel size of the General Office may have fluctuated in the post-Deng era judging from the changing number of senior administrators in charge of this body. When the CMC Secretariat was abolished following the ouster of Yang Baibing in 1992, the number of General Office deputy directors nearly doubled from 3–4 in the early 1990s to 5–6 in the late 1990s and early 2000s. This has subsequently fallen back to four deputy directors in 2011. The length of tenure of CMC General Office directors increased from around two years on average during the Maoist era to four years under Jiang and Hu.

Wang Guanzhong has had the longest tenure for a General Office director since the 1980s, having served for six years between 2007 and 2012, when he was promoted to become a deputy chief of the General Staff. Wang is the consummate CMC insider as he has served most of his career within the organization. He began as a secretary to Yang Shangkun, who was CMC executive vice-chairman during the 1980s. In 1996, Wang returned to work in CMC for the next sixteen years. He first served in the comprehensive planning bureau and then was assigned to the CMC General Office as deputy director in 2001 and became director six years later.[25]

The chairman and vice-chairmen have their own offices with a small staff of secretaries and personal advisors. When Deng Xiaoping and Jiang Zemin were in charge, their chief personal secretaries became powerful figures within the CMC administrative system.[26] However, Hu Jintao does not appear to have followed their tradition by appointing any of his top personal aides to a senior CMC administrative post.

CMC Meetings and the Role of Special Working Groups

Meetings and conferences are the lifeblood of the CMC and are essential for policy coordination, formulation, and dissemination. These gatherings come in several different forms:

- **CMC Standing Conference (*Junwei changwu huiyi*):** The standing conference is a regular meeting of senior CMC officials that would include the chairman, vice-chairmen, and members or their deputies if they are unable to attend. The attendance of the chairman appears to be sporadic and depends on his level of experience and the agenda items. Chairmen at the beginning of their appointments appear to participate more frequently in order to understand how to oversee their military responsibilities. In the chairman's absence, the executive vice-chairman chairs the meeting. The conference deals with major administrative matters, such as passing decrees and approving regulations, but is also active in policymaking.[27] Decisions on key military and defense issues are often taken at these meetings and ratified at enlarged CMC gatherings. There is little public reporting of these meetings so it is difficult to know how regularly they happen. Liu Huaqing mentions these meetings in his memoirs, suggesting that they may occur once every few months, although they could convene more frequently if there are important and pressing issues that need to be discussed by the CMC. Before the 1980s, the standing conference was occasionally referred to as the Work Conference (办公会议). These name changes do not appear to have had any noticeable impact on the functioning of the CMC.

- **CMC "Knocking Heads" Conference (*Junwei pengtou huiyi*):** These are brief working meetings intended as a forum for the exchange of information among senior CMC and PLA officers. They were especially popular during the 1960s and 1970s, but have been held less frequently since the 1980s.

- **CMC Discussion Conference (*Junwei zuotan huiyi*):** These sessions run for upward of several days and are held to allow CMC leaders and high-ranking military chiefs to candidly discuss major political, military and foreign policy issues. They are often held shortly after CCP plenums. At one of these discussion meetings in October 1984, for example, the CMC leadership decided to give preliminary approval for the demobilization of a million troops and to allow military units to take part in commercial activities.[28]

- **CMC Plenary Conference (*Junwei quanti huiyi*):** These annual plenary sessions were occasionally convened during the Maoist years. They were usually held around the end of the year to review the past twelve months' work and to set out priorities for the following year. They were replaced by enlarged CMC conferences in the 1980s.[29]

- **CMC Operational Conference (*Junwei zuozhan huiyi*):** These operational conferences appear to take place very infrequently and occur when major war-fighting and combat decisions are required. For example, these operational conferences were convened in 1958 when the CMC leadership met to decide on the artillery shelling of Jinmen Island in the Taiwan Strait and the 1978–1979 border conflict with Vietnam.[30] In his memoirs, Liu Huaqing refers to a CMC operational conference in June 1993 to translate new national military strategic guidelines into operational doctrine and practice.[31]

- **CMC Enlarged Conference (*Junwei kuoda huiyi*):** These enlarged conferences come in two forms: annual year-end review sessions and extraordinary meetings to unveil major initiatives. Since the early 1980s, the annual enlarged meetings are held at the end of each year and are attended by several hundred top commanders from around the country to receive their work directions for the following year. These meetings are equivalent to the CCP's annual plenary session and the national economic work conference that is also held around the same time. Extraordinary enlarged conferences take place once or twice every decade and are convened to announce major organizational reforms or shifts in the country's security posture. The most important of these meetings include the first enlarged conference in 1954 that ratified the PLA's peacetime organizational structure, a 1975 meeting that paved the way for a major streamlining of the armed forces, an enlarged session in 1985 that announced the reduction of one million troops and the PLA's strategic shift to a post–Cold War footing, and a 1993 conference that introduced a new set of national military strategic guidelines that has subsequently defined the nature and direction of the PLA's modernization program.

- **CMC Emergency Meeting (*Junwei jinji huiyi*):** These impromptu meetings are convened in response to sudden major crises. Only two CMC emergency meetings have so far been publicly disclosed, both of which occurred in the spring of 1999. The first was on 25 April 1999 when Jiang Zemin instructed CMC Vice-Chairman Zhang Wannian to convene and chair an emergency CMC session that same day in response to a large-scale protest by supporters of the Falungong directly in front of the central leadership compound in Zhongnanhai. Jiang wanted the PLA, and especially the Beijing Garrison and PAP, to be mobilized to protect domestic order.[32] The second CMC emergency meeting took place on 8 May following the U.S. bombing of the Chinese embassy in Belgrade.

The CMC session, which Zhang Wannian described as an "emergency CMC enlarged meeting," followed immediately after a Politburo emergency meeting and was used to convey the instructions from this earlier meeting to the CMC leadership for onward dissemination to the rest of the PLA. A number of organizational traits can be gleaned from these two emergency meetings. First, they are convened on the orders of the CMC chairman, but are presided over by the CMC executive vice-chairman. It is unclear who the other meeting participants are, but as they are convened with little notification, it is likely that it would be a small group that would include the CMC vice-chairmen, senior officials in the CMC administrative apparatus, and senior commanders from the general headquarters departments. Second, they are usually held in conjunction with an emergency Politburo session, especially if the matter concerns political issues. Third, these emergency meetings are quickly followed up by a CMC standing conference that would bring in the rest of the CMC leadership, such as the heads of the general departments and service arms, for discussion.

As these meetings primarily deal with defense-related issues, the attendees are predominately military personnel. Senior civilian leaders sometimes participate in the enlarged conferences and give speeches. CCP general secretary Hu Yaobang attended the 1985 enlarged session, for example, and Li Peng also occasionally took part in some of these CMC events when he was premier.

When the CMC decides to undertake major policy initiatives, it organizes special work groups and committees drawn from the PLA bureaucracy to formulate policy recommendations. Some of the most important of these entities include:

- **Drafting group for the five-year defense program:** The CMC convenes an all-army leading group once every five years to draw up a military and defense science and technology five-year program that parallels the country's national five-year plan.[33] The CMC establishes the leading group at the beginning of the last year of the existing plan with a CMC vice-chairman as the head. In the 1990s, the heads of the PLA General Staff Department (GSD) and General Logistics Department (GLD) were the deputy heads of this group, but it is likely that the General Armament Department (GAD) director will also have been included since the end of the 1990s. Members of the leading group include deputy heads of the GSD,

TABLE 3.2 Enlarged Sessions and Other Important Meetings of the CMC, 1989–2013

Date of meeting	Type of meeting	Participants	Key issues discussed
November 1989	Special enlarged conference	Deng Xiaoping, Jiang Zemin, all CMC members, commanders and political commissars of PLA general departments, service arms, Military Regions, key academies	Deng Xiaoping retires as CMC chairman and Jiang Zemin takes charge
January 1991	Enlarged annual conference	Jiang Zemin, all CMC members, commanders and political commissars of PLA general departments, service arms, Military Regions, key academies	
December 1991	Enlarged annual conference	Jiang Zemin, all CMC members, commanders and political commissars of PLA general departments, service arms, Military Regions, key academies	
April 1992	Enlarged conference	Jiang Zemin, all CMC members, commanders and political commissars of PLA general departments, service arms, Military Regions, key academies	Review of Deng Xiaoping's tour of Southern China; Jiang Zemin emphasizes urgent need to improve weapons and defense science and technology development
November 1992	Enlarged annual conference	Jiang Zemin, all CMC members, commanders and political commissars of PLA general departments, service arms, Military Regions, key academies	Prominent attention paid to Deng's remarks on new leadership following Fourteenth CCP Congress and his views on Hong Kong issue
January 1993	Enlarged annual conference	Jiang Zemin, all CMC members, commanders and political commissars of PLA general departments, service arms, Military Regions, key academies	"Military strategic guidelines for the new era" unveiled by Jiang Zemin in keynote speech
June 1993	Special operational conference	Jiang Zemin, all CMC members, commanders and political commissars of PLA general departments, service arms, Military Regions	Translating MSG into operational guidelines for development of combat capabilities and long-term force modernization
December 1994	Enlarged annual conference	Jiang Zemin, all CMC members, commanders and political commissars of PLA general departments, service arms, Military Regions, key academies	Prominent attention to cadre selection and evaluation
December 1995	Enlarged annual conference	Jiang Zemin, all CMC members, commanders and political commissars of PLA general departments, service arms, Military Regions, key academies	Jiang Zemin makes keynote speech emphasizing the importance of political and ideological work

Date of meeting	Type of meeting	Participants	Key issues discussed
December 1996	Enlarged annual conference	Jiang Zemin, all CMC members, commanders and political commissars of PLA general departments, service arms, Military Regions, key academies	PLA organizational reform and force reductions
December 1997	Enlarged annual conference	Jiang Zemin, all CMC members, commanders and political commissars of PLA general departments, service arms, Military Regions, key academies	Development of high-quality military personnel and defense science and technology; Jiang Zemin talks of importance of winning future hi-tech wars
April 1998	Enlarged conference	Jiang Zemin, Hu Jintao, all CMC members, commanders and political Commissars of PLA general departments, service arms, Military Regions, key academies	Promoting advanced weapons development and PLA organizational reform
25 April 1999	Emergency meeting		Emergency deployment on anti-Falungong work; specific request for anti-Falungong struggle
8 May 1999	Emergency meeting		Convey messages from Politburo emergency meeting following the bombing of the Chinese embassy in Belgrade for dissemination to rest of PLA
December 1999	Enlarged annual conference	Jiang Zemin, Hu Jintao, all CMC members, commanders and political Commissars of PLA general departments, service arms, Military Regions, key academies	Decision made on actively promoting military revolution with Chinese characteristics, especially the building of an informatized PLA
December 2000	Enlarged annual conference	Jiang Zemin, Hu Jintao, all CMC members, commanders and political Commissars of PLA general departments, service arms, Military Regions, key academies	Development of military informatization
December 2002	Enlarged annual conference	Jiang Zemin, Hu Jintao, all CMC members, commanders and political Commissars of PLA general departments, service arms, Military Regions, key academies	
July 2003	Enlarged conference	Jiang Zemin, Hu Jintao, all CMC members, commanders and political Commissars of PLA general departments, service arms, Military Regions, key academies	Structural and organizational reform, including decision to cut PLA by 200,000 personnel that is announced in Sept. 2003

Date of meeting	Type of meeting	Participants	Key issues discussed
September 2004	Enlarged conference	Jiang Zemin, Hu Jintao, all CMC members, commanders and political Commissars of PLA general departments, service arms, Military Regions, key academies	Jiang Zemin hands over CMC chairmanship to Hu Jintao
December 2004	Enlarged annual conference	Hu Jintao, all CMC members, commanders and political commissars of PLA general departments, service arms, Military Regions, key academies	Hu Jintao presides as CMC chairman for first time and unveils "historic missions of the armed forces in the new period of the new century"
December 2005	Enlarged annual conference	Hu Jintao, all CMC members, commanders and political commissars of PLA general departments, service arms, Military Regions, key academies	Hu Jintao unveils military version of his "scientific development" concept
December 2006	Enlarged annual conference	Hu Jintao, all CMC members, commanders and political commissars of PLA general departments, service arms, Military Regions, key academies	
December 2007	Enlarged annual conference	Hu Jintao, all CMC members, commanders and political commissars of PLA general departments, service arms, Military Regions, key academies	Taiwan Strait, especially concern over unstable and uncertain developments regarding upcoming Taiwan presidential election
December 2008	Enlarged annual conference	Hu Jintao, all CMC members, commanders and political commissars of PLA general departments, service arms, Military Regions, key academies	Worries raised about global and Chinese economic situation that could threaten domestic social stability
December 2009	Enlarged annual conference	Hu Jintao, all CMC members, commanders and political commissars of PLA general departments, service arms, Military Regions, key academies	Hu Jintao speech on accelerating the "transformation of combat power"
December 2010	Enlarged annual conference	Hu Jintao, all CMC members, commanders and political commissars of PLA general departments, service arms, Military Regions, key academies	Civil-military integration
December 2011	Enlarged annual conference	Hu Jintao, all CMC members, commanders and political commissars of PLA general departments, service arms, Military Regions, key academies	Training reforms
November 2012	Enlarged conference	Hu Jintao, Xi Jinping, all CMC members, commanders and political commissars of PLA general departments, service arms, Military Regions, key academies	Transfer of CMC chairmanship from Hu Jintao to Xi Jinping

TABLE 3.3 Categories of CMC Meetings

Conference type	Frequency	Participants	Nature of meeting
Standing conference	Once every few months	CMC chairman (occasionally), CMC vice-chairmen and CMC members	Administrative and policy coordination and decisionmaking
"Knocking heads" conference	Irregular	CMC chairman (occasionally), vice-chairmen, members and commanders and political commissars of major PLA central and regional commands	Information exchange
Discussion conference	Irregular	CMC chairman (occasionally), vice-chairmen, members and commanders and political commissars of major PLA central and regional commands	Open discussion of major policy issues, before adoption as official policy
Plenary conference	No longer meets	CMC chairman, vice-chairmen, members and commanders and political commissars of major PLA central and regional commands	Review annual work goals and lay out next year's work priorities
Operational conference	Very infrequently, usually during periods of crisis or war	CMC chairman, vice-chairmen, members and commanders and political commissars of major PLA central and regional commands	Decisions on major operational matters
Annual enlarged conference	Annually at year's end	CMC chairman, vice-chairmen, members and commanders and political commissars of major PLA central and regional commands	Review annual work goals and lay out next year's work priorities
Special enlarged conference	Irregular, but usually once every five to ten years	CMC chairman, vice-chairmen, members, commanders and political commissars of major PLA central and regional commands, and group army-level commanders	Announce major strategic initiatives and force restructuring

General Political Department (GPD), GLD, State Administration for Science, Technology, and Industry for National Defense (SASTIND), Academy of Military Sciences (AMS) president, a National Defense University representative, and the director or deputy director of the CMC General Office. Among the key concerns of this leading group is defense and weapons modernization, defense science and technology (S&T) research and development, organizational reforms within the PLA, and defense budget allocations. This planning process takes around twelve months to complete and is divided into three stages: a survey period (*diaocha jieduan*) to collect information; discussion of specialized topics (*zhuanti lunzheng jieduan*);[34] and a comprehensive discussion (*zonghe lunzheng jieduan*) of all the key issues that will go into the program. A draft plan is then drawn up by around September and presented at a CMC standing conference before the final version is submitted to the annual CMC enlarged conference at the beginning of each year for ratification before it is approved by the CMC.

- **Committees and working groups on military strategy, training, and force restructuring:** When major changes to military strategies, operational doctrines, and general threat assessments are required, the CMC organizes ad hoc leading groups to formulate general outlines that are then passed to the general departments for implementation. A CMC Defense Science, Technology and Armaments System Reform Leading Group was set up in 1988, for example, to coordinate with key PLA and defense industry organizations on reforming the defense science, technology, and industrial research, development, and acquisition system.[35]

- **Working and inspection groups on financial and economic discipline:** Since the mid-1980s, the CMC has regularly organized special working and inspection groups to oversee campaigns to audit military units. These inspection activities were especially intensive during the 1980s and 1990s when the PLA was extensively engaged in commercial business operations and corruption was rife.[36] But these CMC inspection groups have continued to be regularly convened and deployed for economic and political audits around the PLA. In 2011, for example, the CMC Discipline Inspection Commission conducted a detailed economic and political investigation of the PLA Air Force's leadership organs, including its party committee and general headquarters departments.[37]

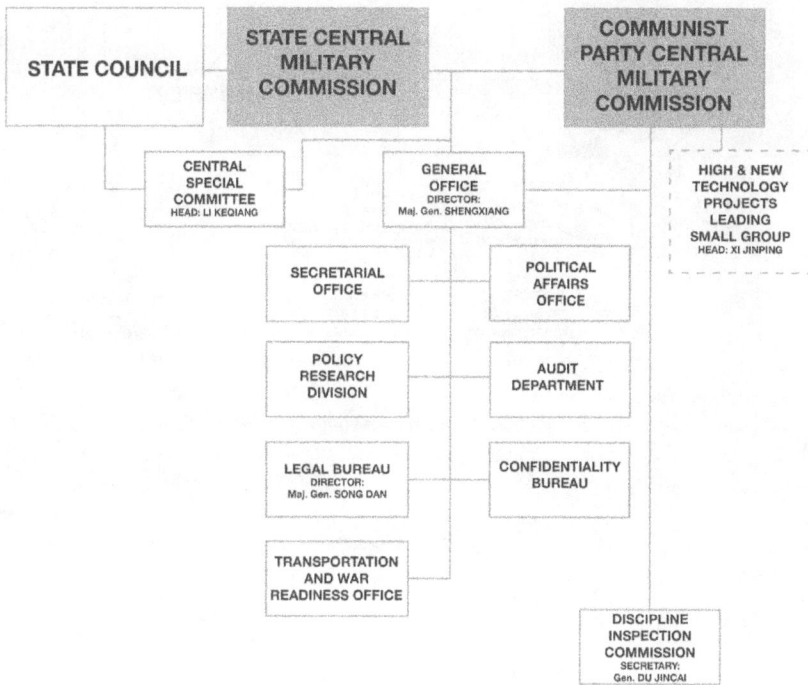

FIGURE 3.1 The Organizational Structure of the Central Military Commision, 2014

The Locus of Power and Military Oversight within the CMC: The Key Role of the Vice-Chairmen

To make the CMC more capable, professional, and institutionalized, the roles of the vice-chairmen have become increasingly important while the status of ordinary commission members appears to be peripheral. After Deng Xiaoping ordered the CMC to be streamlined in the early 1980s with a major pruning in the bloated ranks of its commission members (*weiyuan*), he elevated the authority and influence of the vice-chairmen (*fuzhuxi*) and deputy secretaries-general (*fumishuzhang*).[38] There was an important distinction made during this period between vice-chairmen and deputy secretaries-general. The vice-chairmen were senior civilian leaders who had general oversight of the CMC and the PLA. During the late 1980s, then CCP general secretary Zhao Ziyang was the CMC first vice-chairman while Yang Shangkun was the CMC executive vice-chairman and CMC secretary-general. They were given decisionmaking authority for general (*yiban*) CMC matters, but Deng had sole authority to decide major issues.[39]

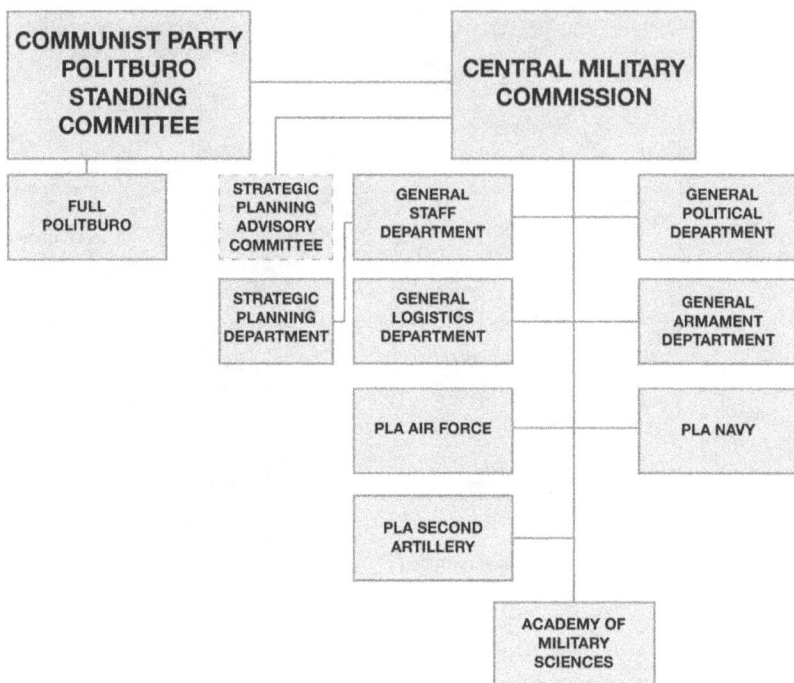

FIGURE 3.2 The CMC and Its Relationship with the PLA and Communist Party

Below the vice-chairmen were the secretary-general and deputy secretaries-general. They were responsible for the operational management of the CMC, which included:

1. Overseeing the daily administration of the organization, especially taking charge of key meetings;
2. Conducting research and investigation of major military issues;
3. Monitoring the mood and thinking across the entire military establishment, in particular among senior officers in central and regional commands;
4. Coordinating with the PLA general departments.[40]

Yang Shangkun also held the position of CMC secretary-general and was assisted by two deputy secretaries-general. Liu Huaqing and Hong Xuezhi were highly experienced senior military officers. They assumed operational oversight of the management of the military establishment.

These steps to institutionalize the running of the CMC were disrupted by the political fallout from the Tiananmen Square crackdown in 1989. In November 1989, Deng decided to formally step down as CMC chairman and appointed Shanghai CCP general secretary Jiang Zemin as his replacement. In addition, Yang Shangkun took over as the sole executive vice-chairman and his half brother and head of the PLA General Political Department, Yang Baibing, assumed the title of CMC secretary-general.

This was a hurried and poorly conceived succession process that created considerable political tensions within the CMC and party-army relations. Jiang was an inexperienced political outsider with little military background, and struggled to effectively take the reins of power of an organization whose power and authority rested overwhelmingly on the prestige, experience, and dominant influence of its chairman. Jiang was also undermined by having the Yangs serve as his principal advisors on the CMC as they saw themselves as rivals for control of the CMC. This led to several years of political tension and intrigue within the CMC, which eventually ended at the Thirteenth CCP Congress in 1992 when the Yangs were forced into early retirement and the position of secretary-general and its deputy slots were abolished.

Following the Yang affair, Deng Xiaoping sought to put the stalled institutionalization of the CMC back on track. Immediately after the Thirteenth CCP Congress, he wrote a letter to the new Politburo to provide guidance on the personnel arrangements of the new CMC leadership, highlighting the prominent role the CMC vice-chairmen would play in supporting the work of the chairman. "From now on under Jiang Zemin's leadership, the two comrades Liu Huaqing and Zhang Zhen will be responsible for the daily work of the CMC. From my understanding, comrades Liu Huaqing and Zhang Zhen are the most informed on the army."[41]

This power-sharing arrangement appears to have become firmly institutionalized since these earlier hesitant days. In 1995, the number of CMC military vice-chairmen was doubled from two to four as Jiang appointed his own handpicked military loyalists, Zhang Wannian and Chi Haotian, who replaced Liu and Zhang Zhen at the Fifteenth CCP Congress in 1997. While Guo Boxiong, Xu Caihou, and Cao Gangchuan were appointed as vice-chairmen in 2002 to replace Zhang Wannian and Chi Haotian, Hu had not yet received his chairmanship. But Guo and Xu were considered to be loyal allies of Hu's as their terms were extended at the Seventeenth CCP Congress in 2007, while Cao was retired. Fan Changlong and Xu Qiliang replaced Guo and Xu at the Eighteenth CCP Congress in 2012.

Xi Jinping would almost certainly have handpicked Fan and Xu because they would play an instrumental role in the consolidation of his power and authority over the PLA. Fan's service record would suggest that he had limited interaction with Xi before his CMC appointment. Fan was the commander of Ji'nan Military Region between 2004 and 2012 before his move to Beijing. Xu's career path though has overlapped on a number of occasions with Xi's, which would indicate that he may have deeper connections with the CMC chairman. In the early 1990s, Xu served in Fuzhou when Xi was party secretary and Xu was also a CMC member and PLA Air Force (PLAAF) commander when Xi was a CMC vice-chairman from 2011 to 2012, which meant that they regularly met in CMC-related activities. Xu is the first PLAAF officer to serve as a CMC vice-chairman, which has given the air force a major boost in its influence in military bureaucratic politics.

The roles and responsibilities of the vice-chairmen have evolved over time. During the Liu Huaqing–Zhang Zhen period, Liu was primarily responsible for the defense science, technology, and industry portfolio along with arms-trade matters, while Zhang oversaw military modernization and some political issues. Under Zhang Wannian and Chi Haotian, the former took charge of military modernization issues while Chi was responsible for political issues. In the Guo-Xu-Cao period, Guo and Cao presided over professional and military modernization matters while Xu managed the political portfolio.

Another important institutional procedure introduced in the late 1990s was the appointment of successors to the CMC chairman to the position of CMC first vice-chairman one or two years before they would formally take over that slot to provide them with on-the-job training. This occurred with Hu Jintao in 1998 and Xi Jinping in 2010, although the exact timing of this transitional process depends on prevailing political circumstances.

Compared to the vice-chairmen, the ordinary members of the CMC appear to have only a secondary role in the affairs and decisionmaking of this body. These members are the directors of the four PLA general departments, defense minister, and, as of 2005, the commanders of the air force, navy, and Second Artillery. While these senior military leaders attend key CMC meetings such as the CMC standing conference and are appointed to

TABLE 3.4 CMC Vice-Chairmen, 1992–Present

Time period	CMC Vice-Chairmen (Principal work portfolios)	Notes
14th CCP Central Committee, 1992–1995	Liu Huaqing (professional, modernization & defense science, technology, industrial affairs) Zhang Zhen (professional & political affairs)	Liu and Zhang were appointed by Deng Xiaoping
14th CCP Central Committee, 1995–1997	Liu Huaqing (professional, modernization & defense science, technology, industrial affairs) Zhang Zhen (professional & political affairs) Chi Haotian (political affairs) Zhang Wannian (professional & modernization affairs)	Chi and Zhang were politically close to Jiang Zemin
15th CCP Central Committee, 1997–2002	Chi Haotian (political affairs) Zhang Wannian (professional & modernization affairs)	Chi and Zhang were appointed by Jiang Zemin
16th CCP Central Committee, 2002–2007	Guo Boxiong (professional & modernization affairs) Xu Caihou (political affairs) Cao Gangchuan (defense science, technology, industrial affairs)	Guo and Xu were politically close to both Jiang Zemin and Hu Jintao
17th CCP Central Committee, 2007–2012	Guo Boxiong (professional & modernization affairs) Xu Caihou (political affairs)	Guo and Xu were appointed by Hu Jintao
18th CCP Central Committee, 2012–2017	Fan Changlong (professional & modernization affairs) Xu Qiliang (political affairs)	Fan and Xu were appointed by Xi Jinping

the ad hoc leading small groups, they do not appear to be closely involved in the CMC's operational management. Key decisions appear instead to originate from deliberations between the CMC vice-chairmen and chairman.

The role and importance of CMC administrative officials would appear to depend on their political standing with the CMC leadership, especially with the chairman. For example, the CMC General Office director in the early 2000s was Lt. Gen. Jia Tingan, who was Jiang Zemin's principal secretary. The CMC General Office director is the CMC's most senior administrative officer and is a two-star lieutenant general, while his deputies are one-star major generals.

Hu Jintao, the CMC, and the Emergence of Civil-Military Coordination Gaps

Questions have been raised over the extent to which Hu Jintao was able to exert authority over the PLA when he was CMC chairman from 2002 to 2012. These doubts stem from several publicized incidents during his tenure in which the military appeared to have taken actions that Hu and the civilian authorities were either not consulted on or were unaware of.[42]

One event in the first term of Hu's rule that sparked concerns over a gap in party-army coordination was an antisatellite test in 2007 in which the PLA used a modified ballistic missile to destroy one of its own satellites in space. After the incident became public, the international community pressed the Chinese government for an explanation. The Chinese Ministry of Foreign Affairs waited nearly two weeks before it acknowledged that China had conducted the test, which led to speculation as to whether the PLA was acting independently and without seeking approval from the civilian authorities.[43] It is very unlikely, though, the military was acting in a rogue capacity as no senior military officer faced any sanctions over the test. Indeed, Chen Bingde, the director of GAD, which was in overall charge of the event, was subsequently promoted to take charge of the GSD.

A second incident that led to renewed worries about civil-military friction occurred in the summer of 2010 when senior Chinese military officials and serving and retired strategists belonging to military think tanks made widely publicized statements aggressively criticizing the U.S. and Republic of Korea for conducting naval exercises in international waters near China. Following remarks by Gen. Ma Xiaotian, a deputy chief of the general staff, who said that China was "strongly opposed" to the maneuvers, the Chinese Foreign Ministry adjusted its initially mild concerns to a more forceful warning that the U.S. needed Chinese permission before it could send its naval forces near Chinese waters.

A third case was the maiden test flight of J-20 fighter aircraft in January 2011, which appeared to catch Hu Jintao unaware when he was asked about the event during a meeting with visiting U.S. Defense Secretary Robert Gates. None of Hu's aides in the meeting with Gates appeared to have any knowledge of the J-20 flight, even though it had been reported on the Internet before the meeting.[44] A fourth incident, arising from the 2008 Wenchuan earthquake, offers another wrinkle in the style of Hu Jintao's military leadership.

Immediately following the earthquake, Premier Wen Jiabao took charge of the central government's response as head of the National Earthquake Relief Headquarters, which included representatives from the CMC and PLA commands. Wen ordered the PLA to dispatch large numbers of troops and equipment, as it was the only Chinese organization capable of carrying out major rescue operations. While the PLA was an important player in the emergency disaster response, only the CMC has the authority to order major military movements. This led to questions as to whether the premier and the central government had overstepped their authority in giving operational instructions to military units. In one instruction given by Wen two days after the earthquake, the PLA was ordered to send sixty helicopters to help with rescue operations. In justifying this decision, Wen pointed out that "we must use all our forces, and save lives at whatever the cost. Life is the most precious thing; we must be amenable to the people and history."[45]

One reason why Wen gave the orders for major military reinforcements was that he had taken full charge of the disaster response operations from the outset. By contrast, it took Hu several days before he decided to visit the earthquake region and take command of military operations. After Hu finally did visit Sichuan, the party and military propaganda apparatus launched a full-court media campaign to show that Hu was in command of operations. This incident highlights a particular feature of Hu's military rule: that he was sometimes hesitant and slow to take charge. This points to coordination problems arising from Hu's management style.

Were these incidents an indicator of coordination gaps and management style issues attributable to Hu's approach in running the CMC or reflective of more serious challenges posed by an assertive military establishment seeking greater independence and influence in important policy areas? Some observers have suggested that these and other similar actions under Hu's rule showed a lack of civilian control over the PLA, which would certainly be a serious development in Chinese civil-military relations.[46] A more likely explanation is that Hu's indecisive and hands-off management style at the CMC had led to coordination and communication problems, especially in "hard" military issues such as weapons development, military strategy, and military operations in which Hu had shown limited interest.[47]

From an organizational perspective, Hu's limited interest in professional military matters was shown by a reduction in the numbers of senior military officials in key CMC positions. There were only two CMC vice-chairmen since the Seventeenth CCP Congress and the number of CMC deputy directors has also decreased. Moreover, Hu did not appear to have placed any of his own closely trusted aides onto the CMC unlike Deng Xiaoping and Jiang Zemin, who appointed their personal secretaries to key CMC administrative slots. Hu's principal secretary, Ling Jihua, remained within the CCP apparatus serving as the deputy head of the CCP General Office.[48] This suggests complacency rather than more sinister concerns over a rogue military.

The CMC in the Making of Military Strategy, Weapons Development, and the Modernization of the Defense Technology and Industrial Base

The CMC has been playing a proactive and hands-on role in overseeing the country's defense modernization since the late 1980s, especially in two key areas: defining the country's national military strategy and guiding weapons development and broader defense technological and industrial transformation. While the development of military capabilities is one of the CMC's chief responsibilities, it had seriously neglected this area between the 1960s and the 1980s as it was consumed by internal political challenges.

Deng began to pay attention to defense modernization from the mid-1980s as part of an overall effort to streamline the military establishment and adapt to changing international strategic conditions and long-term trends in science and technology. Deng appointed Liu Huaqing as a CMC deputy secretary-general in 1987 to spearhead this reform. Liu's initial focus was on the reform of the weapons research and development system.[49] The CMC standing conference approved the establishment of a CMC Defense Science, Technology and Armaments System Reform Leading Group in 1988 to coordinate with key PLA and defense industry organizations and come up with a study to provide recommendations to the CMC leadership. This leading group, which was made up of senior representatives from the GSD, GLD, and Commission of Science, Technology, and Industry for National Defense (COSTIND), met twice a week for two months in the summer of 1988, and its findings were discussed at a CMC standing conference in August 1988. While Liu was keen to pursue major structural reforms, there was fierce resistance to any attempt to change the status quo. The CMC meeting decided that the problems that the defense S&T system faced were extremely complicated and difficult to address and more research was required. It became apparent to Liu that the time was not yet ripe to undertake any major reforms of the defense S&T apparatus.

The conditions for serious reform finally began to emerge with the 1990–1991 First Gulf War. The Chinese civilian and military leaderships were profoundly impressed by the role high-technology weaponry had played in allowing the U.S. and its allies to easily defeat Iraq. During the Gulf War campaign, the CMC convened special seminars to brief senior leaders on the global state of military technologies and the implications for China. Liu Huaqing pointed out that at a seminar to discuss electronic warfare capabilities, Jiang spoke of the need to pay greater attention to science and technology and to address the huge technology gulf between China and the West. Over the following months, Liu and his colleagues on the CMC held numerous meetings and came up with policy recommendations to speed up the pace of weapons development. At a CMC enlarged meeting in 1992, Jiang emphasized the need to step up weapons and S&T development. The Politburo also held a special meeting to approve this new initiative and the State Council began to increase allocations for investment in defense S&T. Liu commented that these events showed that "the spring for weapons development had finally arrived."[50]

The Gulf War and other changes in the regional and international strategic situation, especially worrying political developments and U.S. arms sales to Taiwan, also prompted the CMC leadership to reassess the country's national military strategy or military strategic guidelines (MSG—*junshi zhanlüe fangzhen*), which are the principles drawn up by the national leadership to guide the planning, development, and utilization of the armed forces.[51] The revision of the MSG took place between 1991 and 1992, apparently led by the AMS acting under the direct instructions of the CMC with Yang Shangkun in charge.[52] The new set of MSG was unveiled at the annual enlarged CMC conference in January 1993.[53] Jiang Zemin gave a major speech to provide details of the "military strategic guidelines for the new era" that pointed out that major international, regional, and domestic changes necessitated the first change to the MSG since the early 1980s. According to Liu, the CMC then convened a special operations conference (*zuozhan huiyi*) in June 1993 to translate the new MSG into operational guidelines to provide strategic directions and principles for the development of military combat capabilities and long-term force modernization.[54] Jiang also gave a major speech at this meeting.

A major initiative in Chinese national military strategy on "historic missions of the armed forces in the new period of the new century" was also unveiled at the CMC's annual enlarged meeting in December 2004 shortly after Hu took over as CMC chairman. The new missions, focusing on more nontraditional security issues, are intended to better align the PLA's activities with the CCP's evolving goals.

Another major external crisis that drew the CMC into a direct hands-on role in overseeing weapons development matters took place in 1999. Although the PLA and the country's defense industry had been ramping up their defense modernization efforts since the early 1990s amid deepening fears by the Chinese authorities that Taiwan was moving toward independence, much of this effort was directed at the development of regular conventional forces such as armored fighting vehicles, combat aircraft, and warships. The bombing of the Chinese embassy in Belgrade in May 1999 by a U.S. B-2 bomber led the Chinese authorities, and specifically the CMC leadership, to call for intensified efforts to develop these major weapons systems, which the PLA also term "assassin's mace" (*shashoujian*) capabilities. According to Gen. Zhang Wannian, who was CMC vice-chairman at the time, immediately following the embassy bombing, the CMC convened an emergency enlarged meeting and one of the key decisions made was to "accelerate the development of *shashoujian* armaments."[55]

Zhang pointed out that Jiang Zemin was especially insistent on the need to step up the pace of development of *shashoujian* mega-projects (*zhongda gongcheng*), saying that "what the enemy (*diren*) is most fearful of, this is what we should be developing."[56] As the "enemy" was the United States, the implication was that the defense and strategic S&T system should be engaged in developing asymmetric capabilities targeting U.S. vulnerabilities.[57]

To ensure that these major weapons projects would receive priority attention, the CMC established a New/High Technology and Engineering Leadership Small Group (*Zhongyang junwei xin'gao keji gongcheng lingdao xiaozu*) in 1999 with the CMC chairman as its head. This coordinating body is responsible for providing top-level unified leadership and management of the development of high-technology weapons systems.[58] This leading group appears to have similar characteristics and roles as the Central Special Committee, which was established in the early 1960s to manage the development of the country's nuclear weapons and strategic launch capabilities.[59]

The Early Tenure of Xi Jinping as Commander in Chief:
The Return of a Strong and Effective Leader and CMC?

At the Eighteenth Party Congress in November 2012, Xi Jinping took over from Hu Jintao as CMC chairman. There was some uncertainty in the run-up to the congress as to whether Hu would relinquish his power and hold on to his post as Jiang Zemin did a decade earlier, which led to two subsequent years of uneasy power sharing between the two leaders. In the end, Hu quietly stepped down from all his positions (he did not officially retire from his state CMC position until March 2013), allowing for a smooth transfer of authority to Xi.

In his first year as CMC chairman, Xi was portrayed by the Chinese propaganda apparatus as being intensively engaged in military matters and providing strategic vision. Xi crisscrossed the country conducting high-profile visits of military facilities and spending plenty of time meeting with troops and conducting on-the-ground investigations. He reportedly made eleven military visits between November 2012 and December 2013, ranging from an air force base in Xinjiang in Northwest China to naval facilities in Hainan Island and Qingdao in Shandong province, including the *Liaoning* aircraft carrier.[60] By comparison, Hu Jintao in his first year as CMC chairman only made a handful of visits to military installations.[61]

Xi has moved quickly to promote his vision of the central role military power plays in China's rise as a great power through his promotion of a "strong China dream" that goes hand in hand with a "strong military dream." Xi has pointed out that "in order to achieve the great rejuvenation of the Chinese nation, it is necessary to uphold the unity of making our country prosperous and our armed forces powerful."[62] A key dimension in Xi's call for military strengthening is for the PLA to step up its preparations for "military struggle," which means enhancing its combat readiness and further accelerating the pace of military building.[63]

A deepening concern that China is facing an increasingly complicated external threat environment is the primary driver behind Xi's demand for a more battle-capable military and defense industrial establishment. Writing in *Qiushi*, an authoritative Communist Party journal, Gen. Sun Sijing, political commissar of the Academy of Military Sciences, noted that "facing the strategic rivalry between the big powers, intense maritime competition, and frequent local turbulences, our national security environment is getting more complex, more sensitive, and more uncertain, and the task of safeguarding national sovereignty, security, territorial integrity and guaranteeing our nation's peaceful development is getting more arduous. Chairman Xi scientifically studied and determined the international strategic situation and the national security environment, and came up with the goal of strengthening the military from the strategic high plane of fulfilling the Chinese dream."[64]

Hand in hand with this stepped-up effort to enhance the PLA's combat capabilities has been a concerted effort by Xi to impose stricter political and fiscal discipline and tackle corruption and other vices in the rank-and-file, which is part of a broader campaign also being waged in the civilian arena. Xi has used the CMC apparatus to launch and oversee this rectification and cleanup drive, rather than the usual practice of delegating authority to the General Political Department. He has, for example, sought to beef up the CMC's ability to organize inspection teams that are dispatched to grassroots units to conduct detailed investigations and audits, especially targeting senior officials for decadent misbehavior.[65] This has included the establishment of a CMC leading group on inspection work headed by CMC Vice-Chairman Xu Qiliang, which is responsible for building up a comprehensive inspection system.[66]

A central focus of this inspection apparatus is to target high-level corruption. "Both tigers and flies should be chased down," according to instructions laying down the work of these inspection groups. "Tigers" refers to senior officials. The instructions add that inspectors should engage in "shock and awe" tactics to deal with corrupt officials.[67] Besides this newly expanded inspection system, the CMC also has a well-established discipline inspection commission that conducts anticorruption investigations.

The use of these aggressive strategies reflects concern by Xi and the military leadership about widespread corruption within the PLA. At a conference on disciplinary inspection work within the PLA in January 2014, Xu Qiliang said that the PLA needed to step up its anticorruption work, especially focusing on areas that are most at risk, such as military construction projects and weapons research, production, and procurement.[68] The highlighting of the construction sector as a focal point for malpractices may have been a reference to the arrest in 2012 of Lt. Gen. Gu Junshang, a deputy director of the GLD, who was found to have taken kickbacks on RMB 2 billion of property deals involving military real estate holdings.[69] The biggest military "tiger" to fall is Gen. Xu Caihou, who was detained in 2014 for taking "extremely large" bribes.[70] The case against Xu, according to a CCP Central Committee announcement, was that his actions were "serious and had a vile impact." There have also been allegations that former CMC Vice-Chairman Gen. Guo Boxiong is being investigated for corruption, which if true means that the CMC under Hu Jintao's tenure would have a deeply tarnished record of having its top two military leaders brought down by corruption.

Another political vehicle used by the CMC are so-called democratic life meetings in which military personnel are required to engage in Maoist-style criticisms and self-criticisms of themselves and colleagues with the goal of bolstering the Communist Party's legitimacy. The CMC held a "democratic life" meeting in July 2013 in which Xi took part.[71] Xi has placed experienced and trusted commissars in key CMC slots to oversee this political tightening. Xu Qiliang is the senior CMC official responsible for political affairs, while CMC General Office Director Qin Shengxiang also is likely to play a leading role as he has served most of his career in the General Political Department.

In another sign that Xi is seeking to be a far more decisive military leader than his predecessors, he included the restructuring of the military command system as a key component of a broader reform program of the Chinese economic and social systems that was unveiled at the Third Plenum of the Eighteenth Party Congress in November 2013. The plenum communiqué pointed out that the PLA's long-standing army-dominated leadership system needed to undergo far-reaching reform, in particular focusing on the development of a joint operational command system under the CMC as well as at the Military Region level. Japanese media accounts suggested that the reforms would lead to the reduction of Military Region commands from seven to five and that they would become joint service commands.[72] The Chinese Defense Ministry called the report and other domestic media stories about the establishment of a pilot joint operational command structure baseless speculation, although it added that the PLA is moving toward the eventual creation of a joint operational command.[73]

Strong bureaucratic opposition from the ground forces has been one of the primary reasons the PLA has been unable so far to implement a joint command system even as other militaries, especially in advanced countries, have adopted these operational models. If Xi has been able to overcome this entrenched resistance from the ground forces, this would represent an early and major political victory that would bode well for the rest of his tenure as commander in chief. To support the case that the ground forces have finally lost out in the interservice wars, Xu Qiliang, a former PLA Air Force commander, explained in an article on the significance of the Third Plenum for military reforms that the time had come to "lay stress on strengthening the building of the navy, the air force, and the Second Artillery" and "promote the well-balanced power development of various services and arms."[74]

While the Third Plenum communiqué contained few specific details about this proposed joint operational command structure, one possible option is the elevation and expansion of the Strategic Planning Department (SPD) that resides under the GSD but which also has ties to the CMC through a strategic planning advisory committee.[75] The SPD was established in 2011 with the goal of improving coordination across the competing general departments and service arms on policy planning, resource allocations and drafting of development plans. When the SPD was first set up, CMC Vice-Chairman Gen. Guo Boxiong said that "it has very important meaning for strengthening the strategic management functions of the CMC."[76] If the SPD were to be upgraded in this push toward a more joint command system, a key player could be Lt. Gen. Wang Guanzhong, who was promoted from CMC General Office director in 2012 to become a deputy chief of the General Staff. One of Wang's responsibilities is oversight of the SPD.

Notes

1. See Tai Ming Cheung, "The Influence of the Gun: China's Central Military Commission and Its Relationship with the Military, Party, and State Decision-Making Systems," in *The Making of Chinese Foreign and Security Policy: 1978–2000*, ed. David Lampton (Stanford, CA: Stanford University Press, 2001); and David Shambaugh, "The Pinnacle of the Pyramid: The Central Military Commission," in *The People's Liberation Army as Organization: Reference Volume 1.0*, eds. James C. Mulvenon and Andrew N. D. Yang (Santa Monica, CA: RAND Corporation, 2002).

2. Liu Huaqing [刘华清], *Memoirs of Liu Huaqing* [刘华清回忆录] (Beijing: Liberation Army Press [解放军出版社], 2004); *Biography of Zhang Wannian* [张万年传] (Beijing: Liberation Army Press [解放军出版社], 2011); and Bo Xuezheng [傅学正], "Daily Work in the CMC General Office" [在中央军委办公厅工作的日子], *World Party History* [党史天地] (January 2006): 8–16.

3. Zhao Qi [赵琦], "A Major Indication of a Perfect State System: A Visit to Yang Dezhi and Other NPC Deputies on the Occasion of the Birth of the State Central Military Commission" [国家体制完善的一个重要标志——就国家中央军委诞生访杨得志等人大代表], *Outlook* [瞭望] (July 20, 1983): 11.

4. See Wang Yongsheng and Li Yuping [王永生, 李玉平], "Historical Background and Past Composition of the Chinese Communist Party Central Military

Commission" [历届中共中央军事委员会的组成及历史背景], *Military History* [军事历史], no. 6 (2007): 11–14.

5. For the Soviet case, see Central Intelligence Agency, *The Higher Military Council of the USSR* (July 1964, declassified June 2007). For the North Korean case, see Pak Yong-taek, *The Enhanced Position of the North Korean Military and Its Influence on Policymaking* (Seoul: Korea Institute for Defense Analyses, 2008).

6. "China Publishes Jiang Zemin's Letter of Resignation," Xinhua, September 19, 2004. See also James Mulvenon, "The King Is Dead! Long Live the King! The CMC Leadership Transition from Jiang to Hu," *China Leadership Monitor*, no. 13 (Winter 2005).

7. See Tai Ming Cheung, "The Special One: The Central Special Committee and the Structure, Process, and Leadership of the Chinese Defense and Strategic Dual-Use Science, Technology and Industrial Triangle," unpublished conference paper, July 2012.

8. *Selected Works of Deng Xiaoping, 1975–1982* (Beijing: Foreign Languages Press, 1984), 386.

9. Peter Feaver, *Armed Servants: Agency, Oversight, and Civil-Military Relations* (Cambridge, MA: Harvard University Press, 2003), 75–87.

10. Susan Shirk, *The Political Logic of Economic Reform in China* (Berkeley: University of California Press, 1993), 57–62.

11. Michael D. Swaine, *The Role of the Chinese Military in National Security Policymaking* (Santa Monica, CA: Rand Corp., 1996), 52.

12. Wang and Li, "Historical Background and Past Composition of the Chinese Communist Party Central Military Commission," 14.

13. Zhao, "A Major Indication of a Perfect State System," 11.

14. Yao Yanjin, Lai Mingchuan, and Wang Yamin [姚延进, 赖铭传, 王亚民], eds., *Research on Military Organizational Structure* [军事组织体制研究] (Beijing: National Defense University Press [国防大学出版社], 1997), 371.

15. See Kao Li, "The Seven Discussion Meetings of the National Party Committee Secretaries-General and General Office Directors in the New Era," *Secretarial Work* [秘书工作], no. 10 (2005): 51–52.

16. Bo, "Daily Work in the CMC General Office," 14.

17. Interview with senior PLA officer, Beijing, 1999.

18. This is an estimate by Huazhengtong, a Chinese media and communications affairs website, http://jigou.infomix.com.cn/showOrgan.aspx?Type=0&institutionCode=INST00000000003.

19. Bo, "Daily Work in the CMC General Office," 9. These administrative functions are similar to those of the general offices in the State Council and the Party Central Committee. The State Council General Office is responsible for the following functions:

> Preparing the meetings of the State Council;
> Organizing the implementation of resolutions made at these meetings;
> Organizing the draft of notices or announcements for the State Council;

Reporting to the head of the State Council for decisions on research projects and requests from provincial governments and from ministries within the State Council;

Coordinating the work of related ministries and reporting to the head of the State Council on any disputes, along with opinions on possible solutions;

Assisting in the administration of events and important matters that require the direct involvement of the State Council;

Handling all incoming correspondence, receiving group visits, and making timely reports to the head of the State Council on suggestions arising from this interaction;

Investigating, conducting research, inspecting and supervising the enforcement of the State Council's decisions and directives.

Directory of China's Government Structure (Hong Kong: Hong Kong Commercial Daily Press, 1997), 10–11.

20. "Xiao Xiangrong [萧向荣]," in *Biographies of Liberation Army Generals* [解放军将领传], Single Spark Editorial Committee [星火燎原编辑部] (Beijing: Liberation Army Press [解放军出版社], 1988), 254. Xiao was one of the first CMC General Office directors in the early 1950s and was also the longest serving in this post.

21. This includes the *chengyuejian* (reading materials for superiors), *zhuangyuejian* (commentaries on reading materials), and *junban jianbao* (CMC bulletin). Ibid.

22. Bo, "Daily Work in the CMC General Office," 9.

23. Ibid., 16.

24. Interviews with PLA officers, Beijing, 1987–1990. See also Swaine, *The Role of the Chinese Military in National Security Policymaking*, 68.

25. "Deputy Chief of General Staff Wang Guanzhong" [王冠中任中国人民解放军副总参谋长], *Ta Kung Pao* [大公報], October 23, 2012.

26. For a broad analysis of the secretarial system, see "A Brief History of the Work of Secretaries in the Chinese Communist Party (1921–1949)," *Chinese Law and Government* 30, no. 3 (May–June 1997); and Wei Li, *The Chinese Staff System: A Mechanism for Bureaucratic Control and Integration* (Berkeley: Institute for East Asian Studies, University of California, 1994).

27. For details, see Liu's memoirs.

28. Jiang Siyi, Yang Guoyu, and Yang Zhihua [姜思毅, 杨国宇, 杨志华], eds., *Chinese People's Liberation Army Encyclopedia* [中国人民解放大事典] (Tianjin: Tianjin People's Publishing House [天津人民出版社], 1992), 1871.

29. The last reported CMC plenary session was held in December 1977. *Chinese People's Liberation Army Sixty-Year Event Record* [中国人民解放军六十年大事记] (Beijing: Military Science Publishing House [军事科学出版社], 1988), 676.

30. Zhang Shude [张树德], ed., *Documentary of Major Decisions Made by Mao Zedong and the People's Republic* [毛泽东与共和国重大决策纪实] (Wuhan: Hubei People's Press [湖北人民出版社], 2009).

31. Liu, *Memoirs*, 636.

32. *Biography of Zhang Wannian*, 54–55.

33. See Liu's *Memoirs*, 580–590, and Zhang's *Biography*, 77–85, for extensive details of this five-year drafting process.

34. For the Ninth Five-Year Plan, thirty-three topics were put forward as important areas for discussion. The leading group delegated analysis and discussion of these topics to PLA units specializing in these areas. *Biography of Zhang Wannian*, 80.

35. Liu, *Memoirs*, 555.

36. See Tai Ming Cheung, *China's Entrepreneurial Army* (Oxford: Oxford University Press, 2001); and "Yang Shangkun at PLA Financial Discipline Meeting," Xinhua, March 11, 1986.

37. "CMC Inspection Team Comes to the Air Force and Unfolds Inspection Work," *Kongjun bao* [空军报], February 25, 2011: 1.

38. *Selected Works of Deng Xiaoping, 1975–1982* (Beijing: Foreign Languages Press, 1984), 386.

39. Liu, *Memoirs*, 527.

40. Ibid., 529

41. Ibid., 630.

42. Andrew Scobell, "Is There a Civil-Military Gap in China's Peaceful Rise?," *Parameters* 39 (Summer 2009): 4–22.

43. See James Mulvenon, "Rogue Warriors? A Puzzled Look at the Chinese ASAT Test," *China Leadership Monitor*, no. 20 (Winter 2007); and Eric Hagt, "China's ASAT Test: Strategic Response," *China Security* 3, no. 1 (Winter 2007): 31–51.

44. John Pomfret, "Chinese Army Tests Jet during Gates Visit," *Washington Post*, January 12, 2011; and Elizabeth Bumiller and Michael Wines, "Chinese Army Test Jet as Gates Visits," *New York Times*, January 12, 2011.

45. "Chinese Premier Orders Deployment of 90 More Helicopters for Quake Relief," Xinhua, May 14, 2008.

46. Scobell, "Is There a Civil-Military Gap in China's Peaceful Rise?," 19.

47. For a PLA assessment of Hu's contributions to Chinese military thinking and defense modernization, see Tang Xiaohua and Geng Dexing [汤晓华，耿德兴], "The Study of Hu Jintao's Important Explications on Development of National Defense and Armed Forces" [胡锦涛关于国防和军队建设重要论述研究], *China Military Science* [中国军事科学], no. 2 (2010).

48. Cheng Li, "The New Military Elite," in *Civil-Military Relations in Today's China*, eds. David Finkelstein and Kirsten Gunness (Armonk, NY: East Gate, 2007), 68.

49. Liu, *Memoirs*, 555–560.

50. Ibid., 667.

51. David M. Finkelstein, "China's National Military Strategy: An Overview of the 'Military Strategic Guidelines,'" in *Right Sizing the People's Liberation Army: Exploring the Contours of China's Military*, eds. Roy Kamphausen and Andrew Scobell (Carlisle Barracks, PA: U.S. Army War College, 2007), 82.

52. Liu, *Memoirs*, 636. For further discussion of the key role the CMC has played in the drafting of the PLA's operational doctrines since 1949, see Yang Zhiyuan [杨志远], "Innovative Development in Compiling and Revising PLA's Operational Doctrines

and Its Implications" [我军编修作战条令的创新发展及启示心理战本质：相对于肉体战的 "精神战"], *China Military Science* [中国军事科学], no. 6 (June 2009): 112–118.

53. "Our Army Heads to the Sun: The 1993 CMC Enlarged Meeting," Xinhua, December 18, 2007.

54. Liu, *Memoirs*, 636.

55. *Biography of Zhang Wannian*, 416.

56. Ibid., 419.

57. There has been plenty of analysis of Chinese efforts to develop asymmetric weapons capabilities. For a provocative Chinese assessment, see Qiao Liang and Wang Xiangsui [乔良, 王湘穗], *Unrestricted Warfare* [超限战] (Beijing: Liberation Army Literature and Arts Publishing House [解放军文艺出版社], 1999).

58. Zhou Bisong [周碧松], *Research on the Path for the Construction of Weapons with Chinese Characteristics* [中国特色武器装备建设道路研究] (Beijing: National Defense University Press [国防大学出版社], 2012), 39.

59. See Cheung, "The Special One."

60. "Record of Advancement of National Defense and Army Building by Party General Secretary Xi Jinping," Xinhua, December 27, 2013.

61. During his first year as CMC chairman from September 2004 to August 2005, Hu only made one trip whose primary purpose was to inspect military facilities, which was to the Ji'nan Military Region in April 2005. He also made short side visits to see military personnel and installations during regional visits that included Macau (December 2004), Shanxi (July 2005), and Hubei (August 2005). Hu also presided over a number of military-related activities in Beijing, such as attending military-related conferences and meeting with foreign defense dignitaries. One reason for Hu's apparent limited engagement with the military in this period was that he had already served as CMC vice-chairman for seven years.

62. "Xi Jinping Stresses during His Inspection of Guangzhou Military Region the Need to Uphold the Unity of Making Our Country Prosperous and Our Armed Forces Powerful and Strive to Consolidate National Defense and Build a Strong Army," Xinhua, December 12, 2012.

63. "Chinese Military Leaders Call for Enhancing Combat Preparedness," Xinhua, February 6, 2013.

64. Sun Sijing [孙思敬], "The Strong Military Path Requires That Military Theory with Chinese Characteristics Be Taken as a Guide" [强军之路要以中国特色军事理论为先导], *Qiushi* [求是], August 1, 2013.

65. "Army Disciplinary Inspection Eyes Leading Officials," Xinhua, November 19, 2013.

66. "Central Military Commission Issues 'Decision of the Central Military Commission on Unfolding Inspection Work' and the 'Regulations of the Central Military Commission on Inspection Work (Trial)'; Xu Qiliang Chairs a Meeting to Make Implementation Arrangements," Xinhua, October 29, 2013.

67. "China Strengthens Military Inspections Targeting Corruption," Xinhua, October 29, 2013.

68. See "CMC Vice Chairman Stresses Effective Anti-Corruption," Xinhua, January 16, 2014.

69. Wang Heyan [王和岩], "Investigation of GLD Deputy Director Gu Junshang Lasted Two Years" [总后副部长谷俊山被查已有两年], *Caixin* [财新], January 14, 2014.

70. "Xu Caihou Confesses to Taking Bribe," Xinhua, October 28, 2014.

71. "Record of Advancement of National Defense and Army Building by Party General Secretary Xi Jinping," Xinhua, December 27, 2013.

72. "China Plans Military Reform to Enhance Its Readiness," *Mainichi Shimbun*, January 2, 2014.

73. "Ministry of National Defense Clarifies Rumors about 'Joint Operational Command,'" *China Military Online*, January 6, 2014.

74. Xu Qiliang [许其亮], "Firmly Push Forward Reform of National Defense and the Armed Forces" [坚定不移推进国防和军队改革], *People's Daily* [人民日报], November 21, 2013.

75. "Inaugural Meeting of PLA Strategic Planning Department Held in Beijing; Guo Boxiong Attends and Speaks," Xinhua, November 22, 2011.

76. Ibid.

4 Top Leaders and the PLA:
The Different Styles of Jiang, Hu, and Xi

Nan Li

A S A PARTY-ARMY SUBORDINATE TO THE LEADERSHIP
of the Chinese Communist Party (CCP), the People's Liberation
Army (PLA) differs from Chinese civilian ministries under the State Council
that report to the premier. Instead, the PLA reports to the Central Military
Commission (CMC), chaired by the CCP general secretary and staffed almost
entirely by military officers.[1] Key policy decisions that affect the party, state,
and military are made collectively by the CCP Politburo Standing Committee (PBSC), which currently consists of seven civilian members and is chaired
by the CCP general secretary. There has not been a PLA officer on the PBSC
since 1997. Instead, the CCP general secretary represents PLA views in PBSC
discussions and conveys PBSC decisions back to the CMC for implementation
by the PLA. This arrangement limits institutionalized channels for top-level
civil-military policy coordination and places a premium on the CCP general
secretary's role in ensuring coordination of civilian and military policies and
civilian (party) control of the PLA.

Many of the institutional practices that helped coordinate policy and
ensure the PLA's loyalty to CCP orders that existed during the first four
decades of the PRC have gradually broken down. First- and second-genera-
tion leaders such as Mao and Deng relied on extensive personal networks in
the PLA to "command the gun" and coordinate policies, based on their revolutionary legitimacy and the narrative that "they founded the PLA." Third-
and fourth-generation leaders such as Jiang and Hu lacked such networks

because they had never served in the PLA. (Fifth-generation leader Xi Jinping, who served for three years as secretary to then-Defense Minister Geng Biao from 1979 to 1982, is a partial exception.) During the revolution and the initial decades of the PRC, civilian cadres often served as political commissars and military officers rotated into government positions. However, the CCP's increasing emphasis on formal credentials and technical expertise (and a parallel emphasis on military professionalism) has ended this cross-institutional circulation of civilian and military elites. PLA political commissar positions are now filled by career uniformed officers, who are required to be loyal to the party but are also charged by PLA *Political Work Regulations* to defend and serve the institutional interests of the PLA.[2] Other policy coordination measures such as military representation on leading small groups for national security affairs, foreign affairs, and Taiwan affairs have proven inadequate. It remains to be seen whether the newly established National Security Commission can improve coordination.

As a result of these changes, civil-military policy coordination and party control of the PLA now rest heavily on the CCP general secretary in his role as chairman of the CMC. This chapter examines the relationship between CCP general secretaries and the PLA by comparing the leadership styles of Jiang, Hu, and Xi. Although the importance of this relationship is obvious, it is not well understood. A better understanding may help clarify the relative weight of the PLA in national security decisionmaking.

To operationalize the different styles of top leaders in a manner that can be verified or falsified by empirical evidence, this chapter identifies two major ideal types: currying favor and imposing will. Currying favor means that top leaders seek to build military support by doing what the PLA wants. They hesitate to order the PLA to do things it does not want to do or to intervene in military matters to stop the PLA from doing things it wants to do. Conversely, imposing will means that top leaders are willing to order the PLA to do things it does not want to do, or to prevent it from doing things it does want to do. Imposing will may be unpopular with some or all of the military, but it may be necessary to serve the larger good at the expense of special, vested interests within the PLA.

This chapter argues that although Jiang usually curried favor with the PLA from 1989 to 1997, he imposed his will more during the period from 1997 to 2004. In comparison, Hu largely curried favor with the PLA as CCP general secretary and CMC chairman from 2004 to 2012. After becoming the CMC chairman in 2012, Xi has also curried favor with the PLA, but major indicators show Xi is capable of imposing his will on the PLA.

There are three caveats. First, greater civil-military institutionalization in post-Deng China has imposed more constraints on the role of personalities in affecting policy outcomes. Nevertheless, areas of discretion remain where different personal styles do make a difference, particularly in top-level interagency coordination and civilian oversight of the PLA. Analyzing the role of personal styles does not deny progress in institutionalization. The literature on bureaucracy indicates that informal, personal politics can make a difference in highly institutionalized bureaucratic settings under certain conditions.[3]

Second, this chapter focuses on these two ideal types because they are the most typical and the most likely to affect outcomes. Most analysis highlights the CCP general secretary's role in representing PLA views and interests in civilian settings such as PBSC meetings, suggesting efforts to "curry favor" with the PLA. However, party general secretaries may also represent the views and interests of civilians in military settings such as CMC meetings, "imposing will" by ordering the PLA to do things it may not want to do or preventing the PLA from doing things it wants to do. These two ideal types are also consistent with the Chinese classical governance philosophy of both "bestowing favor" and "inspiring awe (through imposing will)" (shi'en and shuwei, or enweibingju), two very different but necessary requisites for becoming a competent leader. The chapter will analyze nuances in empirical cases that the two ideal types may not explain fully.

Third, the empirical evidence used to illustrate the different styles of Jiang, Hu, and Xi mostly involves military policy decisions with important implications for national security. These examples are not national security or crisis management decisions, nor are they routine bureaucratic decisions. As a result, the number of decisions available as evidence is limited. A major reason for selecting these examples is that relatively more information is available about them. To the extent that different types of issues and decisions may make a difference in the PLA's role in influencing national security decisions,[4] the findings may also serve as a starting point for examining how the PLA's influence on different types of issues and decisions varies.

The next three sections of the chapter discuss the different styles of Jiang, Hu, and Xi, presenting empirical evidence on how they interacted with the PLA. The conclusion then addresses what accounts for the different styles of Jiang, Hu, and Xi.

Jiang and the PLA: From Currying Favor to Imposing His Will

Jiang became party general secretary and CMC chairman in 1989. With no military experience and few close connections in the PLA, Jiang was quite successful in exploiting his position as CMC chairman to consolidate his power. The CMC chairman has the final say in all major military decisions, from allocating budget and appointing senior officers to deploying troops and controlling employment of nuclear weapons. Jiang's relationship with the PLA can be roughly divided into two periods: a "consolidation" period from 1989 to 1997 where he curried favor with the PLA, followed by an "initiative" period from 1998 to 2004 where Jiang was more likely to impose his will on the PLA.

Currying Favor

Jiang's efforts to curry favor with the PLA can be clearly identified in the areas of defense budget, senior officer appointments, and cultivating relationships.

China's defense budget has enjoyed double-digit growth most years since Jiang became CMC chairman. This is a sharp contrast to the earlier period, when the defense budget steadily declined in real terms as Deng shifted resources toward economic development and required the "army to be patient." As a result, the PLA was asked to go into business on a massive scale to make up for spending shortfalls under a policy of "self-development, self-perfection."[5]

Some analysts argue that Jiang initiated the post-1989 defense budget increases to reward the PLA for its action during the 1989 Tiananmen crisis. While Jiang had incentives to curry favor with the PLA by increasing defense expenditures, lobbying by senior PLA officers may have played a more important role. After becoming a CMC vice-chairman in 1992, General Liu Huaqing asked "experts" to calculate the cost to upgrade armaments for the navy, air force, and army mechanized forces, concluding that the defense budget should be doubled or tripled. Liu also suggested that the salaries and benefits for military personnel were too low compared with the civilian sector, and that the "practical difficulties" (referring to poor living and working conditions and inability to have dependents live with officers) of those in basic-level units were "unresolvable." These factors made it difficult to attract and retain high-quality personnel. Liu went to Jiang, Premier Li Peng, and Vice-Premier

Yao Yilin several times to "reflect the difficulties of the army" and to "provide a credible and accurate basis for the Party Center to make policy."[6]

Liu and Zhang Zhen, another uniformed CMC vice-chairman, also met with Zhu Rongji (who succeeded Yao as vice-premier in charge of finance) to discuss the budget. This lobbying quickly produced positive results. The 1993 defense budget increase allowed for hefty salary improvements for PLA personnel, particularly those in basic-level units. This set a precedent and "played a positive role in preserving the stability of the army."[7]

Jiang also curried favor with the PLA by approving the appointments of a large number of senior officers as well as selecting who would fill key positions. *PLA Officers' Service Regulations* requires the CMC chairman's authorization for appointments of all officers at and above the division leader grade (*shiji*). From 1989 to 2004, Jiang's fifteen-year tenure as CMC chairman, 81 officers gained the rank of full general (three-star, or *shangjiang*), an average of slightly less than 11 every two years. Jiang interviewed some candidates for senior positions before approving their appointments, but promotion recommendations came from military professionals in the CMC.[8] Jiang's knowledge of senior appointees was scanty due to his limited exposure to them; as a result, his personal ties with the officers he appointed may not have been that strong. Whatever networks Jiang attempted to develop within the PLA are not comparable to those of Mao and Deng, because the latter were tested by numerous military and political life-and-death battles.

On the other hand, approving the appointments of senior officers may create a superior-subordinate relationship. Jiang's 1997 revamping of the CMC, for instance, probably made it easier for him to impose his will on the PLA. The retirement of PLA elders such as Liu Huaqing and Zhang Zhen and filling the two CMC vice-chairman positions with younger officers Zhang Wannian and Chi Haotian may have removed a constraint stemming from deference to the elders.

Jiang also curried favor with the PLA by demonstrating respect for the PLA as an institution and by cultivating and maintaining good relations with PLA leaders. This involved showing respect for PLA veterans, listening to officers' concerns on major issues, honoring PLA heroes and traditions, and conducting regular inspection tours of basic-level PLA units.[9] In a culture that highly values attention and sensitivity to and investment in relationships, this likely contributed to more positive and rewarding interactions between Jiang and the PLA. Jiang may also have curried favor with the PLA by allowing it to drive the decision to conduct military exercises during the Taiwan Strait crisis of 1995–1996.[10] By doing what the PLA wanted in the areas of defense budget, personnel appointments, and building relationships in his early years as CMC chairman, Jiang accumulated substantial political capital with PLA leaders.

"Imposing Will" on the PLA

After 1997, when Deng died and PLA elders Liu Huaqing and Zhang Zhen retired, Jiang began to impose his will on the PLA.

In 1998, Jiang required the PLA to divest most of its business activities. The PLA was highly divided on the issue of divestiture, which gave Jiang allies in the PLA. But although some senior officers were concerned about corruption and the corrosive effects of business activities on PLA combat readiness, the mainstream view was to reform PLA business activities by separating them from combat units and retaining the revenue they generated. Zhang Zhen wrote that many comrades "see more the benefits of production and business but see less the harm they produce."[11]

Jiang wrote that when he first became CMC chairman, he wanted to get the PLA out of business activities.[12] This shows Jiang had a "will" on this issue even before the negative effects of business activities on PLA combat readiness began to divide the PLA. He was unable to impose his will because it was Deng who had allowed the PLA to go into business,[13] because many children of PLA elders were involved, and because PLA units were poorly funded. After 1997, he felt secure enough to push divestiture without fear of displeasing Deng and the PLA elders. Rapid economic growth also made it possible to allocate more funding to the PLA. Moreover, divestiture increased political control over the PLA by cutting off its sources of extra-budgetary income. Although some PLA officers supported divestiture, the PLA was united in wanting compensation in the form of a higher defense budget, and was reportedly disappointed by the budget increase that it received.[14]

Jiang also endorsed policies to downsize the PLA by 500,000 billets from 1997 on and another 200,000 from 2003 on. As early as in 1993, Jiang advanced the new PLA strategic principle of preparing for fighting and winning "local war under high-tech conditions," but was not able to follow up with concrete policy initiatives. After 1997, he felt more secure to introduce bold and concrete policies. To justify downsizings, Jiang introduced the concept of "leapfrogging development" in 1997 by shifting the emphasis of military modernization from mechanization (adding new hardware platforms) to informatization (developing information-technologies-based networks and software) to narrow the technological gap with more advanced militaries. This led to the CMC's endorsement of a policy of dual-transformation (mechanization and informatization) of the PLA in late 2002.[15]

While some in the PLA leadership supported downsizing to free up funds for technology-based modernization, these policies were mostly unpopular in the PLA, mainly because the PLA remained a military heavily vested in manpower rather than technology. These two rounds of downsizing represent critical cases that show Jiang made the PLA take actions it would not otherwise have taken.

Jiang also may have prevented the PLA from taking actions it wanted. He made the decision not to reserve a PBSC seat for a senior PLA officer after Liu Huaqing's retirement in 1997. This removed the PLA's ability to have a direct voice and vote on national policy decisions.

After the 1999 accidental U.S. bombing of the Chinese embassy in Belgrade where the PLA defense attaché was seriously wounded, and the 2001 EP-3 incident where a PLA Navy (PLAN) pilot was lost, the PLA demanded harsh reprisals. In the case of EP-3 incident, the PLA wanted the U.S. crew detained in Hainan to be court-martialed. Jiang eventually persuaded senior PLA officers to agree to his position that China would demand an apology from the United States and then release the U.S. crew.[16]

Similarly, after the 1995–1996 Taiwan Strait crisis, Jiang refused to endorse the aircraft carrier program that Liu Huaqing had lobbied for,[17] arguing that carriers were not that useful for a military conflict over Taiwan.[18] These cases show that after 1997, Jiang felt more secure and was relatively successful in imposing his will on the PLA.

Hu and the PLA: From Currying Favor to Currying Favor

Hu Jintao took over the position of party general secretary in 2002 and of CMC chairman in 2004. Like Jiang, Hu had weak military credentials, with no service experience and few close connections in the PLA. Hu also curried favor with the PLA through increases in the defense budget and regularly appointing senior officers. PLA personnel also received a 100 percent salary increase in 2006 and were issued better-quality uniforms. Salaries of PLA personnel were raised substantially again in 2008 and 2011.[19] In 2004, Hu approved a change to the CMC that added the PLAN, the PLA Air Force (PLAAF), and the Second Artillery (China's strategic rocket force) commanders as ex officio members. Hu had also paid many visits to basic-level units, attended and delivered speeches at party congresses of major PLA institutions, and maintained good relations with senior officers.

A central challenge in analyzing the relationship between Hu and the PLA is that it is difficult to identify a clear example where Hu was able to impose his will on the PLA by making the PLA do things it did not want to do or by preventing the PLA from doing things it wanted to do. Hu highlighted the need for the PLA to "enhance the capabilities to cope with multiple types of security threat and fulfill diversified military missions," calling on the PLA to devote more energy and resources to nontraditional security missions. This guidance was codified in the "new historic missions" that Hu approved in 2004. The PLA's participation in 2008 Sichuan earthquake relief operations and the PLAN's counter-piracy mission in the Gulf of Aden since late 2008 are both examples that deserve scrutiny.

Because disaster relief has been a traditional PLA mission, the quick mobilization of about 120,000 PLA men to participate in the Sichuan earthquake relief in May 2008 might not seem like a new departure. However, the deployment revealed serious force structure, training, equipment, and interagency issues that may have made the PLA more reluctant to conduct these missions. The forces mobilized were largely quick-reaction units (*kuaifan budui*) and strategic reserve forces (*zhanlüe yubei dui*), or elite army divisions, paratroopers, and PLAN marines trained to fight conventional wars. They were issued light tools such as spades and picks that were ineffective in removing large concrete pieces of collapsed buildings. More importantly, Premier Wen Jiabao asked senior PLA officers to undertake tasks that they perceived as recklessly risking the lives of their soldiers, leading some PLA officers to conclude that Wen "does not understand the army."[20]

Hu could have exploited this moment of PLA vulnerability due to poor performance to impose his will, which he probably tried to do initially. The December 2008 CMC meeting, for instance, allegedly reached agreement that the PLA should be downsized substantially, eliminating some group armies and Military Region (MR) bureaucracies by consolidating the seven MRs into four, and by establishing an army headquarters to command all the remaining army units. To enhance party-army coordination, each MR was to be led by a regional military commission modeled after the CMC, chaired by a regional party leader.[21] This reorganization plan, however, was not executed.

The PLAN's counter-piracy mission in the Gulf of Aden was first requested by the Ministry of Transportation agency that oversees the safety of commercial shipping. The PLA's desire to remedy its deficiencies revealed by the Sichuan earthquake relief may be an important reason for the more forthcoming PLA cooperation and coordination with the state authorities. The PLAN has also been acquiring more warships capable of far-seas operations and was interested in opportunities to expose itself to conditions in the far seas to gain operational experience. Therefore, Hu's order for the PLAN to conduct this mission should not be counted as an example where Hu imposed his will on the PLA.[22]

A final case is the first test flight of the J-20 stealth fighter during Defense Secretary Robert Gates' visit to China in January 2011. The puzzle is whether Hu knew about the test flight in advance, because he looked surprised and had to consult an aide when Gates raised the issue in their meeting. One answer is that Hu did not know about the test flight because top leaders are mainly concerned with decisions of larger, strategic importance, not routine issues such as the timing of test flights. While this is plausible, there are a few reasons and some anecdotal evidence to support an alternative answer, that Hu might have known about the test in advance.

As CMC chairman, Hu would be kept informed of major progress in research and development of strategically important weapons. Hu, for instance, attended the ceremony to commission two new nuclear submarines in 2006.[23] There are also reports that Xi Jinping, the newly appointed vice-chairman of the CMC, was at the Chengdu airport on January 7, 2011, to inspect the new J-20.[24] Finally, from the perspective of Chinese culture, Hu may have tried to be polite to Gates by looking surprised. If Hu had answered "yes" to Gates' inquiry, it would have amounted to an affront that may have made the distinguished guest "lose face."

It is possible that senior PLA officers, but not Hu, initiated the idea to conduct the J-20's first test flight at the same time as Gates' visit. Hu probably went along with the idea, because he did not want to say "no" to the PLA, or impose his will on the PLA. These examples show that Hu curried favor with the PLA much more than he imposed his will on it.

Xi and the PLA: From Currying Favor to Imposing His Will?

Even though Xi served in the PLA for three years from 1979 to 1982, his tenure was too short to cultivate a personal network in the PLA. Like his predecessors, Xi also curried favor with the PLA after he became CMC chairman in 2012. Double-digit defense budget increases have continued, and senior officers were promoted to the rank of full general in November 2012, July 2013, and July 2014.[25] Xi has also regularly inspected troops, including a tour of Sanya Naval Base in Hainan on April 9, 2013, a visit to the PLAAF headquarters on April 14, 2014, a meeting with delegates to the Second Artillery Party Congress on December 5, 2012, and inspection of a division of the Thirty-first Group Army in Fujian on July 30, 2014.[26] Moreover, Xi has aligned his preferences with those of the PLA, endorsing the "dream of a strong military"(*qiangjun meng*),[27] and supporting a harder-line policy over maritime disputes in China's near seas, including establishing an air defense identification zone (ADIZ) over the East China Sea.[28]

While currying favor with the PLA and serving as CMC chairman for only two years, however, Xi has also taken measures to reduce special privileges and combat corruption in the PLA, which may have upset many in the PLA. For instance, Xi has ordered retired officers to return illicit houses and apartments that they occupy or have a much higher market rental rate automatically deducted from their pension.[29] Because these low-cost properties can be rented out or even sold for a high profit, such a policy is highly unpopular among those who occupy these properties, but highly popular among those (likely active-duty officers) who are entitled to a house or an apartment but do not have one yet.[30]

Moreover, Xi has issued regulations intended not only to eliminate petty graft such as business-related extravagant dining, excessive alcohol consumption, and luxurious hotels, but also to ban senior officers from corruption-related practices. These include interference in officer appointment and promotion decisions made by lower-level party committees, and intervening in project contracts, equipment procurement, and military land disposal in exchange for valuable gifts, money, and stock shares. These regulations also admonish senior officers to "strictly discipline" family members and personal aides to ensure proper behavior.[31]

More importantly, Xi has put these regulations into practice. On June 30, 2014, the CCP Politburo decided to expel from the party General Xu Caihou, who served as a CMC member (1999–2004) and vice-chairman (2004–2012), and hand him over to prosecutors on charges of "using his office to provide help for others in promotions, and accepting bribes directly or through his family."[32] Xu allegedly took several million dollars of bribes from Gu Junshan, a senior officer accused of corruption, and played a key role in Gu's promotion to the position of deputy chief of the PLA's General Logistics Department (GLD), despite objections by the GLD leadership.[33] Moreover, Xu allegedly attempted to block a GLD request to investigate Gu for corruption.[34] In both cases, Xu had apparently "interfered" in decisions of a lower-level party committee in exchange for money. Similarly, Gu reportedly embezzled tens of millions of dollars that he could use to pay for bribes by pocketing kickbacks from the sale of military land while serving as head of GLD's Infrastructure Construction and Barracks Department.[35]

Because many senior officers may be affected by these anti-special privileges and anticorruption campaigns, these cases represent major indicators that Xi can "impose his will," or order the PLA to do things many in the PLA may not want to do. These cases can also be regarded as a process where Xi attempts to fight special interests in the PLA in order to consolidate his authority. During the period when Xu was undergoing an internal investigation, for instance, fifty-three senior officers pledged their support for Xi's military policy in *PLA Daily*.[36] By consolidating his authority in the PLA, Xi apparently intends to impose his ultimate will on the PLA, which is to restructure the PLA through downsizing and reorganization.

Currently, the army dominates the PLA structure and consumes substantial PLA resources. The army's dominance is so overwhelming that unlike other services, it does not even have a headquarters in Beijing. As a result, the PLA general departments must devote their organizational resources to army functions. Both the General Staff Department (GSD) and General Armament Department (GAD), for instance, have specialized departments and agencies dedicated to army issues,[37] but not for other services. Such an army bias may distort the functions of the PLA general departments, which constitute the CMC's command and coordination institutions, inhibiting greater jointness. At the regional level, the command and control structure of seven MRs, roughly comparable to the U.S. regional combatant commands, are also army-centric. Senior navy, air force, and Second Artillery officers may serve symbolically as deputy commanders of MRs, but they are not fully integrated because they cannot become full MR commanders. Similarly, officers from other services may find it difficult to penetrate MR staff departments, which are largely dominated by army officers.

As most of China's land border disputes have been settled by diplomacy, and the responsibility of domestic security has largely been shifted to the reinforced People's Armed Police, an army-dominated PLA structure looks increasingly irrational. In the meantime, most of China's maritime territorial disputes remain unresolved, and the major threat to China's security is perceived by many Chinese analysts to come from the maritime direction. Moreover, China's development interests are growing in the far seas and overseas. Therefore, restructuring the PLA in order to provide security for China's growing maritime interests is likely to become a major challenge for Xi.

In the Decision to Deepen Reforms passed by the CCP's Third Plenum in 2013, Xi outlined his plan to restructure the PLA. The Decision, for instance, proposes to "perfect leadership and management systems of respective services, and improve the CMC's joint operations command institutions and theater (regional) joint operations command systems." Moreover, the Decision highlights the need to "optimize the scale and structure of the military, and adjust and improve the ratio among services."[38] In an article to flesh out the Decision, CMC Vice-Chairman Xu Qiliang also highlights the need to "emphatically strengthen the construction of navy, air force, and Second Artillery units."[39]

All these imply that the next phase of China's military reform may involve substantial downsizing of the army, establishing an army headquarters to contain and manage the remaining army units, and expanding the other services. This change should enhance the equal status among services, making it easier for the CMC's command institutions and regional-level command and control structure to become genuinely joint.

But because restructuring the PLA in favor of the non-army services may be controversial and unpopular in an army-dominated PLA, whether Xi can follow through with his plan can be a critical test of whether he can impose his will on the PLA. The anti-special privileges and anticorruption campaigns, however, show that Xi can impose his will on the PLA if needed. Moreover, Xi has outlined his plan in the Third Plenum Decision, which suggests that he is serious about restructuring the PLA. The credibility cost of not implementing his plan as China's top leader should also incentivize Xi to impose his will on the PLA.

Conclusion

This chapter shows that although Jiang curried favor with the PLA from 1989 to 1997, he imposed his will during the period from 1997 to 2004. In comparison, Hu mostly curried favor with the PLA during his tenure as China's top leader from 2004 to 2012. After succeeding Hu in 2012, Xi has also curried favor with the PLA, but major indicators show Xi is capable of imposing his will on the PLA if needed.

What accounts for the different styles of Jiang, Hu, and Xi in dealing with the PLA? One explanation has to do with the relative influence of retired CCP leaders and PLA elders. From 1989 to 1997, for instance, Jiang had to be cautious because Deng was still alive and attempted to influence military policy by appointing PLA elders Liu Huaqing and Zhang Zhen as CMC vice-chairmen to "assist" Jiang in military work, and by having Wang Ruilin, his former personal aide, join the CMC as a member. As a result, Jiang had to defer to the elders in all major policy decisions. By 1997, Deng had died and both Liu and Zhang were retired. Jiang's own appointees began to dominate the CMC. As a result, Jiang felt more secure and moved to introduce bold military policies, imposing his will on the PLA.

When Hu became the CCP general secretary in 2002, he had to defer to Jiang to deal with the PLA because Jiang stayed on as the CMC chairman for two years. Even after Hu became the CMC chairman in 2004, he still had to work with a CMC dominated by Jiang's appointees. This explanation suggests that Hu therefore had to be cautious and defer major decisions to Jiang and "his men" in the CMC until Hu left office in 2012.

Xi assumed the CMC chairman position at the same time that he became CCP general secretary in November 2012, and therefore did not have to contend with a predecessor who retained the top CMC position. Moreover, the majority (eight members) of the twelve-member CMC retired in 2012, allowing Xi to fill the CMC with his own appointees.[40] Both factors gave him the confidence to impose his will on the PLA.

While having some merit, this explanation is inadequate. First, Jiang and his CMC appointees are not comparable to Deng and PLA elders in status and prestige. Their influence on Jiang's successors should therefore be much smaller than the influence of Deng and PLA elders on Jiang. Also, major members of the previous CMC can shift their support to the new top leader. Xi, for instance, can impose his will on the PLA seemingly without deference to senior CMC members known as "Hu's appointees," such as Xu Qiliang, Chang Wanquan, and Wu Shengli. Xi even took on Xu Caihou, an alleged protégé of Jiang.

A more persuasive explanation has to do with different personalities between Jiang, Hu, and Xi, mostly shaped by different life and career experiences. Jiang's personality of being willing to impose his will may be shaped by a life and career experience that highlights executive responsibilities. First, Jiang can claim revolutionary credentials because he joined the CCP before 1949. For most of his career after 1949, Jiang held major executive positions that involved independent and sometime unpopular decisions. Jiang, for instance, served as manager of three different factories in 1950s. He was director of two major research institutes of China's First Ministry of Machine-Building Industry in 1960s, and served as a bureau chief of the same ministry in 1970s. He was put in charge of two national commissions that supervised imports and exports and foreign direct investment, and served as China's minister of electronics industry in the early 1980s. From 1985 to 1989, he served as mayor and party secretary of Shanghai, one of China's largest and most economically dynamic cities.

In contrast, Hu's personality of currying favor and leadership style of avoiding conflict may be shaped by a life and career experience that requires caution rather than independent decisions. A humble but also "exploitative class" family background such as a small-scale tea merchant in the age of "class struggle," for instance, demanded caution and may not have instilled a lot of self-confidence. Hu worked as a political instructor in Tsinghua University in the mid-1960s, a technical assistant and a personal secretary in a hydraulic project in Gansu province in the late 1960s and early 1970s, a section head of the Construction Commission of Gansu province in the late 1970s, secretary of the Gansu Communist Youth League (CYL) in the early 1980s, and general secretary of China's CYL from 1982 to 1985. Most of these are staff positions that do not require independent decisions, but instead demand careful conformity with bureaucratic supervisors. The positions of provincial and national CYL secretaries may sound more important, but their responsibilities mainly involve propaganda and ideological work among youth rather than executive leadership.

From 1985 to 1992, however, Hu held the positions of party secretaries of Guizhou province and Tibet Autonomous Region. While these are major leadership positions that require executive responsibilities, these provinces were relatively poor and backward. Hu's six years managing two different provinces also seems to be rather short by Chinese bureaucratic standards. This time was further shortened by reports that Hu had to stay mostly in Chengdu during his term as Tibet's party secretary because he suffered from high altitude sickness. By 1992, Hu moved to Beijing to become a full-time CCP Politburo member.

Unlike Hu and Jiang, Xi had served in the PLA for three years. Xi's father was founder of a major red army base in northern China, which offered a safe haven for the main Red Army units that had been decimated by the tumultuous Long March by late 1935. While PLA-related personal experience and family connections may give Xi political capital in dealing with the PLA, other aspects of Xi's life and career experience gain more respect from China's ruling elites, including senior PLA officers. A prominent and privileged family background may foster self-confidence in Xi, but this background is also mitigated by sixteen years of family misfortune. Xi's father, for instance, was out of political favor as early as 1962, when Xi was only nine. In 1969, Xi moved to a village in loess-covered northern Shaanxi as a sent-down youth, and lived and worked in one of the poorest regions of China for seven years. The son of a major "capitalist roader" in China, Xi had to make all the tough decisions on his own. Xi applied for CCP membership ten times but was rejected repeatedly before his hard work eventually allowed him to become party secretary of his village.[41]

In twenty-five years from 1982 to 2007, Xi held major executive positions that require independent decisions. Xi, for instance, served as party secretary of a county in Hebei province from 1982 to 1985. He then moved to Fujian province and worked there for seventeen years from 1985 to 2002, serving as mayor or party secretary of two cities and one prefecture, and then governor and party secretary of the province. From 2002 to 2007, Xi was governor and party secretary of Zhejiang province. Both Fujian and Zhejiang are large, economically dynamic coastal provinces. In 2007, Xi took over as party secretary of Shanghai, but moved to Beijing to become a new member of the CCP Politburo Standing Committee after a few months. It is likely that twenty-five years of executive experience has played a crucial role in shaping Xi's personality as a leader able to impose his will if he needs to do so.

Notes

1. A state CMC chaired by the president technically exists, but in practice the positions of president and CCP general secretary are usually held by the same person and the state CMC membership parallels that of the party CMC.

2. See Nan Li, *Chinese Civil-Military Relations in the Post-Deng Era: Implications for Crisis Management and Naval Modernization*, China Maritime Studies 4 (Newport, RI: U.S. Naval War College Press, 2010); and Michael Kiselycznyk and Phillip C. Saunders, *Civil-Military Relations in China: Assessing the PLA's Role in Elite Politics*,

INSS China Strategic Perspectives 2 (Washington, DC: National Defense University, 2012).

3. See Michel Crozier, *The Bureaucratic Phenomenon* (Chicago: University of Chicago Press, 1964), 109–111; and Anthony Downs, *Inside Bureaucracy* (Boston: Little, Brown, 1967), 61–64.

4. See the chapter by Kardon and Saunders in this volume.

5. See Zhang Zhen [张震], *Memoirs of Zhang Zhen, Vol. 2* [张震回忆录，下册] (Beijing: Liberation Army Press [解放军出版社], 2003), 399.

6. See Liu Huaqing [刘华清], *Memoirs of Liu Huaqing* [刘华清回忆录] (Beijing: Liberation Army Press [解放军出版社], 2004), 585.

7. Zhang, *Memoirs*, 373–374.

8. Personnel policies concerning senior officers had largely been worked out by Zhang Zhen, Liu Huaqing, and Yu Yongbo (CMC member and head of the General Political Department) and approved by Jiang during the 1992–1997 period. See Zhang, *Memoirs*, 377–378.

9. You Ji, "Jiang Zemin's Command of the Military," *The China Journal*, no. 45 (January 2001); and James Mulvenon, "China: Conditional Compliance," in *Coercion and Governance: The Declining Political Role of the Military in Asia*, ed. Muthiah Alagappa (Stanford, CA: Stanford University Press, 2001), 318.

10. See Andrew Scobell, *China's Use of Military Force: Beyond the Great Wall and the Long March* (New York: Cambridge University Press, 2003), chap. 8.

11. Zhang, *Memoirs*, 406.

12. Jiang Zemin [江泽民], "The Army Must Stop All Its Business Activities" [军队必须停止一切经商活动], collected in Jiang Zemin, *On National Defense and Army Construction* [论国防和军队建设] (Beijing: Liberation Army Press [解放军出版社], 2002). The speech was delivered on July 21, 1998, at a CMC meeting.

13. Even though first CMC vice-chair Zhao Ziyang was believed to be responsible for the policy, Zhao was likely to have consulted Deng, who was then the CMC chair.

14. For detailed discussions of the rise and decline of PLA's business activities, see James Mulvenon, *Soldiers of Fortune: The Rise and Fall of the Chinese Military-Business Complex, 1978–1998* (Armonk, NY: M. E. Sharpe, 2001); and Tai Ming Cheung, *China's Entrepreneurial Army* (Oxford: Oxford University Press, 2001).

15. See Army Construction Research Institute of National Defense University [国防大学军队建设研究所], *A Reader for Studying Jiang Zemin's Thought on National Defense and Army Construction* [江泽民国防和军队建设思想学习读本] (Beijing: CCP History Press [中共党史出版社], 2002), 56, 232–244.

16. Conversations with informed sources in Guangzhou and Beijing in 2003.

17. See Liu, *Memoirs of Liu Huaqing*, 477–481. Liu was PLAN commander from 1982 to 1987 and a CMC member and vice-chair from 1987 to 1997.

18. Jiang even removed a commanding officer of the PLAN South Sea Fleet for advocating aircraft carriers to resolve the Spratlys issue to him during an inspection tour of the fleet. Conversation with informed sources in Guangzhou in 2003. See also "Phoenix Net's Special Interview with Ma Xinchun: Aircraft Carrier Should Have

Been Developed 10 Years Ago" [凤凰网专访马辛春: 十年前就该造航母], *Phoenix Net*, October 14, 2009. Ma Xinchun is the former commander of the PLAN North Sea Fleet. In the interview, Ma notes that someone was criticized for advocating aircraft carriers ten years earlier. He actually refers to an incident where a North Sea Fleet senior officer was reprimanded by Jiang at a National People's Congress annual meeting for advocating aircraft carriers.

19. "Details of Raising Salaries for the PLA" [解放军加薪详情], *Global Times* [环球时报], March 2, 2011.

20. For details, see Li, *Chinese Civil-Military Relations*, 26–32.

21. Conversations with informed sources in Beijing in 2009.

22. For details, see Li, *Chinese Civil-Military Relations*, 32–33.

23. "Two New-Type Nuclear Submarines Entered Service in 2006: Chairman Hu Personally Conferred the Flag" [海军2006年服役两艘新型核潜艇，胡主席亲自授旗], *People's Daily* [人民日报], May 18, 2009.

24. "Xi Jinping Inspects J-20 Aircraft of Chengdu Aircraft Corporation on January 7" [习近平1月7日视察成飞J-20飞机], *Ming Pao* [明报], January 8, 2011.

25. See *PLA Daily* [解放军报], November 23, 2012, July 31, 2013, and July 11, 2014.

26. For inspection tours, see "Xi Jinping Lays out Overall Arrangement for Military Reform: Break down Barriers against System of Systems, and Strategize Transformation of Three Services" [习近平布局军队改革：破体系壁垒，谋三军转型], *People's Daily Online* [人民网], August 8, 2014; and "Xi Jinping Inspects Naval Units in Sanya" [习近平视察海军驻三亚部队], *PLA Daily* [解放军报], April 11, 2014.

27. "Xi Jinping: Constructing a Modern Military Force System of Systems with Chinese Characteristics" [习近平: 构建中国特色现代军事力量体系], *People's Daily* [人民日报], August 15, 2014.

28. An ADIZ is likely an agenda that is preferred by PLAAF. For a discussion of "air operations to safeguard maritime interests and rights" [维护海洋权益空中行动] and "far-seas air offensive and defensive system of systems operations capabilities" [远海空中攻防体系作战能力], see Ma Xiaotian [马晓天], "Assiduously Enhance the Capabilities of Air Force Units to Fight and Win War" [努力提高空军部队能打仗打胜仗能力], *PLA Daily* [解放军报], April 2, 2014. Ma is commander of the PLAAF.

29. See "Four General Departments and CMC Disciplinary Inspection Commission Issue Notice, Requiring Strengthening of Forceful Measures to Clear-up Housing of Departed and Retired Cadres That Violates Regulations" [四总部军委纪委发出通知，要求强化刚性措施清理离退休干部违规住房], *PLA Daily* [解放军报], July 26, 2014.

30. See "Great Housing Clearance of the Chinese Military" [中国军队大清房], *Southern Weekend* [南方周末], August 14, 2014.

31. See "CMC Has Issued Ten Regulations to Strengthen Construction of Its Own Work Style" [中央军委引发关于加强自身作风建设十项规定], *Xinhuanet* [新华网], December 21, 2012.

32. "CCP Center Decides to Expel Xu Caihou from the Party" [中共中央决定给与徐才厚开除党籍处分], *Xinhuanet* [新华网], June 20, 2014.

33. See "Senior General on Corruption Charges," *South China Morning Post*, March 31, 2014.

34. "Xi Strikes Hard at Military Graft and Corruption by Heavily Punishing Gu Junshan" [习严打军队贪腐，重惩谷俊山], *Ming Pao* [明报], March 11, 2013; and "Leader in China Aims at Military with Graft Case," *New York Times*, April 1, 2014.

35. See "Senior General on Corruption Charges."

36. See *PLA Daily* [解放军报], March 7, 2014, April 2, 2014, and April 17, 2014.

37. These include GSD's Army Aviation Department and agencies dedicated to army functional arms such as armor, artillery, and engineering, and GAD's Army Armament Scientific Research and Order and Procurement Department.

38. "The Decision of the CCP Center on Major Issues Concerning Comprehensively Deepening Reforms" [中共中央关于全面深化改革若干重大问题的决定], *Xinhuanet* [新华网], November 15, 2013.

39. "Xu Qiliang: Unswervingly Advance National Defense and Military Reform" [许其亮: 坚定不移推进国防和军队改革], *People's Daily* [人民日报], November 21, 2013.

40. Xi served as a civilian vice-chairman of the CMC from 2010 to 2012, and thus likely had a significant role in shaping which military officers were appointed to the CMC to replace the eight members who retired in 2012.

41. "Xi Jinping: How I Went into Politics" [习近平: 我是如何跨入政界的], *Chinese Sons and Daughters* [中华儿女], no. 7 (2000).

PART II
THE PLA IN POLICY AND CRISIS

5   The PLA Role in China's Foreign Policy and Crisis Behavior

Michael D. Swaine

IN EXAMINING THE ORIGINS, CHARACTERISTICS, AND likely future course of a "more assertive" China, many analysts point to the supposedly growing role of the Chinese military (or People's Liberation Army—PLA) in Beijing's overall foreign policymaking and in the origins and evolution of political-military crises between China and other countries. For such observers, the PLA—as a conservative, highly nationalistic, and increasingly capable and confident actor in the Chinese political system—is the main, if not sole, force behind a range of more assertive and/or confrontational actions and crises undertaken by the Chinese government in recent years. These include deployment of large numbers of ballistic missiles opposite Taiwan, widespread cyber-attacks on the U.S. government, official criticism of U.S. military exercises in the Western Pacific, more vigorous challenges to U.S. military surveillance along China's maritime periphery, testing new weapons during visits to China by U.S. officials, and various confrontations with neighboring states over disputed maritime territories. Some observers view the PLA as an interest group that pressures the civilian Chinese leadership to adopt a more assertive stance toward Washington overall, thereby influencing the leadership succession process.[1]

While at least some senior PLA officers have probably played an important role in instigating or intensifying several of these actions, clear and conclusive evidence of the precise role of the military in China's foreign policy formulation and implementation remains elusive. Indeed, very little is known about China's military-related policy decisionmaking structure and process in general, both in normal times and especially during political-military crises. Most available information on civil-military relations, the foreign policy process, and crisis management decisionmaking relates to the organizational structures involved, not to those internal formal and informal processes that produce both policy and crisis decisions. More is known about interactions between major bureaucratic players at the ministerial level and below than about interactions among the most senior civilian and military leadership and their staffs.[2]

Moreover, it is extremely difficult to verify what little information is available. Some sources (such as many Hong Kong and Taiwan media) are notoriously unreliable; others (such as interviewees) are highly subjective, possibly biased, and often are relating information from secondhand sources.

This chapter summarizes and assesses what is reliably known, on an unclassified level, about the role of the PLA in China's foreign policy processes and in China's political-military crisis behavior. The first section provides a look at the organizational and procedural relationship of the PLA to the foreign policy process in particular. This includes an examination of both senior-level interactions and those occurring at subordinate, operational levels. The second section examines the PLA's role in crisis decisionmaking and implementation, focusing on five areas of relevance. The chapter concludes with a summary and some general observations.

The Chinese Military and the Foreign Policy Process

The Overall Policy Process: Civilian Party Control and a Professional Military

As Alice Miller's chapter discusses, the PLA has a highly limited position of power within the elite leadership structure. Nevertheless, some outside analysts believe that the PLA is a major source of hyper-nationalist views and a strong, increasingly influential proponent of a tougher, more confrontational policy stance toward the United States and any other power that might threaten China's major security and foreign policy interests.[3]

The PLA, like most other militaries, is a highly nationalist organization committed to a vigilant defense of national sovereignty and territorial integrity. Military figures have exerted sporadic influence over specific foreign-policy-related issues by expressing their views publicly. However, it is far from clear that such views translate into a cohesive, widespread, and explicitly enunciated PLA institutional "interest" or result in concerted, autonomous military pressure on senior civilian party leaders. Both civilian and military elites in China have a common commitment to regime survival and to increasingly institutionalized norms of policy formulation. Most elites support pragmatic, development-oriented policies designed to sustain or expand social order, regime unity, social prosperity, and national power and prestige.[4]

More importantly, the civilian CCP leadership makes the final decisions on fundamental national security-related policy issues—both civilian and military—by virtue of their predominant political power in the Chinese party-state system. The Politburo Standing Committee (PBSC) defines China's basic security interests and the PLA's basic defense mission and political line, albeit no doubt with significant input from senior military leaders. Moreover, the CCP leadership exercises ultimate control over the deployment of PLA forces in wartime and determines the PLA's budget and resource base.[5] Examples include party decisions to divest the PLA from its involvement in profit-making business activities; to pursue a noncoercive approach toward Taiwan and other territorial disputes; to reduce the overall size of the PLA; to make military modernization subordinate to overall economic development in China's reform strategy; and to restructure China's defense industry complex.[6]

As part of this decisionmaking system, the PLA undoubtedly advocates its professional interests within the definition of its missions, for example, ensuring national defense, preserving territorial integrity, attaining national reunification, achieving great power status, and maintaining domestic social order. But there is little if any evidence that it dictates *basic* strategy or policy outcomes, including those relating to national security. Today, most party-army interactions over key policy issues, whether foreign or domestic, almost certainly occur through institutional channels, and possibly on occasion via a small number of personal interactions. This is certainly true in the foreign policy realm.

Upper-Level Decisionmaking: Limited Yet Significant Influence
At senior levels, the civil-military interactions most relevant to PRC foreign policy occur primarily through the CCP's Central Military Commission (CMC) and several CCP leading small groups associated with foreign policy issues. Policy contacts between the senior military and the PBSC usually

occur via the CCP general secretary and his putative successor (when present), as civilian leaders of the CMC. China has no equivalent of the civilian U.S. secretary of defense—and the larger Office of the Secretary of Defense (OSD)—to determine basic defense policy and facilitate interactions with the top civilian political leadership. The CCP general secretary combines the roles of both commander in chief and secretary of defense, albeit without the same power that would accrue to such an individual in the U.S. system, given the collective nature of the Chinese party leadership. Moreover, most of the duties of the U.S. defense secretary are performed not by the CCP general secretary, but by the two most senior PLA officers, as vice-chairmen of the CMC. The nominal Chinese minister of defense interacts with foreign counterparts, but lacks the power of the CMC vice-chairmen and has a lower grade in the PLA structure.

The two CMC vice-chairmen usually enjoy close access to the CCP general secretary on many military-related policy issues, likely including those relating to foreign policy. Both also exert some influence on foreign policy via their membership in the Politburo, to the extent that body addresses such matters. However, the exact nature of these high-level civil-military interactions is unknown to outside observers.[7] To a considerable extent, such interactions probably depend on the personalities and relationships of the individuals involved.[8]

Despite its authority and senior membership, the CMC is not a final decisionmaking body for formulation of *fundamental* national strategy or policy (as opposed to the creation and implementation of lower-level civil-military or purely military policies). The CMC usually functions as a de facto leading small group (LSG), providing policy advice and recommendations on *military-related* foreign policy topics to the civilian leadership (primarily via the CMC chairman), coordinating basic policy views and actions among its constituent members and their subordinate organs, and serving as a consensus-building apparatus.

Military input into the foreign policy process also occurs via several relevant LSGs that oversee foreign policy and military-related issues. These include the Foreign Affairs LSG, the National Security LSG, and the Taiwan Affairs LSG. All three of these LSGs contain senior PLA officers. PLA representatives usually consist of at least one senior CMC member (possibly the minister of defense or a CMC vice-chairman) and the senior PLA officer responsible for military intelligence and foreign relations.

The LSGs do not make final decisions regarding most fundamental policy matters. They usually function as senior-level advisory, communication, coordinating, supervising, and consensus-building bodies *on major national policy issues.*[9] In many cases, policy recommendations offered to the PBSC by the LSGs and the CMC are accepted with little debate, partly because the other PBSC members possess very limited knowledge of the specific areas managed by each LSG. Nonetheless, the PBSC retains final authority on all major decisions.[10]

Thus, given the advisory and coordinating role of LSGs, PLA representatives on foreign policy-related LSGs likely represent military viewpoints concerning policy implementation and policy coordination, provide intelligence, and at times offer military-related policy recommendations. In light of this, "the FALSG is not intended to serve as *the* forum for military input into critical foreign policy decisions."[11] Such high-level input is likely provided first and foremost via the CMC, through the CCP general secretary, and to a likely lesser extent via the Politburo, through the two most senior PLA officers and CMC vice-chairmen.[12]

The General Office of the CCP Central Committee (CCP CC GO) is an administrative organ that might facilitate civil-military coordination on foreign affairs-related issues. The CCP CC GO has responsibility for maintaining constant contact and continuously coordinating information between the leading civilian party organs and various party bodies within the military, including the CMC, subordinate CMC departments, and party committees within the PLA regional commands. Thus, the CCP CC GO probably coordinates and facilitates routine bureaucratic information flows between party organizations within the foreign affairs and defense sectors, as well as higher-level contacts among senior members of both organizations, in their capacity as Politburo members. Whether this information flow is an integral part of the decisionmaking process is unclear.[13]

In November 2013, the Third Plenum of the CCP National Party Congress decided to establish a National Security Commission (*Guojia anquan weiyuanhui*) to improve coordination on domestic and international security issues. The Politburo approved its creation in January 2014, and the new body met for the first time on April 15, 2014, with Xi Jinping as chairman and Prime Minister Li Keqiang and National People's Congress chairman Zhang Dejiang as vice-chairmen.[14] The National Security Commission (NSC) will have a standing committee and report to the Politburo and the Politburo Standing

Committee. Its charter is to "coordinate major matters and important tasks involving national security." The relationship between the NSC, the CMC, the LSGs, and the CCP CC GO is unclear at this point, as is the nature and extent of PLA representation on the new body.[15] One source claims that a new PLA joint operation command center for East China Sea operations provides situation reports directly to the NSC and that Li Zhanshu, director of the CCP Central Committee's General Office, has responsibility for foreign affairs related to national security.[16]

Subordinate Foreign Affairs–Related PLA Activities: Considerable Independence

While the senior CCP leadership exercises ultimate power over basic foreign and defense policy, it apparently does not exert clear and decisive control over all military actions with implications for China's foreign relations. Two overlapping areas are especially notable: civil-military coordination on specific military-related activities that impinge on foreign policy and civilian oversight of military operations beyond China's territorial borders.

The former includes a wide array of Chinese military actions that, while purely military, could nonetheless exert a significant impact on Beijing's foreign relations. Examples include many actions mentioned in the Introduction, such as testing advanced weapons systems or other military actions that might concern or offend other nations.[17]

The latter includes deployments of Chinese warships into or near the territorial waters of other countries, interceptions by PLA ships and aircraft of foreign surveillance vessels operating near China, and military exercises outside China's borders.[18]

In the United States and many other Western countries, such potentially disruptive, foreign policy-related military actions are usually coordinated beforehand with (and in some cases approved by) senior civilian national security or diplomatic officials, as part of a well-established interagency vetting and oversight process usually administered—in the U.S. case—by the National Security Council (NSC). In contrast, knowledgeable officials, scholars, and PLA officers state that no clear regulations or orders currently exist to ensure such advance coordination between civilian and military authorities.[19] Chinese advocates of establishing a National Security Commission hope that it will increase information sharing and improve coordination.

In the past, the lack of formal regulations did not pose a major problem. Paramount party leaders such as Mao Zedong and Deng Xiaoping possessed a clear knowledge of how the PLA operates, knew the top PLA leadership personally, and held the authority to demand—and receive—consultation by military authorities on important foreign policy-related military activities.[20]

Today, even though senior party leaders likely formally approve all major military-related policies and programs, such individuals do not possess the political clout, knowledge of military issues, or personal influence and charisma to ensure control over the details of military activities in many areas with foreign policy implications. Moreover, the CMC and LSGs do not routinely address lower-level military issues. While the CCP general secretary, as CMC chairman, is probably kept informed of major PLA weapons, training, and exercise programs and perhaps even the outlines of some important operational issues, he is almost certainly not told beforehand of specific military actions, such as individual weapons tests and exercises, small-scale military "patrols" or training exercises outside of China's borders, or the "rules of engagement" guiding interceptions of foreign surveillance vessels. CMC meetings reportedly do not address such operational military issues.[21]

Moreover, the extent to which the party general secretary and other PBSC members have demanded information on specific PLA operations, exercises, and training practices outside of China's borders is not known. It is possible, and even likely, that in the apparent absence of an explicit requirement, such information is rarely requested and rarely provided to senior party leaders, including those responsible for foreign affairs. As a result, the PLA probably enjoys considerable latitude in all these areas.

In addition, the military system itself is apparently not structured to ensure that such matters are brought to the attention of the PLA's foreign affairs system. Many of the activities undertaken by the military that pose potential problems for the United States—including both the testing of major weapons and deployments of PLA assets beyond China's borders—come under either the Operations Department (作战部) or the Military Training and Service Arms Department (军训与兵种部) of the PLA General Staff Department (GSD). According to a very knowledgeable Chinese officer, these departments are senior in the PLA hierarchy to those GSD units in charge of foreign affairs (外事办公室) and intelligence (情报部). As a result, they routinely do not consult with such units when deploying assets or conducting military tests or exercises. The GSD's foreign affairs office is primarily responsible for military exchanges with foreign countries, not assessments of the diplomatic impact of military actions. In other words, no organization within the PLA has the authority and responsibility to routinely demand and receive notice of PLA activities that might impact China's foreign relations.[22]

One possible avenue of coordination between the PLA and the CCP leadership on such matters resides in the staff secretary or assistant to the CMC chairman, mentioned above. This individual is reportedly responsible for keeping the CMC chairman informed of PLA policies and actions, among other duties.[23] However, the specific nature of his responsibilities in this area remains unclear to outsiders, and it is not known whether he, or anyone else within the military system, is charged with informing the CMC chairman of PLA activities that might affect China's diplomatic relationships. Even less is known about the extent of interaction, if any, between the CMC secretary and senior staffers within the foreign affairs system.

Given PLA's resistance to sharing information about military capabilities and operations, it is quite possible that little if any regular contact occurs between any parts of the Chinese military and China's foreign affairs system regarding military activities relevant to foreign policy.

The Chinese Military in Political-Military Crises: An Excessively Autonomous Actor?

Very little detailed, reliable information exists regarding Chinese crisis decisionmaking in general and the military's role in particular, especially concerning the informal and high-level dimensions of the decisionmaking process. Much of the information presented in this section is derived from interviews with both civilian and military Chinese scholars and analysts conducted by the author and other analysts—especially Bonnie Glaser and Alastair Iain Johnston—and from the literature on past political-military crises. The latter includes some findings of an ongoing collaborative project on crisis management.

Many of the observations are tentative and subject to future clarification and correction. Nonetheless, enough is known about certain aspects of the role of the PLA in foreign political-military crises to draw an overall picture of the decision process, and to identify significant gaps or gray areas in our knowledge.

This section covers five areas relevant to the military's role in crisis decisionmaking: upper-level participants and processes, lower-level actors, intelligence and information flows and preexisting plans, research institutes, and unplanned or uncontrolled behavior.

Within each area, general features of the crisis decisionmaking structure and process often provide the larger context and background for assessment of the military's role and presence.

Upper-Level Participants and Processes: A Largely Informal,
Oligarchic Process Led by the CCP General Secretary
The critical senior players in China's formal crisis decisionmaking process overlap considerably with those in the foreign policy process. They include:

- The CCP general secretary, who almost always simultaneously holds the positions of PRC president and chairman of the Central Military Commission.
- At least some of the remaining members of the Politburo Standing Committee (PBSC)—and quite possibly informal subgroups among them.
- Senior leaders responsible for aspects of foreign relations within relevant party, state, and military institutions—including the State Council, CCP Politburo, CCP Central Committee, CCP International Liaison Department, General Staff Department and CMC members, minister of foreign affairs, minister of state security, and leading officials responsible for propaganda affairs (primarily to handle public opinion).
- Individual, trusted senior advisers of the CCP general secretary, including but not limited to top-level officials close to him.

Among these individuals, PBSC members perform the primary decisionmaking role in any major political-military crisis. And within that body, the CCP general secretary, as in normal times, acts as "first among equals"—organizing meetings, selecting participants of ad hoc bodies, directing decisions, and appointing overseers responsible for implementing major decisions made at the top. However, all key decisions—including those that could involve confrontations or conflicts with foreign powers—are usually made by the PBSC as a group.

Subordinate or secondary players in a crisis include civilian and military individuals charged with implementing decisions and less formal players who can influence senior leadership views as the crisis unfolds. The former include subordinate civilian agencies and military units (both central and local) as well as leadership staffs and secretaries. The latter include the media, the public, and perhaps scholars, both civilian and military. The role of retired party and military elders in advising (formally or informally) active leaders remains obscure and the subject of considerable speculation.

The crisis decisionmaking structure and process, especially at senior levels where key decisions are made, are apparently largely informal and ad hoc, rather than institutionalized and regularized. The entire process involves subjective judgments by top leaders and relies on personal relationships, especially between the CCP general secretary, his PBSC colleagues, and his personal advisers. That said, certain features and patterns are apparent based on the study of the post–Deng Xiaoping era.

According to interviews, the CCP general secretary usually convenes an ad hoc enlarged PBSC meeting at the onset of a political-military crisis. This normally includes all members of the PBSC, plus additional relevant senior leaders (both military and civilian) and trusted senior advisers. When the crisis involves significant military issues, participants probably include one or both of the two uniformed vice-chairmen of the CMC and possibly their senior staff.[24] Additional participants (beyond the PBSC) are usually designated by the general secretary.[25]

The purpose of this initial senior-level meeting is to understand and determine the features and significance of the crisis, and to agree upon a set of principles and guidelines for handling it. For example, in this meeting, the leadership will often identify what political and/or policy interests are at stake, what dangers the crisis presents, and what outcomes are desired. It will also set out some key parameters for subsequent crisis management, for example, to exchange tit for tat with the other side, to only employ military force in response to a use of force, and so forth.[26]

Convening such an enlarged PBSC meeting at the initial stage of a crisis follows from two features or requirements of the system: 1) the overall collective nature of the party leadership, which demands that the general secretary and his colleagues all provide their input and become vested in any major decisions made; and 2) the general need of the top leaders to obtain relevant information (including military intelligence) and advice regarding the unfolding crisis. As a result, even though a major crisis with a foreign power might require quick and decisive action, the oligarchic nature of China's current leadership system can result in delayed responses as top leaders convene, obtain information, deliberate, and hammer out a basic consensus position. Indeed, such delays have been evident in recent Sino-U.S. political military crises.[27]

In this process, senior military leaders within the CMC and GSD likely play an important role in providing military information, supplying intelligence, and offering assessments on national security and military issues. The role of senior military leaders in making basic decisions during a crisis was arguably more critical in the 1990s and earlier, when senior PLA leaders were members of the PBSC or more experienced elder cadres. Yet their role could still prove critical today if a crisis includes a major military dimension.[28]

In addition to convening an enlarged PBSC meeting, the CCP general secretary will also usually establish or delegate a working-level group or groups to manage and oversee the crisis for the senior leadership, and to provide advice as needed.

In an unanticipated crisis (such as the 2001 EP-3 incident or the 1999 bombing of the Belgrade embassy), the general secretary might order the creation of an ad hoc interagency crisis working group whose membership would be determined on the basis of the nature of the crisis. In the case of an anticipated or ongoing crisis (such as the slow-motion North Korean nuclear crisis), it is more likely that a relevant CCP leading small group, such as the Foreign Affairs LSG (FALSG), the National Security LSG (NSLSG), or the Taiwan Affairs LSG (TALSG), would be delegated to manage the crisis on a continuous basis in support of the senior leaders.

In some instances, however, an ad hoc working group and one or more LSGs might both play a role in crisis management, depending on the preferences of the general secretary and the PBSC. In particular, an LSG might be involved in crisis decisionmaking if the general secretary or other members of the PBSC had become dissatisfied with the advice and support provided by the ad hoc working group.[29]

Whether an ad hoc or an existing LSG (or both), this working group would usually operate under the leadership of a single PBSC member. In the case of the ad hoc group, the specific member selected to perform this leadership function, and the composition of the working group, would be determined by the general secretary (for example, Jiang Zemin apparently designated Hu Jintao to head what was probably an ad hoc working group to manage the EP-3 incident) and report directly to the PBSC. The group's functions would primarily consist of advising and carrying out the directives of the PBSC and coordinating the actions of relevant organizations. Membership would include the heads of all relevant organizations involved in the crisis, as well as additional participants from the enlarged PBSC meeting. This would almost certainly include one or more PLA representatives, and especially the senior PLA officer responsible for military intelligence.

The general secretary might also convene other informal discussion groups or individual meetings in the early stages of a crisis to gather different opinions and to provide advice. These ad hoc bodies or fora would meet separately from any crisis working group, PBSC, CMC, or LSG meetings, and could also include PLA representatives. However, the existence and composition of such informal entities would depend on the personal leadership style of the CCP general secretary. Jiang Zemin was known to seek advice from outside normal bureaucratic channels during normal policy deliberations and in crisis situations. In contrast, Hu Jintao generally depended on the existing bureaucracy for advice.[30]

Lower-Level Actors: Crisis Working Groups
under the Foreign Affairs System

Once a crisis working group (or groups) is established at the top, crisis teams are set up in relevant party offices, government ministries, and the PLA to carry out the orders of senior civilian and military leaders. Such teams are likely formed in both anticipated and unanticipated crises. During the EP-3 crisis and the embassy bombing incident, both the PLA General Staff and the Ministry of Foreign Affairs (MFA) set up crisis teams to handle information and monitor the situation. Similar crisis teams also exist to handle the ongoing North Korea nuclear crisis.

Chinese sources indicate that the Ministry of Foreign Affairs calls an emergency meeting and sets up an ad hoc team to deal with every major potential foreign crisis, even if no leadership-level crisis working group has been established. If a crisis extends over many days or weeks, the Foreign Affairs Office (FAO) of the CCP Central Committee might convene meetings that include mid-level or high-level officials from the PLA and relevant government ministries, as well as directors of Chinese think tanks and outside experts. It likely distills and forwards information from various bureaucracies to the leadership, sometimes with policy recommendations attached.[31] The FAO usually includes both MFA and PLA representatives. The extent to which the new National Security Commission may take on some of these FAO roles is still unclear.

Intelligence and Information Flows and Preexisting
Plans: Critical Avenues of Military Influence

During a crisis, leadership decisions and resulting actions often depend on the timeliness and quality of information and intelligence received. There are three main branches through which information and intelligence flows through the Chinese system in a crisis: the party, the military, and the government. Within each branch, intelligence and other reports by crisis management teams within ministries, offices, and the PLA/GSD are funneled upward to one of three general offices within the Central Committee, the CMC, and the State Council. Each general office reviews reports to determine if they need to be forwarded to the Politburo and the ad hoc crisis working group or LSG managing the crisis. The general office directors play an influential role in this process because they are the ultimate arbiters of whether a document is sufficiently critical and time sensitive to pass on to the senior leadership. However, despite the oversight exercised at various levels in the chain of command, some Chinese crisis management experts have indicated that these reports often discuss issues rather than present options, thus engendering further debate within the LSGs and PBSC and delaying timely decisionmaking.[32]

In addition to these formal channels, a small number of urgent intelligence and other reports by senior officials may be sent directly to the senior leadership, but it is unclear under what circumstances this occurs. For example, some reports signed by the foreign minister are reportedly submitted directly to the Politburo or to a select number of PBSC members and need not pass through the State Council General Office. This direct channel may be used more frequently during a crisis than during routine times.

Perhaps most notably, all three of the above branches operate independently in providing intelligence. Thus, no single set of integrated intelligence is provided to senior Chinese leaders in a crisis. The lack of a mechanism for adjudicating among the various sources of incoming information often results in the PBSC delaying decisions while attempting to decipher the actual conditions on the ground.[33] Whether the new NSC will play a role in coordinating, prioritizing, or filtering the flow of intelligence to senior leaders is unclear at this point.

Interagency bureaucratic competition aggravates coordination problems, with different actors seeking to promote their particular interpretation or interests in a crisis. Communication between the MFA and the military is especially problematic. It is likely that very little sharing of intelligence occurs between them, thus further inhibiting effective crisis management.[34]

154 The PLA in Policy and Crisis

Some Chinese and outside sources state that senior party leaders some-times rely heavily on intelligence provided by the PLA (via the CMC or GSD—see below), at least in the early stages of a military-related crisis, largely because no other branches are able to provide timely information, and per-haps also because the MFA does not enjoy the reputation or official rank of the CMC. However, as in other governments, initial intelligence is often incor-rect and must be adjusted or corrected using information provided by other agencies.

In a crisis, military intelligence is passed up the chain of command to the GSD, which then provides the information to the CMC General Office and at times directly to the Politburo or PBSC. Within the PLA, there is usually a strict hierarchy from the bottom to the top. Normally information has to go through every level before it gets to the top. When critical intelligence reaches the top, the CMC usually holds a meeting to discuss what it has received and submits a report to the ad hoc crisis group under the PBSC.

However, in very urgent situations, the CMC may be bypassed. For example, in the case of the 1999 Belgrade embassy bombing, Chinese sources indicate there was insufficient time to hold a CMC meeting to receive information, assess the situation, and provide military views to the PBSC; the CMC was informed of the incident after a PBSC meeting was held. The GSD does not usually bypass the CMC entirely, but it does routinely report information simultaneously to the PBSC and the CMC. In other words, the GSD apparently has an established channel to the PBSC that it might use in a crisis. The most senior military lead-ers would probably be informed of such direct reporting, especially given the fact that all such leaders are members of the CMC.

The absence of integrated intelligence, the presence of direct lines of com-munication to the PBSC, and the existence of personal advisers to the party general secretary mean that lower-level units and individuals can exert a dis-proportionate influence over crisis assessments and decisions made at the top. For instance, during the crises triggered by the Belgrade embassy bombing and the EP-3 incident, Jiang Zemin reportedly relied considerably on the senior PLA officer in charge of military intelligence and foreign issues (Xiong Guangkai), a trusted advisor.[35]

As in other countries, the military can also influence decisionmak-ing, especially during the early stages of a crisis, via preexisting operational plans drawn up to cover possible military contingencies. For example, dur-ing the 1995–1996 Taiwan Strait crisis, a preapproved PLA operational plan involving exercises and missile firings near Taiwan was put forth (and ultimately accepted) as a ready means of expressing Beijing's resolve. This plan was reportedly never reexamined as the crisis evolved.[36] If true, at least two implications can be drawn: first, the existence of such preexisting plans might provide the PLA with considerable leverage over the evolution of a crisis. Second, they could also create difficulties for the senior civilian leadership by limiting their options and locking them into a particular response, especially if few other immediate options for conveying resolve are readily available.[37]

Research Institutes: Occasional Sources
of Expert Analysis and Advice

Reports by research institutes or think tanks are not submitted directly to the senior leadership unless: 1) a top leader directly tasks a research institute to produce a report; 2) an individual researcher has a personal connection to a leader's staff; or 3) a specific report is judged to be urgent by a person in a position of authority. In a crisis, military think tanks such as the Academy of Military Sciences (AMS) are likely tasked to provide assessments and recommendations regarding relevant military issues. Such organizations also analyze potential future crises and assess the impact of a crisis after it concludes to synthesize lessons learned. Other nonmilitary research entities can play a similar role. For example, in a prolonged crisis, the FAO might task both civilian and military research institutes to analyze specific questions. However, Chinese governmental actors—especially those within the PLA—tend to be biased against relying on outside experts for policy advice or assessments. According to some Chinese crisis management experts, this results in an insufficient level of input from think-tank scholars during crises.

Unplanned or Uncontrolled Behavior:
A Major Source of Instability

Intense political-military crises can involve unplanned or uncontrolled behavior by government and military actors that influences developments before, during, and after the event. In a defense-related area, PLA actions can play an important role in precipitating and shaping the course of a crisis in ways unintended by the senior civilian leadership. This is largely because local PLA entities are not necessarily under the close direction of the senior civilian (or perhaps even military) leadership and can at times take actions that run counter to the overall intent and strategy behind PRC foreign policy.

Possible examples of such unplanned or uncoordinated behavior include: PLAN submarine incursions into Japanese territorial waters during November 2004; PLAN or PLAN-related "aggressive" ship or aircraft maneuvers in or over contested waters or within the PRC exclusive economic zone (EEZ) at various intervals during the past fifteen years; military clashes in the South China Sea in 1974 and 1988; the surfacing of a PLAN submarine within the defense perimeter of a U.S. carrier in 2007; and the refusal to give safe harbor to two U.S. mine-sweepers during a storm in 2007, along with the last-minute denial of a request for a visit by the *Kitty Hawk* to the port of Hong Kong a few days later.[38]

The military could also influence the course of a crisis indirectly through comments, statements, or articles in China's increasingly raucous public media and cyber sphere. These avenues of expression are open to a growing number and variety of Chinese citizens, including retired or semi-retired military scholars and officers. In a crisis with military dimensions, such military commentators could shape public views significantly.[39] That said, in a serious crisis, the senior party leadership would almost certainly seek to control, guide, or (more likely) censor military views, especially those not in accord with their approach or policies. Military officers or scholars who ignored such efforts would be doing so at their peril.[40]

Finally, the potential adverse impact of unplanned or uncontrolled behavior by the PLA on crisis management is likely reinforced due to problems of military signaling during a crisis. According to a leading Chinese crisis management specialist, the Chinese military's ability to engage in external signaling is underdeveloped and largely limited to military signaling on the Taiwan issue. As a result, attempts to convey benign intentions during a crisis may be undermined by actions or misleading messages conveyed by local or even central PLA actors.[41] This potential problem is compounded by the apparent fact that China tends not to coordinate diplomatic and military moves when signaling in the early stages of a crisis. If the crisis is predominantly diplomatic, Chinese officials tend not to employ the PLA to reinforce diplomatic messages. That China tends to wait until a crisis intensifies before sending military signals contrasts with U.S. behavior, and is a potential source of misunderstanding.[42]

Summary and Conclusions

Many aspects of the interaction between the military and China's foreign policy decisionmaking process remain unknown or only dimly understood by outsiders. We know almost nothing about the scope, frequency, and policy impact of personal interactions that might occur between the most senior civilian party and military leaders regarding foreign policy issues. We also know very little about the possible role, if any, of individuals such as the secretary to the CMC chairman and the director of the CCP CC GO in coordinating between specific military actions and elements of PRC foreign policy and diplomatic relations. We do not know to what degree the CCP general secretary or other senior civilian party leaders are kept informed of the progress of military programs with significant implications for China's foreign relations.

Many features of the PLA's role in political-military crises are also either poorly understood or unknown to outside observers. This is partly due to the generally secretive nature of decisionmaking in China, especially at senior levels, and partly because much of the crisis decisionmaking process apparently involves ad hoc or informal organizations and interactions. For example, little is known about the scope and type of interactions among the party general secretary, other members of the PBSC, and both the ad hoc crisis working group and LSG(s) that support the leadership in a crisis.

Even less is known about crisis management interactions that undoubtedly occur between senior civilian party leaders and the most senior military officers, via the above-mentioned enlarged PBSC meeting and the subordinate working groups, or through personal contacts. Senior military officers are almost certainly present in both types of organizations to provide critical advice, information, and intelligence during crises, in some cases (e.g., Xiong Guangkai) as personal associates of PBSC members. Moreover, up until at least the 1990s, senior PLA officers apparently played very key roles in shaping basic decisions taken by the general secretary or the entire PBSC during political-military crises. This was largely because of their "elder" status or party position as PBSC members, or as a result of the highly militarized nature of particular crises.

Despite significant areas of uncertainty regarding the military's role in both foreign policy and political-military crisis decisionmaking, certain general observations can be made with a fairly high level of certainty, based on interviews and written sources.

First, China's overall leadership system is centered on a party-based oligarchic, consensus-driven structure that reflects a balance of "constituencies" among the party, government, geographical regions, public security organs, and the military. Within this system, senior leadership bodies such as the

Politburo are organized to serve as arenas for balanced and rational decision-making among various institutional and geographic interests. Although leadership competition continues, it is not based, as during the Mao and Deng eras, on largely informal, personal, and vertically organized factions, but instead on an increasingly established lattice of institutions and processes that operate on the basis of largely consensus-oriented, codified norms.

Second, today's PLA wields far less political power at the top of this system than it did during the Mao Zedong and Deng Xiaoping eras. Ultimate decisionmaking authority regarding fundamental foreign and defense policies resides in the CCP Politburo Standing Committee, which contains no military representative. The two most senior PLA officers may exert some influence on major foreign policy decisions in their capacity as Politburo members, but such influence is diluted by the fact that the Politburo is a large body (usually over twenty members) and wields far less power over basic policy decisions than the PBSC. The extent to which the top two PLA leaders exert informal influence over foreign policy issues via their personal relationships with senior civilian party leaders such as the CCP general secretary likely depends on the specific personalities and relationships of the individuals involved. That said, both CMC military vice-chairmen undoubtedly play critical roles in managing a crisis involving military issues or requiring military intelligence (such as the EP-3 incident), at the very least by advising and shaping the views of the general secretary and the entire PBSC.

Third, individual senior PLA officers likely express their views on specific defense-related aspects of elements of foreign policy primarily via the CMC-centered system. However, senior PLA officers have at times exerted influence over the stance taken by the Foreign Ministry on specific foreign-policy-related issues, largely by expressing their views publicly. Many PLA officers often have little regard for what they view as the excessively accommodating stance toward other countries (and especially the United States) taken by the Ministry of Foreign Affairs. However, such views do not necessarily constitute a cohesive, clearly defined, and widely supported military "interest" distinct from and opposed to those of civilian organizations; nor do such views necessarily translate into a pattern of autonomous and continuous pressure on the senior civilian party leadership, whether on foreign policy issues or during political-military crises. Unlike the military in many other developing countries, the PLA does not behave as an entirely separate institutional force in Chinese power politics and within senior policy channels. Its mandate is almost exclusively defined by its professional responsibilities.

Fourth, those entities that provide regularized institutional channels between the senior military leadership and senior civilian officials with authority over foreign policy (i.e., the CMC and relevant LSGs) perform primarily advisory, coordinating, and consensus-building functions on major foreign or domestic national policy issues. In carrying out these functions, the PLA serves as one organization among many, under the leadership of civilian party figures. Nevertheless, such organizations can at times exert significant influence over both major and (especially) lesser types of foreign policy and crisis decisions made by the PBSC. Of these organizations, the CMC offers the strongest avenue for high-level military influence on foreign policy and political-military crises, albeit largely via the civilian CCP general secretary.

Fifth, despite its ultimate authority over all major aspects of foreign policy, China's civilian party leadership most likely does not exert clear and decisive control over two types of military activities with significant implications for PRC foreign relations and political-military crises: specific military tests and other actions (regardless of location) and military operations undertaken outside of China's territorial borders. Before the creation of the NSC, the PRC party-state system lacked the structures and processes to coordinate such activities with China's foreign affairs and diplomatic structures, either before or during a specific crisis. The lack of adequate cross-agency civil-military communication and coordination and limited senior civilian oversight of PLA activities beyond China's borders can both trigger political-military crises and undermine senior-level crisis management efforts. The NSC's ability to address these issues is unclear.

These conclusions indicate that it is incorrect to suggest that the Chinese military today wields decisive, or even significant, influence over fundamental aspects of PRC foreign policy on an ongoing basis or during political-military crises. The few official avenues of high-level influence on foreign policy and crises the PLA does enjoy—via the CMC, the Politburo, and the LSGs—are highly limited, and largely dependent on a single figure, the CCP general secretary. Although the two military vice-chairmen of the CMC undoubtedly exert informal influence at senior levels, little is known of such interactions. Any such influence is almost certainly either based on limited personal ties with senior party figures or mediated and diluted by the formal processes of the CMC and the Politburo.

In contrast, the military can exert significant influence over specific foreign and diplomatic actions at lower levels via its access to public media and due to the lack of coordinating mechanisms between specific military actions and foreign policy. At lower levels of the crisis decisionmaking system, PLA officers and analysts reportedly play important, sometimes critical, roles as providers of intelligence and analysis, overseers of military aspects of crisis behavior, and creators of contingency plans used in a political-military crisis, and via membership in ad hoc and leadership working groups, the CCP CC FAO, advisory and management teams formed within the GSD or other PLA agencies, military intelligence and planning units, and military research organs.

At the same time, little is known about the level and type of influence exerted on crisis decisionmaking in general by such lower-level individuals and their organizations, given both the highly secretive nature of intra-PLA processes and the fragmented and stovepiped structure of the overall crisis decisionmaking system. Information sharing and coordination during a crisis between military players and their civilian counterparts within the MFA or party system is usually either poor or nonexistent.

The absence of an NSC-type system in China to coordinate between civilian and military entities presented a significant problem for PRC foreign policy and for the management of future crises, especially given the expanded scope of PLA activities and the increasing PLA presence beyond China's territorial borders. The need to establish clear and authoritative procedures for coordinating foreign and defense policy and managing crises at both senior and lower levels of the policy process was likely a significant motivation for establishing the new NSC.[43] In the past, high-level policy coordination on all but the most major issues was weak and excessively dependent on the CCP general secretary and his relationship with the two uniformed CMC vice-chairmen. At lower levels, coordination between military actions and foreign policy or diplomacy was virtually nonexistent, increasing the likelihood of political-military crises.

The extent to which the NSC improves information sharing and policy coordination will be a critical factor in its ability to rectify the weaknesses described above. The PBSC's role as the supreme decisionmaking body also raises questions about whether the NSC will have decisionmaking authority during a crisis. The NSC may end up playing a role similar to the CMC and the LSGs: gathering information and making recommendations to the PBSC and then coordinating implementation of collective decisions made by the seven members of the PBSC. Better information sharing and coordinated policy recommendations may help upgrade the quality of PBSC decisions on foreign policy and national security issues and improve policy implementation. However, the need to achieve consensus among the seven PBSC members is still likely to delay Chinese responses significantly during a major crisis.

Notes

This chapter is adapted from "China's Assertive Behavior–Part Three: The Role of the Military in Foreign Policy," *China Leadership Monitor*, no. 36 (Winter 2012), and "China's Assertive Behavior–Part Four: The Role of the Military in Foreign Crises," *China Leadership Monitor*, no. 37 (Spring 2012). I am indebted to Audrye Wong for her research assistance and to Phillip Saunders for his invaluable help in revising the chapter.

1. See Cheng Li, "China's Midterm Jockeying: Gearing Up for 2012 (Part 3: Military Leaders)," *China Leadership Monitor*, no. 33 (Summer 2010). Li states, "The Chinese military . . . remains a very important interest group in the country. The PLA's need to advance its own bureaucratic interests makes the Chinese military, collectively and on an individual basis, an influential powerbroker that may carry enormous weight in Chinese politics generally and especially in CCP leadership transitions."

2. David Shambaugh, *Modernizing China's Military: Progress, Problems, and Prospects* (Berkeley: University of California Press, 2002), 46–47; Alice Miller, "The CCP Central Committee's Leading Small Groups," *China Leadership Monitor*, no. 26 (Fall 2008): 6; Qi Zhou, "Organization, Structure and Image in the Making of Chinese Foreign Policy since the Early 1990s," Ph.D. dissertation submitted to Johns Hopkins University, Baltimore, Maryland, March 2008, introduction, 109.

3. Li, "China's Midterm Jockeying"; and Susan L. Shirk, *China: Fragile Superpower* (New York: Oxford University Press, 2007), 9, 66–77. Shirk states: "The military's perspective on Japan, Taiwan, and the United States generally is more hawkish than that of civilian officials, according to interviews, and military voices constrain China's policies on these controversial issues," 75.

4. See Shambaugh, *Modernizing China's Military*; and David Shambaugh, *China's Communist Party: Atrophy and Adaptation* (Washington, DC: Woodrow Wilson Center Press, 2009)

5. Shambaugh, *China's Communist Party*; and Dennis Blasko, *The Chinese Army Today: Tradition and Transformation for the 21st Century* (New York: Routledge, 2006).

6. Zhou, "Organization, Structure and Image," 115–116 (on subordination of military modernization to economic development and the reduction of the size of the PLA), 117–118 (on ending profit-making activities); Blasko, *The Chinese Army Today*, 6–8; Shambaugh, *Modernizing China's Military*, 31, 230–241; James C. Mulvenon, *Soldiers*

of Fortune: The Rise and Fall of the Chinese Military-Business Complex, 1978–1998 (Armonk, NY: M.E. Sharpe, 2001); David M. Lampton, *Same Bed, Different Dreams: Managing U.S.-China Relations, 1989–2000* (Berkeley: University of California Press, 2001), 72–73; and the Alice Miller and Tai Ming Cheung chapters in this volume.

7. For details on their roles and responsibilities, see Michael D. Swaine, *The Role of the Chinese Military in National Security Policymaking* (Santa Monica, CA: RAND, 1998), 41; and Shambaugh, *Modernizing China's Military*, 117.

8. A CMC secretary or assistant for military affairs may also play a significant role in shaping policy interactions between the CCP general secretary—whom he apparently serves—and the senior PLA leadership.

9. In addition to Swaine, *The Role of the Chinese Military*, and Zhou, "Organization, Structure and Image," 131–171, see A. Doak Barnett, *The Making of Foreign Policy in China* (SAIS Papers in International Affairs, no. 9, 1985); Carol Lee Hamrin, "The Party Leadership System," in *Bureaucracy, Politics, and Decision Making in Post-Mao China*, eds. Kenneth G. Lieberthal and David M. Lampton (Berkeley: University of California Press, 1992), 103; and Wei Li, *The Chinese Staff System: A Mechanism for Bureaucratic Control and Integration* (Berkeley: Institute of East Asian Studies, University of California, 1994), 33–34.

10. Swaine, *The Role of the Chinese Military*, 22.

11. Ibid.

12. As Qi Zhou states ("Organization, Structure and Image," 122): "The Chinese military must speak in one voice even though it comprises many departments. When a policy is under deliberation, representatives are encouraged to voice opinions at the meetings of the various agencies. . . . But when the military reports on intelligence analysis or provides policy recommendations, there is only one channel through which the military can reach the Standing Committee of the Politburo, that is, the CMC. The CMC unifies the voice of the military before it reports to the Politburo. On any decision related to the armed forces, the final decision is dominated by the Politburo. The military is merely one of several different bureaucracies whose voice can be heard by the top leaders through reports, though on strategic issues, the voice of the military is considered extremely important."

13. As with other important party, state, and military organs, the amount of influence exerted on policy issues by the CCP CC GO depends considerably on the personal stature and influence of its top leader. Historically, the CCP CC GO has been led by very influential party figures such as Wen Jiabao and Zeng Qinghong. See Swaine, *The Role of the Chinese Military*, 33.

14. "The CPC Central Committee Political Bureau Opens a Meeting to Study and Decide the Organizational Structure of the Central National Security Committee and Review the Implementation of the Central Authorities' Eight Regulations" [中共中央政治局召开会议研究决定中央国家安全委员会设置审议贯彻执行中央项规定情况报告], Xinhua [新华], January 24, 2014; "Xi Jinping Chairs First Meeting of CPC Central Committee's National Security Commission" [习近平主持召开中央国家安全委员会第次会议], Xinhua [新华], April 15, 2014.

15. MND spokesman Yang Yujun declined to answer a question on PLA representation on the NSC, stating only that the PLA "will coordinate closely with relevant departments based on unified arrangements and do a good job together in maintaining the nation's security." MND News Conference, April 24, 2014.

16. "China Establishes East China Sea Joint Operation Command Center," *Kanwa Defense Review*, no. 119 (September 1, 2014): 2–3.

17. See James Mulvenon, "Rogue Warriors? A Puzzled Look at the ASAT Test," *China Leadership Monitor*, no. 20 (Winter 2007); and Andrew Scobell, "The J-20 Episode and Civil-Military Relations in China," testimony before the U.S.-China Economic and Security Review Commission, March 10, 2011.

18. For specific examples, see Mark Valencia, "The Impeccable Incident: Truth and Consequences," *China Security* 5, no. 2 (Spring 2009); Stacy A. Pedrozo, "China's Active Defense Strategy and Its Regional Impact," statement before the U.S.-China Economic and Security Review Commission, January 27, 2010; and Christopher D. Yung et al., *China's Out of Area Naval Operations: Case Studies, Trajectories, Obstacles, and Potential Solutions*, INSS China Strategic Perspectives 3 (December 2010).

19. See Wu Xinbo, "Managing Crisis and Sustaining Peace between China and the United States," United States Institute of Peace (2008), 25, www.usip.org/files/resources/PW61_FinalApr16.pdf; and Wu Xinbo, "Understanding Chinese and U.S. Crisis Behavior," *Washington Quarterly* 31, no. 1 (Winter 2007–2008): 72.

20. Ellis Joffe, *The Chinese Army after Mao* (Cambridge, MA: Harvard University Press, 1987); Michael Swaine, *The Military & Political Succession in China: Leadership, Institutions, Beliefs* (Santa Monica, CA: RAND, 1992), 16–21, 28–33; and Swaine, *The Role of the Chinese Military*, 35–36; 77–78.

21. Discussions with Chinese scholars and military analysts.

22. Discussion with a senior PLA officer.

23. Swaine, *The Role of the Chinese Military*, 43; and Shambaugh, *Modernizing China's Military*, 121. Shambaugh states: The CMC General Office "contains a number of administrative secretaries (*mishu*), although each [CMC member] has his own personal *mishu* as well."

24. Both of these senior PLA officers are usually also members of the Politburo or the CCP Secretariat.

25. For more on the CMC and the role of the vice-chairmen, see Gong Li, Men Honghua, and Sun Dongfang [宫力, 门洪华, 孙东方], "China's Diplomatic Decision-making Mechanism: Changes and Evolution since 1949" [中国外交决策机制变迁研究 (1949～2009年)], *World Economics and Politics* [世界经济与政治] (November 2009): 44–54; Zhou, "Organization, Structure and Image," 109–122 (on military involvement in foreign policy, CMC) and 131–188 (on leading small groups in Chinese foreign policy); Nan Li, *Chinese Civil-Military Relations: The Transformation of the People's Liberation Army* (New York: Routledge, 2006), 2; Lu Ning, *The Dynamics of Foreign-Policy Decisionmaking in China*, 2nd ed. (Boulder, CO: Westview, 2000), 11; David Bachman, "Structure and Process in the Making of Chinese Foreign Policy," in *China and the World: Chinese Foreign Policy Faces the New Millennium*, 4th ed., ed. Samuel

Kim (Boulder, CO: Westview, 1998); Swaine, *The Role of the Chinese Military*; Hamrin, "The Party Leadership System," 114; and Kenneth Lieberthal, *Governing China: From Revolution through Reform* (New York: W. W. Norton, 1995), 213.

26. According to Chinese observers, these assessments usually adhere to Mao Zedong's guideline for handling confrontations with foreign powers: "on just grounds, to our advantage, and with restraint" (有理, 有利, 有节). China's leaders seek to determine the basic principles involved in a crisis, and then determine some key guidelines for managing it, including thresholds for certain actions. See Michael Swaine, "Understanding the Historical Record," in *Managing Sino-American Crises: Case Studies and Analysis*, eds. Michael Swaine and Zhang Tuosheng, with Danielle F. S. Cohen (Washington, DC: Carnegie Endowment for International Peace, 2006), 23–24.

27. For example, following the April 2001 EP-3 incident, the Chinese government did not respond for many hours to repeated attempts by the U.S. embassy to establish contact. See John Keefe, *Anatomy of the EP-3 Incident, April 2001* (Alexandria, VA: CNA Corporation, 2001); and Zhang Tuosheng, "The Sino-American Aircraft Collision: Lessons for Crisis Management," in *Managing Sino-American Crises*, 394–395.

28. Jiang Zemin reportedly interacted closely with fellow PBSC member Li Peng and PLA elders Liu Huaqing and Zhang Zhen to make all major decisions during the 1995–1996 Taiwan Strait crisis. Senior PLA officer Zhang Wannian reportedly played a critical role as the lead implementer of the senior leadership's military-related decisions during the crisis. However, Jiang, as head of the CMC and party general secretary, almost certainly approved all the military exercises and missile "tests." See Robert L. Suettinger, *Beyond Tiananmen: The Politics of U.S.-China Relations, 1989–2000* (Washington, DC: Brookings Institution, 2003), 200–263; and Michael Swaine, "Chinese Decision-Making Regarding Taiwan: 1979–2000," in *The Making of Chinese Foreign and Security Policy in the Era of Reform*, ed. David M. Lampton (Stanford, CA: Stanford University Press, 2001), 293–294.

29. LSG(s) would usually operate in parallel with the ad hoc crisis working group in supporting the senior leadership during a crisis. Coordination between LSGs and any ad hoc group would usually be facilitated by the CCP Central Committee's Foreign Affairs Office (FAO), which acts as staff for foreign affairs–related LSGs. Based on interviews conducted by Bonnie Glaser.

30. Ibid.

31. Ibid.

32. Alastair Iain Johnston, "The Development of International Crisis Management Theory in the People's Republic of China" (unpublished manuscript, December 2011).

33. Ibid. For example, during the EP-3 incident, the three main sources of intelligence for the senior leadership were the MSS, the PLA General Staff, and the Ministry of Foreign Affairs; they did not coordinate or talk to one another, and sometimes apparently refused to share information, according to interviews conducted by Bonnie Glaser.

34. Interviews conducted by Bonnie Glaser and Alastair Iain Johnston, "The Development of International Crisis Management Theory."

35. Xiong reportedly briefed the PBSC during both crises; in the case of the embassy bombing, he persuaded Jiang that the attack could not have been accidental and advocated a tough response. Information based on interviews conducted by Bonnie Glaser. For information on Xiong's role, see James Mulvenon, "'Ding, Dong, The Witch is Dead!': Foreign Policy and Military Intelligence Assessments after the Retirement of General Xiong Guangkai," *China Leadership Monitor*, no. 17 (Winter 2006).

36. Swaine, "Chinese Decision-Making Regarding Taiwan."

37. See Andrew Scobell, Arthur Shuh-fan Ding, Phillip C. Saunders, and Scott W. Harold, eds., *The PLA and Contingency Planning in China* (Washington, DC: National Defense University Press, 2015).

38. See Michael Swaine and M. Taylor Fravel, "China's Assertive Behavior Part Two: The Maritime Periphery," *China Leadership Monitor*, no. 35 (Summer 2011); Linda Jakobson and Dean Knox, *New Foreign Policy Actors in China*, SIPRI Policy Paper 26 (Stockholm: SIPRI, September 2010), 15–16; Peter A. Dutton, "International Law and the November 2004 'Han Incident,'" in *China's Future Nuclear Submarine Force*, eds. Andrew Erickson et al. (Newport, RI: Naval Institute Press, 2007), 162–211; Bonnie Glaser and Daniel Murphy, "China and the USS *Kitty Hawk*," *CSIS Critical Questions*, December 6, 2007; U.S. Department of Defense, *Annual Report to Congress: Military and Security Developments Involving the People's Republic of China 2008* (Washington, DC: U.S. Government Printing Office, 2008); and Lu, *The Dynamics of Foreign-Policy Decisionmaking in China*, 126–127.

39. Jakobson and Knox, *New Foreign Policy Actors in China*, 14. PLA publications played a key role after the EP-3 incident in claiming that the U.S. plane "veered" toward the Chinese fighter and caused the crash. Such accounts may have fueled public outrage and possibly shaped the MFA's early statements. See James Mulvenon, "Civil-Military Relations and the EP-3 Crisis: A Content Analysis," *China Leadership Monitor*, no. 1 (Winter 2002).

40. See Bonnie Glaser's discussion of the leadership response to Maj. Gen. Luo Yuan's 2009 remarks about Taiwan's "peaceful separation" in her chapter in this volume.

41. Interview cited in Johnston, "The Development of International Crisis Management Theory."

42. Ibid. Johnston suggests that this could create problems in a crisis if the other side resorts to military means early on, as Washington often does. In such circumstances, "Chinese decision-makers may believe the situation has evolved more quickly than expected to a serious military crisis and thus over-react."

43. See Bonnie S. Glaser, "China's National Security Leading Group and the Ongoing Debate on Creating a National Security Council" (unpublished manuscript, April 1, 2003); and Joel Wuthnow, *Decoding China's New "National Security Commission"* (Alexandria, VA: CNA China Studies, November 2013).

6   The PLA Role in China's Taiwan Policymaking

Bonnie S. Glaser

FOREIGN ANALYSTS HAVE LONG WORRIED THAT THE People's Liberation Army (PLA) could assume a prominent role within China, from which it could promote an aggressive foreign policy platform. As the PLA's technical and operational capabilities have increased over the past decade, these fears have only grown. One of the foremost concerns about PLA modernization is its potential effect on Beijing's policy toward Taiwan. As the military balance tips in favor of the mainland, many fear that the PLA could push the central leadership in Beijing to impose a decisive cross-Strait resolution through force. Such a position could be advocated either as a consequence of a return of the Democratic Progressive Party (DPP) to power in Taiwan that is accompanied by efforts to press for independence or a refusal by a Kuomintang (KMT) government to negotiate terms of reunification with the mainland.

Given that Taiwan remains the most important mission for which the PLA must plan and a rallying point for all Chinese, it is only logical that the PLA would harbor certain preferences concerning Taiwan policy. Such preferences may include less accommodation toward Taiwan and use of military means to warn Taiwan's leaders against crossing Chinese redlines. Past examples, such as the 1995–1996 Taiwan Strait crisis, support such a conclusion. In fact, some analysts believe the PLA is a staunch advocate of a hard line toward Taiwan and perceived U.S. interference in cross-Strait relations.[1] Yet, while PLA officers have on occasion lobbied China's top leaders to take a tougher stance toward Taiwan, there is no evidence that the PLA has ever acted in contradiction to orders, and PLA efforts to influence Taiwan policy appear to operate within the constraints placed upon the PLA by the Chinese Communist Party (CCP).

This chapter will address the PLA's role in China's Taiwan policymaking process and the cross-Strait relationship. Ten channels are identified through which the PLA seeks influence China's Taiwan policy or are used by the central authorities as an instrument of policy toward Taiwan: 1) institutional representation; 2) intelligence and research; 3) military procurement; 4) military exercises; 5) official statements; 6) defense white papers and other official documents; 7) media exposure; 8) informal mechanisms; 9) cultural and social exchanges; and 10) military-to-military exchanges with third countries. Although efforts by the Chinese military to exert influence are apparent, it is difficult to demonstrate a direct causal impact on policy. Therefore, while it can be concluded that the PLA employs various means to influence policy toward Taiwan, its actual influence cannot be proven and remains somewhat of a mystery. A tentative conclusion suggested by the evidence is that when cross-Strait tensions are high, PLA influence on policy toward Taiwan increases. After mid-2008, with the easing of cross-Strait tensions, the PLA's influence on Chinese policy toward Taiwan has diminished somewhat, although it still plays an important role. Another conclusion is that although at times the military prefers a more muscular expression of China's Taiwan policy than civilian organs, the PLA's policy preferences are rarely contrary to those advocated by other actors or to existing PRC policy.

Channel One: Institutional Representation

Central Military Commission
Important decisions on policy toward Taiwan are made by the Politburo Standing Committee (PBSC), where the PLA has not enjoyed representation since the Fifteenth Party Congress in 1997. PLA interests are represented by PBSC members who concomitantly hold positions on the Central Military Commission (CMC). The CMC is the key mechanism for facilitating coordination among all military organs and between those organs and the senior PLA leadership.[2] Among its many responsibilities, the policy-related tasks of the CMC include formulating and executing programs for the modernization of the armed forces, and providing advice to the top party-state leadership on

national defense and national security affairs and developments in trends in international security.

Since the Eighteenth Party Congress in 2012 Xi Jinping has served as general secretary of the CCP and chairman of the CMC. Ten uniformed military officers sit on the CMC, including two vice-chairmen, the minister of national defense, the directors of the four general departments, and the commanders of the Second Artillery, navy, and air force. When the larger Politburo meets to deliberate on issues related to Taiwan, two PLA vice-chairmen—General Fan Changlong and Air Force General Xu Qiliang—have seats at the table.

CMC meetings offer senior PLA brass critically important opportunities to engage top party leaders positioned to defend military interests on the PBSC. Through the CMC, the PLA is able to highlight the defense aspects of Taiwan policy. High-ranking PLA generals can also convey their views and concerns as members of the CMC Executive Committee, an informal body made up of the CMC chairman and vice-chairmen.[3] Although there are other forums focused on Taiwan, the CMC is a venue where uniformed officers comprise the majority of members and where the PLA likely feels most comfortable airing its views. It may also be the setting where differences between civilians and the military emerge. During Jiang Zemin's tenure, there were reportedly serious disagreements between Jiang and top PLA officers over Taiwan policy.[4] According to Tai Ming Cheung, in the first half of 1993 the CMC ordered PLA policy planners and intelligence analysts to conduct a comprehensive reexamination of cross-Strait relations. The results, adopted by the PLA leadership during a May 1993 meeting, were alarming and conveyed the warning that Taiwan was committed to establishing a separate state. After lengthy deliberations, the party leadership adopted a conciliatory approach to Taiwan. However, the PBSC and CMC also ordered the PLA to begin upgrading preparations for a Taiwan contingency, in the event that the conciliatory approach should fail.[5] While the PLA may not have gained support for a tougher policy toward Taiwan, it appears that the military's sense of urgency may have influenced party decisionmakers and secured some of the PLA's goals.

According to PLA sources, the process of developing a policy proposal in the PLA begins with the convening of an informal discussion group either by the General Staff Department or the CMC. Participants may include representatives from other CCP and government organs, including the Ministry of Foreign Affairs (MFA). Once a policy option is developed it is presented to the CMC for approval and then forwarded to the PBSC. Chinese experts say that such an informal discussion group was formed in 1995–1996 to produce planning options for the conduct of military exercises against Taiwan. The MFA, Taiwan Affairs Office (TAO), CCP Foreign Affairs Office, and other government and party organs develop policy proposals based on a similar process and include PLA participants when the policy under consideration affects PLA equities or otherwise requires military input. The PLA's clout is greater, however, when it takes the lead as convener of the discussion group.[6]

Leading Small Groups

The CCP Central Committee's leading small groups (LSGs) are another important set of institutions that involve the PLA in the policymaking process on Taiwan issues. LSGs are not decisionmaking bodies, but are communication and coordination mechanisms that ensure the flow of information and forge consensus across various parts of the Chinese system. They also make policy recommendations that are forwarded to the PBSC for deliberation. According to Chinese interviewees who have worked in LSG staff offices, the vast majority of policy proposals agreed upon within an LSG are subsequently endorsed by the top leadership.

Three LSGs discuss Taiwan, either directly or indirectly: the TALSG, the Foreign Affairs Leading Small Group (FALSG), and the National Security Leading Small Group (NSLSG). The full memberships of the LSGs are not public, but official media occasionally mention leaders in connection with their LSG activities. The PLA has one or two representatives on all three LSGs.[7] The CMC is convened more regularly and more often than the LSGs, supporting the contention that the LSGs are not the primary forum for PLA input into decisionmaking on Taiwan or other issues.

The TALSG focuses exclusively on Taiwan, advising the PBSC of developments in Taiwan, assessing the efficacy of Chinese policy, and recommending policy adjustments. It is chaired by the CCP general secretary, who serves as the "bridge leader" within the top leadership on Taiwan issues.[8] At TALSG meetings, the PLA can present its evaluation of the cross-Strait environment and suggest particular policy options prior to the referral of an important issue to the PBSC for a final decision. Once major policy decisions are made, the TALSG oversees implementation throughout the relevant state and party organs, which may offer the PLA the chance to influence how directives are carried out.

As with all the LSGs, membership in the TALSG is based on position and portfolio, not on personal connections. Based on precedent, the PLA likely has two members: a vice-chairman of the CMC (Fan Changlong) and the deputy chief of the PLA General Staff with responsibility for intelligence (Sun Jianguo).[9] New membership slates of the TALSG, the FALSG, and the NSLSG are appointed every five years, soon after a party conference to coincide with changes in leadership. New appointments may also be made as needed, for example when a current member is replaced within the institution he represents.[10]

The FALSG, headed by the CCP general secretary in recent years, has two PLA representatives: the minister of defense, who is a CMC member (currently Chang Wanquan), and the deputy chief of the PLA General Staff who oversees intelligence (Sun Jianguo). The FALSG likely addresses Beijing's handling of the Taiwan issue with foreign countries and international institutions, on issues such as China's response to U.S. arms sales to Taiwan. As with the TALSG, the PLA can likely use this venue to introduce and frame a problem or opportunity, along with policy options, prior to referral of the issue to the PBSC for final consideration. The NSLSG, which was established in 2000, is believed to have similar or identical membership to the FALSG and the PLA is also represented by the minister of defense and the deputy chief of the PLA General Staff.[11]

Zhang Zhijun, director of the CCP Central Committee's Taiwan Affairs Office (TAO), is also a member of the NSLSG, indicating that Taiwan is sometimes discussed there. While the ability of the PLA to influence policy through any one group may be limited, representation on the TALSG, FALSG, and NSLSG offers important opportunities to register the PLA's positions and concerns about Taiwan.

National People's Congress

Another institutional channel for PLA participation in national security discussions is the group deliberations at the annual sessions of the National People's Congress (NPC). PLA deputies hold group discussions on the government work report delivered by the premier and exchange views on important PLA tasks. By convention, the PLA delegation to the NPC is visited every year by the CCP general secretary and other top party and military leaders.[12] Before military outspokenness in the media became commonplace in 2009–2010, the annual NPC meeting provided PLA deputies an opportunity to comment to the media, a means of shaping public and elite views on Taiwan and an indirect pathway to influence policy. In 2006, after Taiwan's President Chen Shui-bian disbanded the National Unification Council and terminated the National Unification Guidelines, the PRC-owned Hong Kong press agency reported that "stopping and opposing 'Taiwan independence'" was "a focus of attention during the 'two sessions'"—the NPC and the Chinese People's Political Consultative Conference (CPPCC). Lt. Gen. Li Yuanzheng, a PLA deputy to the NPC, spoke about the antisecession law that the NPC had passed the year before, and warned that the mainland would "act according to the law."[13]

Government Agencies

The PLA may also exercise some influence within the civilian government organizations that implement Taiwan policy, including the State Council's TAO, which serves as the staff office for the TALSG, coordinating TALSG meetings and preparing background material. It has a number of other official functions, such as drafting and implementing guidelines, policies, and laws related to Taiwan affairs. The TAO also analyzes cross-Strait developments and "takes charge of relevant preparations for negotiations and agreements with Taiwan authorities and its authorized public organizations."[14] PLA Major General Wang Zaixi served as the vice minister of the TAO during the mid-2000s, giving the PLA direct access to the main civilian organization in charge of coordinating and implementing policy toward Taiwan. Wang, who initially was in charge of research and later shifted to responsibility for propaganda, likely helped to coordinate with the military and represent PLA's interests during Chen Shui-bian's rule in Taiwan, a period of great uncertainty in cross-Strait relations. Between 2007 and late 2013, Wang Zaixi served as vice-minister of the Association for Relations Across the Taiwan Strait (ARATS), the quasi-official organization that handles technical and business matters with Taiwan, including cross-Strait negotiations.

A source of indirect PLA influence in ARATS is military officers who serve as advisers. For example, Maj. Gen. Chen Zhiya was appointed to the Second Board of Directors on June 4, 2008.[15] Chen is the son of General Chen Geng and an influential operator who served as the secretary-general of the China Foundation for International Strategic Studies (CFISS), a semi-independent research organization with ties to both senior party and PLA officials.

Channel Two: Intelligence and Research

The PLA may be able to influence Taiwan policy through a number of bottom-up efforts. Perhaps the most important is intelligence collection and analysis, which is conducted by a number of different PLA entities and affiliated research institutions. Such research and reporting can depict the cross-Strait environment in a light favorable to the PLA, and may also advocate preferred policy options. Given that reunification of Taiwan or prevention of its de jure independence is a central PLA mission, Taiwan remains a key focus of military intelligence, research, and analysis. PLA intelligence and analysis can potentially influence the thinking of senior military and party leaders and affect policy outcomes.

The General Staff Department (GSD) has been described as "the chief executive arm of the CMC," and is responsible for information gathering and analysis, and developing military policies that support China's overall Taiwan policy.[16] The GSD Operations Department exercises line authority over all GSD strategic research, analysis, and intelligence producers, including the Second, Third, and Fourth Departments. The Second Department (military intelligence) is considered superior to others as a source of defense analysis.[17] The Second Department houses the foremost PLA intelligence analysis think tank, the China Institute for International Strategic Studies (CIISS). According to an official description, CIISS "offers consultancy and policy advice to and undertakes the task of preparing research papers for relevant departments of the Chinese government, the army, and other institutions." It is staffed with some hundred research personnel, drawn from "active and retired officers, diplomats, experts, and scholars."[18] The CIISS chairman is typically a deputy chief of staff, whose portfolio includes foreign intelligence. Its current head is Gen. Sun Jianguo. CFISS, which is connected to the GSD Second Department, also conducts Taiwan research, including research on a cross-Strait military confidence-building mechanism.

The GSD Operations Department is also responsible for formulating war plans and is in operational control of PLA combat units. It has reportedly played an influential role in crafting the PLA's Taiwan policy since the early 1990s.[19]

The PLA also manages the Academy of Military Sciences (AMS) and National Defense University (NDU), which are directly subordinate to the CMC. Their activities are confined primarily to research and analysis of strategic issues, not intelligence collection. AMS is the PLA's premier doctrinal research and development institute, focusing on studies of military strategy, operations, and tactics; military systems; military history; and foreign militaries.[20] The operational focus of AMS research and its responsibility for development of defense doctrine and analysis of war-fighting capabilities make its work on Taiwan especially important. The largest of the PLA's research institutes, AMS receives assignments from the GSD and the CMC, and also consults with the PLA general departments and coordinates work throughout the PLA. In addition to research and reports for PLA leadership, AMS researchers have also been known to ghost-write speeches for PLA leaders and serve on temporary and permanent ad hoc groups tasked with drafting documents such as defense white papers.[21]

Whereas AMS does not focus on student education, NDU is the PLA's primary professional military education institution. NDU's student body comprises senior commanders, staff officers, and researchers and civilians from different government organizations.[22] Unlike AMS, which has done significant work on future warfare, NDU is traditionally more focused on present military challenges.[23] Nevertheless, both AMS and NDU are important generators of new ideas and research in defense trends, and presumably do extensive work on Taiwan. During the 1990s, NDU and AMS were at the vanguard of efforts to update China's military doctrine. In 1999, they published several "campaign outlines," which detailed a new doctrine for "joint operations."[24] In the late 1990s, AMS was involved in discussions on potential political reforms, along with central bureaucracies and think tanks.[25] Such projects would have certainly weighed the PLA's role in regards to Beijing's overall Taiwan strategy.

The General Political Department (GPD) also does important work on Taiwan. While the GPD is not believed to be as intimately involved in military planning as the GSD, its Liaison Department gathers and analyzes political and economic intelligence concerning Taiwan. The Liaison Department is said to play an important role in the war between China and Taiwan for diplomatic recognition by other countries, which has cooled down since Ma Ying-jeou's election and declaration of a diplomatic truce.[26] The Liaison Department, also known as the China Association for International Friendly Contact (CAIFC), oversees the Centre for Peace and Development Studies (CPD). The CPD, which conducts both intelligence collection and analysis, has special expertise in Taiwan dating to the pre- and immediate post-Liberation period. In addition, the PLA Navy (PLAN) and PLA Air Force (PLAAF) both have research units that conduct analysis on Taiwan.

The PLA's disparate intelligence collection and analysis and research institutions are an important tool the PLA can use to influence Taiwan policy.

Their work likely influences how central leaders assess the cross-Strait environment and provides policy options that protect and advance the PLA's interests. During periods of increased tension across the Taiwan Strait, the exercise of PLA influence through this channel is likely significant. Most PLA analysis is channeled through the CMC General Office, which summarizes and distributes reports to relevant defense and foreign policy organs. On rare occasions reports are delivered directly to PBSC members, usually in response to a direct tasking from a member.[27] The PLA may occasionally provide strategic analysis on Taiwan to the TAO, which serves as the staff office for the TALSG, or to the CCP Foreign Affairs Office. High-ranking PLA officials with membership on the TALSG, FALSG, or CMC likely use PLA research to bolster support for particular policies among their civilian counterparts.

Channel Three: Military Procurement

Military procurement is another means by which the PLA can influence Chinese policy toward Taiwan. Procurement issues are deliberated primarily in the CMC. Key procurement decisions beginning from the late 1990s indicate that procurement and strategy toward Taiwan converged. This suggests that the PLA and top civilian party members agreed on many important aspects of Beijing's Taiwan policy.

Throughout the 1990s, the PLA lacked a credible deterrent against Taiwan independence and U.S. intervention in the event of conflict. As the perceived threat of Taiwan independence grew, particularly after the U.S. deployed two aircraft carriers to the area around the Taiwan Strait in 1996, PLA procurement decisions reflected the priority attached to deterring Taiwan secession and the possibility that the PLA might have to fight the U.S. in a relatively short timeframe. The decision was made to focus on development of near-term capabilities, while postponing certain long-range capabilities that were not relevant for Taiwan missions. For example, the PLA procured hundreds of Russian multirole fighters such as the Su-30, while focusing less on capabilities such as modern strategic bombers and aerial refueling.[28] PLA officers advocated additional conventional strike options, such as ballistic and cruise missiles, which, in concert with strike aircraft provide more flexible attack options in a Taiwan contingency.[29] The PLAN also assumed a more important role in the PLA's defense strategy, expanding its surface and sub-surface platforms.

Grim assessments of cross-Strait developments in the mid-1990s gave the PLA the opportunity to lobby for expanded defense budgets and new military purchases. With improvements in the cross-Strait environment since mid-2008, coupled with the PLA's own rapid military improvements, the PLA increasingly has the luxury of developing indigenous technology and capabilities for missions other than Taiwan. Yet even the decision to develop aircraft carriers may have been made with Taiwan in mind. While many analysts consider aircraft carriers superfluous in a Taiwan conflict, some PLA advocates such as Liu Huaqing have argued that an aircraft carrier would play an important role in a Taiwan contingency.[30] Such advocacy may have influenced Beijing's decision to refurbish the *Varyag* and procure indigenously built aircraft carriers. While the PLA may be preparing for a potential conflict with the United States, Taiwan would most certainly provide the spark. Taiwan scenarios will continue to weigh heavily in PLA procurement, giving the PLA the opportunity to frame the threat and lay out a procurement strategy in response for party leaders.

Channel Four: Military Exercises

PLA military exercises are important policy instruments that can be used by the central leadership to intimidate Taiwan's government and voters, and to signal disapproval of policy decisions made by Taipei that threaten Chinese interests. When concerns in the Chinese military about Taiwan independence behavior intensify, the PLA may advocate conducting exercises aimed against Taiwan, thereby influencing overall Taiwan policy. Before the mid-1990s Taiwan Strait crisis, military strategists had already been advocating provocative displays of force as a component of the PLA's new strategy of local war under high-technology conditions.[31] Following then Taiwan President Lee Teng-hui's controversial trip to the United States in 1995, Jiang Zemin was reportedly under pressure from elements within the PLA to "stand firm against the Americans and Lee Teng-hui."[32] PLA officers argued that Lee's visit was evidence that the conciliatory approach had failed. In their view, military intimidation was necessary to warn Lee and deter him from making further moves. PLA officers made a number of passionate public statements denouncing Taiwan independence and announcing the PLA's readiness to protect China's territorial integrity.

The PLA subsequently carried out a series of missile tests and military exercises in the Taiwan Strait in July 1995 and March 1996. The missile firings preceded Taiwan's legislative elections in December 1995 and the first direct popular presidential election in March 1996. While some interpret the exercises as evidence of PLA influence over the central leadership,[33] Jiang Zemin and other civilian leaders were likely also resolved to adopt tougher measures against Taiwan. Nevertheless, Jiang did not want the exercises to escalate into a larger conflict with the United States. With this in mind, the "purpose, scale, time, and venue" of the exercises were announced beforehand.[34] The PLA undoubtedly provided advice and options to the PBSC. There is no evidence that PLA officials on the CMC disagreed with the ultimate decisions; PLA leaders may have shared Jiang's concern to keep the exercises from escalating into a military conflict.

Renewed efforts by Taiwan's leaders to challenge mainland China's sovereignty over Taiwan in the late 1990s and early 2000s were again met with warnings from Beijing in the form of military exercises. Just a few weeks after Lee Teng-hui's July 9, 1999, declaration that a "special state-to-state relationship" existed between Taiwan and the mainland, PLAAF aircraft crossed the centerline of the Strait for the first time. Shortly afterward, in the run up to and immediately following Chen Shui-bian's May 2000 inauguration, the PLA carried out three exercises in eastern China between April and June.[35] These maneuvers served as a backstop for the oral threats issued by then Chinese Premier Zhu Rongji, who warned the people of Taiwan on the eve of the vote that "the election of the independence candidate would mean war."

In September 2004, the PLAAF carried out a massive air exercise near the centerline of the Strait during which thirty sorties involving several different models of aircraft were flown. One theory held that the show of force was intended to influence Taiwan's Legislative Yuan elections and the upcoming U.S. presidential elections.[36] While these exercises were likely an example of the top leadership's use of the military as an instrument of Chinese policy toward Taiwan, they may also demonstrate bottom-up influence on policy by the PLA and showcase the PLA role in implementing policy.

The failure of Chinese military exercises to prevent Taiwan voters from electing Lee Teng-hui in 1996 and Chen Shui-bian in 2000 or deter those leaders from pursuing provocative policies toward the mainland during their terms in office may have convinced both the civilian and military leadership in Beijing that such exercises were ineffective and even counterproductive. Analysis of open-source reporting of PLA named exercises in recent years indicates that training has since been directed at several potential contingencies, with Taiwan being only one of the many possible scenarios.[37] Even before the election of Ma Ying-jeou as Taiwan president in March 2008 and the subsequent easing of cross-Strait tensions, PLA exercises began to emphasize missions other than Taiwan and implementation of operational concepts such as joint operations under informatized conditions and in complex electromagnetic environments.

Between 2006 and 2012, it is difficult to find exercises overtly and explicitly aimed at intimidating Taiwan. The shift away from conducting major exercises targeting Taiwan even before tensions lowered in cross-Strait relations may be a result of Beijing's conclusion that overt displays of force were not necessary during a period of improving cross-Strait ties. There was no longer an urgent need to employ military maneuvers to intimidate Taiwan. Instead, restraint in military exercises became part of a new policy toward the island designed to signal a softer stance. Perhaps as a goodwill gesture to Ma Ying-jeou for pledging to not pursue Taiwan independence and accepting the 1992 consensus on "one China," Beijing deliberately stopped conducting major military exercises in the Nanjing MR opposite Taiwan in 2009, opting instead to hold the annual exercise further away.[38] "Stride 2009" and "Mission Action 2010," two of the largest trans-regional exercises ever held, specifically avoided moving units into the Nanjing MR or moving to amphibious training areas as might be expected if the scenario were to depict follow-on forces preparing to conduct second-wave amphibious assaults as part of a larger campaign. Exercises carried out in the Nanjing MR in 2009 were small and did not appear specifically directed at a Taiwan scenario. "Joint 2008," the only publicized exercise that year that included amphibious operations, was conducted as far from Taiwan as possible, with PLA troops moving from the Ji'nan MR to the Shenyang MR.[39]

The trend of restraint was broken with the launch of the "Mission Action 2013" series of exercises on September 16, 2013. In contrast to previous trans-regional exercises in which the PLA took great care to distance its activities from Taiwan, "Mission Action 2013" was conducted across the Taiwan Strait in the Guangdong and Nanjing MRs. The exercises tested "long-range three-dimensional projection of soldiers into *unfamiliar areas* several thousand kilometers away by air, ship and railway."[40] The final phase of the exercise tested amphibious assault training.[41] Despite speculation that the exercises was intended to prepare for conflict over the Senkakus, there were signals that the PLA explicitly intended to intimidate Taiwan. During the final phase of the exercise, held on October 11, 2013, CCTV footage of the exercise headquarters prominently displayed a map of Taiwan with military bases marked.[42] This happened five days after President Xi Jinping's meeting with Taiwan envoy Vincent Siew at the Asia-Pacific Economic Cooperation (APEC) 2013 summit, in which Xi declared that political talks could not be postponed indefinitely.[43] The timing suggests that the PLA was playing a role in a broader initiative to pressure President Ma Ying-jeou to move beyond economic talks.[44]

Although there is no direct evidence that the PLA advocated conducting exercises in a manner less intimidating to Taiwan, the military may have initiated a proposal to move major exercises out of the Nanjing MR from 2006 to 2012 in order to participate in the new policy of offering positive inducements to Taiwan. The PLA may also have pushed for a return to its traditional role in coercing Taiwan as Xi Jinping made political talks a priority. Whether due to bottom-up efforts from the PLA or top-down instruction from the central leadership, both the restraint from 2006 to 2012 and the pressure afterward illustrate compatibility between senior military and civilian leaders in their approaches to Taiwan.

Channel Five: Official Statements

Official statements are both an instrument of Chinese policy toward Taiwan (and toward the United States regarding its policy on Taiwan) as well as a logical means that the PLA can use to attempt to shape and influence policy toward Taiwan. The PLA's Ministry of National Defense (MND) began to hold monthly press conferences in April 2008, in part to highlight PLA transparency, but also to increase the public voice of the military on a range of issues.[45] When Taiwan is raised in press briefings, MND spokesmen issue carefully prepared responses that reiterate official policy, although in some cases they expand on policy, providing insights into the preferences of the military. For example, during a 2010 press conference, in reference to discussion about potential cross-Strait dialogue on military confidence-building measures (CBMs), an MND spokesman said that "the mainland and Taiwan can make contact and exchanges on military issues at a proper time," so as to maintain stability in the region. Preparations "should be done step by step and starting from the easy ones," and "peaceful development of cross-Strait relations conforms to the fundamental interests of people on both sides and represents their common aspirations."[46] This position was consistent with, yet also elaborated on, Hu Jintao's six points delivered in December 2009.[47]

Like their counterparts in the MFA, MND spokesmen criticize U.S. arms sales to Taiwan whenever questions regarding possible sales are posed or after an arms sale decision or transfer is announced. There is a pattern, at least in the cases of the October 2008, January 2010, and September 2011 U.S. arms sales packages to Taiwan, that MND condemnation is slighter harsher than the wording used by the MFA. In September 2011, the MFA spokesman warned that the sales would "damage" bilateral ties, exchanges, and "cooperation in the military, security and other fields."[48] The MND spokesman declared that the sales would "severely damage" bilateral and military ties.[49] In January 2010, the MFA warned that the sales would have a "serious and negative impact" on a range of bilateral exchanges.[50] On the same occasion, the MND spokesman not only warned of "serious harm" to the military and bilateral relationship, but also accused the U.S. of "perfidy."[51] In October 2008, a Chinese MFA spokesman said that the arms package would "gravely harm" bilateral ties.[52] The MND spokesman maintained that the arms package had "poisoned" the atmosphere between the two militaries.[53]

Public remarks by high-ranking PLA officials about U.S. policy toward Taiwan in 2011—especially those made directly to American counterparts or an American audience—were unusually harsh, suggesting that the Chinese military may have favored a stronger response than its civilian counterparts. For example, in May 2011, while visiting Washington D.C., Chief of the PLA General Staff Chen Bingde used particularly tough language to criticize the Taiwan Relations Act, calling it "hegemonic" and a form of interference in China's internal affairs. Chen also mischaracterized, perhaps deliberately, statements made to him about Taiwan by Secretary of State Clinton and several members of the U.S. Congress. Yet Gen. Chen also expressed a pragmatic position that China's reaction to U.S. arms sales to Taiwan would hinge on the nature of the weapons sold, a stance not heard from civilian officials or MFA spokesmen.[54] It is impossible to assess whether Chen Bingde's statements were prepared in advance and coordinated within the Chinese system. They may not have been thoroughly vetted, though they may represent a consensus reached within the Chinese military.

According to PLA and civilian researchers, the Chinese military is not necessarily pressing internally for a harsher response to U.S. arms sales to Taiwan than in the past, but it is resisting taking guidance from the MFA, which previously took the lead in drafting Beijing's response.

Channel Six: Defense White Papers
and Other Official Documents

One of the most important products of PLA intelligence and research is the biennial Defense White Paper, which regularly includes an assessment of the cross-Strait situation. The report is drafted by an interagency team of experts from the GSD, the AMS, the MFA, and the State Council Information Office. The drafting team is usually led by the military participants from the GSD and the AMS who prepare the initial outline of the document and coordinate all the meetings of the group. The final document is approved by the PBSC. According to Major General Chen Zhou, the principal coordinator of China's defense white papers, the document serves three distinct functions: it builds confidence and resolves doubts abroad; it raises national defense awareness domestically; and it deters and warns adversaries.[55]

As regards Taiwan, the defense white papers unify thinking internally and set the tone of the overall assessment of the cross-Strait environment, including the degree of danger of Taiwan independence and the threat posed by U.S. arms sales to Taiwan. Since the PLA has the lead in drafting and coordinating the document, the military exerts some influence in shaping the contents and language, but in the end the paper is a consensus document and represents a compromise among the government, party, and military. Defense white papers are therefore both a top-down instrument of policy and a bottom-up means for the PLA to promote the military's assessment of cross-Strait affairs in support of the PLA's preferred policies.

The 2004 white paper came at a time of heightened cross-Strait tensions, and reflected PRC concern about Chen Shui-bian's reelection and the holding of a referendum. It portrayed the cross-Strait situation as "grim" and described the "separatist activities of the 'Taiwan independence' forces" as "the biggest immediate threat to China's sovereignty and territorial integrity as well as peace and stability on both sides of the Taiwan Straits and the Asia-Pacific region as a whole." Citing the "sacred responsibility" of the Chinese armed forces to prevent splitting of the country by "Taiwan independence" forces, the white paper warned that "a reckless attempt that constitutes a major incident of 'Taiwan independence'" would be "resolutely and thoroughly" crushed by the Chinese people and armed forces.[56]

The 2004 white paper was issued while the antisecession law (ASL) was being drafted. It is plausible that there was interchange between those individuals involved in drafting each document. The PLA likely had a significant voice in the debates over the tone and content of both documents. According to Jing Huang and Xiaoting Li, before the drafting of the ASL an internal debate took place over the possible formulation of a "unification law." Policymakers were unsure whether the PLA could fulfill such an obligation given the possibility of U.S. involvement. Jiang Zemin, who had stepped down as party secretary but retained his position as CMC chairman, reportedly asked his top generals whether the PLA was "ready and confident" that it could win a war over Taiwan given potential U.S. intervention. Uncertainty over such a prospect restricted the law to preventing Taiwanese independence.[57] It is unclear how hard PLA officials may have pushed for a unification law.

The 2010 Defense White Paper noted that "significant and positive progress" had been achieved in cross-Strait relations.[58] It also contained a passage proposing military CBMs, or what Chinese sources term a "military security mechanism of mutual trust." The preceding year, Major General Luo Yuan, deputy head of the World Military Research Institute at the AMS, advocated cross-Strait military CBMs.[59] Luo argued that cross-Strait military CBMs would show Taiwan "an even deeper sense of the mainland's good will and sincerity" and would "reduce the clamor and bluster of the 'Taiwanese independence' forces." Building on such suggestions, the 2010 white paper concluded that

> the two sides may discuss political relations in the special situation that China is not yet reunified in a pragmatic manner. The two sides can hold contacts and exchanges on military issues at an appropriate time and talk about a military security mechanism of mutual trust, in a bid to act together to adopt measures to further stabilize cross-Strait relations and ease concerns regarding military security. The two sides should hold consultations on the basis of upholding the one-China principle to formally end hostilities and reach a peace agreement.[60]

A proposal to pursue cross-Strait CBMs was first included in an official PRC document in May 2004, when the TAO released a major statement intended to reaffirm the mainland's resolve to prevent Taiwan independence. At the same time, the statement sought to encourage Taiwan to embrace the "one China" concept by offering a number of positive inducements, including establishment of a mutual trust mechanism in the military field.[61] According to senior military researchers, the PLA recommended the inclusion of the CBM proposal as one of the seven "bright futures" that could emerge if Taiwan abandoned the path of Taiwan independence and accepted the "one China" principle. They cited a desire to increase PLA input in decisionmaking on Taiwan policy and to respond to appeals from Taiwan's military to engage in CBMs as motivations. A PLA senior colonel noted that "policy toward Taiwan includes both push and pull," and that "CBMs are part of the pull."[62]

As noted above, Major General Wang Zaixi was vice-minister of the TAO at that time and may have facilitated PLA input in Taiwan policymaking, including the May 2004 statement. During his tenure at the TAO, Wang frequently made harsh statements that may have reflected PLA concerns, but which were also endorsed at higher levels. For example, Wang repeatedly warned Taiwan as the Chen administration pushed forward its plans for referenda. He reminded Taiwan authorities that there was a "bottom line" for the mainland's use of force against Taiwan, as stated in Beijing's February 2000 White Paper on the One-China Principle and the Taiwan Issue.[63] Wang emphasized that China must seize the "precious opportunity of the first fifteen to twenty years of the twenty-first century in which China is likely to have some great achievement" in order to settle the Taiwan issue and warned that a cross-Strait military conflict before 2008 could not be ruled out so long as Chen continued pushing his pro-independence agenda.[64]

Official discussions with Taiwan on cross-Strait CBMs, should they proceed, could provide an opportunity for the PLA to exert greater influence on policy in the context of easing tensions and reconciliation between the two sides of the Strait. Until talks get underway and Beijing's proposed road map for CBMs becomes known, it is impossible to judge PLA influence in the process. One indicator could be the extent to which the proposals of individual military researchers are incorporated into official policy proposals. Luo Yuan, a senior researcher with the AMS and a Chinese People's Political Consultative Conference delegate, has published and lectured extensively on cross-Strait CBMs. According to Luo, "confidence" should be translated as xinren (trust), so that CBMs equal a "measure to establish trust." Trust has to come first, as "security should be protected by relying on the connection of mutual trust with common interests." Without mutual understanding and trust, issuing "detailed lists of measures" can only be empty words. The foundation of trust is the acknowledgment by soldiers on both sides of the Strait of the "principle that both sides of the Strait belong to one China." Luo proposes that CBM discussions proceed from unofficial to official discussions, noting that "with regard to order, it is best to proceed from easy to difficult in an orderly way, step by step. When the conditions are mature, the core questions that both sides are most concerned about can be directly approached." Luo believes that the two sides should address issues upon which they already agree, as well as the most pressing matters and less sensitive nontraditional security questions. In this manner, a consensus can be built gradually, "cultivating trust, before finally launching a joint assault."[65]

Yet Luo is by no means given to compromise on Taiwan. He has criticized the position put forward by many in Taiwan, including President Ma Ying-jeou, that the mainland must adjust its military deployments prior to establishing cross-Strait CBMs. Luo argues that "whether or not the mainland adjusts its military deployment is a topic of discussion, not a prerequisite." He also insists that both sides should make military adjustments: "When the mainland adjusts its military deployment, Taiwan should also adjust its military deployment."[66]

Channel Seven: Media Exposure

In recent years, a more commercially driven press and a dynamic Internet have provided new avenues for the PLA, as well as other bureaucratic players and interest groups, to actively promote its views, including on policy toward Taiwan. Linda Jakobson and Dean Knox, examining the phenomenon of new foreign policy actors in China, wrote that "in recent years the PLA has increasingly tried to influence the public debate about national security issues by publicly disseminating analysis by PLA research institutions as well as allowing officers to write divergent commentaries in prominent newspapers and serve as television commentators."[67] The growing prominence of the PLA in the media may be an effort by the PLA to play a greater role in Taiwan policy, both as a "stick" and "carrot." Individuals from the military may have more personal agendas, ranging from earning extra income to gaining national fame.

PLA writers published articles that staked out tough positions against Taiwan independence after Chen Shui-bian assumed the presidency in Taiwan and began implementing provocative policies. Major General Peng Guang-qian of the AMS stated in a 2003 interview that "He who 'plays with fire' shall perish by it. Taiwan independence means war. This bottom line was made clear long ago. Once this bottom line is touched, we mean what we say and the 1.3 billion people mean what they say." Peng also sought to dissuade Taiwan voters from the belief that the U.S. would protect Taiwan, stating the United States "knows exactly which is more important between the Chinese mainland and Taiwan. Unprofitable deals are not for the U.S. It will not gamble on its national security for the sake of 'Taiwan independence.'"[68]

Retired Major General Luo Yuan enjoys widespread notoriety as an analyst unafraid to speak his mind. Luo's opinions on cross-Strait developments are widely distributed both in print and through media appearances on CCTV and other media platforms, and are monitored beyond the mainland. Luo is a princeling—his father was Luo Qingchang, the Mao-era chief of the CCP's External Liaison Department, which oversaw international intelligence—which may at least in part account for his outspokenness. During Chen Shui-bian's administration, Luo used legal arguments to erode the basis for the planned referendum. He cited the failed attempts at referenda on independence in Northern Ireland and Quebec, noting that the U.S. considered Quebec's request to separate from Canada illegal. Luo referenced UN secretary general Boutros Boutros-Ghali's statement that "If referenda were called at will, allowing the separatist movement to spread, it would be nothing short of legalizing interference in other countries' internal affairs."[69] After Taiwan's January 2012 elections, Luo maintained that Beijing should "vigorously push for peaceful reunification," which was not consistent with the official policy of emphasizing peaceful development across the Strait while working toward the long-term goal of "peaceful reunification."[70]

Retired Admiral Yang Yi, former director of NDU's Institute of Strategic Studies, is another influential PLA media figure who has conveyed stern admonitions against U.S. interference with Taiwan. Yang has blamed the unsteady military-to-military relationship between China and the U.S. on the latter's practice of "persistently and ceaselessly selling arms to Taiwan."[71] In 2009 Yang wrote an article in the *Global Times* warning the United States to stay out of affairs between the mainland and Taiwan, stating, "This is a friendly reminder to the U.S.: please be careful, careful, careful, and don't think Beijing won't dare to declare war with Washington."[72] Shortly after word broke of a pending U.S. arms package to Taiwan in January 2010, Yang suggested that Beijing impose sanctions on U.S. arms companies who sell weapons to Taiwan. Yang was quoted as saying, "Why don't we conduct 'defensive counterattacks' against them? Apart from lodging protests with the

U.S. government and taking the necessary measures, why don't we impose sanctions on these troublemakers?" Yang advised that China should ensure that the economic losses for those companies are much greater than the profits they gain from selling weapons to Taiwan.[73]

Other PLA researchers also strongly condemned the arms sale and called for China to retaliate. In an interview with *Guoji xianqu daobao*, Luo Yuan argued that the arms sale gave China "justified cause" to increase its military spending and accelerate military modernization, saying that "the tiger that does not show its fierceness will be treated like a sick cat."[74] The call for sanctions and other punitive measures against the U.S. was not limited to the PLA; civilian scholars also argued for such steps. Jin Canrong, a professor at People's University, proposed that China impose sanctions on U.S. arms companies and suspend bilateral military dialogue and cooperation.[75]

One day after the Obama administration notified Congress on January 29 of its intent to sell $6.4 billion worth of military equipment to Taiwan, the MFA announced for the first time that sanctions would be levied on the U.S. companies involved in the arms sale (potentially affecting Boeing, Lockheed Martin, Raytheon, and United Technologies). While there is no clear evidence that demands by PLA and civilian scholars influenced the decision, presumably made by China's top leaders, discussions in the media likely put pressure on the government. It should also be noted that despite the declaration of sanctions, the policy was never carried out.

In September 2011, several military researchers and civilian scholars once again called for harsh retribution against the U.S. for approving another arms sale to Taiwan. Luo Yuan suggested China could "learn from Russia," which had vowed to deploy nuclear missiles on its western frontier in response to a U.S. proposal to deploy a missile defense system in central Europe. He also said Beijing should step up its military threat to Taiwan.[76] Such advice was not heeded; China's rhetorical and policy response were more muted than the year before.

In at least one instance, a position taken by a PLA researcher was regarded as out of step with policy and was criticized. In a November 2009 speech at Beijing University, Luo maintained that Ma Ying-jeou's "three no's" (no reunification, no independence, and no use of force) amounted to "peaceful separation" from the mainland.[77] According to Chinese experts, the speech aroused the ire of Chinese leaders, who did not want to disrupt the cross-Strait rapprochement taking place at the time, and Luo was reprimanded. The central leadership's reaction demonstrates the limits to public commentary, including by PLA researchers.

Several factors drive assertive PLA commentary in the media. One is deep-rooted nationalism and a widely held view that China should rectify the injustices it has suffered at the hands of foreigners since the mid-nineteenth century. Another is the commercialization of the Chinese media. Sensational-ist views expressed by Chinese military representatives are welcomed by an increasingly nationalistic Chinese public. This is reinforced by the fact that publishing articles and giving television interviews provide supplemental income for civilian scholars as well as active duty and retired military officers.

Chinese experts and officials privately insist that the opinions expressed by PLA and civilian researchers in the media reflect the views of individuals and their influence on policy is extremely limited. This has been acknowl-edged by Luo Yuan, who commented: "We have a rule in the PLA: it is the Communist Party that commands the guns, never the other way round. . . . It is up to the party to decide foreign policy. And the PLA will never transgress that line." Luo added that the most important military positions are those from the CMC and the PLA's official spokesmen. "The remaining opinions, like my own, are just personal opinions from PLA researchers."[78]

Channel Eight: Informal Mechanisms

Very little is known about the informal mechanisms for promoting PLA influ-ence on Chinese policy on Taiwan or other issues. One such example is partic-ipation in small group meetings with China's top leader. Very few PLA officers have such an opportunity and only rarely. In January 2007, Rear Admiral Yang Yi, then head of NDU's Institute of Strategic Studies, along with a civil-ian scholar, briefed Hu Jintao. It is possible, but not certain, that Taiwan was discussed in the meeting. When Jiang Zemin was CCP general secretary, he occasionally met with scholars, including PLA researchers. In one instance, Chen Zhiya joined retired ambassadors in a discussion with Jiang. Again, it is not known whether Taiwan was discussed.

Another example of an informal mechanism is occasional letters by retired PLA generals to China's top leaders advocating specific actions. For instance, in July 2004, the *Christian Science Monitor* reported that retired generals had urged Jiang Zemin to take action against Taiwan and settle the cross-Strait issue ahead of the 2008 Olympics. The article claimed that pro-military thinkers banked on the assertion that the world would react badly to aggression against Taiwan but that "everyone will get over it."[79] Jiang had supported a policy of imposing a deadline for Taiwan to accept unification. While still head of the CMC, Jiang reportedly told an expanded meeting of the CMC in July 2004 that "although the first twenty years of the twenty-first century represent an important period of strategic opportunities, the possibility of resolving the Taiwan issue during this period cannot be ruled out."[80]

Channel Nine: Cultural and Social Exchanges

Official and unofficial cross-Strait exchanges expanded rapidly after Ma Ying-jeou assumed the presidency in Taiwan in May 2008, and the PLA has been eager to participate in interactions with Taiwan. There are two categories of PLA engagement with Taiwan: 1) participating in Track 2 conferences and meetings with Taiwan civilian scholars and retired military officers; and 2) hosting delegations of retired military officers from Taiwan. The PLA likely views these interactions as a precursor to the establishment of official military links. Through such engagement, the PLA can discuss sensitive topics such as the preconditions for signing a cross-Strait peace accord and implementing military confidence-building measures. Such exchanges also provide an opportunity to increase the PLA's influence over Taiwan policy at a time of relative calm in cross-Strait relations.

PLA-sponsored events have included cultural celebrations, anniversaries and reunions for descendants of Whampoa Military Academy alumni, and golf events for retired generals. In addition to retired PLA officers, participants have included academics, government officials, and members of cultural organizations such as China Whampoa. PLA participants have included Wang Zaixi, former deputy chief of the General Staff Xiong Guangkai, and retired AMS and NDU generals such as Peng Guangqian and Pan Zhenqiang. Another participant in cross-Strait exchanges has been Major General Xin Qi, still on active duty. Xin is also the executive vice-chairman of the China Cultural Development Association, which along with China Whampoa, is an important promoter and facilitator of cross-Strait exchanges. These organizations have helped the two sides find common causes for celebration, such as New Year and Yellow Emperor Worship ceremonies, and historical celebrations such as the anniversary of victory in the Second Sino-Japanese War.

Most such interactions take place on the mainland, but in 2009 a delegation of retired military officers and civilian scholars visited Taiwan to attend a seminar entitled "60 Years Across the Taiwan Strait." The delegation was headed by retired Lieutenant General Li Jijun, the highest-level retired officer to ever visit the island. Conference participants reportedly exchanged a wide range of views on foreign relations, military affairs, politics, and economic issues. There was general agreement that the "1992 consensus" should be the basis for cross-Strait negotiations, however, discussions of "one China" produced differing opinions.[81] Li maintained that Taiwan would be better served by accepting the "one-China" principle as its primary mode of defense, rather than to have half a million troops, and commented that Chinese missiles targeting Taiwan were positive because they served to rein in independence activists.[82]

Attitudes on both sides of the Strait may gradually open to new concepts and ideas as a result of exchanges, which could have long-term implications for policy. For example, following "60 Years Across the Strait" Pan Zhenqiang of NDU said that members of the DPP were more rational than he imagined. According to one report, the PLA was initially reluctant to make contact with the DPP, but slowly began to initiate contact around this time. The report claimed that the PLA started to engage in exchanges with "rational members" of the pan-green camp, and was especially interested in academic groups with local contacts in central and southern Taiwan.[83]

These exchanges are in accord with Chinese policy of promoting cross-Strait military exchanges. A TAO spokesman has expressed the view that cross-Strait military exchanges should develop step by step, dealing with easy things first, and could begin by having cross-Strait exchanges between retired servicemen and relevant experts and academics.[84] Cross-Strait exchanges could serve as a bottom-up vehicle for the PLA to influence popular attitudes on both sides of the Strait and allow the PLA to play a critical role in any steps toward negotiated cross-Strait agreements. Alternatively, cross-Strait exchanges could also be a top-down phenomenon, with the central government viewing the PLA as a useful mechanism to generate positive momentum toward more substantive dialogue on CBMs.

Channel Ten: Military-to-Military Exchanges with Third Countries

Senior PLA officers routinely raise Taiwan when meeting with counterparts from other countries. Their objectives likely include influencing third-country policies toward Taiwan as part of a broader coordinated PRC strategy and, more generally, boosting the role of the PLA in China's foreign relations and highlighting the issues of particular importance to the military. Chinese newspaper reporting on comments by senior PLA officers to foreign military officers on Taiwan mentions briefings on China's position on Taiwan and expressions of appreciation for other countries adhering to a one-China policy.[85] When PRC concerns about Taiwan separatism reached a peak during Chen Shui-bian's term, PLA officers regularly explained the dangers of Taiwan independence to foreign counterparts.[86]

In most cases, PLA messages to foreign counterparts are similar to public statements by officials from the MFA and the TAO and seem to be well-coordinated. During the Chen Shui-bian era, publicly reported statements were quite harsh and sometimes warned that China would not tolerate Taiwan independence, but the wording was not notably tougher than the language used by civilians. For example, on December 14, 2004, Vice-Chairman of the CMC Guo Boxiong reportedly told Russian Defense Minister Sergei Ivanov that the PLA "will never sit idle regarding Taiwan separating from China."[87] The following day, a spokesman for the State Council's Taiwan Affairs Office similarly warned that "if Chen Shui-bian obstinately follows his so-called timetable for Taiwan independence, and schemes to change the position that Taiwan is part of China, the Chinese government and people definitely will not sit idly by."[88]

The PLA suspended or postponed military exchanges with the United States in 2008, 2010, and 2011 after the notification to Congress of U.S. arms sales to Taiwan. It is uncertain, however, whether the PLA pushed for such a response, whether the PLA was united or divided in its position, or whether the civilian PBSC members made decisions in the face of PLA resistance. After the announcement of the 2010 arms sale, a Chinese scholar with close ties to the PLA suggested privately that some members of the Chinese military objected to being the only part of China's bureaucracy to take punitive actions against the U.S. and wanted others to shoulder some of the burden. However in January 2011 the PLA was said to have been reluctant to permit U.S. Defense Secretary Robert Gates to visit China and may have been ordered to do so by Hu Jintao. Some commentators speculated that the test flight of the J-20 stealth fighter during Gates' visit was a signal of the military's dissatisfaction at being compelled to host him despite U.S. unwillingness to accede to China's demands to stop selling arms to Taiwan.[89]

Conclusion

This chapter has identified ten channels through which the PLA seeks to exert influence over China's Taiwan policy or are used by the central authorities as an instrument of policy toward Taiwan. These channels vary in their importance. The CMC is the single most important mechanism available to the PLA because it enables regular and direct communication between China's senior military officers and the CCP general secretary, who in turn is expected to represent the PLA's interests on the PBSC. Two other channels stand out as especially important means that the PLA employs to influence policy toward Taiwan: providing intelligence and research to shape assessments of the cross-Strait situation and drafting defense white papers. Less important pathways available to the PLA to influence policy toward Taiwan include deciding military procurement, conducting military exercises, delivering official MND spokesman statements, conducting exchanges with Taiwan, expressing opinions in the Chinese media, using informal mechanisms such as writing letters to or briefing top leaders, and conveying messages to third countries through military-to-military exchanges.

Overall evidence points to the conclusion that the PLA effectively uses numerous formal and informal means to inject its views into China's Taiwan policymaking process. As a bureaucratic actor, the PLA lobbies for its preferences within the Chinese system. Sometimes the military prefers a more muscular expression of China's Taiwan policy than civilian organs, as in the case of the condemnation of U.S. arms sales to Taiwan. This is especially true when there is a perceived need to deter actions by Taiwan or the United States. However, the PLA's policy preferences are rarely contrary to those advocated by other actors or to existing PRC policy. The Chinese military appears to follow rather than lead policy, at least in this area. A possible exception is when the Chinese leadership pursues a "two-handed strategy," using the PLA to implement the hard hand and other Chinese departments to offer inducements that constitute the soft hand. Such a strategy was apparent, for example, when Jiang Zemin adopted a conciliatory policy while allowing the PLA to build capabilities in support of a military option against Taiwan.

The military's use of exercises has been in lock step with the central government's approach toward Taiwan—conciliatory when Beijing emphasized peaceful development of cross-Strait relations from 2006 to 2012, and intimidating when Beijing stepped up pressure on Taipei to open political talks starting in

2013. The only evidence of pressure for a harsher policy toward Taiwan (or toward the U.S. for selling arms to Taiwan) is occasional nationalistic rhetoric from PLA media figures. Such opinions likely represent the views of individuals, although they may sometimes be endorsed at higher levels of the military. The sanctioning of prominent PLA figures who step out of line, as Luo Yuan did in 2009, suggests that central authorities have set predetermined boundaries on policy debate and the ability of the PLA to change them is limited.

It is not clear that PLA influence on Taiwan policy is on the rise. In fact, the opposite may be true. The role and influence of the PLA have increased significantly in times of crisis or conflict such as the 1999 bombing of the Chinese embassy in Belgrade and the 2001 collision of a Chinese fighter with a U.S. reconnaissance plane.[90] Therefore it is reasonable to speculate that the PLA's influence on policy toward Taiwan was greater during the mid-1990s and the mid-2000s when cross-Strait tensions were high. As cross-Strait relations have improved in recent years, PLA influence may have diminished somewhat. The PLA has found new ways to exert its influence on policy, making goodwill gestures and participating in cross-Strait interactions and exchanges, even as it continues to build military capabilities that could be used against Taiwan. At the same time, there is some evidence that PLA influence on policy toward U.S. arms sales to Taiwan is increasing as the military insists on having a greater say in formulating Beijing's response.

Looking ahead, a negative change in cross-Strait relations could prompt a sudden spike in PLA influence on policymaking toward Taiwan. The election of a DPP president in 2016 who rejects the current understanding between the KMT and the CCP that there is only one China could be one such scenario. One major explanation for PLA advocacy of a tougher posture toward Taiwan in the mid-1990s is that PLA officers grew frustrated with Beijing's Taiwan policy. If Taiwan were to resume steps aimed at achieving de jure independence, repudiate the 1992 consensus on "one China," and dismantle many of the gains achieved by Ma Ying-jeou, it is likely that China's conciliatory policy toward Taiwan would be reexamined and adjusted. The PLA could be expected to play a significant role in this process. As an instrument of policy, the PLA could be called on to once again mobilize large demonstrations of force. In such circumstances, the PLA would likely use the various means described in this chapter to promote its preferences, but it nevertheless can be expected to continue to adhere to the directives of the CCP. The party is likely to remain in command of the gun, in accordance with Mao's dictum.

Notes

The author is deeply grateful to Mei Shanshan, Jackson Nichols, and Thomas Vien for their research assistance in the preparation of this chapter.

1. Noted in Linda Jakobson and Dean Knox, *New Foreign Policy Actors in China*, SIPRI Policy Paper 26 (Stockholm: SIPRI, September 2010), 13.

2. Michael D. Swaine, *The Role of the Chinese Military in National Security Policymaking* (Santa Monica, CA: RAND, 1996), 52.

3. Michael D. Swaine, "Chinese Decision-Making Regarding Taiwan, 1979–2000," in *The Making of Chinese Foreign and Security Policy in the Era of Reform,* ed. David M. Lampton (Stanford, CA: Stanford University Press, 2001), 294.

4. Tai Ming Cheung, "The Influence of the Gun: China's Central Military Commission and Its Relationship with the Military, Party, and State Decision-Making Systems," in *The Making of Chinese Foreign and Security Policy in the Era of Reform*, 67.

5. Ibid., 76.

6. Author interviews in Beijing, July 2003.

7. One of the PLA representatives is usually the relatively low-ranking deputy chief of the General Staff in charge of intelligence.

8. A bridge leader heads a major functional coordination point or gateway (*kou*) between the PBSC and various relevant subordinate organs, coordinating relations between the various parts of the bureaucracy and the top elite. See Kenneth G. Lieberthal, *Governing China* (New York: W.W. Norton, 1995), 188.

9. For one list of the current membership of the TALSG, see http://blog.sina.com.cn/s/blog_4efe65c30102e09i.html. Some sources claim that the PLA has sometimes had only one representative on the TALSG. See, e.g., Jakobson and Knox, *New Foreign Policy Actors in China*, 13; and Guo Ruihua [郭瑞華], *A Study on the Taiwan Affairs Mechanism of the CPC: "Process of Government" Perspective* [中共對台工作機制研究：政府過程的觀點] (PhD dissertation, National Chengchi University, submitted July 2009), http://nccur.lib.nccu.edu.tw/bitstream/140.119/38528/1/60506101.pdf. However, an authoritative source confirmed that as of 2011 the TALSG had two PLA representatives. See Alice Miller's chapter in this volume, Note 12.

10. Alice Miller, "The CCP Central Committee's Leading Small Groups," *China Leadership Monitor*, no. 26 (Fall 2008).

11. Ibid. It is possible that NSLSG responsibilities were transferred to the National Security Commission when that institution was created in November 2013.

12. Peng Mei and Meng Weigang [彭美, 孟卫刚], "Appearances and Remarks of the Nine Standing Committee Members of the Political Bureau during the Two Sessions Demonstrate Their Concern for Social Management, Innovation" [政治局九常委两会足迹 发言关注社会管理创新], *Southern Metropolis Daily* [南方都市报], March 13, 2011.

13. Xu Xiaoqing and Shi Baoyin [许晓青, 史宝银], "Generals Say before National People's Congress: Opposing and Restraining 'Independence' is Nonnegotiable" [人

民大会堂前将军发话: 反"独"制"独"没商量], *China News Service* [中新社], March 5, 2006.

14. "Main Functions," Taiwan Affairs Office of the State Council PRC, www.gwytb.gov.cn/en/Introduction/MainFunctions/201103/t20110316_1789194.htm.

15. The board consists of 173 directors and its members were posted on the Taiwan Affairs Office website. See also Wang Jue and Ge Chong [王珏, 葛沖], "The New ARATS Board of Directors Clearly Shows That It Will Tackle Economic Issues before Political Ones" [海協新理事會突顯先經後政], *Wen Wei Po* [文匯報], June 4, 2008.

16. Cheung, "The Influence of the Gun," 79.

17. Swaine, *The Role of the Chinese Military in National Security Policymaking,* 64.

18. Bates Gill and James Mulvenon, "Chinese Military-Related Think Tanks and Research Institutions," *China Quarterly*, no. 171 (September 2002): 617–624.

19. Cheung, "The Influence of the Gun," 81.

20. Dennis Blasko, *The Chinese Army Today: Tradition and Transformation for the 21st Century* (New York: Routledge, 2006), 30.

21. Gill and Mulvenon, "Chinese Military-Related Think Tanks and Research Institutions."

22. Blasko, *The Chinese Army Today,* 31.

23. Gill and Mulvenon, "Chinese Military-Related Think Tanks and Research Institutions."

24. Evan Medeiros, "'Minding the Gap': Assessing the Trajectory of the PLA's Second Artillery," in *Right Sizing the People's Liberation Army: Exploring the Contours of China's Military*, eds. Roy Kamphausen and Andrew Scobell (Carlisle Barracks, PA: U.S. Army War College, 2007), 147.

25. Nan Li, "PLA Conservative Nationalism," in *The People's Liberation Army and China in Transition*, ed. Stephen J. Flanagan and Michael E. Marti (Washington, D.C.: National Defense University Press, 2003), 73.

26. Cheung, "The Influence of the Gun," 82.

27. Gill and Mulvenon, "Chinese Military-Related Think Tanks and Research Institutions."

28. Phillip C. Saunders and Eric Quam, "Future Force Structure of the Chinese Air Force," in *Right Sizing the People's Liberation Army*, 380.

29. Ibid., 405.

30. Nan Li and Christopher Weuve, "China's Aircraft Carrier Ambitions: An Update," *Naval War College Review* 63, no. 1 (Winter 2010): 17.

31. Cheung, "The Influence of the Gun," 77.

32. Jing Huang and Xiaoting Li, *Inseparable Separation: The Making of China's Taiwan Policy* (Singapore: World Scientific Publishing, 2010), 399.

33. Ibid.

34. Ibid., 192. Jiang's tough stance in 1995–1996 ultimately won him respect and support from within the PLA. Ibid., 399.

35. Ibid., 252.

36. Bonnie Glaser, "Military Confidence-Building Measures: Averting Accidents and Building Trust in the Taiwan Strait," *American Foreign Policy Interest* 27 (2005): 91–104.

37. The author is indebted to Dennis Blasko for the argumentation in the following two paragraphs. See "PLA Ground Force Modernization and Mission Diversification: Underway in All Military Regions," in *Right Sizing The People's Liberation Army*; and "PLA Ground Force Modernization Underway in All Military Regions, Preparing for a Variety of Missions," *Asia Policy*, no. 4 (July 2007): 78–83.

38. Ni Eryan [妮爾硯], "Proactively and Immediately Establish Military Mutual Trust across the Taiwan Strait" [主動及時建立兩岸軍事互信], *Wen Wei Po* [文匯報], May 19, 2009.

39. Dennis Blasko, "Clarity of Intentions: PLA Trans-Regional Exercises since 2006" (unpublished paper, October 2011).

40. Author's italics. "PLA Forces for 'Mission Action—2013A' Launch Long-range Three-dimensional Projection," Ministry of National Defense of the People's Republic of China, September 16, 2013.

41. Andrew Erickson and Phillip Saunders, "Selective Transparency: How the PLA Uses Development, Testing, Deployment, and Exercises as Shaping and Signaling Tools" (unpublished paper, December 2013).

42. "PLA Launches Final Phase of Its Mission Action 2013 Exercise," *Want China Times*, October 6, 2013.

43. Ben Blanchard and James Pomfret, "China's Xi Says Political Solution for Taiwan Can't Wait Forever," Reuters, October 6, 2013.

44. Erickson and Saunders, "Selective Transparency."

45. "Chinese Military Becomes More Transparent with Regular News Briefings," Xinhua, April 28, 2011.

46. "Mainland Will Agree to Cross-Strait Military Security Talks: Defense Spokesman," Xinhua, July 30, 2010.

47. Hu Jintao's six points were presented in a speech on December 31, 2009. One of the points was a call for a dialogue to consider a mechanism to enhance mutual military trust. Xinhua, "Hu Jintao: Work Together to Promote the Peaceful Development of Cross-Strait Relations to Achieve the Great Rejuvenation of the Chinese Nation" [胡锦涛: 携手推动两岸关系和平发展 同心实现中华民族伟大复兴], December 31, 2008.

48. "Foreign Ministry Spokesperson Ma Zhaoxu's Enunciation of China's Solemn Position on the US Government's Announcement of Arms Sales to Taiwan," Ministry of Foreign Affairs of the People's Republic of China, September 21, 2011.

49. "Ministry of Defense Spokesman Geng Yansheng Makes Clear China's Solemn Stance on Announced US Arms Sale to Taiwan," Xinhua, September 22, 2011.

50. "Vice Foreign Minister He Yafei Lodges Solemn Representations with US Ambassador in China over US Announcement of Arms Sales to Taiwan," Xinhua, January 30, 2010.

51. "Defense Ministry Spokesman Comments on US Weapons Sale to Taiwan," Xinhua, January 30, 2010.

52. "Foreign Ministry Spokesman Liu Jianchao Issues Statement on US Government Notifying Congress of Decision to Sell Weapons to Taiwan," Xinhua, October 4, 2008.

53. "Defense Ministry Spokesman Comments on US Government's Notification to Congress of Decision to Sell Weapons to Taiwan," Xinhua, October 4, 2008.

54. Joint Press Conference with Adm. Mullen and Gen. Chen from the Pentagon, May 18, 2011, www.jcs.mil/speech.aspx?ID=1597.

55. Interview with Chen Zhou, *Guangming ribao Online*, April 15, 2011.

56. "China's National Defense in 2004," Information Office of the State Council of the People's Republic of China, December 2004.

57. Policymakers also worried that a unification law could be used to stir up resentment against the mainland on Taiwan and in the international community. See Huang and Li, *Inseparable Separation*, 274–275.

58. "China's National Defense in 2010," Information Office of the State Council of the People's Republic of China, March 31, 2011.

59. See, for example, Luo Yuan [罗援], "Chance to Establish Cross-Strait Military Security Mutual Confidence-Building System Should Not Be Missed" [两岸建立军事安全互信机不可失], *International Pioneer Guide* [国际先驱导报], January 5, 2009.

60. "China's National Defense in 2010."

61. "Taiwan Affairs Office Issues Statement on Current Cross-Straits Relations," Embassy of the People's Republic of China in the United States of America, May 17, 2004.

62. Author interviews in Beijing, August 2004.

63. "Taiwan Affairs Office Deputy Director Wang Zaixu: Taiwan Independence Would Make It All But Impossible to Avoid War" [国台办副主任王在希：台独就是战争武力恐难避免], *Xinhua Net* [新华网], November 18, 2003.

64. Ibid.; Xing Zhigang, "Beijing: Chen Shui-bian May Cause Straits Conflict," *China Daily*, July 30, 2004.

65. Luo, "Chance to Establish Cross-Strait Military Security Mutual Confidence-Building System Should Not Be Missed."

66. Wang Ping, Liu Hsiao-tan, and Huang Cheng [王平, 劉曉丹, 黃政], "Luo Yuan: Cross-Strait Military Mutual Trust Needs to Analyze and Solve Three Mysterious Ideas" [羅援: 兩岸軍事互信 須破三大謎思], *China Commentary News Service* [中國評論通訊社], August 12, 2009.

67. Jacobson and Knox, "New Foreign Policy Actors in China," 14.

68. Huang Hai and Yang Liu [黄海， 杨柳], "PLA Officers on War to Counter Taiwan Independence: Six Prices; War Criminals Cannot Escape Punishment" [解放军军官谈反台独战争：六条代价 战犯必惩], *People's Daily Online* [人民网], December 3, 2003.

69. Ibid.

70. "Luo Yuan: "The Ball Is in Taiwan's Court on Cross-Strait Military Exchanges," *China Times*, March 7, 2012.

71. Dong Ruifeng [董瑞丰], "Outlook for Sino-U.S. Military Relations before the 'Hu-Obama Meeting'" ['胡奥会'前展望中美军事关系], *Outlook* [瞭望] (January 17, 2011), no. 3: 25–27.

72. Minnie Chan, "PLA Admiral Tones Down Hawkish Rhetoric," *South China Morning Post*, February 25, 2011.

73. Tao Shelan [陶社兰], "PLA Rear Admiral Says U.S. Arms Sales to Taiwan 'Will Harm Others without Benefiting Itself'" [解放军少将: 美对台军售完全是'损人不利己'], *China News Service Online* [中国新闻网], January 6, 2010.

74. Lin Jian [林间], "Major General Luo Yuan: Make the U.S. Feel Some Pain over Arms Sale to Taiwan" [罗援少将: 中国反制美对台军售出手要打美痛处], *International Pioneer Guide* [国际先驱导报], January 18, 2009.

75. "Scholar: If the U.S. Begins Arms Sales to Taiwan, China Will Suspend Military-to-Military Dialogue" [学者:美若开启对台军售 中国将暂停两军对话], *Global Times* [环球时报], January 4, 2010.

76. Kathrin Hille, "China Hits at US over Taiwan Arms Deal," *Financial Times*, September 22, 2011.

77. Transcript of PRC State Council TAO news conference, Taiwan Affairs Office, November 25, 2009.

78. Ed Zhang, "General Luo Yuan: The Cool-Headed Hardliner," *South China Morning Post*, March 22, 2011.

79. Robert Marquand, "Would China Invade Taiwan? Retired Chinese Generals Have Urged Military Action Well ahead of 2008 Olympics," *Christian Science Monitor*, July 22, 2004. Additionally, in April 2004 an essay purportedly written by PLAAF General Liu Yazhou caused a sensation by quoting Jiang Zemin to the effect that "there will certainly be a war in the Taiwan Strait." See James Mulvenon, "Anticipation Is Making Me Wait: The 'Inevitability of War' and Deadlines in Cross-Strait Relations," *China Leadership Monitor*, no. 12 (Fall 2004).

80. Xing Ban [荆伴], "Taiwan Issue Will Probably Be Resolved by 2020" [2020年前或解决台問題], *Wen Wei Po* [文匯報], July 15, 2004.

81. "'60 Years Across the Taiwan Strait' Conference Concluded Saturday, Nov. 14," Kuomintang News Network, November 16, 2009.

82. "Near and Yet So Far," *South China Morning Post*, December 2, 2009.

83. Ch'i Le-yi and Yang Fen-ying [亓樂義, 楊芬瑩], "PLA Retired Major General Pan Zhenqiang Says Members of Pan-Green Camp More Rational Than He Imagined" [解放軍退役少將潘振強: 綠營人士比想像中理性], *China Times* [中國時報], March 18, 2010.

84. Liu Chang and Zhao Bo [刘畅, 赵博], "Taiwan Affairs Office: China Agrees the Two Sides of the Strait Should Discuss Establishing a Military and Security Mutual Trust Mechanism at an Appropriate Time" [国台办: 赞成两岸适时探讨军事安全互信机制], Xinhua [新华], March 18, 2010.

85. See, for example, Gen. Chen Bingde's remarks to Venezuelan Defense Minister Carlos José Mata Figueroa expressing China's appreciation for Venezuela's adherence to the one-China policy and its support on issues related to Taiwan and Tibet. "Venezuela, China Vow to Boost Military Ties," Xinhua, November 17, 2010.

86. "China, Russia to Conduct First Joint Military Exercise Next Year," *People's Daily Online* [人民网], December 14, 2004.

87. Ibid.

88. Live News conference by TAO spokesman Li Weiyi, CCTV-4, December 15, 2004.

89. Gady Epstein, "Hu's China, Whose Army?" *Forbes*, January 12, 2011.

90. Michael D. Swaine, "Chinese Crisis Management: Framework for Analysis, Tentative Observations, and Questions for the Future," in *Chinese National Security Decisionmaking under Stress*, eds. Andrew Scobell and Larry M. Wortzel (Carlisle Barracks, PA: U.S. Army War College, 2005), 5–53.

7 The PLA Role in China's DPRK Policy

Andrew Scobell

Introduction

No country has posed a greater challenge for China's foreign policy in the twenty-first century than North Korea. Policies toward the United States and Taiwan have each proven major tests for China, but neither has posed the sustained policy challenge to the same extent as North Korea. The Democratic People's Republic of Korea (DPRK) has proved to be a near constant headache for the People's Republic of China (PRC) since the early 1990s.[1] Unlike cross-Strait relations, which have ameliorated appreciably since 2008, and relations with the United States, which have tended to fluctuate considerably over time, the Pyongyang problem has not abated and appears to be chronic. Beijing's truculent neighbor has conducted nuclear tests (October 2006, May 2009, and February 2012) and missile launches (notably July 2006, July 2009, April 12, 2012, and May 2013). Moreover there have been numerous other provocations, most notably the torpedoing of the *Cheonan* (March 2010) and the shelling of Yeonpyeong Island (November 2010). There has been no respite for China where the DPRK is concerned.

North Korea policy represents an ongoing daunting and sensitive security challenge for China. What are the key characteristics of China's DPRK policy and how does the People's Liberation Army (PLA) influence it? While scholars and analysts have given considerable attention to China's policy toward North Korea, details of and insights into the making of China's policy toward North Korea have proven elusive. While the PLA is believed to have significant influence on and noteworthy involvement in China's relationship with its troublesome neighbor, no clear picture has emerged of the military's role or its mode of influence in the North Korean policy process.[2]

During the Hu Jintao era, the most senior leader with formal responsibility for DPRK policy was Dai Bingguo—a state councilor with extensive diplomatic experience. He had held posts in the International Department of the Chinese Communist Party Central Committee and the Ministry of Foreign Affairs (MFA). Under the leadership of PRC President and CCP General Secretary Xi Jinping, primary responsibility for North Korea appears to have been split between Vice President Li Yuanchao and State Councilor and former Foreign Minister Yang Jiechi.

Both the Central Committee's International Department and State Council's MFA have been key organs in dealing with DPRK policy. The former has been particularly important as the main interlocutor since traditionally the key relationship has been party-to-party (i.e., ties between the CCP and the Korean Workers' Party). Nevertheless, during the past decade the MFA has emerged as an increasingly important player on DPRK policy with two roles: first as the primary instigator and official host organ of the Six Party Talks, and second as the main mechanism for interaction with the United States on Korea matters (see below).

On the surface, the PLA would appear to be a key and influential player in China's North Korea policy. The PRC's only formal alliance is with the DPRK—by the Treaty of Friendship, Co-operation and Mutual Assistance between the People's Republic of China and the Democratic People's Republic of Korea signed in July 1961. The document commits each country to come to the aid of the other if attacked.[3] However, there does not appear to be any real defense coordination mechanism nor do the terms of the treaty ever seem to have been invoked. Moreover, Chinese leaders have on multiple occasions stated publicly and privately that China will not come to Pyongyang's rescue if the Kim regime gets itself into trouble. Thus, the security relationship is perhaps best viewed as a "virtual alliance" with considerable ambiguity as to if and when it might be invoked by Beijing.[4] This alliance was sealed in blood during the 1950s when the Chinese People's Volunteers fought side by side with the Korean People's Army (KPA). Hundreds of thousands of Chinese soldiers gave their lives in the conflict and Chinese troops remained in North Korea until 1958.[5]

Despite this history of comradeship-in-arms, in the twenty-first century the KPA and the PLA act like allies at arm's length. That is, there is limited interaction and cooperation combined with a significant amount of mutual suspicion and aloofness. There is a military-to-military relationship but it appears to be extremely modest. The manifestations of the relationship are largely ceremonial and superficial exchanges of high-level delegations and a small number of KPA officers attending selected PLA professional military education institutions. However, there do not appear to be any military field or command post exercises between the militaries of the kind one might expect between real or even nominal allies.[6] The most routinized and on-going series of bilateral or multilateral field exercises that the PLA conducts are under the auspices of the Shanghai Cooperation Organization with armed forces of member states.[7] By contrast, China's security relationship with North Korea seems dormant.

Assumptions and Propositions in Analyzing China's North Korea Policy

This chapter makes a number of key assumptions that should be articulated at the outset:

1. *Severe inertia afflicts China's policy toward the DPRK.* This inertia is the product of intense risk aversion because Beijing deems the situation to be extremely delicate with policy alterations likely to be severely destabilizing. North Korea's geographic location on China's doorstep presents a serious proximate potential threat to China's political and economic heartland. Moreover, the United States is directly involved as the ally of the Republic of Korea with a military presence on the peninsula and as a long-time staunch critic of Pyongyang's nuclear and missile programs (see assumption #2).[8]

2. *Beijing's DPRK policy is as much about Washington as it is about Pyongyang.* The involvement of the United States raises the stakes for and threat to China. The United States poses an even bigger threat to China than North Korea—militarily and otherwise— going far beyond the geographical bounds of the Korean Peninsula or Northeast China. The stakes are also higher for Beijing—not just the danger of instability or war on China's doorstep but the specter of a wider conflict involving the United States and possibly other countries. Hence, a volatile situation in Korea is much more alarming to Beijing than a cursory analysis would suggest. Despite

this, while the United States is more problematic than North Korea in many ways, Beijing perceives Washington as more malleable than Pyongyang.[9]

3. *The PLA has difficulty exerting major influence on China's DPRK policy.* The PLA has a substantial interest in DPRK policy and holds strong views on the subject but does not seem able to articulate a single formal military position. This is somewhat surprising since the PLA is considered an influential bureaucratic actor in Chinese politics especially on matters central to national security. Moreover, no other issue, save Taiwan, figures so emotionally or prominently for China's military as Korea. The PLA has serious "history" where North Korea is concerned. Some latter-day military leaders firmly believe that the current situation on the Korean Peninsula represents unfinished Chinese business.[10] Emotionally, Chinese soldiers of the twenty-first century feel that the blood and sacrifice of an earlier generation of Chinese fighting men should not have been in vain.[11] The honor and reputation of China's armed forces are on the line. Nevertheless, while Chinese soldiers have strong views and bear the primary responsibility for defending China's security interests on the Korean Peninsula in the event of a contingency, the PLA finds it difficult to influence process and outcome on DPRK policy.

These assumptions prompt the following propositions. *First of all,* there is elite consensus on the top priority of maintaining the status quo because change is deemed likely to be destabilizing and hence dangerous. Thus, Beijing will only launch a new policy initiative in response to a crisis. *Second,* it is essential not to focus narrowly on Beijing's policy toward Pyongyang, but also on the wider context of Beijing's relationship with Washington. Thus, China tends to concentrate its efforts as much if not more on influencing the United States rather than on the DPRK. *Third,* the military's degree of influence is very difficult to gauge, with clear impact on policy hard to discern. Moreover, since there is widespread consensus among civilian and military bureaucracies in Beijing on the priority of sustaining the status quo in Korea, there is little need for the PLA to influence Chinese policy. However, if the PLA does exert influence, it will be extremely challenging to detect unless it is evident in observable shifts in military operations and changes in public rhetoric.

Great Debates, Little Impact, Big Worry

Since the mid-2000s, a lively debate has emerged in China over North Korea policy. Various schools of thought have been identified among Chinese foreign policy analysts.[12] "Realpolitikers" have emerged to challenge the traditional "geostrategists." The former have reportedly questioned the value and utility of China's long-standing quasi-alliance relationship with North Korea. Should Beijing support Pyongyang at all costs because of its geostrategic location at the gateway to China's heartland? The latter still believe that North Korea is a valuable buffer client state keeping South Korea and its ally, the United States, at arm's length. The PLA is believed to be firmly planted in the geostrategist camp.[13] According to General Wang Haidong of the PLA's China Institute for International Strategic Studies, although North Korea's value to Chinese security in 2013 is "very different from what it was during the Korean War," the country continues to have "special importance to China's national security . . . as a strategic buffer."[14]

However, in the final analysis these different schools may not really matter much. First of all, while the differences of opinion appear real, they are held by people one step removed from the decisionmakers themselves. Second, the decisionmakers are in fundamental agreement that the highest priority is maintaining the status quo with the result being policy inertia (as noted above). In the aftermath of the Sunnylands summit in June 2013 between PRC President Xi Jinping and U.S. President Barak Obama, it was widely reported—including by State Councilor Yang Jiechi—both leaders had agreed that denuclearization was the top priority where North Korea was concerned. While official Chinese media have played this up, the reality was that in late 2013 and late 2014 peace and stability continued to be Beijing's foremost priority.[15]

China is most fearful of the prospect of chaos on the Korean Peninsula. Near-term fears about upheaval in North Korea trump Beijing's concerns about a nuclear armed Pyongyang and the possibility of a unified Korea under Seoul's auspices. China has more influence on North Korea than any other country. But this influence is "potential" in the sense that Beijing is extremely unlikely to activate it. This is because China fears that applying pressure to North Korea will either result in Pyongyang distancing itself from Beijing (and hence China will have no influence) or that Chinese pressure tactics will backfire and only make matters worse.[16]

Although China's leaders are not necessarily unreceptive to new thinking on Korea, at the end of the day they remain preoccupied with maintaining stability (internal and external) and focused on promoting their country's great power status. Like a variety of foreign policy issues in recent years, North Korea threatens to besmirch China's prestige. China wants to be viewed as a responsible power and a force for good in the world. But Pyongyang is not akin to Khartoum in Beijing's eyes. After all, North Korea is not a far off Third World state like Sudan. Rather, it is a radioactive Darfur on the doorstep—a humanitarian disaster which is the subject of enormous international attention with a repressive, distasteful dictatorship made all the more complicated because North Korea is a hyper-militarized state armed with ballistic missiles and weapons of mass destruction. Instability immediately across the Yalu directly threatens domestic stability in China's heartland if only due to the potential for many hundreds of thousands of refugees to flood into Manchuria. Beijing is therefore ultrasensitive to any hint of turmoil on the Korean Peninsula.[17]

Case Studies

This chapter examines two case studies of crisis in China's twenty-first century DPRK policy. The first episode is the so-called second nuclear crisis of 2002–2003; the second is the *Cheonan* crisis of 2010. Both crises involved China, the DPRK, the United States, and the ROK, with other states playing supporting roles. The narrative of each case study, from Beijing's perspective, is the story of how China prevented the United States from taking military action against the DPRK. In the former case Beijing's policy decision was to bring the United States (and DPRK) to the negotiating table. In the latter case the policy decision was to divert the ire of the United States (and ROK) away from Pyongyang and toward Beijing. In first instance the PLA seemed to have little discernible role, while in the second instance its role was more obvious and high profile.

The Second Nuclear Crisis (2002–2003)

The second nuclear crisis emerged when the United States reported that North Korea had informed U.S. Assistant Secretary of State James Kelly during an October 2002 visit to Pyongyang that the country possessed a highly enriched uranium (HEU) program. This news, which jolted the world, was followed in

January 2003 by a North Korean declaration that it was withdrawing from the Nuclear Nonproliferation Treaty (NPT).

As tensions rose on the peninsula in early 2003, China worried about the fallout. The United States was making somber statements and appeared to be preparing for war with Iraq. The Bush administration went to the United Nations and made the case to the world that Baghdad was developing weapons of mass destruction (WMD). Washington's "axis of evil" rhetoric—which lumped together Iran, Iraq, and North Korea as three countries deemed hostile to the United States and in the process of acquiring dangerous armaments—raised alarm bells in Beijing. President George W. Bush was on record expressing visceral dislike for North Korea's dictator and suggesting that his administration would take a very proactive approach toward dealing with regimes acquiring WMD "to terrorize nations." Bush insisted, during a November 26, 2001, press conference, that the United States would hold such regimes "accountable." Bush also issued a cryptic warning: "Afghanistan is just the beginning."[18]

As U.S. and coalition forces mobilized, China became increasingly fearful that the United States might be targeting another country for "regime change." After remarkably swift initial battlefield successes in Afghanistan in late 2001 and the dramatic toppling of the Saddam Hussein regime in spring of 2003, Beijing was reeling from the "shock and awe" of high-tech U.S. power projection. Increasingly Chinese leaders worried about how to prevent a U.S. military strike against North Korea. Moreover, Beijing feared that a Bush administration intoxicated by a string of recent victories would pursue nothing short of the end of North Korea. According to an unnamed Chinese official interviewed by Mike Chinoy:

> By early 2003, the situation was very dangerous. My impression was that the Bush administration was so emotional. Many of its policies were not rational. Bush said, 'All options are on the table.' China did not see this statement as an idle threat. Also, we hated to see North Koreans withdraw from the Non-Proliferation Treaty and restart the reactor. Only when China realized the dangers of confrontation, even military confrontation, did China change its low-key manner.[19]

According to multiple analysts interviewed in Beijing in September 2003, fear of what the Bush administration might do was the key motivator pushing Beijing toward a more proactive DPRK policy.[20] Chinese fears of the potential for instability on the peninsula were especially heightened because of the leadership transition underway from the third to the fourth generations during 2002–2003. The powerful desire for a smooth succession from Jiang Zemin to Hu Jintao prompted Beijing to step outside its traditional comfort zone.[21]

Then the Bush administration offered China an opening. During a February 2003 visit to Beijing, Secretary of State Colin Powell suggested that China initiate multilateral talks on North Korea. Two weeks later in New York, Powell held follow-on talks with Chinese Foreign Minister Tang Jiaxuan and pushed more vigorously for a Chinese diplomatic initiative on North Korea, implying it was the only hope for averting an escalating crisis. Around the same time a similar idea was gaining traction in Beijing. Reluctance to taking an activist role was replaced by a growing sense that if China wanted to avoid a showdown in Korea it had no choice but to step up and launch a full-fledged diplomatic initiative.[22]

The policy solution was to bring the United States and North Korea to the negotiating table. This required two separate full-court presses: one in Pyongyang and the other in Washington. For Pyongyang the effort was combination of carrots and sticks. Beijing promised rewards but also hinted at strong-arm tactics. PRC Vice-Premier Qian Qichen visited Pyongyang in early March, exhorting North Korea to come to the negotiating table. But there were also subtle messages like the temporary shutoff of an oil pipeline for a few days in mid-February. China never explicitly stated that the short halt was intended as blackmail but North Korea seemed to take the hint. Moreover, the step was somehow reported and publicized abroad. The result was a perception that Beijing had finally gotten tough with Pyongyang—a very appealing interpretation in Washington, Tokyo, and Seoul. This was most helpful when China was trying to get representatives from all these countries to sit down with North Korea for multilateral talks.[23] It was particularly important because the Bush administration refused to show up for one-on-one talks with Pyongyang, insisting on multiple parties being seated at the table.

This complicated and involved diplomatic initiative was unprecedented in the annals of Chinese diplomatic history. The only comparable move Beijing had taken in the modern era was in Central Asia two years earlier with the founding of the Shanghai Cooperation Organization (SCO). Although the SCO was a Chinese creation, it evolved gradually out of a decade-long series of confidence-building measures among countries that had little animosity toward each other. By contrast, in putting together the Six Party Talks, China was coaxing and cajoling different countries with histories of conflict and deep-rooted mutual distrust and suspicion.[24]

China initially arranged three-party talks involving representatives of North Korea, the United States, and China in Beijing in April 2003. These ultimately led to a first round of the Six Party Talks in August 2003, which added Japan, Russia, and South Korea.

The PLA's Role   The PLA appeared to play only supporting roles in this case. The first role was to reassure and restrain the Korean People's Army. PLA General Xu Caihou, director of the General Political Department (and vice-chair of the Central Military Commission), led a high-level delegation to Pyongyang from August 18 until August 22. This visit, which received considerable visibility in the North Korean media, came five days before the start of the first round of the Six Party Talks.

The second role was to strengthen frontier security and reassure Chinese leaders that the frontier with North Korea was stable and border secure. In mid-2003, the PLA redeployed troops near the border with North Korea. An MFA spokesman insisted that the move was a "normal adjustment carried out after years of preparation." Hong Kong newspapers claimed the troop movements involved as many as 150,000 soldiers and were a signal by Beijing directed at Pyongyang to express displeasure. More likely boosting border security was intended to ameliorate a deteriorating law-and-order situation along the frontier. Similar troop adjustments were made around the same time on China's frontier with Burma.[25]

The Cheonan Crisis (2010)

A second test of China's DPRK policy was the mysterious sinking of the Republic of Korea Navy corvette *Cheonan* on March 26, 2010. Beijing initially appeared to view the tragedy as a minor irritant as it launched an initiative to restart the dormant Six Party Talks. A central element was welcoming Kim Jong-il on an unofficial visit to China on April 20. Aside from being yet another attempt to convince the North Korean leader about the merits of Chinese-style economic reform, the visit signaled that Beijing was making a serious effort to restart multilateral talks. When, on May 20, 2010, an international team of investigators issued a report that concluded the explosion—which split the ROK naval vessel in two and sank it—was caused by a North Korean torpedo, the episode went from mere irritant to major impediment.

Pyongyang vehemently denied any involvement and the situation threatened to derail completely Beijing's initiative to restart the Six Party Talks.

China's muted response to the apparent North Korean provocation angered South Korea. Seoul was irate at what it viewed as Beijing's coddling of Pyongyang. China refused to condemn or criticize North Korea publicly. This included successfully pushing to exclude any mention of Pyongyang in the United Nations Security Council's statement of July 9, 2010, which condemned the sinking of the South Korean naval vessel.

Beijing was slow to respond with a message of condolence to Seoul, as one Chinese scholar noted.[26] Moreover, China did not express any interest in joining the international team of experts from Australia, Sweden, South Korea, the United Kingdom, and the United States assembled to investigate the tragedy announced on April 8, 2010 (of course, it should be noted that China was not explicitly invited to join). While Russia accepted South Korea's invitation to come and independently review the evidence (and sent a 4-person team to Seoul which arrived on May 21), China demurred.[27]

Beijing tried to downplay the incident and its policy focus was on how to manage the reactions of Washington and Seoul. China had been extremely cautious and almost aloof. Beijing was very concerned that the United States and the Republic of Korea would retaliate against the DPRK militarily. If this happened, China feared it could easily provoke a harsh reaction from North Korea and hostilities could very quickly spiral out of control. Indeed, following the Yeonpyeong Island incident on November 23, 2010, when North Korea shelled South Korean civilian and military targets on the island, killing four and wounding sixteen, Beijing feared that war might be imminent on the peninsula. Both the ROK and the DPRK put their armed forces on high alert. Dai Bingguo made a sudden visit to Seoul on November 27, 2010, on the heels of postponing a PRC-ROK foreign ministerial meeting in protest over U.S.-South Korean exercises in the Yellow Sea.[28]

Beijing was well aware that Pyongyang was in the throes of preparations for leadership succession. In this delicate period an ailing Kim Jong-il made arrangements for his twenty-something son, Kim Jong-un, to assume formally the position of his designated successor. Since the younger Kim lacked political experience and was virtually unknown to most North Koreans, his emergence into the spotlight required careful stage management.

The policy solution that emerged in Beijing was to deflect the focus away from the DPRK and toward China. The decision was less a deliberate and carefully chosen course of action and more of a case of unhappy coincidences. The fallout from the *Cheonan* tragedy coincided with a rise in tensions with the United States over the South China Sea and other issues. After an initial honeymoon period between Beijing and the Barack Obama administration, tensions rose in late 2009 and early 2010.

In the first decade of the twenty-first century, although by no means absent from Asia, the United States had a somewhat lower profile in parts of the region because Washington's attention during the Bush administration was so focused on the War on Terror. Moreover, during Obama's first year in office, the United States seemed low-keyed and accommodating to China's interests. As a result some Chinese and other Asians detected a decline or draw-down in American commitment to the region. Beijing in particular may have been surprised by vigorous Asian activism on the part of the Obama administration in 2010.

In a January 12, 2010, address at the East-West Center in Honolulu, Secretary of State Hillary Clinton underscored the strong and enduring U.S. links to Asia. America's chief diplomat then stated: "So I don't think there is any doubt, if there were when this Administration began, that the United States is back in Asia. But I want to underscore that we are back to stay."[29] Beijing appeared to be caught off guard by Washington reasserting itself in Asia. Beijing was particularly irate at Secretary Clinton's remarks at the Association of Southeast Asian Nations (ASEAN) Regional Forum in Hanoi on July 23, 2010, when she articulated an abiding U.S. interest in the South China Sea.

Beijing interpreted this as part of a forceful U.S. "return to Asia" after the United States had seemed to be decreasing its involvement in Southeast Asia and downgrading its commitments in the region during the George W. Bush administration and continuing into the first year of the Barack Obama administration. Indeed, the new administration was perceived in Beijing as being more deferential to China's "core interests" and appeared to be on a path toward conceding a good portion of East Asia to a Chinese sphere of influence. Whatever China's perceptions, the United States had certainly adopted a lower profile in Southeast Asia while it was preoccupied with waging wars in Afghanistan and Iraq. China's response was outrage at what was viewed as overbearing and provocative U.S. military and diplomatic actions.[30]

After a Korean official announced that the United States and South Korea would hold a naval exercise in the Yellow Sea in late July, Chinese protests were loud and shrill. Originally scheduled for early June but postponed in the aftermath of the *Cheonan* incident, the exercises were said to include an aircraft carrier, the USS *George Washington*, and an assortment of other ships and aircraft (the exercise was eventually held in late November in the Sea of Japan). According to a Chinese analyst, Beijing's reaction to the impending drill was unprecedented.[31] What explains China's vocal, vehement, and repeated protests of the planned July U.S.-ROK naval exercises in the Yellow Sea? And why did this contrast starkly with China's understated and mild-mannered response to the sinking of the *Cheonan*?

The different Chinese approaches to these two events can be explained by the reality that Beijing is far more fearful of agitating Pyongyang than it is of antagonizing Washington. While it is common to criticize U.S. policies across the board, public criticisms of North Korea by the Chinese government, while acceptable in recent years, are carefully calibrated.[32] Moreover, from Beijing's perspective, Washington is more susceptible to modifications of policy than Pyongyang—witness the switching of the location of the July naval exercises from the Yellow Sea to the Sea of Japan announced by a South Korean defense official on July 15.

The outrage expressed over the Yellow Sea exercises is best understood as Chinese sensitivity to the world's most powerful armed forces—and ones that are perceived to be adversarial—flexing their muscles on China's doorstep. The outrage was orchestrated but genuine. The parameters for permissible targets of Chinese ire are limited and the United States tends to be considered fair game and a large convenient target for an array of Chinese civilian and military officials and commentators who find it hard to sound off on other, more controversial topics. But this should not obscure the fact that China has become increasingly sensitive to and assertive about its maritime territorial claims. In the summer of 2010, Beijing was not only vocal about the anticipated exercise in the Yellow Sea but also in responses to Secretary Clinton's comments about the South China Sea made at the ASEAN Regional Forum meeting in Hanoi on July 23.

The PLA's Role   The military played roles in both the determination of a policy response to the anticipated U.S. Navy exercise in the Yellow Sea in the latter half of 2010 (see below) and in the implementation of that policy. The PLA's implementation role was two-fold: hawkish rhetoric from active duty and retired military leaders as well as a stepped up schedule of high-visibility military exercises in the region.

The outcry in China against the U.S. naval exercises in the Yellow Sea came from a variety of high-profile civilian and military figures both in and out of official posts. Some of the most hawkish and shrill verbal salvos were delivered by military figures. Their nationalist rhetoric seemed out of proportion to U.S. actions. In part these outbursts reflected real emotion but in part they also appeared to be elements of a well-coordinated campaign to divert U.S. and South Korean attention from North Korea to China. In short, Beijing hijacked the verbiage to serve a larger purpose: distracting Washington and Seoul from their post-*Cheonan* Pyongyang-directed ire.

Certainly, the initial response of Beijing to the announcement of imminent U.S.-ROK exercises, as expressed through the MFA, was mild—urging all involved parties to "maintain calm." But, according to a report in a Hong Kong newspaper, the PLA insisted that China should take a more strident tone toward the exercises and the MFA verbiage soon adopted a more explicit anti-U.S. vein. As a result of the military's lobbying, the MFA declared that China did in fact "strongly oppose" the exercises.[33]

PLA Deputy Chief of General Staff General Ma Xiaotian declared in a July 1, 2010, interview with a Hong Kong television station that China "strongly opposes the drill in the Yellow Sea because of its close proximity to Chinese territorial waters."[34] Two weeks later, retired PLA General Luo Yuan told an interviewer:

> China is a nation of memories and history, and the Yellow Sea has been an area used to invade China during the Opium and Sino-Japanese Wars. . . . What reasons do they [the United States and South Korea] have to conduct a joint military drill right in our front yard and threaten our security? How can China permit this?[35]

This hawkish rhetoric while genuine was also part of a shrewd and coordinated strategy. If there is any doubt, the cool-headed logic of a PLA general officer provides context and insight. Chatting on-line with Chinese netizens on July 29, 2010, Rear Admiral Yin Zhuo spoke at length about the U.S.-ROK exercises. He first addressed what he considered to be immediate U.S. objectives:

> What the United States is up to is very clear. . . . The United States wants to indicate its firm support for South Korea by holding these joint military exercises. . . . Of course, . . . the ultimate objective should also be very clear . . . to intimidate its adversaries, especially North Korea and countries adjacent to North Korea such as Russia and China.

Washington's broader objectives, according to Yin, were to de-nuclearize the Korean Peninsula and stabilize the region. While the United States had been successful in its narrow objectives, it had "failed" in its broader goals. Indeed, in his view, "massive military exercises" were likely to "exacerbate the instability in Northeast Asia."

One netizen asked point blank: "Will there be any battle in the Yellow Sea?"

Yin answered coolly: "There will not be any war in the Yellow Sea. . . . Thus, we need to observe the exercises calmly. Of course, part of their exercises is meant to deter and intimidate us, but that's all it can do. Any war in the Yellow Sea would not be in the interests of the United States. The U.S. forces taking part in the exercises are not for war."[36]

The PLA's involvement was not limited to rhetoric. China's military conducted a series of well-publicized field exercises in the summer of 2010. These were intended to signal China's resolve and preparedness to defend its territory and national interests in the face of what Beijing interpreted as intimidation and gunboat diplomacy by the United States.[37] From the perspective of many Chinese, the United States had become more assertive in the "near seas," notably asserting its right to conduct military activities in the South China Sea and Yellow Sea. Beijing viewed U.S. rhetoric and actions as being intended to militarily threaten or at least intimidate China. A number of prominent officials and analysts expressed the opinion that Washington was taking advantage of purported North Korean provocations to flex its military muscles on China's doorstep.[38]

While some of the exercises appeared to be routine and modest in scope, others seem to have been less routine or expanded in order to counter perceived U.S. heavy-handedness. According to the *South China Morning Post*, July 2010 "was probably one of the busiest months of the year for the People's Liberation Army . . . [with] the largest, most frequent and most intense drills in years."[39] At least three exercises were conducted during July. The first was a six-day live ammunition drill in the East China Sea held early in the month. The second was a two-day supply exercise in the Yellow Sea held mid-month. Codenamed "Warfare 2010," the drill involved transporting equipment and weaponry by ship and by rail. The third was a major naval drill held in the South China Sea a week later. Additional drills were conducted in August 2010. A nighttime aerial exercise was conducted over the Gulf of Bohai early in the month. A second large-scale Ji'nan Military Region drill focused on air defense. The exercise, code named "Vanguard 2010," reportedly involved

12,000 military personnel from air and ground units spread over areas in Henan and Shandong provinces, was also held in early August.[40]

According to a Japanese media report, in early 2011, Pyongyang asked China to conduct a bilateral naval drill. Beijing allegedly declined the offer. This report cannot be verified. In any case there is no record of any bilateral PLA-KPA exercise taking place and no indication that the two militaries have conducted drills together in many years.[41]

Conclusion and Analyses

China's policy responses to the two crises underscore the intractability of Beijing's Pyongyang problem and the extent of its policy inertia on North Korea. It takes a crisis to get movement in Beijing. And even then the policymaking wheels grind laboriously. Beijing's greatest fear is focused on what Washington will do and how a U.S. reaction might exacerbate a crisis.

There is no sympathy for a former comrade-in-arms nor is there any nostalgia for a war long passed evident among the PLA. Twenty-first century Chinese soldiers appear to be intensely nationalist, conservative, and hawkish. Although extremely attentive to trends on the Korean Peninsula and concerned with China's DPRK policy, the PLA does not lead policy change. Its policy role tends to be low-keyed and low-profile. The military informs at the pre-decision phase, advises at the decision phase, and reassures—and, if necessary, provides hawkish rhetoric or forceful actions—in the implementation phase. Moreover, there appears to be very limited interaction between the two militaries. This engagement is of a symbolic and superficial kind rather than substantive or deep.

From Beijing's perspective, the two Korean crises—one in 2003 and other in 2010—were each resolved satisfactorily with successful foreign policy outcomes. The first concluded with the creation of the Six Party Talks—the first ever session was held in Beijing in August 2003 and subsequent sessions followed, enabling Beijing to emerge from the second Korean nuclear crisis. Although no dramatic breakthrough was achieved, that war had been averted was a victory for China and the Six Party Talks became a mechanism for influencing North Korean behavior and for managing the United States and the ROK. The PLA appeared to play a minor but significant role in securing China's unsettled border with the DPRK and reassuring Pyongyang—showing outward solidarity through General Xu's high-profile visit on the eve of the Six Party Talks.

The second crisis had not been fully resolved but the most acute phase passed without escalation. In the latter half of 2010, Beijing was fearful that Washington and Seoul were preparing to punish or at least intimidate Pyongyang. China worried this might trigger a violent reaction from North Korea and escalate into a full-blown conflict. The planned naval exercises by the United States and South Korea provoked nationalist outbursts in China. Beijing utilized this genuine outrage to distract the two allies from their intended target. PLA figures, active duty and retired, played a loud and shrill central role (at least in the implementation phase).

China's relations with North Korea have been strained since the death of Kim Jong-il in December 2011. Beijing's puzzlement over the dynastic succession in Pyongyang turned to shock when the youthful Kim Jong-un executed his elderly uncle in December 2013. Jang Song-taek had been viewed as an important advisor and the regime's key interlocutor with China.

Under Xi Jinping, Beijing has adopted a tougher stance on North Korea—more willing than previous administrations to display its displeasure with North Korea. China has ceremonially downgraded its relationship with North Korea and concurrently moved to mend fences with South Korea—ties were damaged by Beijing's refusal to condemn Pyongyang's provocations among other issues. The PRC hosted a state visit by ROK President Park Geun-hye in mid-2013 and then Xi Jinping reciprocated with a high-profile visit to South Korea in June 2014. The contrast with China's North Korea policy was clear—Kim Jong-un has yet to visit China since succeeding his father as leader. Moreover, Chinese commemorations of the sixtieth anniversary of the Korean War armistice in July 2013 were low key and Beijing dispatched second-tier leaders to Pyongyang: Vice President Li Yuanchao, who is not a member of the Politburo Standing Committee, was the top civilian leader represented China. Meanwhile, the PLA was also represented by a second-tier leader: Lieutenant General Jia Tingan, who, as deputy director of the General Political Department, is not a full member of the CMC. And in March 2014, in an unprecedented event, the PLA received directly from the South Korean military the remains of an estimated four hundred dead Chinese People's Volunteers. In the past such transfers have been done overland via North Korea.[42] Given the sensitivities involved, this signals a dramatic improvement in the climate of Beijing-Seoul relations, is a powerful testament to the sorry state of Beijing-Pyongyang relations, and constitutes a clear PLA snub of the KPA.

Despite continued debate in academic circles and increasing criticism of the DPRK by scholars and policy analysts, China does not appear likely to adopt a major change of policy where North Korea is concerned unless confronted by a serious crisis. The last time Beijing adopted a major new initiative on Korea policy was in 2003 when it launched the Six Party Talks. The impetus at that time was grave concern that Washington was prepared to undertake military action against North Korea. Escalation was averted in 2010 and no comparable level of alarm was detectable in China as of this writing. Indeed Xi Jinping and other senior leaders in Beijing are preoccupied with domestic affairs and sensitive to internal political turbulence in Pyongyang. At this time, maintaining stability both inside China and on its periphery is the highest priority along with sustaining China's status as a responsible great power.

Notes

1. For a brief overview of these turbulent years, see Andrew J. Nathan and Andrew Scobell, *China's Search for Security* (New York: Columbia University Press, 2012), 132–137.

2. This judgment is founded upon the author's prior research. Studies on China's North Korea policy include Bates Gill, *China's North Korea Policy: Assessing Interests and Influences*, Special Report 283 (Washington, DC: United States Institute of Peace, July 2011); Avery Goldstein, "Across the Yalu: China's Interests on the Korean Peninsula in a Changing World," in *New Directions in the Study of Chinese Foreign Policy*, eds. Alastair I. Johnston and Robert S. Ross (Stanford, CA: Stanford University Press, 2006), 131–161; International Crisis Group [ICG], *Fire on the City Gate: Why China Keeps North Korea Close*, Asia Report #254 (Brussels: December 2013); ICG, *Shades of Red: China's Debate Over North Korea*, Asia Report #179 (Brussels: November 2009); ICG, *China and Inter-Korean Clashes in the Yellow Sea*, Asia Report #200 (Brussels: January 2011); Heungkyu Kim, "From a Buffer Zone to a Strategic Burden: Evolving Sino-North Korea Relations during the Hu Jintao Era," *Korean Journal of Defense Analysis* 22, no. 1 (March 2010): 57–74; Dick K. Nanto, Mark E. Manyin, and Kerry Dumbaugh, *China-North Korea Relations* (Washington, DC: Congressional Research Service, January 2010); Andrew Scobell and Mark Cozad, "China's North Korea Policy: Rethink or Recharge?" *Parameters* 44, no. 1 (Spring 2014): 51–64; Andrew Scobell, *China and North Korea: From Comrades-in-Arms to Allies at Arm's Length* (Carlisle Barracks, PA: U.S. Army War College, 2004); David Shambaugh, "China and the Korean Peninsula: Playing for the Long Term," *Washington Quarterly* 26, no. 2 (Spring 2003): 43–56; Scott Snyder, *China's Rise and the Two Koreas: Politics, Economics, Security* (Boulder, CO: Lynne Reinner, 2009); You Ji, "Dealing with the 'North Korea Dilemma': China's Strategic Choices," RSIS Working Paper no. 229 (Singapore: Rajaratnam School of International

Studies, June 21, 2011). According to Bates Gill, "the Chinese People's Liberation Army also has a strong voice in deliberations over policy toward North Korea." See Gill, *China's North Korea Policy*, 7. According to the ICG, the PLA has "substantial influence on DPRK policy." See *Shades of Red*, 6–7.

3. The text of the treaty can be found in *Peking Review* 4, no. 28 (1961): 5.

4. Scobell, *China and North Korea*, 19–20.

5. Ibid., 1–2.

6. On mil-mil relations between China and North Korea, see Scobell and Cozad, "China's North Korea Policy," 56, 60–61; Kenneth W. Allen and Eric A McVadon, *China's Foreign Military Relations* (Washington, DC: Stimson Center, 1999), 67–68; and Scobell, *China and North Korea*, 8–9. Recent scholarship on the PLA's exchanges underscores the absence of a robust mil-mil relationship between China and North Korea. See Heidi Holz and Kenneth Allen, "Military Exchanges with Chinese Characteristics: The People's Liberation Army Experience with Military Relations," in *The PLA at Home and Abroad: Assessing the Operational Capabilities of China's Military*, eds. Roy Kamphausen, David Lai, and Andrew Scobell (Carlisle Barracks, PA: U.S. Army War College, 2010), 429–473. A recent analysis of PLA multilateral exercises reveals none with the KPA. See Dennis J. Blasko, "People's Liberation Army and People's Armed Police Ground Exercises with Foreign Forces, 2002–2009," in *The PLA at Home and Abroad: Assessing the Operational Capabilities of China's Military*, 377–428.

7. Since 2002, China has conducted almost annual military field exercises with assorted SCO member states. These have included not just the PLA and its counterpart armed forces but also the People's Armed Police and their foreign counterparts.

8. Scobell and Cozad, "China's North Korea Policy," 57–58.

9. Scobell, *China and North Korea*, 24–25.

10. Andrew Scobell, "China's Strategic Lessons from the Korean War," *International Journal of Korean Studies* 15, no. 1 (Spring 2011): 22–23.

11. The year 2010 marked the sixtieth anniversary of the outbreak of the Korean War. The commemoration was a sober reminder of a violent episode—seared into China's psyche—a recurrence of which Beijing would strongly prefer to avoid. On the one hand, the war stirs up immense national pride because the intervention of the People's Volunteers signaled the arrival of a strong, new China that could no longer be bullied by great powers. On the other hand, the conflict resurrects memories of untold suffering and great sacrifice that in hindsight call into question whether the outcome was worth the cost. After all, North Korea remains a security problem for China sixty years later.

12. At least two or three opinion groups have been identified. See, for example, Kim, "From a Buffer Zone to a Strategic Burden," and the ICG, *Shades of Red*. For another take on opinion groupings as of 2005, see Andrew Scobell and Michael Chambers, "The Fallout of a Nuclear North Korea," *Current History* 104, no. 683 (September 2005): 292–293.

13. Kim, "From a Buffer Zone to a Strategic Burden," 59–60.

14. Wang Haidong [王海运], "China Must Build Strategic Buffers" [中国有必要建战略稳定带], *Global Times* [环球时报], August 27, 2013.

15. ICG, *Fire on the City Gate*; interviews with civilian and military analysts in Beijing and Shanghai, September 2014.

16. Scobell, *China and North Korea*, 22.

17. This paragraph draws on Scobell and Cozad, "China's North Korea Policy," 53.

18. Cited in Andrew Scobell, "Crouching Korea, Hidden China: Bush Administration Policy toward Pyongyang and Beijing," *Asian Survey* 42, no. 2 (March/April 2002): 366.

19. Quoted in Mike Chinoy, *Meltdown: The Inside Story of the North Korean Nuclear Crisis* (New York: St. Martin's Press, 2008), 165.

20. Scobell, *China and North Korea*, 14.

21. Ibid., 21.

22. Chinoy, *Meltdown*, 165–166.

23. Scobell, *China and North Korea*, 23–24.

24. Ibid., 11–12.

25. Ibid., 24.

26. Shen Dingli, "Lessons from Cheonan," *Zhongguo Wang* [China Net], in English, July 28, 2010, www.china.org.cn/opinion/2010-07/28/content_20587399.htm.

27. Bonnie Glaser and Brad Glosserman, "China's Cheonan Problem," PacNet #31 (June 18, 2010).

28. You, "Dealing with the 'North Korea Dilemma,'" 1.

29. Hillary Rodham Clinton, "Remarks on Regional Architecture in Asia: Principles and Priorities," January 12, 2010.

30. Andrew Scobell and Scott W. Harold, "An 'Assertive' China? Insights from Interviews," *Asian Security* 9, no. 2 (2013): 119–121.

31. Cui Yiliang said: "Five successive expressions of attitude is certainly something that has never happened in the past." See Wang Xiyi [王希怡], "Chinese Government Takes 'Tough Line,' U.S. Carrier 'Turns Around'" [中国政府'强硬'美国航母拐弯], *Guangzhou Daily* [广州日报], July 17, 2010.

32. In response to the third nuclear test in February 2013, Xi Jinping avoided singling out North Korea for condemnation. Instead, two months after the test he issued the following vague warning: "No one should be allowed to throw a region and even the whole world into chaos." ICG, *Fire on the City Gate*, 6.

33. Cary Huang, "PLA Ramped Up China's Stand on US-Korea Drill," *South China Morning Post*, August 6, 2010.

34. *Phoenix TV*, July 1, 2010. For the text and video of Ma's interview, see http://news.ifeng.com/mainland/detail_2010_07/01/1702694_0.shtml.

35. "Major General Luo Yuan Discusses U.S.-ROK Military Exercise in Yellow Sea" [罗援少将谈美韩黄海联合军演], *People's Daily Online* [人民网], July 13, 2010.

36. The quotes in this and the preceding paragraph are from "Major General Yin Zhuo, a Noted Military Expert, Comments on U.S.-South Korean Military Exercises"

[著名军事专家尹卓少将谈韩美联合军演], *People's Daily Online* [人民网], July 29, 2010.

37. According to a U.S. scholar, in August 2010 Ma Xiaotian privately told a U.S. academic delegation headed by a former U.S. admiral that China was especially upset because the U.S.-ROK exercises were to be held in a "new area" closer to Chinese territory than previous exercises. The admiral believed Ma's statement to be incorrect.

38. See the quotes in the text from Major General Yin Zhuo and an additional discussion with Chinese netizens conducted on November 29, 2010. See "Yin Zhuo: 'U.S.-ROK Joint Military Exercises and the Security Situation in Northeast Asia'" [尹卓谈'韩美联合军演及东北亚安全局势'], *People's Daily Online* [人民网], November 29, 2010.

39. Choi Chi-Yuk, "Drills Seen as a Flexing of Muscles," *South China Morning Post*, August 6, 2010.

40. Ibid.; Minnie Chan, "PLA Carries Out Night Drill Near Yellow Sea Based on Scenario of an Attack by the United States," *South China Morning Post*, August 11, 2010; Ma Haoliang [馬浩亮], "The Ji'nan Military Region Has Assumed a Prominent Strategic Position" [濟南軍區戰略地位凸顯], *Ta Kung Pao* [大公報], July 29, 2010; "12,000 Take Part in PLA Air Defense Drills," *China Daily Online*, August 4, 2010; Tao Shelan and Zhao Xiaogang [陶社兰, 赵小刚], "PLA Air Defense Exercise Vanguard 2010 in Full Swing, Emphasis on Air-Ground Confrontation" [解放军前卫-2010防空演练全面展开突出空地对抗], China News Service [中国新闻社], August 4, 2010.

41. "N. Korea Sounded Out China in April about Holding Joint Military Drill," Kyodo, August 7, 2010.

42. "South Korea Begins Repatriating China's Korean War Soldiers," BBC, March 27, 2014, www.bbc.com/news/world-asia-26777173.

8   The Rise of PLA Diplomacy

Eric Hagt

THE ASCENDANCE OF THE PEOPLE'S LIBERATION ARMY (PLA) as a diplomatic player is a lesser-known element in China's growing global presence over the past two decades. A myopic focus on erratic U.S.-China military-to-military relations—often held hostage to political disputes between Washington and Beijing—obscures the PLA's increasingly active military diplomacy around the world. This reflects China's deepening international economic interests and parallels diplomatic efforts on the civilian side. A new global role for the PLA has evolved from mostly pro-forma high-level visits to wide-ranging military-to-military (M2M) activities, including joint exercises, extensive training programs, and security dialogues with numerous countries.[1] While China's military policy remains subject to the guidelines set out by the Communist Party, implementation of M2M is seen as the legitimate purview of the PLA, and affords it a degree of maneuver to set the direction and outlook of military ties with other countries. As such, the evolution of military diplomacy, how the PLA conducts relations with the armed forces of other nations, and the objectives the PLA pursues will have a growing impact on China's larger security environment.

This chapter discusses the nature of the PLA's burgeoning international activity as well as the institutions and individuals within the military that are managing and executing it—which deeply shape the objectives and outcomes of military diplomacy. The PLA's evolving role has consequences both for domestic civil-military relations and for China's larger diplomatic and strategic environment. The PLA is consolidating its influence over the domain of military diplomacy with outcomes that are sometimes incongruent with the objectives of China's foreign affairs system—principally, though not exclusively, the domain of the Ministry of Foreign Affairs. While by no means a simple black-and-white contest, the difference in approach and goals between these two sets of actors exists and has implications for China's expanding foreign relations enterprise. Increased PLA diplomatic activity, even if restricted to military affairs and under the broad direction of the party, will inevitably complicate effective coordination of China's diplomacy.

The Evolving Strategic Context

The basic driver for the expansion of China's military diplomatic activities that began in the early- to mid-1990s was a dramatic shift in perceptions of the international security environment. During the first decades of opening up and reform, China's foreign policy was guided by the principle of maintaining a stable regional and global environment in which China could achieve its ambitious economic development goals. Not only was national defense placed firmly behind the economy, agriculture, and science and technology in the modernization strategy, but security issues in general were given far less priority.[2] China adhered to the *tao guang yang hui* (Bide our time and build up our capabilities) principle and strove to build regional confidence in its image as a peacefully rising power. China settled most border disputes and generally avoided conflict in the region and beyond. Deng Xiaoping was the prime mover behind this national trajectory and his control over the military helped maintain these priorities. The Ministry of Foreign Affairs (MFA) was the dominant face for this development-centric foreign policy approach.[3] As for the PLA, it would "have to wait and be patient." This meant a low profile for the military and minimal participation in external relations. During this time the PLA generally yielded—though sometimes grudgingly—to this dominant national and foreign policy agenda.[4]

Beginning in 1989 and throughout the 1990s, two separate but related shifts occurred with regard to the PLA's role in the nation's development. Both internal and external security conditions began to change dramatically. The nationwide unrest in 1989 that culminated in protests in Tiananmen Square threatened domestic stability and regime legitimacy. The PLA heeded the call of the leadership to crackdown on the demonstrators thus demonstrating its loyalty to the Communist Party. The international reactions to Tiananmen—economic and military sanctions—as well as a number of incidents, including *Yinhe* incident,[5] the 1995–1996 crisis in the Taiwan Strait, and the accidental NATO bombing of the Chinese embassy in Belgrade, led to a reexamination of China's security environment, particularly vis-à-vis the United States. This new domestic and international security landscape underscored the indispensible role of the PLA.[6] Moreover, China's expanding international economic interests and growing reliance on imported energy also sparked debate over the need for a more robust national defense capability.[7]

As a result, Deng's thinking on austerity for national defense was officially abandoned with the presentation of the "dual goals" of economic growth and military modernization.[8] The PLA's claim on national resources and its influence with the CCP leadership rose dramatically. The expansion of the PLA's capabilities and missions has continued and has produced regional reactions now being manifested through heightened disputes over the Senkaku/Diaoyu Islands and the Spratly Islands in the South China Sea, and increased regional tensions.

China's emergence as a major power on the world scene has vastly expanded the demands and opportunities in international relations and diplomacy. In this rising tide of external interaction, both positive and negative, the PLA's own diplomatic activities have proliferated. China's international environment has also grown in complexity, giving security and strategic issues greater weight in Chinese foreign policy, thereby enhancing the PLA's role. The net effect has been to progressively shift the PLA's attention to China's external security environment and the nation's foreign affairs.

PLA Activity Abroad

This reorientation has had several implications. The PLA has been called on to strengthen military-to-military relationships as part of a national diplomatic policy initiative to build strategic partnerships around the world.[9] "China's new military diplomacy should enhance regional security and stability and fulfill obligations to realizing a harmonious world by actively promoting a foreign policy of peace."[10] This has laid the foundation for an expanded role in conducting military diplomacy and other M2M activities. But as guarantor of China's national interests amidst an increasingly complicated security environment, the PLA is also being called on to modernize into an effective fighting force. The

PLA understands that interaction with other militaries can enhance modern-ization by creating opportunities to learn from the armed forces of other coun-tries. This is especially true—though not without reservation—of interactions with the world's advanced nations, such as the United States.

This chapter uses the terms "military diplomacy" and "military-to-military relations" interchangeably. Both terms are meant to incorporate the totality of the PLA's external activities with foreign military and security agencies. The dis-cussion is less focused on a detailed cataloguing of various military-to-military activities—where finer distinctions may be necessary—than on the underlying values and attitudes that shape the PLA's outward behavior. China categorizes its own external activities into three areas: international military diplomacy, military exchanges, and military cooperation. International military diplo-macy involves negotiations on arms control and disarmament treaties; bilateral or multilateral rule-setting that impinges on national security; peace-keeping operations; and military exercises on antiterrorism, maritime search and res-cue, and humanitarian relief. Military exchanges include defense policy talks, educational and functional exchanges, and high-level visits between military officers and defense officials. Military cooperation involves closer collabora-tion between militaries that may encompass defense industry and technological assistance, co-development or integration of weapon systems and war-fighting tactics, military intelligence exchanges, joint military exercises, provision of military infrastructure, military aid and arms sales.[11]

The PLA's M2M activities have grown dramatically over the past two decades and several trends are worth noting (see Table 8.1).[12] First, the nature of contacts with foreign militaries has shifted. While China's military diplomacy has traditionally emphasized high-level visits, the number of functional, train-ing, and educational activities has grown steadily. Perhaps most significantly, joint operational exercises, which began in 2000, have expanded to the point that they may warrant qualifications to China's policy of not having military alliances (discussed below). Second, the growth in M2M has varied between regions: contacts with the United States and Europe have been moderate and have fluctuated according to the state of political relations; in Latin America M2M contacts started from a low level but have grown substantially in all areas;[13] M2M with the Middle East remains at a modest level but has been dom-inated by arms sales; the PLA has long-standing ties to Africa and peacekeep-ing operations have risen steadily; finally, the greatest and most comprehensive increase of M2M activities has been with neighboring countries.

TABLE 8.1 M2M Activity, 2005–2013

Region/Country	High-level visits			Security dialogue			Operational[a]					Educational		
Year	2005–6	2007–8	2009–2010	2005–6[b]	2007–8	2009–2010	2005–6	2007–8	2009–2010	2011–2012	2013[c]	2005–6	2007–8	2009–10
Total	284	270	>227	45	Dialogues increased from 15 to 22 countries between 2005 and 2010		7	11	18	18	17*	500 abroad, 2,000 to China	900 abroad, 4,000 to China	Unpublicized
United States	9	11	6	12			1	1	1	2				
Russia	15	7	14	2			1	2	4	1				
EU	72	58	47	15			5	3	0	0				
Neighboring countries†	82	85	98	14			0	4	6	10				
Africa	55	45	26	2			0	0	1	0				
Middle East & Latin America countries	51	61	36	0			0	0	0	3				
Unpublicized/Uncertain	0	0	50	0			0	0	6	2				

SOURCES:

[a] "Chinese Military Participation in Important Sino-Foreign Joint Training and Exercises" [中国军队参加的主要中外联合训练和演习], Xinhua Online [新华网], July 20, 2009, http://news.xinhuanet.com/ziliao/2009-07/20/content_1173757.htm.

[b] Information Office of the State Council, "China's National Defense in 2006," December 29, 2006, Appendix 3, "Participation in Security Consultations, 2005–2006."

[c] Information Office of the State Council, "The Diversified Employment of China's Armed Forces," April 13, 2013, http://eng.mod.gov.cn/Database/WhitePapers/index.htm.

* There is no available breakdown of operational exercises for 2013.

† Includes 25 countries: Central Asia (Tajikistan, Kazakhstan, Kyrgyzstan, Turkmenistan), Mongolia, Afghanistan, Pakistan, India, Bangladesh, Nepal, 10 ASEAN countries, North Korea, South Korea, Japan, Australia, and New Zealand.

Who's Behind PLA Diplomacy?

Three components are central to understanding how the PLA conducts military diplomacy. The first is the Foreign Affairs Office under the General Staff's Second Department (GSD-FAO). The GSD-FAO is responsible for maintaining an organized, coherent approach to M2M relations and is central to the military's management and philosophy in conducting military diplomacy. Its role has expanded along with overall M2M relations, but its small size limits its effectiveness in managing the large volume of exchanges. The second component includes the individuals and units within the PLA that carry out interactions with other militaries. Over a hundred PLA departments are involved in military training programs alone.[14] These individuals, their backgrounds, experiences, and personalities collectively make up an important element in shaping the PLA's attitudes to foreign armed forces—though such effects are more varying and less predictable. Moreover, the networks formed between officers of the PLA and foreign militaries have implications for PLA interests abroad. The third key component is the senior PLA officers in charge of diplomatic and M2M activities, especially the deputy chief of the General Staff responsible for intelligence and foreign affairs and the director of the GSD-FAO. Given their positions of authority, their personal and professional experience has an important influence on specific events as well as the overall direction of the PLA's external relations.

The Foreign Affairs Office
The PLA maintains a separate and professional corps to handle all external military relations. The GSD-FAO and its subordinate institutions throughout the PLA are specialized organizations that exercise overall control of interactions with foreign militaries, whether as points of contact for foreign military attachés in China, as defense attachés in Chinese embassies abroad, or in coordinating a broad range of functional, educational, and operational joint activities with other armed forces.[15] While the GSD-FAO is the main organization managing PLA diplomacy, it is not the only one. A number of PLA institutions have a degree of autonomy in establishing contact with foreigners—so-called windows—including officers in three academic military institutions (National Defense University, the Academy of Military Sciences, and National University of Defense Technology), various associations affiliated with the PLA,[16] and nineteen operational units spread across the various services that have been certified to receive foreigners (*yingwai budui*).[17] These

organizations do not have complete autonomy; their significant events and activities still remain within the purview of the FAO system. PLA staff working in sensitive areas,[18] in institutes for technical or other special training, and officers that have not received formal political education (commanders below brigade level) are generally off limits to foreigners.[19]

At one level, a clear line is drawn between those approved and those not approved to interact with foreigners. At another level, however, the vast increase in PLA participation in joint exercises and training programs complicates the GSD-FAO's efforts at centralized management over military diplomacy.

The GSD-FAO demonstrates the PLA's unique approach to conducting M2M relations. It currently consists of roughly 120 staff and is divided into regional and functional bureaus. Regional bureaus include the Asia Bureau, the Eurasia Bureau, the North America and Oceania Bureau, and the West Asia and Africa Bureau. Functional bureaus include the Bureau of General Affairs, Bureau of Policy Planning, the Media Bureau, the Antipiracy Bureau (established around 2009),[20] and the Bureau of Arms Control and Military Aid.

The GSD-FAO's mandate is to administer and coordinate the wide range of activities between the PLA and other militaries. This includes liaising with foreign militaries, establishing contacts with foreign counterparts, orchestrating the logistics for visits between the PLA and visiting foreign delegations or for PLA delegations visiting abroad, and generally handling exchanges. Its role has expanded to encompass the coordination of joint military exercises and even participation in the other advisory and planning roles, which has helped to increase its impact on larger strategic issues.[21]

The GSD-FAO's formal responsibilities involve providing administrative assistance in implementing M2M activities initiated by senior PLA leaders. In reality however, the GSD-FAO has much more room to influence the shape and direction of M2M relations writ large. GSD-FAO staff members write analytic reports offering recommendations for development of M2M relations with specific countries. Moreover, the GSD-FAO plays an increasing role in military planning and analysis related to China's evolving external security environment. Three developments have transformed and enhanced the GSD-FAO's role.

Gatekeeper   While the GSD-FAO does not drive policy, its staff is much more than a mere "barbarian handler" as commonly viewed from a U.S. perspective. In its role as the "first line of defense" for PLA external affairs, the

GSD-FAO is positioned to set priorities and the tone in military relations. It holds procedural authority that can have a significant impact on how and to what degree policies and initiatives are carried out. The institutional limits on policymaking by the GSD-FAO appear fairly clear, but a large gray zone exists in implementing directives. Motivated insiders understand how to affect outcomes through the process of transforming policy into action. This may occur by expediting, prioritizing, or impeding certain activities ranging from high-level visits to joint military exercises.[22] The gatekeeper status is even truer in a crisis. Any incident with a foreign military—especially the United States—immediately becomes politically sensitive. Communication channels close down, and the GSD-FAO becomes the only point of contact, isolating and limiting interaction until a decision can be made by the Central Military Commission (CMC) and the higher political system about how to respond. The framing of issues during a crisis and first response has the potential to influence the course of events.

Given these responsibilities, the GSD-FAO is a specialized and in some ways isolated bureaucracy within the PLA. Its personnel are largely derived from the military foreign affairs track within the PLA, a system separate from other command and administrative tracks. Most mid- and lower-level GSD-FAO officers are trained in external relations and languages at specialized colleges (in Nanjing and Luoyang). Many GSD-FAO officers have also been groomed through assignments in lower-level foreign liaison offices in the services, military academic institutions such as National Defense University, or Chinese embassies through the military attaché system. Older generations of GSD-FAO directors and deputy directors have experience working in military intelligence,[23] while many of the younger deputy directors have been educated in civilian and even foreign universities.[24] In short, the GSD-FAO is a separate bureaucracy specialized and extensively trained in managing relationships with foreign militaries.

Formally, the GSD-FAO's scope for influence is narrowly confined to this role of implementer and administrator. One indicator of the GSD-FAO's limited authority is the opportunity for promotion to more powerful positions in the PLA leadership. No former GSD-FAO directors have moved up beyond that position. By and large the GSD-FAO resides outside the command and operational tracks,[25] which contrasts with its counterparts in other countries, such as United States, where defense and service attachés generally have strong combat and operational backgrounds. This separateness and highly specialized GSD-FAO system in the PLA suggests a high degree of compartmentalization of the military's foreign relations.

Expanded Functions   The growing complexity of military diplomacy has shaped the PLA's approach to M2M and enhanced the GSD-FAO's role in carrying it out.[26] The PLA has long accepted the basic premise that it stands to gain more than lose from foreign contact.[27] This is generally true for its relations with all militaries and particularly so regarding advanced countries—though not without caution—including the United States. This has led to a higher demand not only for coordination and planning M2M initiatives, but also for strategic analysis of China's security environment and the PLA's international interests. Despite its somewhat sequestered nature, the GSD-FAO is well-positioned to undertake a leading role in those tasks.

As the first line of defense in handling most foreign military contacts, the GSD-FAO has exposure to a wide range of M2M and foreign affairs issues. This direct and sustained contact with the outside gives the GSD-FAO a unique understanding of external issues. Moreover, the GSD-FAO has a high level of linguistic competence and first-hand access to foreign documents, statements, and other materials. Other institutions with formal responsibility for strategic thinking and planning often lack these advantages. For instance, AMS is a more conservative and insular institution, has limited contact with foreigners, and often lacks adequate knowledge of international affairs and foreign languages. Compared to AMS, NDU is more progressive, better connected with the outside, and generally holds greater expertise on foreign issues. Yet, it too is deficient in the requisite skills to perform wide-ranging, comprehensive analysis. The GSD's Strategic Planning Department has less direct exposure to foreign ideas and lacks the language abilities to read foreign materials and interpret the international context. Given the growing complexity of China's external security environment, understanding and insight about foreign countries and militaries are necessary to help formulate China's strategic thinking and planning. The PLA leadership increasingly requests advice and input from a growing number of actors—including civilian scholars—that can provide such assistance. An organization such as the GSD-FAO that can accomplish these functions has a good chance to play an influential role.

The GSD-FAO's position is also unique in that it has the advantage of access to important policymaking actors. As administrator over most military diplomacy, it has frequent contact with the PLA leadership, and even with the CMC chairman (who is also China's highest political and party leader). Before high-level military diplomatic events, the GSD-FAO is tasked with preparing policy and background briefs for leaders. The GSD-FAO is also the principal agency to consult with China's foreign affairs system (mainly the MFA). While there are deficiencies in the government-military relationship, the GSD-FAO is best informed about China's broader foreign policy planning, which the military must take into account.

Managing the PLA's growing interactions with foreign militaries gives the GSD-FAO an extensive network across various departments and services in the PLA.[28] The GSD-FAO also has the unique ability to second officers from other units for temporary assignments without being stymied by bureaucratic and financial obstacles.[29] While the GSD-FAO is short-staffed and usually overwhelmed with administrative tasks, and therefore lacks the resources to conduct much in-depth research itself, it readily can draw on the expertise of other units on topics such as research, operational planning, doctrine, strategy, command and control, etc.—an authority that AMS, NDU, and other strategic planning offices cannot exercise on a regular basis. As a result, the GSD-FAO has the ability to coordinate critical research on a range of military issues, particularly with regard to China's international strategic and security environment.[30]

Military Exercises

The advent of regular military exercises, particularly those conducted with other countries, marks an important turning point for PLA diplomacy. The PLA's last real combat experience was the border conflict with Vietnam in 1979, so current forces, including most commanding officers, have no actual combat experience. This lends increased emphasis to military exercises, which have become more numerous, sophisticated, and realistic over the past decade.[31] In 2004, Hu Jintao officially presented the idea that the PLA needed to "conduct diversified military tasks" to respond to a variety of security threats.[32] Diversified military tasks (DMT) came to encompass the dual objectives of readying the military for winning local wars under informationized conditions and the "new historic missions" (or, military operations other than war—MOOTW).[33] Although DMT contained important domestic security elements such as antiterrorism, prevention of large-scale social unrest, and disaster relief, it also highlighted the need for the PLA to operate beyond Chinese territory in order to protect China's growing international interests.[34] Obstacles to a more expansive interpretation of this outward orientation remain, such as the long-standing "non-alliance principle." However, the PLA was freed to conduct joint exercises with other militaries. The shift occurred in 2000, when the PLA began small-scale, nonsensitive joint military exercises. These were for the most part antiterrorism exercises within the framework of the Shanghai Cooperation Organization (or with its members), or noncombat exercises, such as search and rescue, with Western and regional nations. But the large-scale, combined operations (naval, air, and ground forces) executed with Russia in 2005 (Peace Mission–2005), effectively removed the barriers to combat exercises with other militaries. It was China's first such undertaking in fifty years, and a clear signal that even if China does not have formal alliances with other countries, the PLA was now willing to conduct combat exercises and work more closely with other major militaries.

This event was a watershed moment for the PLA's gradual shift from an inward-looking perspective to an increasingly outward orientation. This transformation was championed by the GSD-FAO under its energetic and farsighted then-director Zhang Bangdong. Without actual combat experience, military exercises have come to be seen as extremely valuable for operational preparedness. Joint exercises open up a new avenue for the PLA to understand how other militaries operate and how its own capabilities compare. To this end, the GSD-FAO vigorously pursued this unprecedented joint exercise with Russia. This opened a new chapter for the PLA and its capacity to interact substantively with foreign militaries. The continued growth in the PLA's exercises with other militaries since 2005 demonstrates the continued shift in PLA thinking on military cooperation and its importance for PLA combat readiness. Under Xi Jinping's leadership, the emphasis on combat readiness is reflected by an unprecedented seventeen joint exercises in 2013.[35] Significantly, in 2014 the PLA participated for the first time in RIMPAC (Rim of the Pacific exercise), the U.S.-led maritime exercise and the largest multilateral exercise in the region.

As the lead agency in planning and organizing these high-profile joint exercises, the GSD-FAO has gained a pivotal role within the PLA as the frontline organization in taking the PLA global. This gives the GSD-FAO greater visibility and exposure to a wide range of PLA operational commanders and combat units at different levels and in different services and Military Regions. This has helped build a network of contacts on which the GSD-FAO can draw when PLA leadership is seeking input and consultation on a range of strategic and foreign-affairs-related issues.

M2M Leadership

While the GSD-FAO is the most important institution managing M2M, two leadership positions within the PLA play prominent roles: the director of GSD-FAO and the GSD deputy with responsibility for military intelligence and foreign affairs. Their personal experiences and background shape their perceptions of other countries and can have a strong influence on the PLA's approach to M2M.

The second-ranking deputy chief of the General Staff has typically been in charge of the PLA's intelligence departments (including human intelligence or the Second Department, and electronic/signals intelligence, or the Third Department) and foreign affairs bureaucracy, even though the GSD-FAO is nominally under the Ministry of Defense. The major figures who have held this dual portfolio position since the 1990s provide some indication of the potential impact on the PLA's influence in foreign affairs. General Xiong Guangkai famously held this position during a critical period for PLA diplomacy (mid-1990s to mid-2000s), especially with regard to U.S.-China relations. He oversaw the creation of the Military Maritime Consultative Agreement, established the under-secretary-level Defense Consultative Talks, and steered the relationship through the Taiwan crisis (1995–1996), the accidental bombing of the Chinese embassy in Belgrade (1999), and the EP-3 incident (2001). Gen. Xiong is important not only for what happened during the period he oversaw M2M relations, but also because of his particular style. He is a controversial figure in the PLA in part because he changed the nature of the military's ties to the foreign affairs system and in part because he was a consummate political infighter. He built especially close ties with China's Ministry of Foreign Affairs, had a seat in the Foreign Affairs Leading Small Group, and was secretary-general of the Taiwan Affairs Small Leading Group.[36] He greatly elevated the PLA's exposure to and participation in foreign affairs decisionmaking bodies. However, Xiong lacked operational experience, and despite his skill in political turf battles, had less respect within the PLA as a professional soldier.

In contrast, Ma Xiaotian was respected within the PLA due to his formidable operational background, but his relationship with the MFA and the other elements of the civilian foreign affairs system was thought to be far less cordial.[37] Known to be highly capable, intelligent, and charismatic, Ma also habitually disregarded advice from organizations serving him on M2M and foreign affairs. The degree to which the disparity in these two figures translated into concrete differences in policy is uncertain. However, it is probably no accident that politically sensitive M2M relations that require greater coordination with China's foreign affairs system (such as with the United States) did not make a lot of headway under Ma.[38]

Ma Xiaotian's replacement, Qi Jianguo, brought yet another distinctive style to this position. He apparently relied far more on advisors for diplomatic affairs and M2M relations as he was more aware of his deficiencies in these areas.[39] Significantly, his background was in operations, having formerly headed the GSD's Operations Department. His selection for this position strongly suggests a high priority on improving PLA operational competency by learning from other militaries.

The PLA experimented with separating the intelligence and foreign affairs portfolios in 2013. Deputy Chief of the General Staff Lt. Gen. Wang Guanzhong was put in charge of foreign affairs for the PLA. Wang brought more administrative than operational experience to this position. He previously directed the CMC General Office, where he was responsible for speech writing for senior PLA leaders but had little experience with military diplomacy. He is seen by many as confident and less responsive to staff advice on foreign affairs. For example, his speech at the 2014 Shangri-la dialogue was not received well by other nations,[40] and while applauded in Chinese public opinion, internal PLA evaluation regarded it as a diplomat gaffe.[41]

The deputy chief of the General Staff in charge of intelligence, Vice Admiral Sun Jianguo, appeared to no longer have primary responsibility for foreign affairs, although he still met with visiting foreign delegations. The rationale for dividing the portfolio is unclear. The demands of intelligence and diplomacy may simply have grown too much to be effectively managed by a single individual. But several alternative explanations are possible.[42] During Xiong Guangkai's tenure, many in the PLA saw him having a strong agenda that colored both intelligence and foreign affairs activities. An "anything but Xiong" sentiment is known to exist within the PLA and the split may be an outcome of that period. A division of the portfolio may have been an attempt to sterilize intelligence from other influences. The new arrangement also suggested a change in approach to military diplomacy, with less emphasis on intelligence collection and more on the traditional diplomatic role of managing relations and reducing tensions. The question remains open as the portfolio appears to have been recentralized under Vice Admiral Sun in 2014.[43]

The second important PLA leader for M2M relations is the head of GSD-FAO. The work of two past directors amply demonstrates their impact on military diplomacy. Zhang Bangdong, GSD-FAO director from 2003 to 2007, presided over a pivotal period in the PLA's M2M program. He did more than just successfully execute a series of joint military exercises, as noted earlier. Prior to his tenure, the GSD-FAO played no significant role beyond administrative coordinator for the PLA's external affairs. It was, for all intents and purposes, a "barbarian handler." Zhang had strategic vision and recognized that China's changing security environment and the military modernization necessary to meet its new demands required the PLA to become more engaged outside of its borders. The growing basket of M2M activities during his tenure, culminating in the Sino-Russian 2005 Peace Mission joint exercise, not only served broader PLA goals but also helped put the GSD-FAO at the center of those efforts. He played a crucial role in translating this turning tide into substantive change for the military and for his own organization. The PLA made important diplomatic progress and the GSD-FAO carved out for itself a greater role as coordinator and manager of strategic planning.

His successor, Qian Lihua (2007–2013), sought to transform the GSD-FAO from a "foreign affairs staff" to a "strategic advisory staff," a substantive change that would allow it to engage in more research and planning with greater potential for policy impact.[44] He required GSD-FAO officers to rotate among a variety of departments within and outside of the GSD-FAO system rather than remain in one track as they had traditionally done. For instance, a GSD-FAO officer specializing in English and English speaking countries would spend time in the North America bureau, but also work in other regional bureaus in order to understand other regions' perspectives on the United States. Officers should also gain experience in different functional areas, including arms control and antipiracy or spend some time in research departments, or in the news/information department. Qian attempted to nurture more rounded individual talent to meet the rising intellectual and functional demands on GSD-FAO officers.

Rear Admiral Guan Youfei is the current director of the GSD-FAO. Besides his conservative and even strident speeches during his tenure as Defense Ministry spokesman, little is known about Guan's impact on the PLA's diplomatic activity. Perhaps because of his past experience as spokesman, Guan has been willing to meet with foreign scholars and media to promote PLA views about military-to-military relations.[45]

Individuals, Leaders, and Military Diplomacy

In addition to the GSD-FAO and the PLA leaders with explicit responsibility for managing military diplomacy, other individuals within the PLA can crucially influence the direction and the success (or failure) of military diplomacy.[46] These include the growing number of officers throughout the PLA who participate in M2M activities as operational commanders and political commissars, troops involved in joint exercises, trainers for foreign militaries, students, and military academics. The number of individual officers involved in military exchanges has grown in tandem with burgeoning M2M activities. Yet, as a result of the PLA's long history of isolation from foreign armed forces (particularly Western ones), the change in mentality and the competence to interact effectively have not kept pace with the level of exposure.

Until recently, most mid-level officers had limited contact with outsiders and so their impressions and knowledge of other countries were gained indirectly and filtered through the Chinese media and propaganda system. The PLA's conservative, even nationalistic mindset creates the irony that those in regular contact with foreigners and thus most likely to understand foreign countries often fall under suspicion of being too dovish. This phenomenon is particularly relevant in M2M with the United States, given its political sensitivity within the PLA. Thus, the more strident viewpoints in the PLA vis-à-vis the United States tend to be based on faulty assumptions and held by those who have the least experience with the United States. The opposite and more rational perspective posits that the best way to understand the military culture and strategic thought of another country is through firsthand experience. Direct contact can also provide a deeper appreciation for the level of distrust and biases between countries. PLA officers engaged in M2M reflect these competing perspectives about the effects of foreign contact.

Culture and personal experience play important roles in other ways as well. One example is misreading of signals. For instance, PLA officers often complain that many in the United States military lack a basic knowledge of the PLA organization.[47] Lack of appreciation of the significance of bureaucratic position (grade) over military rank in the Chinese system is an example. In the PLA, military ranks are mostly based on an accumulation of years in service while the positions officers hold are usually more important.[48] A mismatch in the ranking of hosts in the United States for Chinese military visits can engender a sense of offense that can have lasting effects.[49] Cultural misinterpretation has led to other issues as well. The junior officers who accompany top Chinese military leaders are often handpicked "favorites" of the PLA leadership and thus fast tracked for promotion. Failure to understand this by an American host can create a gap in expectations. Furthermore, the Chinese have also noted the greater rank and numbers of officers and their entourages in Chinese delegations sent to the United States than vice versa. These obscure bureaucratic politics and cultural issues of "face" are generally lost on the U.S. military. Yet they can have a lasting influence on PLA officers whose limited contact with the United States has been shaped by such experiences.[50]

Training Programs and Institutional Links

One often overlooked dimension of the PLA's international links is the depth and breadth of the military training programs underway with many foreign militaries and an increase in Chinese military aid. In the late 1990s, the CMC decided to strengthen the PLA's overseas training—especially of mid- to high-level commanders—as an important component of military diplomacy.[51] According to official military history sources, a total of 130 PLA units, including universities, colleges, hospitals, factories, and operational units took part in overseas training programs between 1949 and 2005.[52] PLA NDU alone trained more than four thousand foreign military personnel from 150 countries during the period 2004–2010.[53] The PLA Air Force Academy opened its simulation facilities to foreign military personnel in 2009. There are programs with countries in Europe, Latin American, the Middle East and Asia, and Africa. The PLA has also aided other armed forces in building military academies and establishing their own training programs.

Training programs and institution building are notable because they represent a conscious shift beginning in the early 1990s in Chinese military assistance from supplying material (armaments and money) to building personal and institutional affiliations.[54] This is in essence establishing a form of soft power for the PLA. It is a smart strategy that is developing the PLA's connections with a new generation of officers, many of whom eventually go on to positions of leadership and influence in their respective military organizations. For instance, from 2000 to 2012, the PLA Air Force Academy trained 755 foreign military personnel from 74 countries, among whom 30 were subsequently promoted to full general. The PLA's training programs with Africa go back to the 1950s and many of the young officers trained in China subsequently moved into senior ranks. These historical M2M contacts provide a great potential for advantage and influence for the PLA in Sino-African relations. While numerous institutions across the PLA are involved in these programs, the GSD-FAO is in overall charge of them. The GSD-FAO's functional role as mediators, organizers, managers, and even operators of these programs gives it a uniquely influential status in China's military diplomacy.

Implications for PLA's New Course

The preceding discussion has outlined the PLA's proliferation of diplomatic activity and the role of the principal institutions and leaders as the PLA retools for a wider regional and even global orientation. What, if any, are the implications of this trend for China's broader foreign policy? An exhaustive analysis of the PLA's influence in foreign policy is beyond the scope of this chapter. But several general observations are noteworthy. First, the PLA's presence around the world is creating facts on the ground that have the potential to complicate China's external image and foreign policy. Even if the PLA's viewpoint and/or interests do not differ substantially from those of other national actors, China has many moving parts in its foreign diplomacy, all of whose behavior and actions require harmonizing. Second, where military methods—and to some degree interests—do diverge from those of civilian actors, as on the issue of U.S. arms sales to Taiwan, coordination is even more difficult. This section draws on several examples to illustrate how the PLA's position on specific foreign policy issues or its activities abroad have affected China's foreign relations.

U.S.-China Relations and Taiwan

When military diplomacy becomes more political, as it invariably does in relations with other major powers, the PLA must coordinate and often take a back seat to other actors in the foreign and security policy decisionmaking system, particularly the MFA. The most politically sensitive bilateral relation of all is the U.S.-China relationship and with respect to specific military interests, China's handling of U.S. arms sales to Taiwan. This issue reflects the differences between the PLA and the MFA in terms of their cultures, methods, and diplomatic goals.[55]

Aside from substantive issues, basic bureaucratic differences have implications for coordination between the PLA and the MFA. From the PLA's perspective, there is a mismatch of rank in dealing with their counterparts in the MFA. China's foreign minister has a civilian bureaucratic rank at the same level as the PLA's deputy chief of General Staff, and lower than the chief of the General Staff. Thus, the PLA GSD, as an institution, has a higher bureaucratic rank than the MFA, which can lead to friction when the PLA GSD must interface with the MFA on a routine basis.[56] This difference matters to the PLA, an organization with a deeply ingrained sense of rank hierarchy.[57]

The PLA sees the MFA merely as an administrative organization, handling the affairs of state as directed by senior CCP leaders. This is partly due to a decline in strong and charismatic leadership at the foreign minister and state councilor for foreign affairs level.[58] The PLA therefore looks to influence channels higher up as a more effective means in shaping policy outcomes to its liking. Moreover, the MFA is viewed as strategically shortsighted and inconsistent in its policy agenda, which is focused on building bilateral relations and multilateral arrangements.

PLA-MFA differences over Taiwan arms sales and M2M relations with the United States underscore this problem. From the PLA perspective, the MFA plays the U.S.-China M2M card for reasons not closely linked to military relations and their inherent security considerations. Thus, once the ostensible purpose of punishing the United States for arms sales to Taiwan by curtailing M2M relations is accomplished, the MFA has a propensity to get the M2M relationship back on track as soon as possible to avoid lasting damage. The PLA mindset is both longer term and more strategic. The military does not see any reason for reversing policy if the principles have not fundamentally changed (meaning, U.S. arms sales to Taiwan will likely continue). The PLA objects to the policy flip-flopping as it sends the wrong signal and makes the PLA look unprofessional. In broad terms, the MFA is more concerned with maintaining stable relations with the United States, while the PLA wants progress on the larger strategic issue of reducing or ending U.S. arms sales.

At a deeper level, the PLA views this changeable policy behavior as symptomatic of the MFA's organizational culture. The turnover rate within the MFA is much higher than in many other bodies in the Chinese system.[59] This contrasts with a much lower turnover rate in the GSD-FAO office, which allows officers to develop knowledge that spans many years and political events, providing more continuity and a longer-term strategic approach.[60] The

MFA also lacks the military expertise and basic information about PLA capabilities and operations necessary for informed views on military and security issues. For example, all the directors and most of the staff in the MFA's Department of Arms Control are transferred from other MFA departments that have little to do with security and military affairs. PLA critics argue that these MFA weaknesses contribute to a fluid policy environment detrimental to national security matters that demand longer continuity.[61]

That is not to say that the PLA and the MFA do not work together. The GSD-FAO and its subordinate regional and functional bureaus have routine contact with counterparts in the MFA, the State Council, and the Central Committee. However, cooperation and coordination vary across offices. In some areas such as antipiracy a good working relationship exists, but ties are poor in other areas such as arms control and African affairs.[62]

The PLA and MFA are clearly at odds in objectives and methods over some issues, such as M2M and U.S. arms sales to Taiwan, which are at the heart of relations with the United States.[63] Nevertheless, the PLA is playing an increasingly visible role, and not necessarily a detrimental one, in stable U.S.-China M2M relations. The cooling of rhetoric over Taiwan arms sales in 2011 supports this idea.[64] In part, this more moderate response conforms to the debate within PLA think tanks about rethinking the method and measure of reaction to incidents that "harm China's core interests."[65] The discussion is principally in the context of Taiwan arms sales, but fundamentally recognizes that severing M2M over specific incidents of "strategic disagreement" is too blunt an instrument. A far more nuanced approach is required, one that is proportionate to the act and allows for more flexibility and refinement in signaling the PLA's position.[66] It is uncertain how widely this debate is occurring inside the PLA, though it is clearly evident within NDU and the Academy of Military Sciences and their affiliated think tanks.[67] The discussion appears to be less about the cost-benefit of greater openness in M2M relations or even delinking M2M ties from perceived challenges to China's security interests. Rather, the discourse revolves around the need for greater rationality in the use of military diplomacy and whether using it as a tool of punishment is in the PLA's interests.

While an internal shift in the PLA's own position on M2M with United States may have been a factor behind the muted response to the 2011 Taiwan arms sale, recent events highlight the role of an unequivocal civilian decision to stabilize and improve the bilateral military relationship.[68] Presidents Barack Obama and Hu Jintao agreed to improve M2M relations, a decision the PLA publicly supported.[69] Xi Jinping clearly articulated a top leadership commitment to improved M2M relations at the Sunnylands summit in June 2013.[70] The PLA appears to be implementing this commitment as the pace of M2M activity has been stepped up along with a broadening in the scope of interactions to include things such as general staff talks and PLA participation in RIMPAC.[71] There is still much mutual suspicion and an increasing sense of competition between the two militaries, but the PLA seems to be using this new framework to try to create opportunities to learn more from the U.S. military and is therefore reluctant to cut off all contacts when an incident occurs that displeases it. These developments point to the importance of civilian decisionmaking over the politically sensitive U.S.-China relationship and its M2M component, but also show a realignment of military diplomacy to a more traditional role of building and strengthening relationships.

Friction: Expanding Space for PLA Influence

The PLA also affects China's external relations in other ways. In many instances, it is inaccurate to portray PLA interests and behavior as necessarily different from, much less in contravention of, China's larger diplomatic efforts. Nevertheless, the PLA's mere presence often drives events in unexpected ways, sometimes forcing other foreign policy actors, principally the MFA, to respond to its actions. As PLA overseas exercises and deployments increase, this diplomatic friction is becoming a bigger problem.

For instance, the PLA reportedly used helicopter patrols near a disputed part of the Sino-Indian border to halt a number of Indian construction activities between 2009 and 2010.[72] This alarmed the Indians enough to initiate a negotiation mechanism in 2011 that included the militaries of both sides. The respective foreign ministries coordinated the talks, but direct action by the PLA played the principal role in setting the agenda.[73] In this way, the PLA's central role in this issue boosted the incentives of the other side—India in this case—to bring the PLA into the negotiations, in effect creating a diplomatic seat for the PLA, where Sino-Indian border talks were previously dominated by the MFA. More recently, the border stand-offs during both Li Keqiang's visit to India in 2013 and Xi Jinping's September 2014 visit have raised questions about the timing of these military incidents, the level of civil-military coordination, and China's intentions toward India.[74]

A high level of friction can also be seen in the lack of coordination between the PLA and the MFA on the diplomatic impact of weapons testing.

The 2007 ASAT test, likely done without any coordination with the MFA, led to an embarrassing diplomatic blunder with strong condemnation by the international community. The J-20 stealth fighter test during U.S. Secretary of Defense Robert Gates' 2011 visit to China was another such display. Outbursts by Rear Admiral Guan Youfei, then deputy director of the Foreign Affairs Office of GSD, during the 2010 Strategic & Economic Dialogue as well as the exchange between Maj. Gen. Zhu Chenghu and Secretary Gates a month later led many to suspect the PLA had a different agenda for strategic talks with the United States.[75] While the PLA may be constrained in direct efforts to influence foreign diplomacy, it often does so indirectly, whether by accident or design.

While there is little evidence of a PLA agenda independent of China's broader diplomatic goals, discrepancies between the two are increasingly a reality, particularly where the PLA has a strong presence and interests. One notable example is China's close M2M relations with Turkey. Both militaries stand to gain from the collaboration with the potential for substantial weapons sales and joint exercises. Since Turkey is a NATO ally, however, the relationship is controversial, raising concerns in Western capitals about Chinese intentions. Moreover, from the Chinese perspective, Turkey's stance on China's Muslim Uyghurs has been problematic. Pan-Turkism is a vision that has been voiced by some Turkish political figures and by a number of Turkish generals as well. Nevertheless, the two sides signed agreements in 2010 to develop a strategic partnership and conducted joint exercises.[76] Turkey subsequently announced plans to purchase Chinese surface-to-air missiles, alarming other NATO countries.[77] The complicated mix of politics, trade, and military ties in Sino-Turkey relations does not lend itself well to a coherent set of policy priorities.

Xi Jinping and the Road Ahead

This chapter argues that the PLA's perspective on and role in China's diplomatic activities has undergone a fundamental shift. This is a consequence of China's changing economic, political, and security role within an evolving international environment over the past two decades. Many of these changes occurred incrementally during Jiang Zemin's and Hu Jintao's time in office. Several years into the Xi Jinping era, it is worth considering the impact the Xi administration and recent events are having on the PLA and military diplomacy.

Under Xi Jinping, the PLA's external role has become more active and visible but also more complicated and ambiguous. Several variables have influenced these trends. Perhaps foremost is Xi's tone on military, security, and sovereignty issues. In an important 2012 speech, Xi emphasized that China will maintain regional stability (*weiwen*) under the prerequisite of safeguarding China's sovereignty, security, and territorial integrity,[78] which others have summarized as *weiquan*, or protection of China's rights and interests.[79] This position differs from that of previous Chinese leaders, who emphasized maintaining good neighborly relations and regional stability while shelving territorial disputes. This highlights an inherent tension between China's need to protect its maritime rights and to maintain regional stability.[80] Given the PLA's role as the ultimate guarantor of China's maritime rights, Xi's statement has a direct bearing on PLA responsibilities.

Xi Jinping has also called on the PLA to step up its effectiveness as a fighting force, emphasizing the importance of combat readiness and a PLA that can "fight and win wars."[81] Xi's statements contrast notably with Hu Jintao's emphasis on noncombat operations such as peacekeeping, disaster relief, and antipiracy operations. Xi's emphasis on *weiquan* and improving PLA combat capability complicates PLA use of military diplomacy to improve ties with neighboring countries.

A third noteworthy change under Xi has been what PLA officers call a new stress on "substance over form."[82] This is part of an austerity campaign that was launched when Xi took over the CMC chairmanship, but it is also a vigorous attempt to promote effective and competent leadership at all levels of the PLA. It is a call for results, not talk and has had several consequences. First, it has boosted the PLA's confidence to pursue a forward-looking diplomatic agenda. The PLA is now engaged in more international defense fora than ever before and is conducting an unprecedented level of bilateral and multilateral joint military exercises.[83] PLA officers involved in multilateral events speak of a proliferation of activity, with much less red tape and restrictive approval procedures.[84] This includes a stepping up of the pace of M2M activity with the United States since the Sunnylands summit and Xi's support for a "new model of major power relations" between the two countries.[85] Urging substance over form has also led to a greater appetite to host and even lead multilateral activities. The PLA Navy hosted the Western Pacific Naval Symposium for the first time in April 2014. The Xiangshan Forum held in November 2014, originally a modest event, was upgraded to a high-level security forum that may aspire

to rival the Shangri-la Dialogue. The recently convened Conference on Interaction and Confidence-Building Measures in Asia is a regional security forum
chaired by China. There have even been suggestions that China's antipiracy
operations might expand from the Gulf of Aden to other regions such as the
Nigerian coast, perhaps in conjunction with the U.S. Navy.[86] However, China
has shown an increasing tendency to favor multilateral fora where it has a
leading role while downgrading and even avoiding those dominated by the
United States.[87]

This chapter should not end without mentioning the growing impact
of public opinion on China's external relations. As James Reilly points out
in his book *Smart Society, Strong State*, in an authoritarian system, regime
legitimacy rests in large part on a high level of responsiveness to public opinion.[88] Although public opinion is mostly focused on domestic politics, China's
increasing interactions with the region (and beyond) blur the line between
internal and external issues. Public opinion has deeply affected Sino-Japanese
relations since the mid-1990s. Its influence is now being felt across a wider
range of foreign policy issues, including the PLA's role in external relations.
While public opinion does not necessarily push the PLA in a more assertive
direction, it increasingly constrains options for how China can response to
external developments.

There are contending lines of thought about China's strategic posture,
with some eager to enforce China's rights and interests with military might,
and others far more wary of a muscular foreign and security policy.[89] Military
diplomacy reflects this competition of visions. If military diplomacy seeks to
strengthen relations, promote understanding and trust, and dampen regional
anxiety over China's military modernization program, recent Chinese diplomatic and military actions have made these tasks more difficult. Whether
due to the changing security environment, Xi Jinping's renewed emphasis
on combat readiness and protection of maritime interests, or a public opinion that increasingly constrains action and demands a response to perceived
national slights, Chinese military diplomacy is becoming more active, but
also potentially less persuasive.

Notes

1. The U.S. military uses "combined exercise" to refer to bilateral or multilateral exercises with other countries, but the PLA uses "joint exercise" to refer to both

exercises involving more than one service and exercises with other countries. This chapter follows the PLA terminology.

2. The Taiwan issue is the exception, but before 1995–1996 was only simmering at a relatively low level.

3. This role was animated by the strong legacy of having charismatic and influential leaders such as Zhou Enlai and Qian Qichen dominate the Ministry of Foreign Affairs and the foreign affairs portfolio.

4. Evidence includes the slashing of PLA budgets and reductions in troop numbers during the 1980s. The PLA directly yielded to the MFA on several occasions, including a 1978 incident with Japan over the Diaoyu/Senkaku Islands when the MFA insisted the PLA not take aggressive action. The PLA did not support China's signing of the Declaration of Conduct of Parties in the South China Sea in 1992. Interviews with MFA officials, July 2011, Beijing. The DOC was signed by the vice foreign minister, but is not referred to in official Ministry of National Defense documents. See "Ministry of Defense: China Has Indisputable Rights over the Spratly Islands and Nearby Islands" [国防部: 中国对南沙群岛及附近海域有无可争辩的主权], *Xinhua Online* [新华网], September 28, 2014.

5. In 1993, the U.S. Navy forced a Chinese container ship, the *Yinhe*, into a Saudi Arabian port to search for the chemical weapon precursors it was allegedly carrying.

6. Brian Francis Lafferty, "Buildup: Chinese Defense Budgets in the Reform Era, 1978 to Present" (Ph.D. dissertation, Columbia University, 2009).

7. Zhang Wenmu, "Sea Power and China's Strategic Choices," *China Security* (Summer 2006): 21.

8. Report to the Seventeenth CCP National Congress declared the strategic goal of "making [China] prosperous (富国) and the armed forces powerful (强军)."

9. Bates Gill, *Rising Star: China's New Security Concept* (Washington, DC: Brookings Institution, 2007).

10. Maj. Gen. Qian Lihua [钱利华], "China's New Military Diplomacy: Review and Outlook" [新中国军事外交: 回顾与前瞻], *PLA Daily* [解放军报], February 28, 2011.

11. Han Xiandong and Kim Soonsoo [韩献栋, 金淳洙], "China's Military Diplomacy and New Conception of Security" [中国军事外交与新安全观], *Contemporary International Relations* [现代国际关系], no. 2 (2008); and Yang Yi [杨毅], "Strategic Adjustment of China's Defense and Military Building" [中国国防与军队建设的战略性调整], *World Economy and Politics* [世界经济与政治], no. 11 (2008).

12. Shirley Kan, "U.S.-China Military Contacts: Issues for Congress," *CRS Report for Congress RL32496*, Congressional Research Service, Library of Congress, Washington, DC (July 29, 2014); Office of the Secretary of Defense, "Military and Security Developments Involving the People's Republic of China," *Annual Report to Congress (2013)*; Kenneth Allen and Eric McVadon, *China's Foreign Military Relations* (Washington, DC: Harry L. Stimson Center, 1999); China's Defense White Papers; and numerous Chinese sources.

13. Evan Ellis, "The Rise of China in the Americas," in *Reconceptualizing Security in the Americas in the Twenty-first Century*, eds. Bruce M. Bagley, Jonathan D. Rosen, and Hanna Samir Kassab (Lanham, MD: Lexington Books, 2014).

14. Interview with PLA officers, Beijing, August, 2012.

15. Technically, the CMC, the four General Departments, and the defense-related academies have the authority to independently have contacts with foreign entities. Decisions on high-level exchanges are usually made by the CMC.

16. These include the China Institute for International Strategic Studies and the Foundation for International Strategic Studies under the GSD's Intelligence Department, and the China Association for International Friendly Contact under the GPD. Other organizations that facilitate PLA contacts with foreigners include the China Association for Military Sciences and the China Arms Control and Disarmament Association, hosted under the MFA but with close connections to the PLA. See Bates Gill and James Mulvenon, "Chinese Military-Related Think Tanks and Research Institutions," *China Quarterly*, no. 171 (September 2002): 617–624.

17. Zhou Feng [周峰], "PLA's Window: Chinese Army's Steady Steps toward Further Opening-up" [迎外部队：军队对外开放步履铿锵], *PLA Daily* [解放军报], December 18, 2008.

18. Interviews with PLA officers, Beijing, August 2011.

19. Interviews with PLA officers from NDU. Rules governing PLA officer interaction with foreigners have been in place for some time but regulations recently published by the CMC formalize them. "China Issues Revised Regulations on PLA Discipline," *China Daily*, June 3, 2010.

20. Ibid.

21. According to Wen Bing, the GSD-FAO is the leading agency in coordinating China's Defense Whitepaper. "Wen Bing Discusses the Drafting Process of Defense White Paper" [温冰介绍国防白皮书编制过程：对每个词都要很准地把握], *People's Daily Online* [人民网], April 1, 2011.

22. Interviews with PLA officers, Beijing, August 2010. The GSD-FAO is understaffed and some actions are the result of lack of manpower rather than overt planning.

23. Chai Chengwen, GSD-FAO director (1969–1982), was the deputy director of the GSD Second Department.

24. Maj. Gen. Zhan Maohai, former director (2000–2003), graduated from the University of International Business and Economics; Maj. Gen. Zhang Bangdong, former director (2003–2007), graduated from the Beijing Broadcasting University and studied at Harvard University.

25. Roughly one-fifth of GSD-FAO officers have served in combat-oriented field units. Interviews with PLA officers, Beijing, August 2012.

26. This section largely derives from interviews with PLA officers at NDU, Beijing, July–August 2011.

27. This is a viewpoint almost universally held by PLA officers interviewed.

28. Moreover, the GSD-FAO maintains authority over trips abroad, a highly sought-after perk.

29. The PLA has strong bureaucratic boundaries: salaries and duties are under strict personnel management. The GSD-FAO can second officers without formally affecting structure or budgetary issues. Interviews with PLA officers, Beijing, January 2013.

30. One example is the GSD-FAO's central role in coordinating the drafting of the Defense White Paper. "Wen Bing Discusses the Drafting Process of Defense White Paper."

31. "PLA Comprehensively Promotes Reform of Combat Training" [中国军队全面推进对抗训练改革], *Xinhua Online* [新华网], November 26, 2012; "Efforts to Promote Transition to Military Exercises under Conditions of Informatization" [努力推进军事训练向信息化条件下转变], December 27, 2007, and "China to Hold 40 Military Exercises Directed at Hotspot Regions" [我国今年将举行近40场军演 场合直指热点区域], *Sina.com*, February 27, 2013.

32. Zhang Xiaotong [张晓彤], "New Progress in National Defense and Army Building since the Sixteenth National Congress of the CCP" [十六大以来国防与军队建设的新进展], Party Literature Research Centre of the CCCPC, October 31, 2012, www.wxyjs.org.cn/rdzt_550/yjsbdslzk/201210/t20121031_136514.htm.

33. For an overview, see Andrew Scobell, "Discourse in 3-D: The PLA's Evolving Doctrine, Circa 2009," in *PLA at Home and Abroad: Assessing the Operational Capabilities of China's Military*, eds. Roy Kamphausen, David Lai, and Andrew Scobell (Carlisle Barracks, PA: U.S Army War College, 2010).

34. Wang Guang [王光], "From 'Territory of Borders' to 'Territory of Interests'" [从"领土边疆"投向"利益边疆"], *PLA Daily* [解放军报], November 22, 2012.

35. Total joint exercises are as follows: 2 in 2002, 3 in 2003, 5 in 2004, 4 in 2005, 3 in 2006, 9 in 2007, 2 in 2008, 6 in 2009, 11 in 2010, 5 in 2011, 10 in 2012, and 17 in 2013. Figures are derived from China's Defense White Papers and "Highlights in China's Military Diplomacy in 2013" [2013中国军事外交亮点纷呈], *Xinhua Online* [新华网], December 26, 2013.

36. "Structural Analysis of General Staff Leadership, 1987–2009" [1987–2009年总参谋部领导人事结构分析], May 9, 2009, http://club.xilu.com/xinguancha/msgview-950389-93900.html.

37. Zhang Qinsheng, who held this position between Xiong Guangkai and Ma Xiaotian, is not discussed due to his very brief tenure.

38. Based on interviews with PLA officers, Beijing, July 2011. However, the linkage between personality and policy should be taken as only one possible factor. External events such as major arms packages to Taiwan in 2007, 2008, 2010, and 2011 undoubtedly played a role as well.

39. Interviews with PLA officers, Beijing, January 2013.

40. Banyan, "Dust-up at the Shangri-La," *The Economist,* June 1, 2014.

41. Interviews with PLA officer, August 2014.

42. Interviews with PLA officers, August 2014.

43. Personal communication from a U.S. scholar, February 2015.

44. Interviews with PLA officers, Beijing, January 2013.

45. Personal communication from a U.S. scholar.

46. Interviews with PLA officers, Beijing, July 2011.

47. This problem is partly inherent in any contact between two distinct military systems, but also stems from the high degree of rotation present in the American FAO system.

48. For instance, even though the heads of the four General Departments may sometimes hold the military rank of lieutenant general, their positions are more important than the head of a military region, who may be a full general.

49. One case noted by PLA officers is the visit to the United States by Yu Yongbo, the third-ranking member on the CMC and top political commissar of the PLA, who was hosted by Under Secretary of Defense for Readiness Bernard Rostker. See Kan, "U.S.-China Military Contacts."

50. Interviews with PLA officers, August 2010 and 2011.

51. Shan Xu and Guo Kai [山旭, 郭凯], "Foreign Military Elites Enter Classes of China's PLA Air Force: Eating, Living and Studying Together" [外军精英走进中国空军课堂: 同吃同住同学习], *Outlook Oriental Weekly* [东方周刊], July 23, 2012.

52. Institute of Military History at Academy of Military Sciences [军科院军史所], *Concise Military History of the PRC* [中华人民共和国军事史要] (Beijing: Academy of Military Science Press [军事科学出版社], 2005).

53. "PLA NDU College of Defense Studies Reveals It Has Already Trained 4,000 Foreign Military Personnel" [国防大学防务学院揭秘已培训4000多名外国军官], Chinanews.com, September 5, 2010.

54. According to a former director of the Foreign Military Education and Exchange Center of Nanjing Army Command Academy. Wang Cunfu [王存富], "Remembering Thirty Years of Training Foreign Military Personnel" [难忘外训三十年], *China Military News Net* [中国军网], March 16, 2011.

55. The term "MFA" may be a slight oversimplification as other civilian actors play roles in foreign policymaking, including the state councilor, small leading groups, the Central Committee Foreign Affairs Office, and the National Security Commission.

56. GSD-FAO bureaus correspond directly with MFA bureaus that are functionally equivalent, but lower in bureaucratic rank and have an equal rank to the vice foreign minister's office. Interview with MFA staff, Beijing, August, 2011.

57. The political status of CMC vice-chairmen is below that of Politburo members, but above that of the state councilor. The status of ordinary CMC members is immediately below state councilor, which means all CMC members are of higher rank than all ministerial positions (except the Ministry of Defense).

58. Past foreign ministers and state councilors from Chen Yi through Qian Qichen and perhaps Li Zhaoxing are regarded as much more influential than recent foreign minister Yang Jiechi and state councilor Dai Bingguo, who did not have the same political clout even though they maintained similar access. Interviews, July–August, 2011.

59. For instance, the Arms Control Department in the MFA has replaced its director every 2–4 years since the mid-1990s. The actual turnover of its staff is even faster. Many MFA officers spend roughly half their time in the national MFA office and half overseas; promotion is determined in significant part by overseas appointments. Directors include Sha Zhukang (1997–2001), Liu Jieyi (2001–2005), Zhang Yan (2005–2007), Cheng Jingye (2007–2011), and Wang Qun since early 2012.

60. Interview with PLA officer, Beijing, August 2011.

61. Interview with PLA officer, Beijing, February 2010.

62. Interview with PLA officer, Beijing, July 2011.

63. This is a separate issue from their respective stances on arms sales or other national security affairs. Within the PLA is a range of positions from softer to harderline and the MFA can be more strident than the PLA in its position.

64. Response to the Taiwan arms sales announcements in late 2008 and 2010 were strident and comprehensive. The reaction to the 2011 sale was decidedly toned down. See, "American Experts Say China's Reaction to This Arms Deal Unexpectedly Mild" [美国专家称中国对美台军售反应温和出乎意料], *Sina.com*, September 27, 2011. This may reflect the view that China successfully moved the U.S. side to limit sales to F-16 A/B upgrades rather than F-16 C/D aircraft.

65. Interviews with PLA officers, Beijing, July 2011.

66. For instance in the Taiwan arms sales case, rather than a knee-jerk reaction of severing all ties, the reaction should be based on a specific set of parameters that depend on the types of weapons, their numbers, and other contexts.

67. The NDU Institute of Strategic Studies and the NDU Strategic Studies Department are likely studying these issues. The AMS has broached the possibility of establishing institutional contacts with foreign militaries that would weather the political impact on M2M relations. The China Foundation for International and Strategic Studies under AMS, and to a lesser degree the GPD Liaison Department also have an interest in military diplomacy.

68. PLA officers frequently speak of a diversity of views—even highly contentious—especially with respect to U.S.-China M2M relations. Another way to see this is that the civilian decision helped tip the debate within the PLA.

69. General Chen Bingde emphasized the importance of the CCP leadership commitment to improve bilateral and M2M relations with the United States in his May 18, 2011, speech at the U.S. National Defense University.

70. Xi articulated a vision for "new type of major country relations" and as a critical part of that, a "new type of military-to-military relations." See *Remarks by President Obama and President Xi Jinping of the People's Republic of China After Bilateral Meeting*, Office of the Press Secretary, White House, June 8, 2013.

71. Kan, "U.S.-China Military Contacts."

72. "Indian Press Cooked Up So-called 'Report on PLA Invasion'" [印煤炒作所谓'中国军队入侵报告'], *Sina.com*, January 12, 2011.

73. "China and India Establish Border Dispute Management Mechanism," *Global Times*, September 29, 2011.

74. Shannon Tiezzi, "China, India End Military Stand-Off along Disputed Border," *The Diplomat*, October 1, 2014.

75. "Top Chinese and American Military Leaders Bicker in Singapore: Zhu Chenghu Points Finger at Gates" [中美军方高层在新加坡激烈交锋 朱成虎怒斥盖茨], *Oriental News* [东方网], June 10, 2010; John Pomfret, "In Chinese Admiral's Outburst, A Lingering Distrust of U.S.," *Washington Post*, June 8, 2010.

76. "China and Turkey Announce Establishment of Strategic Cooperation," www.sina.com.cn, October 8, 2010; and Yitzhak Shichor, "Military Cooperation between Beijing and Ankara," *China Brief* 9 (April 16, 2009).

77. Although the deal is unlikely to be consummated. See Denise Der, "Why Turkey May Not Buy Chinese Missile Systems After All," *The Diplomat,* May 7, 2014.

78. "Xi Jinping's Talk at the World Peace Forum" [习近平在 "世界和平论坛" 开幕式上的致辞], *China.com.cn* [中国网], July 9, 2012. Xi reiterated his thinking in 2013: "Xi Jinping at Eighth Collective Study Session of the Politburo" [习近平在中共中央政治局第八次集体学习时强调], *People's Daily* [人民日报], August 1, 2013.

79. Teng Jianqun [滕建群], "Safeguarding Stability or Rights, an Inevitable Choice for China's Diplomacy" [中国外交必须的抉择: 维稳还是维权], *Lianhe zaobao* [联合早报], August 7, 2012.

80. Taylor Fravel, "Xi Jinping and China's Maritime Disputes," *The Diplomat,* August 15, 2013; and Phillip C. Saunders, "China's Juggling Act: Balancing Stability and Territorial Claims," *PacNet,* no. 33 (April 29, 2014).

81. Edward Wong, "China's Communist Party Chief Acts to Bolster Military," *New York Times,* December 14, 2012.

82. Interviews with PLA officer, August 2013 and 2014.

83. "Highlights in China's Military Diplomacy in 2013" [2013中国军事外交亮点纷呈], *Xinhua Online* [新华网], December 26, 2013.

84. Interviews with PLA officers, August 2014.

85. Bonnie Glaser and Jacqueline Vitello, "US-China Relations: Sizing Each Other Up at Sunnylands," *Comparative Connections* 15, no. 2 (September 2013).

86. Such cooperation remains problematic in many ways. Interviews with PLA officers, August 2014.

87. China's active engagement in and even leading a number of fora as mentioned above stands in stark contrast to its reluctance to send senior PLA officers to attend the Track 1.5 Shangri-la Dialogue.

88. James Reilly, *Strong Society, Smart State: The Rise of Public Opinion in China's Japan Policy* (New York: Columbia University Press, 2012).

89. Interviews with PLA Officer, August 2013.

PART III
THE PLA AND OTHER ACTORS IN TERRITORIAL DISPUTES

9 The PLA and National Security Decisionmaking: Insights from China's Territorial and Maritime Disputes

M. Taylor Fravel

A CENTRAL QUESTION IN THE STUDY OF CHINA'S FOR-eign policy is the role of the PLA in national security decisionmaking. Many observers have argued that PLA influence at least partly accounts for the more active and assertive posture China adopted following the 2008 global financial crisis. As Joshua Kurlantzick writes, "At times, the PLA appears to have initiated or escalated international disputes—against the wishes of the top leadership in Beijing—in order to push Chinese policy in a more hawkish direction."[1] Kurlantzick captures a sentiment in the media that the influence of the PLA on policymaking in Beijing accounts for China's recent behavior.[2]

Nevertheless, assessments of the PLA's influence in national security decisionmaking are often based on conjecture or speculation, not facts. This chapter seeks to illuminate this question by examining one specific issue area, territorial disputes. Territorial disputes arguably offer an easy test for observing the PLA's influence on decisionmaking. The defense of China's sovereignty and territorial integrity has been one of the PLA's core missions since the founding of the PRC in 1949 (in addition to defense of the CCP's rule). Many of China's uses of force have involved the defense of territorial claims, such as the 1962 war with India.[3] As a result, territorial disputes should be one policy arena where the influence of the PLA can be observed and identified.

This chapter argues that the PLA's role in decisionmaking on China's territorial disputes has been limited to bureaucratic influence within existing policymaking structures and processes. With the partial exception of China's interpretation of the rights of coastal states under the UN Convention on the Law of the Sea (UNCLOS), the PLA has not played a significant role in influencing the initiation of China's territorial disputes, in the content of these claims, or in how China has chosen to defend them. Instead, China's behavior in territorial disputes, including its recent assertiveness in the South China Sea and East China Sea, reflects the consensus of China's top party leaders to respond to what are seen as challenges and provocations from other states. In other words, the PLA and China's leaders share the same preferences for a robust but nonmilitarized defense of China's claims in these disputes. Little evidence exists to support the view that the PLA has escalated these disputes against the wishes of top leaders. As other scholars have argued, the PLA remains subordinate to the party through existing mechanisms of party (or civilian) control.[4]

This chapter proceeds as follows. First, it reviews the challenges that scholars and analysts must confront when seeking to determine the influence of the PLA on national security decisionmaking in China. Second, it examines the general ways the PLA might influence China's policies on territorial disputes, including the initiation and content of specific territorial claims as well as China's approach to managing and defending its current claims. Third, to create a baseline for the analysis of recent events, it reviews the PLA's role in China's past territorial disputes. Fourth, it examines the role of the PLA in recent territorial and maritime disputes, including China's interpretation of the rights of coastal states under UNCLOS as well as the conflicts in the South China Sea and East China Sea. Overall, the findings support other recent studies regarding the role of the PLA in national security decisionmaking.[5]

Analytical Challenges

Scholars or analysts who seek to identify the influence of the PLA on policymaking in China must overcome a variety of analytical challenges, including the kinds of influence that the PLA could exercise, the types of policies over which the PLA might exert influence, and the evidentiary basis for determining whether influence has been exercised. Each is discussed below.

The first challenge is to define the concept of influence. What motivates a great deal of concern about the nature and degree of the PLA's influence over policy today is the fear that the PLA might be able to capture the state in certain policy domains, which may push China to adopt more "assertive" or "hawkish" policies than it otherwise would have adopted in the absence of pressure from the PLA. Nevertheless, as a key actor within the Chinese Communist Party (CCP), the PLA could also exert influence through existing institutional or bureaucratic channels, such as the Central Military Commission (CMC) or leading small groups established by the party or the state to coordinate policy.

As a result, it may be useful to identify two types of potential influence over policy. The first draws on traditional conceptions of relational power and could be called *capturing influence*. That is, through lobbying or independent action outside existing bureaucratic channels, the PLA could push the party-state to adopt a specific policy that party leaders do not want and would not have otherwise adopted without pressure or manipulation by the PLA. By definition, such influence would represent an act of disobedience and a violation of party norms. The second type of influence draws on research in bureaucratic politics and could be described as *bureaucratic influence*. That is, the PLA helps shape the content of a given policy through lobbying or independent action. The key difference is that in the bureaucratic view the PLA is only one of many actors that provide input and the final decision is taken by the party-state. Bureaucratic influence would include the PLA's influence over tactical and operational matters, including how specific policies are implemented in the military arena. The potential for this type of influence has increased as the PLA's autonomy within the party system has grown over the past twenty-five years.

A second analytical challenge concerns the types of policies over which the PLA can exert influence. The core concern revolves around whether the PLA is exerting influence beyond its military and defense portfolio to advance parochial interests at the expense of the party-state. At the level of grand strategy, for example, the PLA could seek to influence nonmilitary issues such as the overall guiding principles for Chinese foreign policy beyond the role of the armed forces as reflected in party guidelines.[6] Similarly, decisions to use force lie beyond the PLA's military domain due to their implications for overall national interests, and would be made by China's top leaders on the Politburo Standing Committee. In a specific foreign policy issue with a military component such as nonproliferation, for example, the PLA could seek to prevent China's accession to key international agreements such as the Comprehensive Test Ban Treaty.[7]

Taken together, these two challenges require precision about the type of influence being exercised and the issue over which it is being exercised. In the jargon of political science, analysts must clearly and precisely define the "dependent variable." Determining whether the PLA has actually exercised influence over national security decisionmaking involves an even more difficult analytical challenge: distinguishing between a potential PLA role in *shaping* policy and a PLA role in *implementing* policy. A visible PLA role in implementing China's approach to a particular issue does not necessarily mean that the PLA played an important role in shaping the content of policy. The PLA may simply be carrying out the instructions of the party-state. Likewise, lack of a visible PLA role in China's approach to a particular issue does not necessarily mean that the PLA did not play a role in influencing China's policy on that issue. The PLA may have shaped the policies that were adopted even if it does not help implement them. Finally, "aggressive" or "hawkish" behavior is not necessarily evidence of PLA influence on national security policy. China's top leaders might have adopted such policies for other reasons or because they share the PLA's preferences on the issue at hand.

Given this challenge, how should analysts proceed? How do we "know" that the PLA has influenced a particular policy? No simple solutions exist. Nevertheless, the following approach may be useful. First, state clearly and precisely the nature of potential PLA influence and the policy issue affected. Second, bring evidence to bear that demonstrates the PLA role in the formulation of policy. If the data permit, direct evidence is better than circumstantial evidence. The consistency of policy decisions with known or assumed PLA preferences is not direct evidence of PLA policy influence. Third, consider carefully alternative explanations. If China might have had strong reasons to adopt a particular policy that can be attributed to other factors, then this suggests that the influence of the PLA was not high and, at a minimum, that the PLA did not capture the party-state's position on this particular policy.

Pathways of PLA Influence in Territorial and Maritime Disputes

How might the PLA influence China's policies in its territorial and maritime disputes? It might do so in three different ways. First, the PLA could push for China to initiate a new claim to a piece of territory. Second, as the initiation of disputes is relatively infrequent, the PLA could push for China to alter the scope or content of an existing claim. That is, the PLA could push the state to claim additional land in an existing dispute or additional rights within a maritime jurisdiction. Both types of influence would reflect instances where the PLA would be moving beyond the military domain to change national policy.

Third, in an existing dispute, the PLA could push for a change in China's strategy for managing its claims. In general, a state can pursue three generic strategies for managing its territorial claims.[8] First, it can pursue a strategy of cooperation, which excludes threats or uses of force and involves an offer to either transfer control of contested land or drop existing claims to territory. Second, a state can pursue a strategy of escalation, engaging in coercive diplomacy to achieve a favorable outcome at the negotiating table or using force to seize contested land. Finally, a state can adopt a delaying strategy, which involves maintaining a state's claim to a piece of land but neither offering concessions or using force. Given these strategies, the PLA could influence China's policies in its territorial disputes in several ways. The PLA could seek to prevent China from pursuing a strategy of cooperation and offering compromises or territorial concessions to another state in an existing dispute. The PLA could push for threats or uses of force in an existing dispute. Finally, when a delaying strategy is being pursued, the PLA could lobby for demonstrations or exercises of sovereignty, such as a more aggressive patrolling posture.

The PLA in Past Territorial Disputes

A review of the PLA's role in shaping China's policies in territorial disputes demonstrates that its influence has been limited and mostly bureaucratic.

Since 1949, China has participated in twenty-three territorial disputes and six maritime rights disputes. Although many of these trace their origins to the Qing dynasty, most of the disputes arose for the PRC in the early 1950s during the process of consolidating China's boundaries after the civil war. No evidence exists that the PLA played a prominent role in the decisions to initiate these territorial claims. Similarly, no evidence exists that the PLA played a role in the PRC's first claim to the Senkakus, which was issued in December 1970. (As discussed below, evidence does exist to suggest that the PLA has played a role in shaping China's interpretation of the rights of coastal states and foreign military activities in the EEZ under UNCLOS.)

Since 1949, China has offered territorial concessions twenty-five times in seventeen of its disputes. No evidence exists that the PLA blocked or limited any of these compromises.[9] Anecdotal evidence suggests that the PLA delayed compromise in the boundary negotiations with Vietnam in the 1990s by refusing to participate in the joint working group created to negotiate with Vietnam. The PLA reportedly objected to offering concessions to a country with which it fought an embarrassing and costly war in 1979. Nevertheless, when Jiang Zemin announced in 1997 that land border negotiations would be completed by 1999, the PLA was either unable or unwilling to block this agreement.[10]

Since 1949, China has used force sixteen times in six of its territorial disputes. Consistent with the CCP chain of command, most decisions to use force were made by top party leaders, not by senior PLA officers in opposition to the instructions or intent of the party. Nevertheless, the PLA appeared to play a prominent and leading role in the decision to use force in three disputes. The first concerns a brief clash with India in September and October 1967 at two different mountain passes along the line of actual control, Nathu La and Cho La.[11] The clash occurred amid competition between China and India to consolidate their positions at the passes and resulted in PLA troops firing on Indian soldiers erecting a barbed wire fence. During three days of fighting, thirty-six Indian and an unknown number of Chinese soldiers were killed. The account of the clash by the commander of the Tibetan Military District, Wang Chenghan, suggests that it had not been authorized by the CMC, much less top party leaders.[12] As a result, the PLA's actions in the clash had the potential to capture China's policy in the dispute with India. Nevertheless, senior party leaders acted quickly to prevent further hostilities.

A second case involves a significant PLA role in the 1988 decision to occupy some of the land features China claimed in the South China Sea. Amid growing tensions in the South China Sea, including the occupation of features by Vietnam and other claimants, the PLAN in cooperation with the State Oceanographic Administration submitted a plan calling for the occupation of nine vacant features in the South China Sea.[13] This represents a form of bureaucratic influence, as the PLA submitted a plan for entry into the Spratlys that was vetted and approved by both the CMC and state organs. In the clash itself, the local commander reportedly opened fire without receiving permission from the General Staff Department, violating China's guideline for the engagement to "not fire the first shot."[14]

In a third case, the PLA may have a played a central role in the occupation of Mischief Reef in late 1994. Although the occupation was consistent with the

1988 plan (to seize vacant features), the action may not have been authorized and may have been undertaken independently by the Guangzhou Military Region in collaboration with the South Sea Fleet.[15]

At the same time, evidence exists that party leaders have overruled the PLA on several occasions. The first concerns General Su Yu's ambitious plan as chief of the General Staff to seize all the islands off the coast of Fujian and Zhejiang that remained under Nationalist control in the 1950s. Mao's opposition to Su Yu's plan was likely one factor that resulted in his demotion and transfer to the Academy of Military Sciences in 1958.[16] Su Yu's plan was never implemented. A second example occurred after the first few clashes between Chinese and Indian troops on the China-India border in August and October 1959. Front-line commanders repeatedly sought permission to attack Indian positions, which Beijing refused. A third example occurred during the clash with Vietnam over Johnson Reef in March 1988. After the clash, the CMC denied a request from the local commander to assault other features under Vietnamese control.[17]

Why has the PLA played such a limited role? The short and over-simplified answer is the structure of civil-military relations, namely, that the PLA is a party-army under the leadership of the CCP and not a national army supervised by the state. The PLA, most of the time, conducts operations within procedures established by the party and in support of the party's objectives, not the PLA's own goals.[18]

The PLA in China's Recent Territorial and Maritime Disputes

Similarly, the role of the PLA in China's territorial disputes over the past few years suggests limited, largely bureaucratic influence. Consistent with bureaucratic influence, the PLA appears to have played a role in the evolution of China's interpretation of provisions of UNCLOS. In the summer of 2010, the PLA appeared to capture China's policy regarding China's objection to U.S. naval exercises in the Yellow Sea with the carrier *George Washington*. Nevertheless, little evidence exists to support the assertion that the PLA influenced strategic decisions in China's polices on the various disputes in the South China Sea and East China Sea. Instead, China's more assertive policies can largely be explained in terms of the interactive nature of these disputes, which are prone to spirals of instability.

Maritime Jurisdiction and the Interpretation
of Coastal States Rights in the EEZ

Although China signed and later ratified UNCLOS, Beijing has adopted domestic legislation and policy positions that challenge some of its provisions. In particular, China seeks to limit foreign military activities in waters that it claims in two ways. First, China asserts that foreign military ships must request prior permission for "innocent passage" in China's territorial seas (that is, within waters 12 nm from its coast). By contrast, Article 17 of UNCLOS states that all ships "enjoy the right of innocent passage" without prior permission. Although UNCLOS does prohibit military activities in the territorial seas such as weapons exercises and intelligence gathering, it does not prohibit the movement of military vessels. China's requirement of prior permission is contained both in its 1992 law on territorial seas and in a note submitted with its instrument of ratification in 1996.

Second, China opposes military activities in its 200-nm EEZ for two different reasons. China views all military-related surveys as "marine scientific research" over which a state can claim jurisdiction in its EEZ. As a result, China opposes intelligence-gathering by foreign countries in these waters, which has resulted in the 2001 *Bodwitch* and 2009 *Impeccable* confrontations.[19] China has also challenged the freedom of navigation by military vessels within the EEZ as being inconsistent with "peaceful purposes" provisions in UNCLOS (88, 141, 301). This relies on a broad interpretation of these articles, which are typically interpreted as referring to aggressive actions outlined by the UN Charter, not intelligence activity, exercises, or other nonaggressive actions.[20]

What role did the PLA play in the evolution of these positions held by China? Although a definitive answer remains elusive, the UNCLOS negotiating record provides one clue and suggests that the PLA's role in China's desire to restrict innocent passage in the territorial seas was limited. During the negotiations over UNCLOS in the 1970s, China expressed concerns about the scope of innocent passage and argued that only nonmilitary vessels could enjoy this right.[21] Attempts to include language regarding prior notification failed to receive a majority vote, but it was a position that China actively supported. At this time, China's stance was probably informed by its traditional conception of national sovereignty when applied in the maritime domain and not the specific views of the PLA. In fact, it is unclear if the PLA even participated in the Chinese negotiating team or would have been able to exert much influence over it.

The PLA has probably played a greater role in China's positions on military activities in its EEZ. The PLA's position on these issues appears to have been formed by the mid-1990s, when it was raised in the talks that resulted in the Military Maritime Consultative Agreement with the United States that was signed in January 1998.[22] At this time, Chinese international legal scholars did not raise the issue of restrictions on military activities in the EEZ in their own analysis of China's 1998 EEZ law.[23] This gap between the public writings of China's legal scholars and the positions of the PLA in defense talks with the United States suggests that, in a manner consistent with bureaucratic influence, the PLA helped to shape China's position on the rights of coastal states in the EEZ.

To be sure, the PLA has actively sought to enforce its interpretation of state's rights in the EEZ. In 2001, the PLA sought to enforce its interpretation of the limitations on foreign military activities, first when a PLAN frigate challenged and threatened the USNS *Bodwitch* in the Yellow Sea in March 2001 and then when a PLAN aviation fighter collided with a U.S. EP-3 flying 70 miles south-southwest of Hainan. Similar challenges occurred in 2002 and several times in 2009. Analysis of the 2001 incidents suggests there was little if any coordination between the PLA and either the state or the top party leaders, suggesting that the PLA may have been trying to shape the content of China's policy on this issue by how it implemented the policy of intercepting surveillance flights.[24] In 2004 and 2005, PLA scholars detailed China's position in *Marine Policy*, an important international journal on maritime affairs.[25] These military scholars were the first to offer detailed arguments in support of the interpretation that the PLA had been implementing, again suggesting a degree of PLA influence over the evolving content of China's interpretation of the rights of coastal states in the EEZ. The role of the PLA in the 2009 *Impeccable* incident is consistent with bureaucratic influence. According to You Ji, the plan to confront the USNS survey ship was approved by both the Foreign Affairs Leading Small Group and the CMC, indicating coordination between key party and military bodies.[26] The actual confrontation involved fishermen, boats from two civil maritime law enforcement agencies, and the PLAN, again consistent with high-level coordination including the military and a number of state agencies. Given the military focus of the *Impeccable*'s activities, it is likely that the PLA raised the issue within China's policymaking process in a way consistent with bureaucratic influence, just as PLAN lawyers helped to shape China's overall position on the EEZ. Nevertheless, it was not an unauthorized operation taken without knowledge of key party leaders.

Perhaps the clearest example of the PLA influencing national security policy in territorial and maritime disputes concerns China's objections to U.S. and Korean naval exercises in the Yellow Sea in the summer of 2010. Although the exercises were designed to signal American resolve to deter North Korea following the sinking of the South Korean ship the *Cheonan*, China viewed them as threatening because of their proximity to China.[27] China did not oppose the exercises when they were first announced, but changed its policy in response to pressure from public opinion, which was shaped partly by military academic commentators and by comments that Deputy Chief of Staff General Ma Xiaotian made in a television interview.

The PLA's influence in this case is demonstrated by reviewing the chain of events. On June 8, 2010, *Huanqiu shibao* (Global Times), published a report from the South Korean Yonhap News Agency about upcoming U.S.-South Korean exercises in the Yellow Sea. In the report, *Huanqiu shibao* interviewed several Chinese military commentators, who described the exercises as provocative. The report did not state where in the Yellow Sea the exercises would occur. On the same day, *Huanqiu shibao* published an editorial that stated "emotionally, the Chinese people cannot accept the presence of the U.S. aircraft carrier in the Yellow Sea."[28] The first Ministry of Foreign Affairs (MFA) comment on the exercises, also on June 8, was to call "for calmness and restraint from all parties concerned to avoid further escalation of tension."[29] In other words, China had not yet formulated a position on the exercises.

The following day, June 9, attention to the exercises in the Chinese media increased. *Huanqiu shibao* published the results of an online poll from its website, in which more than 96 percent of respondents agreed that the exercises "pose a threat to China."[30] In the weeks that followed, the story spread and additional military commentators like retired Major General Luo Yuan began to weigh in, expressing opposition to the exercises. On June 22, 2010, the MFA issued a second statement on potential U.S. exercises in the Yellow Sea. Again, the statement indicated that China had not yet formed a clear position. According to Qin Gang, "We are very concerned about the relevant report and are following the development closely. . . . Relevant parties should stay calm, exercise restraint and refrain from doing things that could aggravate tension and harm the interest of nations in the region."[31]

Amid the growing media attention, a statement by PLA Deputy Chief of Staff Ma Xiaotian helped harden China's position. In what appeared to be an impromptu interview in the lobby of a hotel or office building, Ma answered a few questions from a Phoenix Television reporter.[32] In particular, Ma asserted that China was not merely "concerned" about the exercises, but "extremely opposed" (*feichang fandui*) to them because they were "close to Chinese territorial waters."[33] Ma's statement appeared to catalyze a change in China's declaratory position. On July 6, Foreign Ministry spokesperson Qin Gang stated, "We have taken note of the remarks of Deputy Chief of General Staff Ma Xiaotian. We will follow closely the situation and make further statements accordingly."[34] Two days later, Qin Gang used much stronger language that appeared to endorse the position articulated by General Ma. He stated that China "resolutely opposed" (*jianjue fandui*) the presence of "foreign ships" in the Yellow Sea and "other coastal waters [*jinhai*]" that would influence "China's security interests."[35] Thus, in approximately one month, China's position evolved from a "call for calmness and restraint" to "resolute opposition." This shift can be attributed to the PLA in the context of a more liberal media environment. A combination of public attention generated by China's unofficial media along with commentary on the issue by retired military officers and statements by senior generals, pushed the MFA to adopt increasingly strong language and, ultimately, opposition to the exercises.[36]

To the degree that the PLA did capture China's policy on this issue, it did not last for long. In November 2010, the United States announced that it would conduct another exercise in the Yellow Sea with an aircraft carrier. The MFA responded quickly to register China's objections. However, its statement backtracked from the language used in July 2010 in two ways. First, it stated only "opposition" to the exercises, dropping "resolute" and "extreme" as modifiers of China's position. Second, it referred only to China's EEZ and not its "coastal waters," thereby framing its objection within the UNCLOS framework. This left open the possibility that the exercise might be confined to South Korea's EEZ, which does not overlap with China's entirely in this area.

In sum, the PLA has exercised largely bureaucratic influence regarding China's position on maritime jurisdiction. The PLA did capture policy during the summer of 2010 regarding China's position on U.S. naval exercises in the Yellow Sea, appearing to compel the MFA to change its articulation of China's position. However, this change in China's position was revised only a few months later, limiting the PLA's influence.

The South China Sea

Since 2006, and especially from 2009, China has adopted a more active and assertive approach to managing its claims to contested islands and disputed maritime rights in the South China Sea.[37] Nevertheless, in the South China Sea, China has relied principally on diplomatic and political tools to advance its claims, not military ones. China has not used its naval forces to seize contested features or nor has it used them directly to threaten or use force against the naval forces of other claimant states. Instead, they have been used indirectly, largely through general displays of presence to signal resolve. The possibility remains, however, that the PLA advocated a hardening of the policy and an emphasis on consolidating China's claims, but given the issues at stake and the dynamics of the disputes, China's leaders likely shared the PLA's preferences on the South China Sea.

In the past few years, China has taken a range of actions to strengthen its claims in the various disputes over sovereignty and maritime rights in the South China Sea. Diplomatically, China has sought to actively defend its claims when challenged by others. Between 2006 and 2008, Chinese diplomats challenged the legality of foreign-invested hydrocarbon exploration and development projects in Vietnam in waters where China claimed maritime rights. In May 2009, China submitted a note along with a map of the infamous "nine-dashed line" (*jiu duan xian*) to the UN after Vietnam and Malaysia formally expanded their claims to maritime rights by asserting extended continental shelf rights in the South China Sea, especially in waters around the disputed islands and coral reefs. Politically, China used the activities of civil maritime law enforcement agencies to demonstrate and exercise its sovereignty in these waters. Starting in 2008, the South Sea regional fisheries administration bureau began to increase its presence in these waters. In 2009, it detained an unprecedented number of Vietnamese boats and fishermen. At the same time, vessels from the State Oceanic Administration's China Marine Surveillance Force (*Haijian budui*) began to increase its presence around the Spratlys. In the first half of 2011, it began to openly challenge seismic surveys conducted by the Philippines and Vietnam, cutting the towed cables of a Vietnamese ship in late May 2011.[38]

In the South China Sea, however, the PLA has played a secondary role and not a primary one. As the brief review of China's actions above demonstrates, China has not sought to actively defend its claims through use of its armed forces, especially the PLAN. Instead, the PLA has played a secondary role, namely, to underscore China's ability to defend its claims by force, if necessary. China has done so through a series of large-scale military exercises, especially in 2010. In March 2010, the North Sea Fleet conducted a long-distance exercise with a task force of six ships, including one destroyer, three frigates, a tanker, and a salvage vessel. The task force traveled from Qingdao through the Miyako Strait and then turned south, passing through the Bashi Channel between Taiwan and the Philippines before stopping at Fiery Cross Reef in the South China Sea.[39] According to the deputy commander of the North Sea Fleet, one purpose of the exercise was "to protect China's maritime territorial integrity through long-distance naval projection."[40] In July 2010, the South Sea Fleet organized a large-scale live-ammunition exercise in an undisclosed (though likely undisputed) location in the South China Sea that involved China's most advanced vessels from all three fleets. Although the exercise was held to promote the "transformation in military training" and the operational concept of "a system of systems operations," Chief of the General Staff Chen Bingde also noted the broader context in which it occurred at the time: "we should pay a high degree of attention to developments and changes in situations and tasks to carry out preparations for military struggle."[41] In November 2010, the South Sea Fleet organized an amphibious landing exercise named *Jiaolong*-2010 involving more than 1,800 marines, which was observed by more than 200 foreign military officers.[42] More recently, continuing this trend, the PLAN conducted highly publicized cruises and exercises in the South China Sea in 2013 and in 2014. In both instances, vessels stopped at James Shoal in the southernmost reaches of the South China Sea near Malaysia, while state media publicized oath-swearing ceremonies whereby PLAN sailors pledged to defend Chinese territory.[43] Similarly, in December 2013, the *Liaoning* aircraft carrier conducted its first long-range training exercise when it traveled from its homeport in Qingdao to the Yulin naval base on Hainan Island adjacent to the South China Sea. Although the carrier stayed relatively close to the Chinese coast and avoided disputed waters, its presence nevertheless sent another general signal of China's resolve to defend its claims.[44] Nevertheless, China has not sought to use its growing naval power to compel other states to accede to its demands, to enforce its sovereignty claims directly, or to seize contested features.

The secondary role of the PLA was underscored by the standoff over Scarborough Shoal in April 2012. According to a mainland publication, the decision to dispatch maritime law enforcement vessels to protect the Chinese fishermen found by the Philippines inside the shoal was made within civilian channels by the MFA. When the incident occurred, Chinese fishermen used their satellite phones to send a distress signal, which was received by vessels from China Marine Surveillance, a maritime law enforcement body under the State Oceanic Administration (and now part of the newly established China Coast Guard). The incident was then reported to the MFA via the SOA's headquarters in Beijing. Following a decision by China's top leaders, a command post was established within the China Marine Surveillance force, whose ships were instructed to aid the Chinese fishermen in the shoal.[45] Although the PLA and CMS reportedly have a close working relationship, focused primarily on information sharing and limited joint training, Chinese sources indicate that the initial decision in the crisis were made by civilian leaders and not military ones. In addition, in order to limit the potential for escalation, Chinese naval vessels were never deployed close to the shoal. Noted Chinese military historian Xu Yan describes this as "naval forces on the second line, coast guard forces on the first line" (*haijun erxian, haijing yixian*), or placing naval vessels over the horizon in an "overwatch" position.[46] Similarly, when China deployed the *HD-981* deep-water semi-submersible drilling rig to the Paracel Islands in May 2014, it also deployed some naval vessels nearby in addition to much larger numbers of China Coast Guard vessels.[47]

In the Scarborough standoff, top military leaders indicated their support for the government's approach. In an impromptu television interview, a Phoenix TV reporter tried to interview General Ma Xiaotian in early June 2012 at a conference on cyber security in Beijing.[48] In particular, Ma said: "The question you ask is very sensitive. We have the ability to defend our waters, but at the moment we are not yet ready to use military force to go defend [our waters]. If we were to do so, it would be as a last resort. Now we are still conducting bilateral talks, using diplomatic means and some civilian [i.e., law enforcement] means to resolve the conflict. This way is the best."[49] Ma's statement countered rumors that Chinese forces in the Guangzhou Military Region had been placed an alert (indicating preparations to use force) and highlighted the consensus between party and military elites.[50] Earlier, in May 2012, Defense Minister Liang Guanglie also underscored the importance of a diplomatic solution to the standoff in a meeting in late May with his Philippine counterpart, Voltaire Gazmin. Although PLA-affiliated media commentators such as retired General Luo Yuan have called for China to adopt a more forceful response, active-duty general officers such as Ma Xiaotian and Liang Guanglie have not.

Even though the PLA has not played a more active role in China's assertiveness in the South China Sea in the past few years, the possibility remains that

China adopted this approach in response to PLA pressure that outside analysts cannot observe. Nevertheless, this is unlikely for two reasons. Although PLA-affiliated commentators write frequently on the issue, they often seem to write in reaction to events. This suggests that they are responding to developments, not driving decisionmaking. In any case, whether commentators such as Luo Yuan speak for the PLA as a whole remains unclear and is unlikely.[51] More importantly, however, China's assertiveness in these disputes can be explained as a reaction to the actions by other claimants to strengthen and bolster their own claims. In other words, PLA influence over decisionmaking is not necessary to explain the policies and positions China's government and party leaders would have adopted anyway. From Beijing's perspective, it has faced many challenges to its claims in the past few years. These challenges, not PLA pressure, offer a superior explanation for China's assertiveness, as one can clearly link China's policies to the actions of other states. China's detention of Vietnamese fishermen in 2009, for example, occurred as the number of Vietnamese fishing around the Paracels increased dramatically. Likewise, China's interference with seismic surveys being conducted by Vietnam and the Philippines in the first half of 2011 were a response to the launch of new survey activities by both countries. Finally, the standoff at Scarborough occurred when the Philippines distributed photos of its armed soldiers inspecting Chinese fishing boats within the shoal.

Evidence from key authoritative Chinese newspapers suggests little divergence between the PLA and the party in the South China Sea disputes. Figure 9.1 plots the number of articles per year in the *People's Daily* (the CCP's main newspaper) and the *PLA Daily* (the PLA's main newspaper) with the word "Spratlys" (*Nansha*) in the title. As Figure 9.1 shows, there is a strong correlation between articles on the Spratlys in both the *PLA Daily* and the *People's Daily*. Although the *PLA Daily* consistently publishes more articles on the Spratlys, many of these reflect "soft" coverage emphasizing the hardship and contributions of the troops garrisoned on the seven features.

One area where the PLA has almost certainly exerted influence concerns China's refusal to clarify the meaning of the nine-dashed line. Although the line has been used on Chinese maps since before the founding of the PRC, the Chinese government has never clarified its meaning. The importance of clarifying the line increased after China submitted a map with the line to the UN in May 2009. Whether the line indicates a claim to the enclosed land features in a manner consistent with international law or whether it indicates other

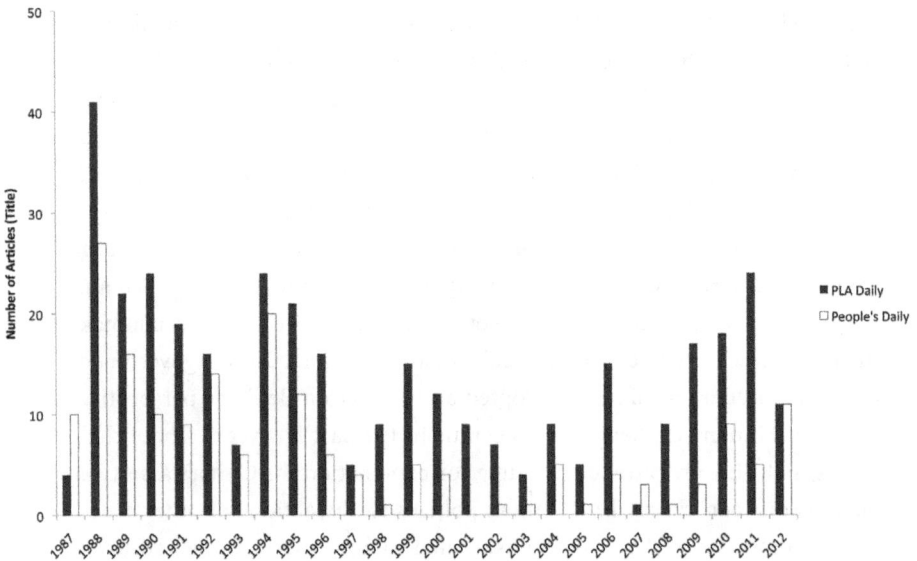

FIGURE 9.1   Articles on the Spratly Islands

types of rights, such as historic rights or even sovereignty, is an important issue that shapes the perceptions and responses of other claimants. At least some in the PLA believe the line represents historic rights or a traditional form of sovereignty, views that would be inconsistent with UNCLOS. The *PLA Daily* openly referred to the line as China's "traditional maritime boundary" (*chuantong haijiang xian*).[52] This phrase has appeared ten times in this paper, including eight times in 2009 and 2011. By contrast, the *People's Daily* has never used this language to describe China's claims in the South China Sea. Thus, the PLA may be exerting a form of bureaucratic influence that prevents China from issuing a definition of the line that is inconsistent with what appears to be the PLA's definition (or at least the definition of some in the PLA). Other relevant actors, including the Bureau of Fisheries Administration and the State Oceanographic Administration, appear to maintain similar historic definitions of the line, indicating that China may prefer ambiguity for a variety of reasons and not just in response to pressure from the PLA.

The East China Sea
The East China Sea involves several disputes between China and Japan over the sovereignty of the Senkaku (Diaoyu) Islands and over maritime jurisdiction in the East China Sea. China also contests Japan's claim to maritime rights from Okinotorishima in the Western Pacific, but does not claim

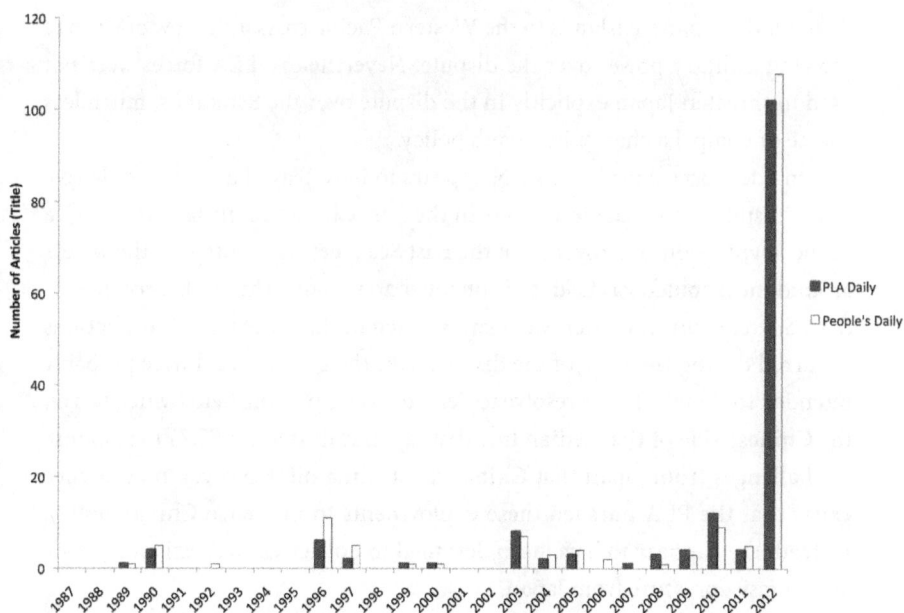

FIGURE 9.2   Articles on the Senkaku/Diaoyu Islands

sovereignty over the atoll itself. Although this dispute was largely dormant for much of the past two decades, it has become a focal point of tension between China and Japan since 2010.

Before September 2010, China had pursued a largely passive approach to the dispute over the Senkakus. Indeed, China sought to minimize attention to the dispute. As shown in Figure 9.2, the dispute was rarely discussed in articles in either the *People's Daily* or the *PLA Daily* until the crisis with Japan in 2012. Typically, an article would appear simply noting that China had restated its claim in response to some event involving the disputed islands or in response to a Japanese claim. In the mid-2000s, China began to play a more active role in limiting the potential for escalation in the dispute by preventing Chinese activists from sailing to the islands from ports on the mainland and detaining *baodiao* (Defend the Diaoyu Islands Movement) activists during the 2005 protests against Japan.[53]

During this period, the PLA played no visible role in the dispute over the Senkakus. Almost no public reports exist of PLAN vessels approaching the 12 nm territorial waters around the islands or even the broader 24 nm contiguous zone. Similarly, PLAAF reconnaissance flights that approach Japan's ADIZ in the East China Sea usually occur several hundred kilometers from the islands themselves.[54] The PLA has played a direct role, as the transit of PLAN ships through the Japanese islands to the Western Pacific casts a shadow of China's growing military power over the dispute. Nevertheless, PLA forces were not used to threaten Japan explicitly in the dispute over the Senkakus, much less coerce or compel a change in Japan's policy.

On a few occasions, the PLAN appears to have played a more visible role in the dispute over maritime rights in the East China Sea. In January 2005, a single *Sovremenny* destroyer from the East Sea Fleet was spotted in the waters around the disputed gas field. In September 2005, a five-ship task force including a *Sovremenny* destroyer was again spotted in these waters.[55] These actions occurred during the peak of the dispute over the gas field and were probably intended to signal China's resolve to defend its claim to the field (which lies on the Chinese side of the median line that Japan claims as its EEZ) in response to challenges from Japan that China was stealing oil. However, no evidence exists that the PLA pursued these deployments to influence China's policy. Instead, they appear to have been designed to bolster China's existing policy and to resist pressure from Japan.

Likewise, little evidence exists to suggest that China's harsh response to Japan's detention of a Chinese fishing boat and its crew in September 2010 reflected PLA influence over government policy. The crisis began on September 7, when a Chinese fishing vessel entered the territorial seas around the Senkaku Islands, refused instructions to halt, and rammed a Japanese Coast Guard vessel. Although Japan released the crew and the ship on September 13, it continued to hold the captain and considered prosecuting him under Japanese criminal law. China reacted swiftly. China summoned the Japanese ambassador at least once a day, often in the middle of the night, from September 8 to September 11. China also postponed negotiations over the East China Sea (September 11), cancelled a slew of high-level visits (September 13), detained four Japanese nationals for entering a military restricted area in Shijiazhuang (September 20), and slowed the shipment of rare earth metals (September 24).[56]

Can PLA influence explain China's forceful response? Probably not. The government's response was likely consistent with the PLA's own preferences, namely, the unconditional return of the captain. However the speed with which the government reacted, and the policies it adopted, suggest that the PLA could not have influenced the policymaking process. Instead, Chinese actions can be explained in terms of what was seen as a change in Japanese policy (of subjecting Chinese citizens detained around the islands to criminal prosecution), an issue that perhaps was especially salient because it occurred just before the sixty-ninth anniversary of the Mukden Incident. Under these conditions, the government probably sought to preempt domestic criticism, perhaps including from the PLA, of failing to defend China's interests by not protecting a Chinese citizen detained by Japan. In contrast to the discussion about the Yellow Sea in June 2010, military commentators such as Luo Yuan, Dai Xu, and others were completely silent during this period. They did not author any articles nor did they apparently give any interviews, at least according to a database of Chinese newspaper articles. Likewise, the blogs and webpages for Luo Yuan and Dai Xu do not include any articles authored or posted in September 2010.[57]

Following the September 2010 crisis, tensions spiked again in 2012 after the Japanese government purchased three of the islands from a private Japanese citizen. The purchase was intended to prevent a deterioration in China-Japan relations, as the right-wing governor of Tokyo, Shintaro Ishihara, had launched a public bid to buy these three island, which he justified in terms of what he viewed as the inability of the national government to defend them. China's reaction to the purchase was rapid and severe: Beijing issued territorial baselines around the islands to demarcate China's territorial waters and then dispatched vessels from the China Marine Surveillance force to "patrol" these waters, directly challenging Japan's claims to sovereignty over the islands. Nationwide protests were permitted on the 15, 16, and 18 of September, while Foreign Ministry officials used exceptionally undiplomatic language to describe the purchase as an "atomic bomb."[58] Since then, China has conducted more than ninety patrols within the 12 nm territorial waters of the islands, always using vessels from civilian agencies, first the China Marine Surveillance force and, after June 2013, the newly established China Coast Guard.

It is of course possible that the PLA pushed hard for a strong and powerful response to the Japanese purchase. Nevertheless, China's top civilian leaders likely shared the same preferences as the PLA. Following Ishihara's public bid in April 2012, the prospect of the purchase had become a diplomatic issue being waged in full view of the public. Moreover, it involved a dispute over sovereignty with Japan, a country with which China has had repeatedly strained ties since the end of the Cold War. The purchase itself occurred shortly after Hu Jintao personally requested that Japanese Prime Minister Noda halt the sale. Finally, it occurred on the eve of a delicate moment in Chinese politics, of the Eighteenth Party Congress, when a significant leadership change would occur, a moment that would heighten China's sensitivity to external threats.[59]

In the crisis itself, the PLA did not appear to be pushing for an even more assertive policy. As shown in Figure 9.2, the number of articles on the Diaoyu Islands in *PLA Daily* was almost identical to those in *People's Daily*, indicating the high level of attention throughout the party-state. In addition, articles in *PLA Daily* did not endorse positions beyond those expressed by top party leaders. For example, on September 12, *PLA Daily* published a signed opinion piece by noted commentator retired General Luo Yuan entitled "China Will Never Concede Half a Step over Territory and Sovereignty."[60] However, the content mirrored closely themes from the MFA statement. Perhaps the most noteworthy piece in *PLA Daily* warned Japan "not to play with fire," but was written by a civilian analyst and remained consistent with China's objective of deterring Japan from taking further steps to consolidate its position.[61] More recently, Lt. Gen. Qi Jianguo, deputy chief of the Headquarters of the General Staff, stated in August 2013 that "the Diaoyu Islands are within the range of [China's] core interests."[62] However, his language mirrored almost to the word a statement from the Ministry of Foreign Affairs in April 2013, which marked the first time that the ministry or any other top government body had suggested that the islands were a core interest.[63]

Overall, military forces have played a secondary role in China's response to the purchase. China has not dispatched any military vessels into the territorial waters around the disputed islands. In October 2012, a PLAN task force returning to China from the Western Pacific entered through the contiguous zone in waters between Yonagunijima and Iriomotejima islands approximately 150 kilometers south of the Senkaku Islands.[64] That same month, eleven vessels from the PLAN, China Marine Surveillance, and the Fisheries Law Enforcement Command conducted a "rights defense" (*weiquan*) joint exercise in the East China Sea near Shanghai.[65] In particular, the exercise simulated how naval vessels would aid and protect Chinese government ships that clashed with patrols from another country, clearly seeking to deter challenges to China's patrols around the islands.[66]

What has garnered the most attention, however, was an incident in January 2013 involving a PLAN frigate and JMSDF destroyer in waters roughly 100 kilometers off the disputed islands. According to Japanese press reports, the Chinese vessel "painted" the Japanese ship with its fire-control radar, which could have been interpreted as the first step in an attack.[67] Needless to say, the incident reflects the potential for tactical or operational military considerations to escalate into a much broader political dispute. The PLA denies that the incident occurred and it did not occur again, suggesting that it was either not part of China's policy in the dispute or that the PLA was overruled by top party leaders.

Finally, the PLA played a direct role in the decision to establish an air defense identification zone (ADIZ) in the East China Sea in November 2013. In this case, the initiative for the policy came from within the PLA, but it was not implemented until approved by China's top leaders. As Shinji Yamaguchi has shown, elements within the PLA first began to propose the establishment of ADIZ in 2008 and 2009. However, the proposal was not approved until after Xi Jinping became general secretary and favored a more proactive foreign policy in China's immediate periphery.[68]

Conclusion

The role of the PLA in national security decisionmaking is one of the most important and most challenging aspects of Chinese foreign policy to study. In the past few years, analysts and observers have speculated that the PLA has sought to push China to adopt more assertive or hawkish foreign policies that China's top leaders would otherwise not have pursued. This chapter has examined the PLA's role in China's behavior in its territorial and maritime disputes, an issue where China has been more assertive in the pursuit of its claims since the mid-2000s and the PLA has opportunities to exert influence.

The evidence does not suggest that the PLA has "captured" national policy in this arena. Instead, the PLA has exercised more limited bureaucratic influence in line with existing national policies. The PLA has not pushed for China to initiate new territorial claims nor to expand the content of its existing claims, with exception of the interpretation of certain aspects of UNCLOS. The PLA has not blocked China's past compromises in territorial disputes, including those throughout the 1990s and in the early 2000s. To the degree that more assertive postures have been adopted in specific disputes, these postures reflect the shared preferences of the PLA and China's top leaders.

Notes

1. Joshua Kurlantzick, "After Deng: On China's Transformation," *The Nation*, October 17, 2011.

2. See, for example, Christopher Bodeen, "Chinese Succession Highlights Military's Role," Associated Press, October 17, 2011; and Jeremy Page, "China's Army Extends Sway," *Wall Street Journal*, October 4, 2010.

3. On China's use of force in territorial disputes, see M. Taylor Fravel, *Strong Borders, Secure Nation: Cooperation and Conflict in China's Territorial Disputes* (Princeton, NJ: Princeton University Press, 2008).

4. Dennis Blasko, *The Chinese Army Today: Tradition and Transformation for the 21st Century* (New York: Routledge, 2006); Michael D. Swaine, "China's Assertive Behavior—Part Three: The Role of the Military in Foreign Policy," *China Leadership Monitor*, no. 34 (Winter 2012); You Ji, "The PLA and Diplomacy: Unraveling Myths about the Military Role in Foreign Policy Making," *Journal of Contemporary China* 23, no. 86 (2013).

5. Swaine, "China's Assertive Behavior—Part Three"; You, "The PLA and Diplomacy."

6. That is, the party determines the overall framework for military strategy.

7. At the same time, the PLA does enjoy a great deal of autonomy over military affairs at the operational level. Swaine, "China's Assertive Behavior—Part Three"; You, "The PLA and Diplomacy."

8. Fravel, *Strong Borders, Secure Nation.*

9. It is possible that the party may not have offered compromises in the first place because of potential opposition from the PLA. Nevertheless, the large number of compromises actually made suggests this is unlikely.

10. Fravel, *Strong Borders, Secure Nation*, 148.

11. Wang Chenghan [王诚汉], *Memoirs of Wang Chenghan* [王诚汉回忆录] (Beijing: Liberation Army Press [解放军出版社], 2004), 482; P. B. Sinha and A. A. Athale, *History of the Conflict with China* (New Delhi: History Division, Ministry of Defence, Government of India, [restricted], 1992), xxiv; G. S. Bajpai, *China's Shadow over Sikkim: The Politics of Intimidation* (New Delhi: Lancer Publishers, 1999), 156–195.

12. Wang, *Memoirs*, 481–482.

13. Liu Huaqing [刘华清], *Memoirs of Liu Huaqing* [刘华清回忆录] (Beijing: Liberation Army Press [解放军出版社], 2004), 534–535; Xu Ge [徐舸], "Steel Anchors Consolidating Maritime Frontiers: Record of the Republic's Naval Battles" [铁锚固海疆: 共和国海战史记] (Beijing: Tide Press [海潮出版社], 1999), 308–325.

14. Xu, "Steel Anchors Consolidating Maritime Frontiers," 312; Lu Ning, *The Dynamics of Foreign-Policy Decisionmaking in China* (Boulder, CO: Westview, 1997), 126.

15. Greg Austin, *China's Ocean Frontier: International Law, Military Force, and National Development* (Canberra: Allen & Unwin, 1998), 91; Fravel, *Strong Borders, Secure Nation*, 296–297.

16. *Su Yu's Biography* [粟裕传], ed. Zhu Ying [朱楹] (Beijing: Contemporary China Press [当代中国出版社], 2000), xxx.

17. Lu, *The Dynamics of Foreign-Policy Decisionmaking in China*, 126.

18. On the party's control of the army, see, for example, David Shambaugh, *Modernizing China's Military: Progress, Problems, and Prospects* (Berkeley: University of California Press, 2002).

19. Raul Pedrozo, "Close Encounters at Sea: The USNS *Impeccable* Incident," *Naval War College Review* 61, no. 3 (2009): 101–111.

20. Erik Franckx, "American and Chinese Views on Navigational Rights of Warships," *Chinese Journal of International Law* 10, no. 1 (2011): 187–206.

21. For an excellent review of China's role in the drafting of UNCLOS, see Zhiguo Gao, "China and the Law of the Sea," in *Freedom of Seas, Passage Rights and the 1982 Law of the Sea Convention*, eds. Myron H. Nordquist, Tommy Thong Bee Koh, and John Norton Moore (Leiden: Martinus Nijhoff, 2009).

22. Interview.

23. See Zou Keyuan, "China's Exclusive Economic Zone and Continental Shelf: Developments, Problems, and Prospects," *Marine Policy* 25, no. 1 (2001): 71–81.

24. At the same time, there was significant regional variation in the pattern by which China intercepted U.S. surveillance flights. The pattern of intercepts was most aggressive in the south, where the EP-3 incident occurred, suggesting that there was not necessarily coordination within the PLA, either. A similar dynamic occurred in 2014, when one particular unit again adopted particularly aggressive intercepts of U.S. surveillance flights near Hainan. Audrey McAvoy, "PACAF Commander: Despite Intercepts, Most East China Sea Encounters Safe," Associated Press, October 9, 2014

25. Ren Xiaofeng and Cheng Xizhong, "A Chinese Perspective," *Marine Policy* 29, no. 2 (2005): 139–146.

26. You, "The PLA and Diplomacy," 16. On the incident, see Pedrozo, "Close Encounters at Sea."

27. On this episode, see also Alastair Iain Johnston, "Stability and Instability in Sino-US Relations: A Response to Yan Xuetong's Superficial Friendship Theory," *Chinese Journal of International Politics* 4, no. 1 (2011): 5–29.

28. "Expert: U.S. Nuclear Aircraft Carrier Conducting Exercises with Korean Military in the Yellow Sea Is Inevitable" [专家: 美核航母开进黄海于韩军军演已不可避免], *Global Times* [环球时报], June 8, 2010; "Editorial: South Korea Should Not Take U.S. Aircraft Carrier into the Yellow Sea" [社评: 韩国休把美航母带入黄海], *Global Times* [环球时报], June 8, 2010.

29. "Foreign Ministry Spokesperson Qin Gang's Regular Press Conference on June 8, 2010," Ministry of Foreign Affairs of the People's Republic of China.

30. "Angered over U.S. Aircraft Carriers Entering the Yellow Sea, Chinese Netizens' Image of Korea is Worrying" [引美航母入黄海激怒中国网友韩国形象堪忧], *Global Times Online* [环球网], June 9, 2010.

31. "Foreign Ministry Spokesperson Qin Gang's Regular Press Conference on June 22, 2010," Ministry of Foreign Affairs of the People's Republic of China.

32. In the interview, Ma was wearing a business suit and not his military uniform.

33. For the text and video of Ma's interview, see http://news.ifeng.com/mainland/detail_2010_07/01/1702694_0.shtml.

34. "Foreign Ministry Spokesperson Qin Gang's Regular Press Conference on July 6, 2010," Ministry of Foreign Affairs of the People's Republic of China, July 7, 2010. For an explicit assertion, based on information provided by unnamed diplomats, that "political pressure from the military community forced the central government to change the text of its official statements several times in the past two months to harden its tone over the US-South Korean joint naval drill near its territorial waters," see Cary Huang, "PLA Ramped up China's Stand on US-Korea Drill," *South China Morning Post*, August 6, 2010.

35. "Foreign Ministry Spokesperson Qin Gang's Regular Press Conference on July 8, 2010," Ministry of Foreign Affairs of the People's Republic of China.

36. At the same time, this chronology indicates that statements by military commentators alone were insufficient as a factor in the change in the MFA's articulation of China's position.

37. For a review of China's actions in these disputes since 2006, see M. Taylor Fravel, "China's Strategy in the South China Sea," *Contemporary Southeast Asia* 33, no. 3 (December 2011).

38. This paragraph draws on ibid.

39. "Chinese Navy's New Strategy in Action," *Strategic Comments* 16 (May 2010); Greg Torode, "Exercises Show PLA Navy's Strength," *South China Morning Post*, April 18, 2010.

40. Quoted in "Chinese Navy's New Strategy in Action."

41. "Grasp Generating Systems Operations, Actively Promote the Transformation in Military Training" [着眼生成体系作战能力，积极推进军事训练转变], *PLA Daily* [解放军报], July 29, 2010.

42. "South Sea Fleet Organizes 'Jiaolong-2010' Live-Fire Exercise" [南海舰队组织'蛟龙-2010'实兵实弹演习], *PLA Daily* [解放军报], November 4, 2010.

43. Bai Ruixue, Gao Yi, and Gan Jun [白瑞雪, 高毅, 甘俊], "From South China Sea to West Pacific: Complete Record of Navy Task Force's Distant Sea Training of Combat-Readiness Patrol" [从南海到西太平洋:海军编队战备巡逻远海训练全记录], Xinhua [新华], April 3, 2013.

44. For a detailed discussion of the carrier's 2013 exercise, see Andrew Erickson and Phillip C. Saunders, "Selective Transparency: How the PLA Uses Development, Testing, Deployment, and Exercises as Shaping and Signaling Tools," (unpublished paper, December 2013).

45. Han Yong and Guan Xiangdong [韩永, 关向东], "Standoff over Huang Yan Island" [对峙黄岩岛], *China Newsweek* [中国新闻周刊], no. 16 (May 2012): 28

46. Xu Yan [徐焰], "Several Decades of Chinese-Philippine Wrangling in the South Sea" [中菲南海争执几十年], *Study Times* [学习时报], May 21, 2012.

47. According to a Vietnamese source, China in early June had deployed "6 warships, 40 coast guard ships, more than 30 transport ships and tugboats, and 34–40 fishing boats." See "Chinese Vessels Try to Scare Vietnam's Ships Further away from Illegal Rig," *TuoiTreNews*, June 9, 2014.

48. This draws on M. Taylor Fravel, "The PLA and the South China Sea," *The Diplomat*, June 17, 2012.

49. For the video, see http://news.ifeng.com/mainland/special/nanhaizhengduan/content-3/detail_2012_05/28/14866227_0.shtml.

50. On the rumors, see Andrew Chubb, "Xinhua Spreading Rumours, Unpopular Military Commentary, and a Witchhunt: The Scarborough Shoal Media Wave Part III (May 11–13)," *South China Sea Conversations* (blog), May 21, 2012.

51. In addition, as Johnston notes, a substantial diversity of opinion exists among the PLA's academic commentators. Johnston, "Stability and Instability in Sino-US Relations," 43–45.

52. "The Navy's Seventh Escort Task Force Enters the Motherland's Traditional Maritime Boundary" [海军第七批护航编队驶入祖国传统海疆线], *PLA Daily* [解放军报], May 3, 2011.

53. M. Taylor Fravel, "Explaining Stability in the Senkaku (Diaoyu) Dispute," in *Getting the Triangle Straight: Managing China-Japan-US Relations*, eds. Gerald Curtis, Ryosei Kokubun, and Jisi Wang (Washington, DC: Brookings Institution Press, 2010). For a detailed account of the protests, see Jessica Chen Weiss, *Powerful Patriots: Nationalist Protest in China's Foreign Relations* (New York: Oxford University Press, 2014).

54. See maps in Japan's annual *Defense of Japan* reports.

55. James C. Bussert, "Oil May Be Focal Point of Sino-Japanese Dispute," *Signal* (November 2006).

56. James J. Przystup, "Japan-China Relations: Troubled Waters," *Comparative Connections* 12, no. 3 (October 2010).

57. Based on a survey of their known blogs.

58. "Remarks by Assistant Foreign Minister Le Yucheng at Symposium Marking the 40th Anniversary of The Normalization of Relations between China and Japan," Ministry of Foreign Affairs of the People's Republic of China, September 28, 2012.

59. Fravel, *Strong Borders, Secure Nation.*

60. Luo Yuan [罗援], "China Will Never Concede Half a Step over Territory and Sovereignty" [中国在领土主权问题上绝不会退让半步], *PLA Daily* [解放军报], September 12, 2012.

61. Yang Xiyu [杨希雨], "The Japanese Government Should Not Play with Fire" [日本政府不要玩火], *PLA Daily* [解放军报], September 11, 2012.

62. Faith Acquino, "Chinese Military Scholar Claims the Senkakus as a 'Core Interest,'" *Japan Daily Press*, August 20, 2013

63. "Foreign Ministry Spokesperson Hua Chunying's Regular Press Conference on April 26, 2013," Ministry of Foreign Affairs of the People's Republic of China.

64. "Chinese Warships Move away from Senkakus, But Tensions Remain," *Asahi Shimbun*, October 17, 2012.

65. "Chinese Navy and Marine Surveillance and the Fisheries Administration Hold Joint Exercise in the East Sea" [中国海军与海监、 渔政在东海举行联合演], *International Online* [国际在线], Oct. 19, 2012.

66. "Content of the Rights Defense Exercise in East Sea on the 19th: Marine Surveillance Boat Collision, China Escort Ships Provide Aid" [19日东海维权演习内容: 海监船遭碰撞 中国护卫舰支援], *New Capital Report* [新京报], October 19, 2012.

67. "China's Use of Fire-control Radar Ramps up Tension in East China Sea," *Asahi Shimbun*, February 6, 2013.

68. Shinji Yamaguchi, "The Foreign Policy of Xi Jinping's Administration and the Establishment of China's Air Defense Identification Zone," NIDS Briefing Memo, September 2014.

10 The PLA Navy Lobby and Its Influence over China's Maritime Sovereignty Policies

Christopher D. Yung

Introduction

Most observers have concluded that the modern Chinese political system is now more collective and consensus oriented and that decisionmakers at the highest levels of the Chinese Communist Party (CCP) prize technical expertise and advice when making important policy decisions.[1] At the same time, the Chinese policymaking process has become somewhat more open and pluralized.[2] This raises the question of how groups in China advocate or lobby for policies that they prefer and how effective those efforts are. This chapter assesses the influence of the People's Liberation Army (PLA) on high-level decisionmaking. It focuses on a specific segment of the PLA, the PLA Navy (PLAN) and affiliated individuals and organizations (referred to as the "PLA Navy lobby"), and on specific policies related to China's "maritime sovereignty."

What Is China's Navy "Lobby"?

A lobby is a group of individuals who use direct or indirect means to collectively or individually advocate policy positions to decisionmakers. A lobby's activities typically seek to benefit their group's collective interests and to portray their group's expertise or responsibilities as contributions to some larger national objective (e.g., enhanced national security). As Isaac Kardon and Phillip Saunders discuss in their chapter, sometimes the PLA leadership lobbies on behalf of widely shared collective interests and sometimes smaller PLA subgroups (such as individual services) lobby on behalf of a narrower set of institutional interests. The PLA Navy lobby constitutes a PLA sub-group that advocates larger naval budgets, seeks policies that emphasize the national importance of Chinese maritime interests and naval capabilities, and offers recommendations based on professional expertise on maritime and naval matters.

Who Belongs to the PLA Navy Lobby?

Admiral Liu Huaqing, PLA Navy commander from 1982 to 1987, could be considered a charter member of the PLA Navy lobby. He personally championed the idea of a Chinese naval strategy, had his staff and experts formulate a draft, and eventually persuaded the Central Military Commission (CMC) to endorse this formulation. Even after his departure from the PLAN and his promotion to the position of vice-chairman of the Central Military Commission, Liu used his considerable experience in naval and maritime affairs to advocate greater emphasis on naval capabilities and Chinese maritime interests. Senior naval officers who have an institutional responsibility to articulate and advocate PLAN interests should be considered ex officio members of the PLA Navy lobby. Current PLA Navy commander Admiral Wu Shengli and Political Commissar Liu Xiaojiang would fit this category. Military scholars such as Rear Admiral Yin Zhuo, who writes and speaks frequently on naval issues in various fora, should also be considered a part of the navy lobby.

The PLA Navy lobby also includes retired officers who advocate policy positions on behalf of the PLAN or as experts with experience working in a particular naval operational area of expertise. Retired PLAN officers are often freer to voice their opinions in public, but usually reflect the views of active duty PLAN personnel. Thus, Rear Admiral (ret.) Zhang Deshen, former PLAN deputy chief of staff, former PLAN Captain Li Jie, and Rear Admiral (ret.) Yang Yi should all be considered part of this lobby. Finally, academics, scholars, and journalists affiliated with PLA Navy institutions (e.g., Vice Admiral Zhang Junshe of the Naval Research Institute) should be considered part of this group because they often reflect the views of the PLA Navy.

This definition excludes representatives of maritime-related state-owned enterprises (such as COSCO shipping), active duty or retired members of the PLA who comment on maritime security affairs but are not part of the PLAN (e.g., General Luo Yuan), and members of other organizations (e.g., the State Oceanic Administration, or SOA) with an interest in maritime affairs and maritime policy, but who are not affiliated with the navy. This distinction between a PLA Navy lobby and a broader maritime or naval lobby matters because groups interested in maritime issues, but not formally affiliated with the navy, can sometimes represent different viewpoints, serve as bureaucratic competitors, and oppose PLA Navy interests.[3]

Maritime Sovereignty Policies

China's maritime sovereignty policies are decided upon at the highest levels of the Chinese Communist Party and involve the protection of Chinese maritime territorial claims and the assertion of Chinese maritime territorial rights. A decision to use force to protect China's claims falls within the category of maritime sovereignty policy, as does a decision to provide resources and procure naval or paramilitary assets to assert China's claims. High-level decisions calling for different agencies to cooperate on maritime sovereignty enforcement or to coordinate related activities would also be considered within the domain of maritime sovereignty policy. Such policies would also include high-level decisions to pursue negotiations to settle maritime territorial claims, to engage in economic sanctions or inducements to help resolve disputes, and to pursue a variety of legal strategies.

Approach and Methodology

This chapter uses three case studies or vignettes to assess whether the PLA Navy lobby influenced CCP maritime sovereignty decisions: the 1988 decision to use force against Vietnam over the Spratly Islands; the decision to acquire an aircraft carrier; and the 2013 decision on centralizing the functions, command and control, and management of China's maritime sovereignty enforcement capabilities. The military tends to have influence in decisions to use force, decisions about what resources are needed to undertake assigned missions, and decisions about military participation in specific missions or general types of operations. The three cases were selected to test the navy lobby's influence in different policymaking environments. In each case, the analysis assesses what the PLA Navy lobby wanted, how it sought to achieve its goals, and the outcome.

The 1988 Spratly Island Case

In his 2004 memoir, Admiral Liu Huaqing, retired vice-chairman of China's CMC, described in detail the thinking that went into the eventual decision to use force against Vietnam in 1988.[4]

> On the evening of 12 February 1988, Vice Chairman Zhao Ziyang had a talk with me. He spent a long time dwelling on the issue of struggle for the Nansha [Spratly] Islands. I briefed him on the situation on those islands. I said that protecting Nansha was primarily a task of the Navy. In recent years, the Navy had dispatched ships and planes on numerous occasions to patrol Nansha or conduct training there. In the first half of that year, an oceanic observation post had been built on Yongshu Reef at the request of the United Nations. In terms of military struggle, the favorable condition was that our naval force was superior in quantity and quality. Our disadvantage was that the area was far away from our base, and this made it difficult for us to conduct air defense, furnish supplies, and defend the islands and reefs there. But these difficulties could be overcome.[5]

Liu argued that Vietnamese encroachment on Chinese territory demanded a military response:

> I geared up the assignment of tasks to proceed with this matter, which was of cardinal importance to our country's sovereignty and interests. Leaders of the PLA General Staff Department, General Logistics Department, and the Navy all placed great importance on this matter. . . . At the numerous meetings I called to study the issue, I told them the following: The present situation is that Vietnam has invaded and occupied isles and reefs of our Nansha Islands and unscrupulously drilled wells to extract oil there. As it has bullied us too much, a struggle is inevitable. This is a just struggle to defend the sovereignty and safeguard the rights and interests of our country. It was provoked by the Vietnamese authorities. We must curb their aggressive ambition, show China's military presence in Nansha, and create as many favorable conditions as possible for the ultimate solution of the Nansha issue.[6]

Liu's assessment of the strategic situation and his presentation to the Chinese civilian and military leadership included an assessment of the kind of struggle China would face:

> In my opinion, the Nansha struggle would be a complicated struggle. Whether a war was to be waged or not, the struggle would be acute and sometime

multiform and intricate. We have to use multiple tactics such as diplomatic, political, military and economic means or select one or two of them to use. Moreover, the Nansha struggle might be a long one. The issue could hardly be solved thoroughly by a single struggle, and many complex factors could boost the aggressive countries' desire to take possession of the things they coveted. Because of this, the struggle between encroachment and anti-encroachment, plunder and counter-plunder, will remain for a long time to come. Plus, the Nansha struggle would be very arduous, and it would bring about many difficulties. But these difficulties would not be hard to overcome. Further, I knew clearly that in this struggle blood and death would be unavoidable, especially in facing the Vietnamese authorities.[7]

Liu argues that his presentation to Zhao Ziyang persuaded the leadership of the seriousness of the situation and the need to take action:

Vice-Chairman Zhao Ziyang listened to my briefing in a very serious manner and asked many questions. His opinion was specific and resolute: We must announce clearly that sovereignty over the Nansha territorial waters is ours. We must increase our military presence in the Nansha area. We must step up our patrol there to show the prowess of our country and our armed forces.[8]

Zhao authorized Liu to conduct operational planning, to provide a risk assessment of any proposed military operation, and to include a range of options from increased patrolling and fortification of the islands to the use of force against Vietnam. He also asked Liu to let the Politburo Standing Committee (PBSC) know what resources the military would need to undertake this mission:

Lastly, he [Zhao] said: 'With regard to this struggle, would you make some studies and give me a written report as soon as possible, specifying where our strength must be reinforced and where improvement must be made.' After I came back, I instructed the General Office of the Central Military Commission to prepare a report on the main points contained in Vice-Chairman Zhao's two talks. I passed the report to the relevant leaders of the PLA's General Staff Department and the General Logistics Department as well as to the Navy so that they could study the matter, draw up a plan, and make preparations for the struggle.[9]

Liu and the PLA then embarked on detailed operational planning on how to conduct the mission:

I studied the issue repeatedly with Deputy Secretary General Hong Xuizhi, Chief of General Staff Chi Haotian, Deputy Director of the General Logistics Department Zhang Bin, Naval Commander Zhang Lianzhong, and Naval Political Commissar Li Yaowen. We took into consideration all possible difficulties and carefully planned all measures to be undertaken. Finally, we drew up a proposal and submitted it to Vice-Chairmen Zhao Ziyang and Yang Shangkun in the name of the chief of the General Staff.[10]

The assessment concluded that the most serious threat to the PLA operation was "not their warships, nor was it their frogmen. It was their warplanes." The Spratlys are "more than 1,000 kilometers away from our mainland." When PLA warplanes reached the operating area "after flying such a long distance, not much fuel would be left. . . . [Therefore] they would not be really combat effective."[11] Vietnam would "have the advantage of a shorter operational flying distance. This would not only prolong their loitering time, but also increase their missile-carrying capacity."[12] If conflict erupted, China's planes "could not give us air and sea superiority and ensure our victory."[13] To resolve this operational problem Liu "contacted comrades of the Ministry of Aeronautics Industry to look into the possibility of developing tanker aircraft."[14] Liu indicates that he convinced the senior civilian leadership to accelerate plans, originally conceived by Deng Xiaoping, to construct an airfield on Woody Island.

Other sources support Liu's claim that as the PLA Navy commander he highlighted the threat of the Nansha situation and got approval to step up PLAN activity in the South China Sea. In his account of the military clashes in the South China Sea, John Garver notes that under Liu the PLA Navy stepped up its naval air patrols of the Spratlys, conducted numerous surveying operations, and in cooperation with the State Oceanic Bureau, submitted a report to the CMC and the State Council advocating a physical military presence on Fiery Cross Shoal.[15] Unofficial accounts of PLA discussions with the PBSC over the Spratly issue highlight the PLAN's significant role in convincing CCP leaders to take action. One author noted that "during 1987, some high-level officers in the Chinese military brought up the Nansha Archipelago many times in speeches, which raised the issue to the level of transformation of naval strategy and adaptation to developments in oceanic undertakings. These officers expressed indignation at the loss of the Nansha Archipelago during the Cultural Revolution. . . . The Navy's call for action in the Nansha Archipelago obtained the support of the many experts in China."[16]

Assessment

The PLAN wanted high-level decisionmakers to take the threat from Vietnam seriously; to give the PLA Navy the resources necessary to address the threat; to authorize study of the tactics and operations necessary to address this situation militarily; to give the PLAN a major role in planning and execution of a counter-encroachment action; and then to authorize execution of the operation.

PLA Navy efforts to achieve its goals first involved building a consensus among the various military players (e.g., the General Staff Department, the General Logistics Department) that the use of force was not only possible, but also justifiable and appropriate. Liu then presented this conclusion to Zhao Ziyang as a unified PLA position. Liu appears to not have presented any alternatives; his military advice went directly to the use of force, the limitations or difficulties that the operation would face, and what the PLA Navy would need to undertake the mission. This approach was particularly effective given Zhao Ziyang's lack of military knowledge and expertise.

The PLA Navy essentially got everything it asked for. It was given permission to undertake the mission as well as a central role in planning the operation, and was the central actor in executing the mission. Admiral Liu identified areas of operational difficulty the PLAN would likely experience and got the PBSC to provide resources to help fix some of those shortcomings. In particular, the CCP leadership agreed to accelerate construction of an airfield in the South China Sea to provide better air support.

The Aircraft Carrier Decision

A second vignette involves Chinese policy debates in the 1980s and 1990s about whether to procure an aircraft carrier. Liu's memoirs reveal that he had long been thinking about the importance of aircraft carriers to China's national defense: "As early as 1970, when I worked in the office of the Leading Group for the Shipbuilding Industry, I organized a special feasibility study for building aircraft carriers as instructed by the higher authorities and submitted a project proposal to them." When Liu became PLAN commander in 1982, the importance of the carrier question was even more apparent and he concluded that China's emerging maritime interests meant he would need to lobby hard for acquisition of a carrier:

> China is a big coastal country with over 3 million square kilometers of "sea territory." At that time, with the development of maritime undertakings

and the change in the mode of sea struggles, the threats from sea we were facing differed vastly from the past. We had to deal with ballistic-missile nuclear-powered submarines and ship-based airforces, both capable of long-range attacks. To meet that requirement, the strength of the Chinese Navy seemed somewhat inadequate. Despite our long coastal defense line, we had only small and medium-sized warships and land-based air units, which were merely capable of short-distance operations. In case of a sea war, all we could do would be to deplore our weakness. By developing aircraft carriers, we could solve this problem.[17]

How did Liu specifically propose going about obtaining or developing an aircraft carrier capability?

With regard to developing carriers, let us suppose that we begin the feasibility studies in the Seventh Five-Year Plan period [1986–1990], do research and conduct preliminary studies of the platform deck and key questions on the aircraft during the Eighth Five-Year Plan period [1991–1995], and decide on the types and models in 2000. This arrangement has the following advantages: First, the annual spending for the present and the following years will not be too much. Second, technologically, it has many advantages. For example, it can stimulate the development of technologies required by the state and by national defense. Third, through preliminary studies, we can get a deeper understanding of the value of carriers and the need for them in war preparations.[18]

Liu argued for aircraft carrier feasibility studies in a report to the Naval Armament and Technology Work Conference in January 1987. Participants included the senior leadership of the Commission of Science, Technology, and Industry for National Defense (COSTIND) and of the PLA General Staff Department's Armament Department. Liu said:

To develop aircraft carriers to meet future war needs, we should do serious research and feasibility studies. Now all countries are paying attention to developing carriers. Whether their goal is to develop attack carriers or carriers for vertical and short-distance takeoff and landing aircraft, the purpose is the same: to meet air defense and sea attack requirements. Indeed they are all paying attention to developing carriers. The United States and the Soviet Union are vigorously doing this; so are relatively developed countries like France, Italy and Britain. A defeated country, Japan, is not allowed to do this because of its constitution. However, if it were to develop carriers, it could easily do it. . . . We have certain financial and technological difficulties. But we do need carriers from a long-term viewpoint. If we don't develop carriers within ten years, we will still have difficulties when we do this after ten years. Because of this, I would like to see feasibility studies in this regard started earlier so the question can be deliberated thoroughly at an early date.[19]

Liu concluded that a Chinese carrier was not intended "to race with the United States and the Soviet Union. The primary goals [were] to meet the needs of struggle against Taiwan, to solve the Nansha Islands disputes, and to safeguard our sea rights and interests." Liu indicated that in peacetime "the carriers could be used to maintain world peace, thereby expanding our international political influence."[20] Finally, Liu concluded that possession of a carrier had significant operational and institutional benefits for the PLAN.

If our Navy had carriers, its quality would change dramatically, and its fighting capacity would greatly increase. This would help raise our military prowess as well as the prestige of our country. Based on this, I asked our research personnel to do feasibility studies with a deep sense of historic responsibility.[21]

Liu's memoirs provide one last glimpse into the argument that he put before the PLA leadership and most likely the PBSC.

On 31 March 1987, I reported to the PLA general departments on two major questions concerning the Navy's armament plan: aircraft carriers and nuclear-powered submarines. These questions, both related to the Navy's core force build up, were of key importance. From a long-term perspective, developing these two items was in the interest of national defense construction. Their development would not only serve our wartime needs, but also add to our deterrent force in peacetime.[22]

John Lewis and Xue Litai confirm Liu's assertion that the PLA Navy argued to the CCP leadership for the development of nuclear submarines and aircraft carriers. By the mid-1980s, Liu had identified four key missions for the navy: to safeguard China's territorial integrity; to conduct a possible blockade of Taiwan; to defeat a sea-based invasion; and to operate survivable nuclear retaliatory forces.[23]

Liu argued that the PLAN needed an aircraft carrier to protect China's interests in Taiwan and in the South China Sea:

Further studies have revealed that, if there is no air cover [provided by ship-borne aircraft], this force can in no way operate outside the scope of the operational radius of land-based aircraft. Also, when studying the Taiwan Strait war, we have found that it would be a grave waste to use land-based aircraft. The reason: Because of the aircraft's limited loitering time, we would need more aircraft and hence, more airports. In addition, our analysis shows that without developing carriers, the Navy still has to develop destroyers and escort ships in order to make up a mobile force at sea. If carriers are developed, these ships can serve as escorts for the carriers and also as mobile combat vessels. Under modern conditions, it is impossible to fight a sea battle without air cover. If we develop carriers, we do not need to increase the total number of aircraft. What we need will be aircraft of a different function. The price of such aircraft may be higher, but will not be too high. As can be seen, developing a carrier force is a question of adjusting the use of armament funds, but it does not need a big increase in the amount of funds. More importantly, if we have carriers we will boost the combat effectiveness of our mobile force at sea.[24]

Liu's argument to the PBSC that aircraft carriers were more cost effective than air bases is a barely disguised plea for a bigger PLAN share of the budget. Most military analysts might question Liu's analysis. A carrier would allow greater aircraft loitering time, but would also invite concentrated attack and risk being lost—a nonexistent risk for PLAAF airbases near Taiwan.

Liu does not describe the CCP leadership's response, but implies that the answer was "no" or at least "not now":

Regrettably, our country's economic strength was insufficient at that time. In early 1984, at the first naval armament and technology work conference, I made this remark: "Quite some time has elapsed since the Navy had the idea of building carriers. Now, our national strength is insufficient for us to do this. It seems that we have to wait for some time."[25]

Assessment

Admiral Liu's biography makes clear what the PLA Navy wanted: an aircraft carrier that could project power to support missions in Taiwan and the South China Sea, military diplomacy, and deterrence. Vice Admiral Zhang Xusan later confirmed Liu's account, stating: "I certainly advocate having an aircraft carrier soon.... When I was [deputy commander of the PLA] Navy I advocated that, and at that time Commander . . . Liu Huaqing advocated it too, but for many reasons it was postponed."[26] In addition to the carrier, the PLA Navy would also need additional destroyers and frigates to serve as escorts and a protective force for the carrier. The carrier's missions would include providing air cover for maritime contingencies close to China (Taiwan) and far away (the southernmost part of the Spratlys). Liu called for further study of requirements and for commissioning feasibility studies. He pleaded for the PLA and the PBSC to act now, because "in ten years" China will still be in the same situation except having wasted ten years.

Admiral Liu and the PLA Navy lobby pursued the aircraft carrier using methods similar to those in the 1998 Spratlys case. Admiral Liu convened several meetings of the PLA to study the problem, gathering the leadership of COSTIND, the General Staff Department's Armament Department, and the leadership of the General Logistics Department. After preliminary research on future PLAN mission requirements, the PLA Navy lobby advanced these arguments at Naval Technology and Requirements work conferences, at working conferences of the PLA General Departments, and then presumably through the Central Military Commission. The navy argued that a carrier would support CCP goals and objectives without violating party restrictions and concerns. When initial efforts failed, the PLAN later sought "friendly guidance" from the PBSC on how to get what it wanted. Hu Jintao's "new historic missions" issued in 2004 subsequently provided a rationale for navy "far seas" operations and a clearer rationale for a carrier.

Although the PLAN did not receive approval to launch an aircraft carrier development program, it appears to have received authorization to acquire a carrier for study. From the mid-1980s to the early 2000s, the PLAN had acquired four aircraft carriers: the HMAS *Melbourne* (1985), the *Kiev* (1988), the *Minsk* (1998), and the *Varyag* (1999). The PLA Navy's stated reason for the purchases were to serve as casinos or entertainment platforms for the public's amusement. However, it now seems apparent that the PLAN purchased the initial three carriers to allow its engineers to study the construction of the ships. The last of the carrier purchases, Ukraine's *Varyag*, lacked engines and other equipment when sold to China in 2000. The ship arrived in China in 2003 after a two year delay and a difficult transit. The *Varyag* then spent close to a decade in the shipyard being reconstructed and configured for operations before it was declared operational in 2012.[27]

Some observers argue that Liu Huaqing was denied permission to acquire an aircraft carrier program due to financial and larger strategic concerns. Nan

Li and Christopher Weuve conclude that despite Liu's strong support for carrier operations, Jiang Zemin was opposed to the idea.[28] At the time China was not heavily dependent on imported raw materials and oil, nor had its overseas economic interests greatly expanded. As a consequence, the PLA's assigned missions were probably narrowly defined, making it difficult to argue for a platform like an aircraft carrier. Jiang may also have been particularly concerned that a carrier purchase was at cross purposes with his larger grand strategy, which emphasized a "soft approach" to China's security and foreign policy.[29] It was during Jiang's tenure that China signed the ASEAN Treaty of Amity and Cooperation, and agreed to work toward some kind of code of conduct in the South China Sea.[30] Ultimately, however, the PLA Navy may not have received permission to pursue carriers during Jiang's tenure because of insufficient funding. As Erickson, Denmark, and Collins conclude, "The PLA budget suffered negative growth during this period; there was not enough money to build destroyers, let alone a carrier. But PLAN experts felt that their work was not in vain, as they had gained a much greater understanding of vital naval systems. They believed that the navy would ultimately build an aircraft carrier, but not for the time being."[31]

The eventual decision to authorize the carrier program came from Jiang's successor, Hu Jintao, who became CCP general secretary in 2002. Hu and Wen Jiabao consulted with the General Armament Department, the PLA Navy, and leaders from relevant industries and experts. The PBSC met (reportedly in August 2004), discussed the PLAN proposal, and eventually decided to authorize the development of aircraft carriers.[32] The leadership endorsed a two-step strategy: reconstructing the *Varyag* to learn how to build and operate an aircraft carrier and then building the second and third aircraft carriers using Chinese technology.[33]

The PLAN eventually secured approval by reshaping the CCP leadership's perception of the international security environment and of the importance of Chinese maritime interests. In 2004, Hu Jintao tasked the PLA with "new historic missions," which included the following: "to ensure military support to continued Chinese communist Party (CCP) rule in Beijing; to defend China's sovereignty, territorial integrity, and national security; to protect China's expanding national interests; and to help ensure a peaceful global environment and promote mutual development."[34] Chinese official writings indicate that drivers of the new missions included "changes in China's security situation, challenges and priorities regarding China's national development, and a desire to realign the tasks of the PLA with the CCP's objectives."[35] Hartnett and Vellucci have described PLA Navy efforts to make the case for the military to take on new and emerging missions far from China's shores.[36] Nan Li notes that the Naval Military Studies Institute published articles arguing for changing the navy's strategic orientation from "near seas active defense" to "far sea operations." This viewpoint resulted from the recognition that China's security interests had to now take into account the emerging dependence on energy imported from abroad, increased reliance on foreign trade and investment, increased merchant fleet activities, and the larger need to secure sea lanes.[37]

This case differs from the Spratly case in that a decision to procure an aircraft carrier would have larger strategic and budgetary consequences. Acquiring an aircraft carrier would have had a large impact on China's defense budget and significant strategic and foreign policy implications. The PLA Navy lobby's success in obtaining a carrier can be considered mixed. Although Liu did not receive permission to launch a carrier development program, the PLAN was authorized to procure retired Australian and former Soviet carriers to learn more about carrier technology. The PLAN eventually obtained permission to rebuild the *Varyag* into an operational carrier and to construct two indigenous carriers. However, the carrier was not procured when the PLA Navy originally wanted it; the PLAN had to wait twenty-five years before it was able to acquire the capability.

The PLA Navy Influence over "Maritime Sovereignty Enforcement" Policies

The third case study involves a series of maritime sovereignty enforcement policies advocated by the navy since the mid-1990s. The first authors and analysts to argue that China needed to develop "sea consciousness" and recognize the link between China's oceans, maritime resources, and China's future prosperity served in the PLA Navy or were affiliated with it.[38] They argued that protection of China's ocean resources and assurance that China would have access to these resources was a PLA Navy responsibility. A 1995 article by an author associated with the Dalian Vessel Academy's Political Department "argued that because global maritime disputes are intensifying, PLAN officers and sailors need to have a new understanding of . . . 'maritime territory consciousness' (*haiyang guotu yishi*)."[39] A PLA Navy lieutenant commander published an article that year "calling for sea consciousness to be spread among the entire nation."[40] Fravel and Liebman note that at this time active duty naval personnel were highlighting the navy's role in securing access to maritime resources.[41] Luo Xianlin, then a PLAN senior captain, wrote a 1994 article that found resonance in later Chinese strategic thinking: "Protecting and developing the ocean's resources is a historic responsibility that our Navy cannot shirk."[42] Liu Zhenhuan, a senior captain with the Naval Research Institute argued in *Modern Navy* that the navy must develop its capability to protect "China's 'maritime territory' and the development of its resources. . . . The scope of China's defense must be enlarged to include the entirety of waters under China's jurisdiction, including the EEZ and the continental shelf."[43]

In recent years, as maritime sovereignty tensions have grown, the PLA Navy lobby has focused its attention on effective responses to encroachment on maritime sovereignty by China's rivals. An effective, coherent, and united response has been hard to achieve because so many agencies and organizations are involved in maritime sovereignty enforcement. In his seminal work *Five Dragons Stirring Up the Sea*, Lyle Goldstein of the China Maritime Studies Institute (CMSI) identified five civilian law enforcement organizations directly involved: the China Maritime Police, China Maritime Surveillance, the Maritime Safety Administration, and the Fisheries Law Enforcement Command (FLEC).[44]

According to the 2010 *Ocean Development Report* by the State Oceanic Administration, these agencies have a general division of labor and set of responsibilities and tasks:

In 1998 the Chinese government undertook reforms of its public affairs administration. . . . According to the [resulting] division of labor, the Maritime Safety Administration [is] responsible for transportation safety at sea; the Fishery Administration is responsible for law enforcement related to the ocean fishery industry; the Maritime Customs Agency is responsible for arresting smugglers; the China Maritime Police, which is part of the Border Control Department, is responsible for safeguarding public safety at sea and for suppressing criminal activities; the Maritime Surveillance Force is responsible for managing the utilization of territorial waters, ocean environmental protection and the defending of ocean rights. According to regulations related to laws in China, the Navy can also participate in certain work and activities related to the infringement of China's ocean rights.[45]

Chinese scholars and observers (both civilian and military) pointed out that the roles and responsibilities of these agencies overlapped and that it was becoming increasingly difficult for Beijing to maintain centralized control over law enforcement activities in waters near China. Chinese observers also noted that the "dragons" were too weak and dispersed to provide effective maritime enforcement capabilities.

The Chinese government recognized these shortcomings:

> To reduce bureaucratic competition and inefficiency, the State Council issued an order calling for enhanced coordination among these [civilian law enforcement] agencies in 2004. The directive called for joint enforcement operations and emergency management at a national level. It also directed the Ministry of Foreign Affairs to make recommendations to the central government when it is necessary to select a lead agency in an emergency related to national maritime security.[46]

The Navy lobby pushed forward its own opinion on how to best manage maritime sovereignty enforcement activities. Admiral Zhang Deshen, a former PLAN deputy chief of staff, called for the National People's Congress to pass a comprehensive law authorizing central control and coordination of the civilian law enforcement activities related to maritime sovereignty violations: "A basic law of the sea is vital because it provides a national framework for taking unified and comprehensive measures to promote the development of maritime resources and to ensure maritime safety."[47] According to Zhang, the law should "make clear the goal and strategy of sea development, draw up a detailed blueprint, and set up an agency to take charge of the role now scattered among several agencies."[48]

Rear Admiral Yin Zhuo went further by advocating centralized control over all civilian law enforcement agencies taking part in maritime law enforcement activities—presumably under the PLA Navy. He claimed that

> at present, China has many departments involved in maritime affairs, each issuing different orders and each doing as it pleases. For example, there are seven or eight departments in charge of law enforcement at sea: the Bureau of Fisheries has fish farming operations, the State Oceanic Administration has maritime patrols, the General Administration of Customs has antismuggling police, the Ministry of Public Security has antismuggling and counter-narcotics, etc. Everybody builds his own boat, everybody sets up his own port station, everybody has his own radar for detection, and everybody has his own

intelligence sources. This not only causes redundant construction and waste of resources, it also leads to an inability to share information and makes cooperation difficult.[49]

Admiral Yin argued that a centralized process was needed to enforce China's maritime sovereignty rights, either by creating a leading small group or multi-ministry commission to coordinate these disparate activities or, failing that, by centralizing these activities under the navy:

> I have suggested the establishment of a State Maritime Strategy Research and Formulation Work Leading Group led by the leaders of the State Council and the Central Military Commission and formed from the National Development and Reform Commission, [along with] the General Staff Department and working with parties formed from relevant ministries and commissions of the State Council, and relevant departments of the General Staff Department and the Navy to carry out concrete research to ensure the harmonization of national maritime strategy. . . . Only through this can we ensure victory in the future.[50]

Senior Captain Li Jie, another frequent commentator on naval and maritime affairs, expressed similar opinions: "scattered maritime law enforcement bodies among different departments are both chaotic and inefficient. The [current territorial disputes] have merely exposed the problem."[51] In a moment of candor, Li indicated that the navy preferred to have civilian law enforcement vessels under its control. "China now faces a complicated situation in maritime diplomacy. . . . China, whose navy functions under the integrated command of the People's Liberation Army, lacks a Coast Guard dedicated to the protection of the maritime boundaries and resources. Instead Coast Guard work is done through well-equipped marine surveillance ships."[52]

Not surprisingly, civilian maritime law enforcement agencies disagreed with navy proposals to centralize management under the military. Wang Hanling, an expert in maritime affairs and international law at the Chinese Academy of Social Sciences (CASS), agreed that decentralization was a problem, but advocated putting all of the disparate agencies and vessels under a single coast guard. He noted that China's maritime forces function separately without proper coordination, weakening China's ability to respond to challenges to maritime sovereignty. Wang argued that the U.S. Coast Guard was the proper model "as they are an 'all-in-one force,' providing military, multi-mission and maritime services to protect the public, environmental and economic security interests, and also [the ability to] patrol international waters."[53]

Former director of the State Oceanic Administration Zhang Dengyi "argued that China should use maritime law enforcement forces . . . to safeguard its sovereignty, rights and interests within that territory. In particular, Zhang called for centralizing all civilian maritime security forces from the center to the localities and enhancing the Chinese maritime police forces' ability to accompany maritime traffic, monitor fishing, expand the force's zone of operations, and effectively safeguard China's maritime rights and interests."[54] Zhang advocated placing these centralized functions under civilian control rather than under the PLA Navy.

Assessment

The PLA Navy had multiple goals. First, it wanted the CCP leadership to take maritime sovereignty issues seriously. The PLA Navy lobby called for the Chinese people and the Chinese leadership to develop a "sea consciousness" that recognized the direct link between access to the oceans and China's continued development. Second, in order to coordinate the disparate activities of many agencies involved in the maritime sovereignty mission, the PLA Navy lobby advocated the passage of a national law centralizing the functions of the wide array of law enforcement agencies. Finally, the PLA Navy lobby wanted the navy to be given the task of managing civilian maritime enforcement functions.

The PLA Navy lobby pursued this objective through a wide range of efforts. First, navy-affiliated authors wrote articles on the importance of sea consciousness and the relationship between China's economic development and unfettered access to the sea. Second, the PLA Navy lobby dispatched its representatives to the National People's Congress to advocate the passage of a national law unifying maritime sovereignty enforcement activities under a single organization. Third, the PLA Navy lobby had prominent spokespeople argue the case in print and on television for the centralization of all maritime sovereignty enforcement activities under the navy. Finally, the PLA Navy commander likely made this case within the Central Military Commission.

As with the aircraft carrier decision, the PLA Navy only got some of what it wanted. There is no question that PBSC members have developed a "maritime territorial conscience" and take maritime sovereignty enforcement seriously. Xi Jinping himself took charge of a leading small group in 2012 to formulate strategies and coordinate government responses to maritime territorial tensions.[55]

Some observers suggest that Hu Jintao initiated the formation of the small group and charged his successor with running it.[56] In any case, top CCP leaders increased attention to maritime sovereignty issues and created new organizations to manage the issue. The leading small group reportedly includes senior officials from the State Oceanic Administration (SOA), the Ministry of Foreign Affairs (MFA), the Ministry of Public Security (MPS), the Ministry of Agriculture (MOA), and the PLA Navy.[57] The National People's Congress passed a law in 2013 authorizing creation of a unified organization to enforce China's maritime sovereignty rights, just as the PLA Navy had been advocating.

While the PLA Navy lobby enjoyed some successes, in other areas it was less successful. State Councilor Ma Kai announced at the National People's Congress in March 2013 that the State Council would create a single agency overseeing maritime sovereignty enforcement, but that agency would not be a military organization.[58] Instead the PBSC decided to centralize enforcement activities under the State Oceanic Administration. The SOA took control over the Maritime Police and Border Control, previously administered under the Ministry of Public Security; the Fisheries Law Enforcement Command (FLEC), previously administered by the Ministry of Agriculture; and the Maritime Antismuggling Police, previously administered by the General Administration of the Customs.[59] All of these agencies have retained their functions but now operate with China's Maritime Surveillance (CMS) force as a single China Coast Guard.[60]

The restructuring plan involved creating a commission—the State Oceanic Commission—to formulate and coordinate maritime sovereignty policy issues.[61] *China Daily* described the commission as "a trans-department coordinating body responsible for China's maritime affairs. . . . It will become the central pivot safeguarding China's interests in the sea. It will play bigger roles than its predecessor, the State Oceanic Administration."[62] Japan's National Institute for Defense Studies (NIDS) notes that "the State Oceanic Commission is composed of several ministries including agriculture, transport, environmental protection, science and technology as well as the SOA. . . . [It is] not an independent body, but a policy coordinating mechanism." NIDS analysts note that the degree of PLA involvement in the State Oceanic Commission and the relationship between the commission and the existing PLA-led National Committee of Border and Coastal Defense are still unclear.[63] One source has speculated that the Committee of Border and Coastal Defense is the supra-ministerial body that will coordinate the activities of the Coast Guard and the PLA Navy, similar to the State Committee on Frontier Border Defense, which coordinates civilian and military work for frontier and border defense.[64] However, there is no hard evidence that this is the case. The State Oceanic Commission appears focused on coordinating China's civilian maritime law enforcement activities rather than integrating civilian and military maritime sovereignty enforcement. The military now has a powerful civilian organization that will compete with the PLA Navy to defend China's maritime sovereignty.

Civilian law enforcement vessels have taken the lead in recent maritime sovereignty enforcement missions. The 2012 Scarborough Shoal stand-off with the Philippines mostly involved China Maritime Surveillance vessels. In May 2014 China dispatched the *HD-981* deep water semi-submersible drilling rig into the exclusive economic zone of Vietnam. The PLA Navy deployed 6 warships, while the Coast Guard deployed 40 Coast Guard designated ships, 30 transport ships, and over 30 fishing boats.[65] In both instances, the PLA Navy served as a backup force in the stand-off. In the latter case, the PLA Navy's presence was clearly intended to deter and, if necessary, defeat any use of force by the Vietnamese military.

PLA Navy officers insist that putting civilian law enforcement vessels at the forefront of maritime sovereignty disputes is a deliberate strategy. Chinese scholars with ties to the Chinese government insist that this approach makes sense: it lowers the risk of a direct confrontation between the PLA Navy and other navies; it affords Beijing a degree of plausible deniability by having a civilian law enforcement vessel with a murky command relationship to Beijing as the principal instrument;[66] and it reduces the risk of escalation in confrontations with foreign vessels since civilian law enforcement vessels tend to be lightly armed. Interviews with the Naval Research Institute, the State Oceanic Administration, and other government-linked think tanks in 2012 suggest that the PLA Navy was an important player in the planning and decisionmaking process, and that it supports the idea that civilian law enforcement vessels should be on the "front line" while the navy and the other military services are "in the rear."[67] The PLA Navy's continued role in backing up the China Coast Guard supports this view.

These arguments suggest that the PLA Navy has accepted that it failed to gain control over civilian law enforcement operations. It put aside its bureaucratic interests to help design a maritime sovereignty enforcement strategy that places civilian law enforcement agencies at the forefront, but which nevertheless still involves a significant role for the PLA Navy in planning, coordination, and operations.

TABLE 10.1 PLA Navy Lobby Policy Preferences and PBSC Responses

PLA Navy lobby policy preference	Policy issue area	PBSC response
Authorization to use lethal force in Spratly dispute (1988)	Military operations	Granted
Obtain additional resources to enhance military readiness for the operation	Military operations	Granted
Permission to lead operational planning	Military operations	Granted
Permission to begin feasibility studies for carrier acquisition	Military acquisition/Strategic investment	Not now/Denied
Authorization to acquire an aircraft carrier	Military acquisition/Strategic investment	Not now/Denied
Authorization to acquire modern surface combatants and submarines	Military acquisition/Strategic investment	Granted
PBSC attention to maritime sovereignty disputes	National security strategy	Granted
Passage of national law	National security strategy	Granted
Centralization of enforcement activities under the PLAN	Interagency coordination and effectiveness	Denied
Important PLAN role in execution of enforcement activities	Interagency coordination and effectiveness	Granted

Overall Assessment

This analysis suggests that the PLA Navy lobby's influence on decisionmaking is mixed. Table 10.1 illustrates where the PLA Navy lobby was able to get what it asked for and where it was told "no" or "not now." A closer examination allows speculation about why the PLA Navy lobby was successful in some issue areas and unsuccessful in others.

In the 1988 Spratly clash, the PLA Navy and PLA leadership were able to frame the issue as a military challenge that demanded a military response. Liu Huaqing appears to have not provided Zhao Ziyang any alternatives to the use of force. Alternative courses of action could have included a demonstration of force or harassment of the Vietnamese military to persuade Vietnam to withdraw its military presence. Liu provided none of these alternatives to the PBSC. Having obtained the PBSC's endorsement to use force, the PLA Navy lobby was able to obtain the resources needed to enhance readiness. Because it was clear that the military was best qualified to provide advice on how to undertake the military operation, the PLA and PLA Navy were given central roles in the planning. The PLA Navy lobby therefore was able to exert a great deal of influence over PBSC decisionmaking in this case.

The PLA Navy lobby's effectiveness at obtaining PBSC endorsement for an aircraft carrier was mixed. Despite the efforts of Liu Huaqing and the PLA Navy, the PLA Navy lobby appears to have been unsuccessful in convincing Jiang Zemin and other members of the PBSC to authorize acquisition of a carrier in the 1990s. It took Hu Jintao's ascension to the post of general secretary, a changed international security environment, improving financial circumstances for China, and alterations in China's foreign and defense policies before the PLA Navy lobby was able to successfully secure authorization to obtain a carrier. Despite the PLA Navy's unquestioned expertise in naval warfare, in understanding the maritime strategic environment, in depicting the potential threats to China's national security, and in understanding the military capabilities of rival states, the Navy lobby was still told "no" or "not now." Liu appears to have gotten a unified PLA position in support of a carrier. His memoirs suggest that he obtained buy in from the PLA General Staff Department, the PLA Logistics Department, COSTIND, and the Naval Armaments Department. Despite a unified PLA position, the answer from the PBSC was still "no." This case reaffirms that the party retains the final word on grand strategy and major budget decisions. In this case, the PBSC decided Jiang's "peaceful rise" approach to Chinese foreign policy outweighed the military need to obtain a specific military capability.

Once the strategic and financial situation changed, and the PLA obtained party endorsement to acquire an aircraft carrier capability, the PLA General Staff Department, the General Armaments Department, and PLA Navy were given a direct role and responsibility to help the PBSC make decisions on related acquisitions (e.g., aircraft, supplies, destroyer or surface combatant development, and submarine development).

The PLA Navy lobby's mixed record in getting the PBSC to agree to centralization of maritime sovereignty enforcement under the PLA Navy also provides an opportunity to speculate about the relative influence of actors within the Chinese political system. The PLA Navy's success in attracting higher-level PBSC attention to the problem is not surprising given increasing Chinese dependence on seaborne trade and extensive writings by PLA Navy and other authors from the mid-1990s arguing that China's future economic development required continued access to the sea and effective management of maritime sovereignty issues. Similarly, the PLA Navy lobby's success in obtaining a national law to begin effective maritime sovereignty enforcement appears to be the result of a consensus by all parties interested in the issue of maritime sovereignty enforcement. The PLA Navy lobby was less successful in obtaining PBSC authorization to control, coordinate, and oversee the activities of civilian actors in the maritime sovereignty enforcement field. This is likely because the civilian agencies involved in maritime sovereignty enforcement have a voice and a vote. The civilian law enforcement agencies argued for centralization, but not under navy control. Those policy advocates won the day.

Each of these agencies and their umbrella ministries represent civilian functions and are answerable to the State Council. Any initiative that attempts to seize hold of these civilian activities and place them under the control of a military entity would be a radical change to the current maritime sovereignty enforcement process and antithetical to the consensus-oriented decisionmaking process in China in general. Centralization of processes involving many agencies and ministries is not unheard of in China. Taylor Fravel's work on China's border defenses suggests that management of the defense of China's frontier provinces involves a similar centralization process among many civilian and military organizations.[68] However, making such an initiative a reality would require a substantial amount of time, a significant amount of bureaucratic horse-trading, the expenditure of political capital throughout the Chinese bureaucracy, arrival at a consensus to organize in this way, and ultimately a decision at the highest levels of the PRC in favor of the proposal.

Because the military reports to the party through the Central Military Commission and civilian paramilitary organizations report to the Politburo via the State Council, reorganizing command and control of civilian paramilitary forces under the PLA Navy was inherently difficult. The failure of the PLA Navy lobby to attain its policy preferences reflects the reality that the PBSC holds for itself the right to set grand strategy and make strategic decisions. Proponents of the maritime civilian law enforcement agencies were more effective than the PLA Navy advocates in arguing their case.

Conclusion

The navy appears to have exerted influence on the central authorities' decisionmaking process through four means: (1) shaping the leadership's understanding of the strategic or security environment; (2) formulating options and giving the PBSC recommendations on the risks involved in conducting military operations; (3) providing advice on how to conduct a military operation once that operation has been approved by the Center; and (4) providing advice on the resources needed to carry out a specific military operation or military operations in general. Given the limited military experience of China's top party leaders, it should not be surprising that the PLA Navy lobby and the PLA in general exercise significant influence on military issues.

The Chinese decisionmaking process relies heavily on consensus building and negotiations, and evidence suggests that the PLAN is often very effective in coalition building. Although the PLA Navy exerts influence and can be an effective bureaucratic player, its mixed success in the cases examined above serves as a reminder that the CCP leadership reserves for itself a monopoly on higher-level strategic policymaking, the right to make major budgetary decisions, and the right to consider alternative views on military policy issues with broader strategic and foreign policy implications.

Notes

1. See David M. Lampton, "The Implementation Problem in China" in *Policy Implementation in Post-Mao China*, ed. David M. Lampton (Berkeley: University of California Press, 1987), 20; Kenneth Lieberthal, "Introduction: The Fragmented Authoritarianism Model and Its Limitations" in *Bureaucracy, Politics, and Decision Making in Post-Mao China*, eds. Kenneth Lieberthal and David Lampton (Berkeley: University of California Press, 1992), 12; and Susan L. Shirk, *The Political Logic of Economic Reform in China* (Berkeley: University of California Press, 1991), 116–128.

2. David M. Lampton, ed., *The Making of Chinese Foreign and Security Policy in the Era of Reform* (Stanford, CA: Stanford University Press, 2001); Linda Jakobson and Dean Knox, *New Foreign Policy Actors in China*, SIPRI Policy Paper 26 (Stockholm: SIPRI, Sept. 2010).

3. For analysis focused on a broader Chinese maritime lobby, see M. Taylor Fravel and Alexander Liebman, "Beyond the Moat: The PLAN's Evolving Interests and Potential Influence"; and Daniel M. Hartnett and Frederic Vellucci, "Toward a Maritime Security Strategy: An Analysis of Chinese Views since the Early 1990s," in *The Chinese Navy: Expanding Capabilities, Evolving Roles*, eds. Phillip C. Saunders, Christopher Yung, Michael Swaine, and Andrew Yang (Washington, DC: NDU Press, 2011), 41–80 and 81–108.

4. This chapter relies heavily on Admiral Liu's memoir because it provides inside details on PLA interactions with top CCP leaders. As Cortez Cooper of RAND

pointed out in a review of an earlier draft of this chapter, Liu excelled in self-promo-tion. Accordingly, other sources are employed to cross-check Liu's account.

5. Liu Huaqing [刘华清], *Memoirs of Liu Huaqing* [刘华清回忆录] (Beijing: Lib-eration Army Press [解放军出版社], 2004), 101.

6. Ibid., 104.

7. Ibid.

8. Ibid., 101.

9. Ibid., 101–102.

10. Ibid., 104–105.

11. Ibid., 107.

12. Ibid.

13. Ibid.

14. Ibid.

15. John Garver, "China's Push through the South China Sea: The Interaction of Bureaucratic and National Interests," *China Quarterly*, no. 132 (December 1992): 1010.

16. Ai Hongren [艾宏仁], *An Inside Look into the Chinese Communist Navy: Advanc-ing toward the Blue Water Challenge* [中共海军透视: 迈向远洋的挑战], translated by Foreign Broadcast Information Service, JPRS-CAR-90-052 (July 16, 1990), 12.

17. Ibid., 55.

18. Ibid., 57.

19. Ibid., 56.

20. Ibid.

21. Ibid.

22. Ibid., 56–57.

23. John Lewis and Xue Litai, *China's Strategic Seapower: The Politics of Force Mod-ernization in the Nuclear Age* (Stanford, CA: Stanford University Press, 1994), 226.

24. Ibid., 56.

25. Ibid., 55.

26. "Former Deputy Commander of the PLA Navy Vice Admiral Zhang Xusan Is Guest of Sina.com" [原海军副司令张序三中将作客新浪], *Warship Knowledge* [舰船知识], July 11, 2005, quoted in Andrew Erickson and Andrew Wilson, "China's Air-craft Carrier Dilemma," *Naval War College Review* 59, no. 4 (Autumn 2006): 19.

27. Bernard Cole, "The Future Chinese Carrier Force," *U.S. Naval Institute News*, May 2013.

28. Nan Li and Christopher Weuve, "China's Aircraft Carrier Ambitions: An Update," *Naval War College Review* 63, no. 1 (Winter 2010).

29. Ibid., 14.

30. Ibid.

31. Andrew Erickson, Abraham Denmark, and Gabriel Collins, "Beijing's 'Starter Carrier' and Future Steps: Alternatives and Implications," *Naval War College Review* 65, no. 1 (Winter 2012): 20.

32. "Chinese Aircraft Carrier Bearing Heavy Responsibility and Having a Long Way to Go, the Future Navigation Not to Be Done Overnight" [中国航母任重道远

未来航程不会一蹴而就], *PLA Daily* [解放军报], September 27, 2012; and Jiang Xiaozhou [江小舟], "China's First Aircraft Carrier 'Liaoning' Commissioned October 1" [中国首航母"辽宁"号十一成军], *The Mirror* [镜报], no. 423 (October 2012).

33. "Chinese Aircraft Carrier Bearing Heavy Responsibility and Having a Long Way to Go"; Jiang, "China's First Aircraft Carrier 'Liaoning' Commissioned October 1"; and Li and Weuve, "China's Aircraft Carrier Ambitions."

34. Daniel Hartnett, "The PLA's Domestic and Foreign Activities and Orientation," testimony before the U.S.-China Economic and Security Review Commission hearing on "China's Military and Security Activities Abroad," Washington, DC, March 4, 2009.

35. Office of the Secretary of Defense, "Military and Security Developments Involving the People's Republic of China," *Annual Report to Congress (2013)*, 17.

36. Hartnett and Vellucci, "Toward a Maritime Security Strategy."

37. Nan Li, "Scanning the Horizon for 'New Historic Missions,'" *Proceedings Magazine* 136 (April 2010).

38. Hartnett and Vellucci, "Toward a Maritime Security Strategy," 83.

39. Ibid., 90–91.

40. Ibid.

41. Fravel and Liebman, "Beyond the Moat," 47.

42. Luo Xianlin [罗仙林], "Ocean Consciousness: A Topic That Cannot Be Avoided" [海洋意识: 一个不能回避的话题], *Modern Navy* [当代海军], no. 5 (1995): 15.

43. Liu Zhenhuan [刘振环] et al., "Enter the New Century of the Ocean, Strengthen China's Navy" [走进海洋世纪强大中国海军], *Modern Navy* [当代海军], no. 1 (2000): 4.

44. Lyle Goldstein, *Five Dragons Stirring Up the Sea: Challenge and Opportunity in China's Improving Maritime Enforcement Capabilities*, China Maritime Studies 5 (Newport, RI: China Maritime Studies Institute, U.S. Naval War College, April 2010), 5–21.

45. State Oceanic Administration [国家海洋局], *China's Ocean Development Report* [中国海洋发展报告] (2010), 456–457.

46. Yang Mingjie, "Sailing on a Harmonious Sea: A Chinese Perspective," *Contemporary International Relations*, April 19, 2011.

47. Wu Jiao, "Deputies Call for a Law of the Sea," *China Daily*, March 15, 2011.

48. Ibid.

49. Hu Xueqin [胡雪琴], "Exclusive Interview with Rear Admiral Yin Zhuo Reveals Secrets about Chinese Aircraft Carrier" [独家专访海军少将尹卓 解密中国航母], *China Economy Weekly* [中国经济周刊] 31 (2011).

50. Ibid.

51. Bai Tiantian, "Government Shake-up for Efficiency," *Global Times*, March 11, 2013. Also see "China to Set up Integrated Law Agency," *Zee News*, March 11, 2013.

52. Ibid.

53. "Changing Tack with Sea Strategy," *People's Daily Online*, May 13, 2009.

54. Hartnett and Vellucci, "Toward a Maritime Security Strategy," 94–95; see Zhang Dengyi [张登义], "Manage and Use the Ocean Wisely, Establish a Strong Maritime Nation" [管好用好海洋，建设海洋强国], *Qiushi* [求是], no. 11 (2010): 46.

55. Li Mingjiang and Zhang Hongzhou, "Restructuring China's Maritime Law Enforcement," *China Daily Mail*, April 10, 2013; Robert Sutter and Chin-hao Huang, "China's Southeast Asia Relations: China's Growing Resolve in the South China Sea," *Comparative Connections*, May 2013; Linda Jakobson, "China's Foreign Policy Dilemma," Lowy Institute, February 5, 2013.

56. Andrew Chubb, "Xi Jinping: A Hardline Nationalist in Control of China?" *Southsea Conversations* (blog), December 14, 2012.

57. Sutter and Huang, "China's Southeast Asia Relations;" Li and Zhang, "Restructuring China's Maritime Law Enforcement."

58. Bai, "Government Shake-Up for Efficiency."

59. "China to Restructure Oceanic Administration, Enhance Maritime Law Enforcement," Xinhua, March 10, 2013; Lyle Morris, "Taming the Five Dragons? China Consolidates Its Maritime Law Enforcement Agencies," *China Brief* 13, no. 7 (March 28, 2013).

60. "China's Maritime Agencies Are Being Brought under a Single Agency," *Global Times*, March 11, 2013.

61. Ryan Martinson, "Power to the Provinces: The Devolution of China's Maritime Rights Protection," *China Brief* 14, no. 17 (September 10, 2014): 4. Also see "National Oceanic Commission Has Big Role to Play," *China Daily*, March 19, 2013.

62. "National Oceanic Commission Has Big Role to Play."

63. *China Security Report 2013* (Tokyo: National Institute for Defense Studies, 2014), 13.

64. "State Oceanic Commission," *Global Security*, www.globalsecurity.org/intell/world/china/soa.htm.

65. As cited in M. Taylor Fravel's chapter in this volume.

66. At the time of these interviews in April 2012, the creation of a Coast Guard under the administration of the State Oceanic Administration had not taken place yet.

67. Author's interviews in Beijing and Shanghai, April 2012.

68. M. Taylor Fravel, "Securing Borders: China's Doctrine and Force Structure for Frontier Defense," *Journal of Strategic Studies* 30, no. 4–5 (August–October 2007): 728–729.

11 The PLA and Maritime Security Actors

Linda Jakobson

Introduction

China's dependency on the seas has risen in tandem with its economic growth. As the maritime environment has become more crucial to China's modernization, senior leaders of the Chinese Communist Party (CCP) have become more aware of the significance of maritime security.[1] They now regard access to the sea as a vital part of China's national security and development policy.[2] China's coastline must not only be protected against military threats, but also considered in terms of foreign trade, resource security, and food security. In late 2012 the Eighteenth CCP National Congress work report set the goal of China becoming a maritime power, calling for enhanced capacity to exploit marine resources, protect the marine environment, and safeguard China's maritime rights and interests.[3]

The 2013 Defense White Paper for the first time devoted an entire subsection to "safeguarding China's maritime rights and interests," stating that "it is an essential national development strategy to . . . build China into a maritime power."[4] The paper adds that the People's Liberation Army (PLA) has an important duty "to resolutely safeguard China's maritime rights and interests."[5] Ongoing military modernization means the PLA now possesses greater capabilities to carry out this duty and has become more willing to use these capabilities.[6]

Two trends in foreign and security policy formulation have affected (and complicated) the PLA's mission of protecting the country's maritime interests and rights. First, the number of actors trying to influence top policy decisionmakers has multiplied.[7] As a consequence of China's dramatically expanded global outreach over the past decade, China's foreign and security policy matters to a growing number of elites and interest groups. In addition to new official foreign policy actors previously unaffected by China's international behavior (such as CCP organs, PLA units, and a broader range of government ministries and agencies), there are new "actors on the margins" who want to shape foreign and security policy and who also participate in implementing Chinese policies.[8] As a result, policymaking is becoming increasingly fragmented and authority over foreign and security policy is fractured.[9] In the maritime domain, the PLA shares responsibility for safeguarding China's maritime rights and interests with several other actors.

Second, many foreign policy actors, both official ones and those on the margins, advocate that China should be "less submissive" in its foreign policy and defend its interests more actively.[10] They support China using its enhanced military and political capabilities to defend maritime interests and territorial sovereignty.

In recent years, China has indeed defended its maritime interests more staunchly. Consequently, China's enhanced military power and how China may use that power in the maritime domain are causing increasing concern among China's neighbors. These concerns are compounded by uncertainty about how China's diverse maritime security actors are coordinated and controlled in defending the nation's maritime interests.[11]

Like many other countries, China has extensive maritime interests. These include claims to territorial sovereignty over islands and coral reefs, claims to exclusive rights to develop maritime resources in its exclusive economic zone (EEZ), and a desire to maintain freedom of navigation on the high seas. Since 2009 Chinese maritime law enforcement agency vessels have substantially increased patrols in disputed waters—which the Chinese regard as their sovereign waters—and chased away and harassed other countries' fishing vessels and the seismic survey vessels of resource companies. In turn, maritime law enforcement vessels of other countries chase away and harass Chinese vessels operating in what they perceive as their own sovereign waters. Numerous incidents have led to heightened tensions between China and its neighbors, and between China and the United States. Outsiders perceive China's actions as assertive and the United States and other countries have warned China not to coerce or "bully" its neighbors. Beijing typically replies that Chinese vessels have not been the provocateurs and that China's actions have always been in response to provocations by others.[12] While in many cases this characterization has been accurate, China's response to what it deems a provocative act has often appeared excessive.[13]

Most of these incidents involve vessels belonging to China's maritime law enforcement agencies rather than the PLA Navy. By giving the primary responsibility for protecting and asserting China's sovereignty in disputed waters to civilian agencies instead of the PLA Navy, China's senior leaders have sought to limit the potential for escalation.[14] Nevertheless, in several incidents a PLA Navy vessel was not far away, in keeping with the policy of "naval forces on the second line, coast guard forces on the first line" (*haijun erxian, haijing yixian*).[15]

The increasing tensions between China and its neighbors in the South and East China Seas run the risk of escalating into military conflict. To form a more nuanced picture of China's intentions and policies it is critical to comprehend the roles and motivations of the diverse actors in the maritime security sphere and how they interact. The relationship between the PLA and the maritime law enforcement agencies is crucial because both are key players in China's maritime security domain. This chapter seeks to enhance understanding of these relationships and the PLA's dealings with other civilian agencies with maritime responsibilities.

Maritime Security Actors

The ultimate authority on maritime security policy in China is the CCP's Politburo Standing Committee (PBSC), the highest decisionmaking body. Decisions are reached based on consensus among the seven Standing Committee members. Consequently, decisionmaking processes are time-consuming and the wording of any guideline or directive is often vague—so vague that the guideline can be used to justify a wide array of sometimes competing policy objectives.[16] In a situation in which lower-level actors do not necessarily have clear guidance on specific maritime issues, some actors, as Thomas Bickford notes, "may be reluctant to act until there is direction from above, while other actors may continue in certain actions until the Standing Committee tells them to stop."[17]

In mid-2012 Xi Jinping was reportedly put in charge of a new leading small group (LSG) focusing on maritime security. The maritime security LSG reportedly includes representatives from the PLA, the Ministry of Land and

Resources, the Ministry of Foreign Affairs, the Ministry of Public Security, and the Ministry of Agriculture.[18] In September 2012, soon after the Japanese government's purchase of the Senkaku/Diaoyu islands, Xi was also made head of a new "Office to Respond to the Diaoyu Crisis."[19]

People's Liberation Army

The PLA shares authority with CCP organs and government entities on decisions pertaining to arms control and proliferation as well as other defense-related policy issues, particularly those related to strategic arms, territorial integrity, and national security. The Central Military Commission (CMC) is the highest CCP body overseeing defense policy and military strategy. In addition to the CMC, the CCP leading small groups provide official channels for senior military leaders to influence foreign and security policy.

The extent to which the PLA exerts influence on China's foreign and security policy is debated among specialists both within and outside China.[20] Top military leaders are political appointees who must follow the party line. The two CMC vice-chairmen are members of the Politburo. All CMC members are full members of the CCP's Central Committee. The PLA is subordinate to the party, not to the state, and as such is an "intrinsically political institution."[21] The prime mission of the PLA is to protect the CCP; in Hu Jintao's words, to "provide critical, powerful backing for the party's consolidation of its ruling status."[22] Nevertheless, PLA leaders also seek to shape the views of the CCP top leadership on foreign and security policy issues that are important to or under the purview of the armed forces.

In essence, today's PLA is both an official foreign policy actor and one on the margins.[23] On the one hand, since the founding of the People's Republic the PLA has been—and still is—a key actor at the highest echelons of power in decisionmaking on specific foreign and security issues. On the other hand, as China's global interests have expanded and authority within China's decisionmaking processes has become fractured, a broader range of actors now seeks to influence policy decisions. The top leadership must take the views of a much more diverse group of elites into consideration. The PLA has sought to get its voice heard by influencing public opinion and the positions of other actors. In doing so it has become a "new foreign policy actor."[24] There are *omnidirectional influences* at play between CCP officials, government bureaucrats, PLA officers, intellectuals, researchers, media representatives, and business executives.[25] Everyone seeks to influence each other and shape public opinion. Awareness of such omnidirectional channels of influence is critical to understanding the PLA's role in the complex national security policy formation process in China.

The PLA's foreign affairs system further contributes to the problem of fractured authority in foreign policy formulation. As Michael Swaine notes,

> Many of the activities undertaken by the military that pose potential problems for the United States . . . come under either the Operations Department or the Military Training and Service Arms Department of the PLA General Staff Department (GSD). According to one very knowledgeable Chinese officer, these departments are senior in the PLA hierarchy to those GSD units in charge of foreign affairs and intelligence. As a result, they routinely do not consult with such units when deploying assets or conducting military tests or exercises. In addition, the GSD's foreign affairs office is primarily responsible for military exchanges with foreign countries, not assessments of the diplomatic impact of military actions. In other words, no organization within the PLA has the authority and responsibility to routinely demand and receive notice of PLA activities that might impact China's foreign policy.[26]

Referring to the PLA as a monolithic or holistic entity is to a certain extent misleading. There is competition for prestige and resources among the various branches of the PLA. The weight of the PLA Navy (PLAN) has likely increased in tandem with the CCP leadership's growing recognition of the importance of maritime security. However, given the dominance of the ground forces within the PLA and the CMC, the PLA Navy is not necessarily the most crucial actor in crafting or finalizing maritime security policies. The navy certainly does not have a monopoly within the PLA on policy decisions pertaining to maritime security.[27] Leading officers of all the forces are involved in crafting maritime security policy.[28]

The CMC, the PLA Navy, the PLA ground forces, and PLA Air Force are all maritime security actors. Numerous other PLA entities are also involved in the maritime sphere, including the General Staff Department, General Political Department, General Logistics Department, General Equipment Department, and the Second Artillery Corps. Moreover, paramilitary organizations such as the People's Armed Police Maritime Border Defense Force and the Maritime Militia also need to be considered as maritime security actors.[29]

Maritime Law Enforcement Agencies

China's maritime law enforcement landscape was transformed by decisions announced at the National People's Congress (NPC) in March 2013. Prior to that there were five civilian maritime law enforcement agencies, each with its own fleet and each subordinate to a different government ministry or agency. The original five agencies were:

- *China Maritime Police* (CMP, *Gong'an bianfang haijing bumen*), belonging to the Border Control Department under the People's Armed Police, which in turn was under a dual command structure (*shuangchong lingdao*) comprising the Ministry of Public Security and the Central Military Commission.[30] In English the CMP was also referred to as China's Coast Guard (*Zhongguo haijing*). It mostly operated small, high-speed vessels armed with machine guns or small cannons.[31] The CMP's responsibilities included protection of and law enforcement in China's maritime territory.[32]

- *China Marine Surveillance* (CMS, *Zhongguo haijian*), a department of the State Oceanic Administration (SOA, *Haiyangju*), which was administered by the Ministry of Land and Resources. The CMS was founded in 1998 with the explicit mission of protecting China's extensive exclusive economic zone (EEZ) from various forms of encroachment.[33] This mandate raised the profile of the SOA and its CMS in recent years even though the SOA, in terms of hierarchy, was only an agency under a ministry.

- *Fisheries Law Enforcement Command* (FLEC, *Zhongguo yuzheng*), a part of the Fisheries Bureau administered under the Ministry of Agriculture. Dwindling fish stocks have created tensions between fishermen and Chinese government agencies that want to limit the catch as well as between the fishermen and government agencies of nearby countries that either want to limit the catch or oppose fishing in disputed waters.

- *Maritime Antismuggling Bureau* (*Haishang jisi jingcha bumen*) under the General Administration of Customs, which operated its own fleet of fast patrol boats.[34]

- *Maritime Safety Administration* (MSA, *Zhongguo haishiju*) was—and remains—under the Ministry of Transportation. Its responsibilities include supervision of maritime traffic control.[35]

Since the early 2000s the five law enforcement agencies were referred to col-
loquially in Chinese publications as the five "sea-stirring dragons."[36] As Lyle
Goldstein notes, many Chinese experts used this term pejoratively because
they viewed the capabilities of China's maritime enforcement authorities as
too weak and dispersed.[37] A group of prestigious Chinese analysts argued,
"in the event of an incident at sea, all the agencies will either rush to assist
or none will. In addition, individual teams with their own systems and construction will lead to . . . a waste of resources."[38] Chinese maritime specialists
repeatedly criticized poor coordination among the five maritime enforcement
agencies, pointing to the need to "overcome the out-dated mindset of self-
ish departmentalism."[39] An active-duty PLA officer alluded to this mentality
when noting that cooperation requires "breaking down the barriers, pooling
resources and sharing information. But information is precious and resources
are exclusive, so this requires cooperating units to have an open mind and
generous spirit."[40]

Before 2013, the urgent need to either enforce new mechanisms to ensure
better cooperation or merge the law enforcement agencies into one body was
a common theme in publications by Chinese analysts.[41] Wang Hanling is one
of many Chinese researchers who cited the U.S. Coast Guard as an "all-in-
one force" model which China ought to adopt to provide military, multi-mission, and maritime services to protect broad national security interests and
to patrol international waters.[42] This approach was to a large extent adopted
when comprehensive government restructuring of maritime law enforcement
agencies was announced at the People's National Congress in March 2013. In
June 2013 the State Council issued guidelines for a new coast guard.[43]

A New Maritime Law Enforcement Agency

The restructuring gave the State Oceanic Administration, which previously
only managed the CMS, administrative control over a new coast guard which
integrated the CMS with the China Maritime Police, the Fisheries Law Enforcement Command, and the Maritime Antismuggling Bureau.[44] It is unclear why
one of the previous five law enforcement agencies, the MSA under the Ministry
of Transportation, was not included in the consolidation plan.

The restructured SOA remains under the administration of the Ministry
of Land and Resources. However, when carrying out maritime law enforcement duties, the SOA operates under a new agency called the Maritime Police
Bureau (*Haijingju*), which is to be operationally guided by the Ministry of

Public Security.[45] It is unclear whether the new Maritime Police Bureau has inherited the former Maritime Police's dual command structure (*shuangchong lingdao*). The Maritime Police previously functioned as part of the People's Armed Police, under the primary command of the Ministry of Public Security and secondary command of the Central Military Commission.[46] If this is still the case, the implication is that any infringement upon national rights and security would result in China's military command structure having a say in the direction of civilian agency operations.

The first director of the Maritime Police Bureau is Meng Hongwei, vice-minister of the Ministry of Public Security. In conjunction with the restructuring, Meng was also appointed deputy director of the reorganized State Oceanic Administration. Officially, the revamped SOA and new Maritime Police Bureau went into operation with much fanfare in July 2013.[47] Chinese media published photos of vessels from the previous enforcement agencies, which had been repainted to bear *Zhongguo haijing* in Chinese characters with "China Coast Guard" painted in English. A "China Coast Guard" sign replaced the 14-year-old "China Marine Surveillance" nameplate.[48]

In reality, the restructuring of the maritime law enforcement agencies was still incomplete by the end of 2014. Initially, the process was slowed down because there was no action plan stipulating how the consolidation should take place.[49] All steps leading up to the restructuring announcement in March 2013 were focused on building a consensus regarding the outcome of the merger, not on the mechanics of the process. When one considers the bureaucratic rivalries among the stakeholders involved, garnering the political support needed for the consolidation of four of five agencies was undoubtedly a complex and time-consuming task.

Lack of an action plan was only one of many severe challenges that have made the restructuring process arduous. At the central government level two factors in particular have hampered the emergence of a unified coast guard. First, coordination has been weak as a result of a power struggle between Meng Hongwei and Liu Cigui, SOA director and party secretary since 2007. According to several SOA officials, the complex leadership structure of the new Coast Guard left Liu embittered.[50] Before the NPC in 2013 Liu had lobbied hard for the SOA to be elevated to ministry status, but instead he was forced to share power with an official from another ministry and one senior to him. In the Chinese bureaucratic hierarchy Meng is a full minister and Liu is only a vice-minister. Second, several senior officials at the three agencies that lost their separate law enforcement agency status were unhappy with the decision and have participated half-heartedly in the restructuring led by the SOA.[51]

The problems the restructuring has faced are reflected in the continuous reference in Chinese media to the former agency fleets instead of the unified "Maritime Police Bureau" fleet.[52] Furthermore, articles published in China make no secret of the fact that "on the inside the Maritime Police Bureau is still not unified."[53] For example, as late as October 2014 a former FLEC employee was quoted as saying, "right now we don't know where we are assigned."[54] Zhou Huawei of Dalian Maritime University and Zhang Tong of Shanghai Maritime University write that maritime law enforcement consolidation is hampered by the lack of a strong legal foundation, difficulty in harmonizing cross-department relationships, and limited skills of enforcement personnel. Zhou and Zhang point out that the new Maritime Police Bureau has centralized enforcement power, but there will still be "multiple administration authorities."[55]

The academics also point out that that the integration is not complete because the MSA is not included. Zhou and Zhang conclude that the Maritime Police Bureau's mission is to shoulder the burden of "maintaining maritime security and guaranteeing China's maritime rights and interests." Thus, "it is necessary to strengthen cooperative relationships with the PLAN and MPS. But this needs long-term development and practice."[56]

As with the former CMS, the restructured SOA's fleet is divided into three regional commands or branches, the North Sea Branch, East Sea Branch, and the South Sea Branch.[57] This division mirrors PLAN fleet organization, facilitating coordination. The three regional commands include eleven Maritime Police Corps with a projected total of 16,296 personnel.[58] During the restructuring the North Sea and East Sea preparatory groups have been located in the SOA's North Sea Bureau and East Sea Bureau respectively. The South Sea preparatory group has been in the office previously used by the South Sea Bureau of the FLEC. By the end of 2014, integration work had only just reached the level of the three sea areas, so the eleven Maritime Police Corps and their detachments had not yet been established.[59]

One of the many uncertainties about China's new maritime law enforcement involves whether the new Maritime Police Bureau fleet will be armed. Some sources suggest that the restructuring will allow previously unarmed units of sea-going law enforcement agencies to become armed. Before 2013 only the vessels of the Maritime Police and the Antismuggling Bureau were lightly armed.[60]

Another uncertainty pertains to the State Oceanic Commission (SOC, *Guojia haiyang weiyuanhui*), announced in March 2013 as a new high-level consultative and coordinating body on maritime operations. The SOA is supposed to carry out the commission's "specific tasks," which have not been made public.[61] Initially, there were public statements predicting that the SOC would have an important role in China's maritime strategy and be responsible for managing interdepartmental relations and emergency plans.[62] As of the end of 2014, the names of commission members had not been made public nor was there news of the commission having convened. Some analysts presume that once it does convene it will be tasked with drawing up an ocean law and national maritime strategy rather than being a high-level coordinator, as initially presumed.

Other Maritime Security Actors

Numerous other government entities under the State Council administer and implement maritime policy in disparate areas such as maritime law enforcement, maritime security, and maritime economic development. The *Ocean Development Report 2013* identifies the following: National Development and Reform Commission (NDRC), Ministry of Foreign Affairs (MFA), Ministry of Public Security, Ministry of Industry and Information Technology, Ministry of Land and Resources, Ministry of Water Resources, Ministry of Environmental Protection, Ministry of Agriculture, Ministry of Science and Technology, General Administration of Customs, Forestry Bureau, National Tourism Association, and Ministry of Transportation.[63]

Many of these government entities have specific maritime-related units. For example, in 2009 the MFA established the Department of Boundary and Ocean Affairs. Its functions include the development of policies concerning land and maritime boundaries, coordination of external work relating to the oceans and seas, management of land boundary delimitation and demarcation with neighboring countries, and engagement in diplomatic negotiations on maritime delimitation and joint development.[64] This department has overlapping areas of authority for maritime issues with the Departments for Asian Affairs, and North American Affairs, both of which are well-established and, according to Chinese interlocutors, have more clout.

Some of the large state-owned enterprises (SOEs), and the national oil and gas companies in particular, are actors on the margins with regard to maritime security policy. Chinese resource companies do not necessarily seek a role in foreign and security policy, but their actions can complicate Chinese diplomacy. By pursuing commercial interests overseas, resource companies can inadvertently entangle foreign and security policy officials in a web of political interests and standoffs with other countries.[65] This characterization applies to large state-owned resource companies that seek to conduct exploration and extract oil, gas, and other resources in the disputed areas in China's near waters.

It is impossible to determine the precise mix of political, nationalist, and commercial motivations influencing the behavior of resource company executives. They have a commercial interest in access to minerals and energy resources in China's near seas, and therefore are portrayed by Chinese analysts and media as generally supporting a firm stance on Chinese territorial claims in the East and South China Seas and strong defense of China's maritime rights. It is not known whether Chinese resource companies actually would rather see China make compromises and pursue joint development of resources. In the present political atmosphere in China, which underlines rights consciousness and rights protection, it would require courage to publicly advocate compromises with neighboring countries over maritime rights.

Finally, fishermen should also be regarded as maritime security actors because they—and the former FLEC—have regularly been involved in maritime incidents in the East and South China Seas, aggravating tensions between China and its neighbors.[66] The FLEC was cited by several Chinese researchers working on maritime issues as the agency that has the "loudest voice encouraging our government to staunchly defend our interests in China's near waters."[67] Patrick Cronin argues that fishermen play a political role by fishing in disputed waters, often citing China's claims to maritime rights as the major reason for their presence.[68] Furthermore, FLEC vessels have escorted fishermen in disputed waters and have provided protection to Chinese fishermen when confronted by vessels from other states.[69]

The PLA and Maritime Law Enforcement Agencies

After the announcement of the consolidation of the agencies in March 2013, a spokesman for the Ministry of Defense emphasized the PLA's intention to strengthen cooperation.[70] This type of statement does not necessarily mean much. Over the past decades there have been innumerable calls for the improvement of civilian-military cooperation by both civilian and military leaders. For example, in a 2014 military publication the commander of the Jiangsu Military Region criticized a "self-interested mindset" and underscored the importance of information sharing to seriously address problems in military and civilian integration.[71] However, this time the ministry statement might be more than empty talk. Since March 2013 there have been indications that institutional interaction between the PLA and the maritime law enforcement agencies is growing.

In the years preceding the 2013 decision to consolidate the "sea-stirring dragons" the PLA already started to modestly cooperate with the agencies, especially with the CMS.[72] Since October 2009 CMS personnel have received training at PLA naval academies, in Nanjing, Anhui, Dalian, and elsewhere.[73] The PLA Naval Command College in Nanjing conducts regular training courses for CMS commanders and political commissars.[74] In January 2011 the PLA Naval Command College in Nanjing and the CMS also jointly established the CMS Education Research Center.[75] In November 2011 the CMS launched a CMS training base at the Bengbu Naval Non-commissioned Officer (NCO) Academy in Anhui, which provides courses tailored to the needs of specific roles relating to the protection of maritime rights.[76] The PLA Naval Academy in Dalian also provides both regular and ad hoc training on an as-needed basis for CMS senior crewmen and core staff.[77] A substantial number of CMS officers and mid-to-senior level NCOs therefore receive training supervised by the PLAN.

The CMS and PLAN have a "deep and long-standing cooperative relationship, and are comrades in arms in battles within China's near waters."[78] Furthermore, according to interviews with mid-level SOA officials and Chinese academics working on maritime issues, political ties exist between SOA Director Liu Cigui and the PLAN leadership, based on their shared view that China should more staunchly defend its sovereignty in disputed areas of the South and East China Seas.[79] In 2010 PLAN Rear Admiral Yin Zhuo publicly lamented the weak status of the SOA as an agency of the Ministry for Land and Resources. Yin said that the SOA does not have "planning power."[80] Even after the restructuring of the agencies was announced there has been indirect criticism of the State Council's decision not to upgrade the SOA to a ministry.[81]

The number of drills the PLA Navy has conducted with maritime law enforcement agency fleets has grown. The first publicized, large-scale joint exercise, dubbed "East Sea collaboration," was held in October 2012 with eleven vessels and eight aircraft. The exercise involved a Chinese territorial enforcement scenario in which fishing vessels were followed, harassed, and hindered by vessels from another country. With backup from the PLAN, CMS and FLEC vessels were employed to enforce China's rights.[82] A subsequent joint exercise was held near Dongguan in November 2013. Participants included local military units, municipal Public Security Bureau personnel, municipal Public Security Frontier Detachment personnel, the Dongguan Maritime Bureau, the Dongguan fishery detachment, and the Huangpu Customs Bureau.[83]

Since the restructuring of the agencies, several joint military-civilian exercises have been held. The most noteworthy took place in the summer of 2014 in waters close to Vietnam. The drill postulated a scenario in which an oil rig was surrounded by foreign fishing boats. It was organized by the PLAN South Sea Fleet and involved more than ten units from the military and the local administrative region, including the PLA Naval Aviation Force, Fisheries Law Enforcement Command, PLA Air Force, China Coast Guard, and the maritime militia. Dozens of vessels and several fighter aircraft were employed.[84]

The exercise had clearly been prompted by the real life standoff in the South China Sea in May 2014 after China National Offshore Oil Corporation (CNOOC) deployed its deep water *HYSY 981* oil rig to a location within Vietnam's EEZ near the disputed Paracel Islands (which China controls but both Vietnam and China claim).[85] Dozens of China Coast Guard vessels fended off attempts by Vietnamese vessels to approach the rig. Water cannon exchanges took place between the Chinese and Vietnamese, and in at least one instance a provincial maritime law enforcement agency vessel from Liaoning (*Haijing 37102*) rammed a Vietnamese vessel. The standoff led to anti-Chinese protests in Vietnam, causing some fatalities.

PLA Navy vessels were in the vicinity of the rig monitoring the situation, but did not actively participate in the defense of the rig. However, according to several Chinese interlocutors familiar with the standoff, the PLA had a key role in coordinating the defense of the rig.[86] The interlocutors emphasized that the professional standards of PLAN officers are considerably higher than officers in the China Coast Guard and without PLAN involvement such a large-scale operation could not have taken place.

In an article about the joint exercise simulating the defense of an oil rig, a former PLAN captain was quoted as saying: "The drill will help the authorities to mount powerful counterattacks as well as threaten Vietnam and other countries involved in territorial disputes, showing them that China is well prepared to repel any possible attack against its oil rigs."[87]

Since the oil rig standoff there have been also been other civilian-military drills. In August 2014, a base under the PLA Navy North Sea Fleet organized exercises with participation from local enforcement units such as the Coast Guard, FLEC, and the Rescue Bureau.[88] The seven drills included a civilian-military maritime denial-and-control operation. In September the PLA Navy East Sea Fleet conducted "large-scale" exercises that incorporated combat support ships, destroyers, naval helicopters, and submarines as well as local law enforcement vessels.[89] That same month the PLA General Staff Headquarters organized metrological exercises, involving meteorological and hydrological troops from different military commands as well as staff of the State Oceanic Administration and China Coast Guard.[90]

The PLA and Other Maritime Security Actors

In its efforts to influence national security decisionmaking the PLA has to compete with numerous other actors—both within the official establishment and on the margins. As mentioned earlier, the PLA is both an official actor in the traditional sense and an actor on the margins. The fracturing of authority in policy formulation pushes PLA officers—as it does all actors—to strive to influence other actors as well as public opinion. PLA officers lobby, they write blogs, they take part in televised debates, and they ardently cultivate good relations with senior editors of *Huanqiu shibao* (the Chinese language edition of *Global Times*).[91] Most of these PLA commentators work in academia, intelligence, and propaganda.[92] Their comments should be viewed as propaganda, directed at both a domestic and international audience with the intent to bolster the PLA's image as a military to be taken seriously. Often their views are quite extreme. But they would not be able to publicly express these views unless they had the support of at least one high-ranking PLA leader.

The heightened importance of maritime security has spurred the PLA to increase its engagement not only with civilian law enforcement agencies and media outlets, but also with government ministries and agencies, state-owned enterprises, and even universities. In 2013, the PLA also signed cooperation agreements related to maritime security with prominent Chinese education institutions, such as Tsinghua University, Peking University, and the Chinese

Academy of Engineering. One such cooperative effort is called the "Ocean, Maritime Rights, and Navy," which is the theme of the PLA–Peking University cooperation.[93]

The 2013 Defense White Paper has an entire section devoted to the role the PLA should adopt to support economic and social development.[94] The paper states that as a result of the integration of China's economy into the world economic system, overseas interests have become an integral component of China's national interests. It notes that "security issues are increasingly prominent, involving overseas energy and resources, strategic sea lines of communication, and Chinese nationals and legal persons overseas."[95]

Though there is scant public information about the interaction between the resource companies and the PLA, the 2013 Defense White Paper explicitly stipulates that the PLAN "provides security support for China's maritime law enforcement, fisheries, and oil and gas exploitation."[96] Wang Peiyun, an oil industry commentator employed by CNOOC, argues that "China's oil and gas security in the South China Sea has been linked with the defense of its sovereignty over its territory."[97] In an industry journal opinion piece, Wang writes: "The South China Sea issue faces the risk of becoming more complex, militarized and internationalized. So, oil and gas exploitation in the disputed areas is an important component that should not be lacking in China's strategy in the South China Sea."[98] Public comments by CNOOC chairman Wang Yilin indicate that he also supports linking protection of China's sovereignty rights to CNOOC's economic objectives.[99] Whether the deployment of CNOOC's oil rig *HYSY 981* to disputed waters in May 2014 was initiated by one of China's national oil companies or by a government entity is not known.[100] According to Chinese sources, including an official working at one of the Central Committee offices, Yang Jiechi, the state counselor in charge of foreign affairs, forwarded the plan to deploy the rig to the senior leadership for approval.[101] The plan had been mooted for a long time, but Yang's predecessor, Dai Bingguo, had refused to pass the plan upward to the senior leadership.[102]

Conclusion

Chinese leadership recognition of the growing significance of the maritime sphere and the emphasis on safeguarding sovereignty in the maritime domain are nudging the PLA to embrace new modes of civil-military engagement. The PLA is reaching out to a diverse set of maritime-related foreign and security policy actors, even those outside the official decisionmaking establishment. Protecting China's maritime rights is their ultimate aim.

The PLA shares this task of protecting China's maritime rights with maritime law enforcement agencies and has increased its interaction with those agencies. The PLAN now provides training to maritime law enforcement personnel at PLAN academies, leads joint exercises at sea with law enforcement vessels, and is available to provide backup support in the event of a serious incident. That the PLA has proactively organized joint drills during 2014 hints at its desire to be more involved at a minimum as a coordinator of maritime law enforcement. According to a June 2014 *PLA Daily* article, the PLA is "actively building a military-police-civilian joint defense mechanism" and "closely coordinating with maritime forces to implement joint rights protection."[103] It could be that this proactive stance was born out of necessity because of the problematic relationship between rivals Liu Cigui (head of SOA) and Meng Hongwei (deputy head of SOA, who in fact outranks Liu in the CCP hierarchy). It could also be, as Chris Yung argues elsewhere in this volume, that the PLA failed in its bid to take control of maritime law enforcement and having accepted its secondary role in maritime law enforcement now wants to be more active.[104]

The decision announced in March 2013 to merge four of the five maritime law enforcement agencies under the leadership of the State Oceanic Administration was driven both from the top down and the bottom up. The decision undoubtedly reflects the Chinese leadership's desire to consolidate control over the agencies. But it was also driven by demands by several actors on the margins—including PLA academics and maritime analysts associated with maritime law enforcement agencies—that China ought to strengthen its capacity to "protect our national maritime security and effectively enforce China's ocean rights."[105] For years maritime specialists publicly criticized poor coordination among the agencies, which stemmed from bureaucratic rivalry and the lack of a single senior decisionmaker at the national level.

Chinese media reports are straightforward when describing the challenges the strengthened law enforcement agency faces.[106] A major uncertainty is how the command structure of the Maritime Police Bureau will function. This is central to an understanding of the interaction between the PLA and the civilian entities responsible for maritime law enforcement. The Maritime Police Bureau, like the People's Armed Police, is a paramilitary organization under the direction of the MPS. Hence the Maritime Police Bureau may have a dual command structure as does the PAP, which is under the unified command of the State Council and Central Military Commission.[107]

Moreover, a major challenge will be to ensure seamless collaboration with the PLA. Although joint exercises are conducted, one can surmise that the PLAN and Maritime Police Bureau still have a way to go to achieve operational "jointness"—"the ability of the military services and other elements of the national security establishments to work together, a critical component of the command-and-control domain."[108] When one considers the challenges the new Maritime Police Bureau fleet is encountering in operating as a unified fleet and adds the difficulties of interoperability within the PLA, civil-military cooperation in the maritime domain will be even more of an uphill struggle. Even though the operation to protect the CNOOC oil rig *HYSY 981* in disputed waters in May 2014 appeared to be well-coordinated, Chinese interlocutors stress that much more training is needed for that scale of operation to be seamlessly executed on a regular basis.

Finally, one can never overemphasize how little outsiders know about the command-and-control structure of the PLA and PLA interaction with paramilitary forces. For all the changes in China, how decisions are made and consensus is reached at the pinnacle of power—within the Politburo Standing Committee and Central Military Commission—remains opaque.

Notes

The author is extremely grateful for research assistance by Eva O'Dea and Dirk van der Kley, Research Associates in 2013 at the Lowy Institute for International Policy, as well interns Masato Kawaguchi, Tracy Tang, and Aimee Yi.

1. Daniel M. Hartnett and Frederic Vellucci write about the emergence of a "sea consciousness" in China and the role of PLA Navy analysts in this awakening. See "Toward a Maritime Security Strategy: An Analysis of Chinese Views since the Early 1990s," in *The Chinese Navy: Expanding Capabilities, Evolving Roles*, eds. Phillip C. Saunders, Christopher Yung, Michael Swaine, and Andrew Yang (Washington, DC: NDU Press, 2011), 81–108; and Christopher Yung's chapter in this volume.

2. Yang Mingjie, "Sailing on a Harmonious Sea: A Chinese Perspective," *Global Asia* 5, no. 4 (Winter 2010).

3. Hu Jintao, *Report of Hu Jintao to the 18th CCP National Congress*, chap. 7, November 16, 2012.

4. China's Ministry of National Defense, *The Diversified Employment of China's Armed Forces*, April 2013, chap. 4.

5. Ibid.

6. M. Taylor Fravel, "Maritime Security in the South China Sea and the Competition over Maritime Rights," in *Cooperation from Strength: The United States, China and the South China Sea*, ed. Patrick M. Cronin (Washington, DC: Center for a New American Security, 2012), 41; and Phillip C. Saunders, "The Role of the Chinese Military in the South China Sea," in *Perspectives on the South China Sea: Diplomatic, Legal, and Security Dimensions of the Dispute*, eds. Murray Hiebert, Gregory B. Poling, and Phuong Nguyen (Washington, DC: Rowman & Littlefield and Center for Strategic and International Studies, 2014), 127–135.

7. Linda Jakobson and Dean Knox, *New Foreign Policy Actors in China*, SIPRI Policy Paper 26 (Stockholm: Stockholm International Peace Research Institute, 2010), 1.

8. Ibid.

9. Ibid., 48.

10. Ibid., 51.

11. Linda Jakobson, *China's Unpredictable Maritime Security Actors* (Sydney: Lowy Institute for International Policy, December 2014).

12. Zhang Yunbi and Cai Hong, "Japan Must Cease Islands Provocations, China Warns," *China Daily USA*, September 11, 2013.

13. See *Dangerous Waters: China-Japan Relations on the Rocks*, International Crisis Group, April 8, 2013, 12.

14. Huang Jun [黄骏], "U.S. Report Says Chinese Navy Already Has Ability to Penetrate the Western Pacific" [美报告称中国海军已有能力深入西太平洋作战], *Eastern Military Affairs* [东方军事], originally published in *Global Times*, August 30, 2011; Fravel states that using naval forces against civilians from other claimant states would indicate greater Chinese assertiveness. See "Maritime Security in the South China Sea and the Competition over Maritime Rights," 43–44.

15. The phrase *haijun erxian, haijing yixian* is from military historian Xu Yan, cited in M. Taylor Fravel's chapter in this volume.

16. Jakobson, *China's Unpredictable Maritime Security Actors*.

17. Thomas J. Bickford, *Uncertain Waters: Thinking about China's Emergence as a Maritime Power* (Washington, DC: Center for Naval Analysis, September 2011), 60.

18. "China Maritime Police Bureau Unveiled" [中国海警局亮剑], *People's Digest* [人民文摘] 9 (2013).

19. Author's conversations with two Chinese officials, Beijing, January 2013.

20. See Jakobson and Knox, *New Foreign Policy Actors*, 12–16; Michael Swaine, "China's Assertive Behavior—Part Three: The Role of the Military in Foreign Policy," *China Leadership Monitor*, no. 36 (Winter 2012): 1.

21. Greg Chaffin, "China's New Military Leadership and the Challenges It Faces: An Interview with Roy Kamphausen," *National Bureau of Asian Research*, January 18, 2013.

22. Hu Jintao [胡锦涛], "Recognizing the PLA's Historic Mission in the New Century" [认清新世纪新阶段我军历史使命], Speech before the Central Military Commission, December 24, 2004. The transcript of the original speech was not officially published.

23. Jakobson and Knox, *New Foreign Policy Actors*, 1.

24. Ibid., 14–15.

25. Ibid., 43, 48.

26. Swaine, "China's Assertive Behavior," 9.

27. Senior researcher at the Academy of Military Sciences, interview with author, Beijing, September 15, 2011.

28. Ibid. See also Bickford, *Uncertain Waters*, 62–63.

29. Bickford, *Uncertain Waters*, 62–68.

30. China's Ministry of Defense website has a detailed description of the People's Armed Police Force, http://eng.mod.gov.cn/ArmedForces/armed.htm.

31. Lyle J. Goldstein, *Five Dragons Stirring Up the Sea: Challenge and Opportunity in China's Improving Maritime Enforcement Capabilities*, China Maritime Studies 5 (Newport, RI: China Maritime Studies Institute, U.S. Naval War College, April 2010), 6.

32. State Oceanic Administration [国家海洋局], *China's Ocean Development Report 2011* [中国海洋发展报告2011] (Beijing: Ocean Press [海洋出版社], 2011), 47.

33. Ibid., 478.

34. Goldstein, *Five Dragons Stirring Up the Sea*, 18.

35. Ibid., 9.

36. For example, "Ease the Pain of the Ocean: A Comprehensive Overview of China's Offshore Ecological Condition" [抚平大海之痛, 中国近海生态环境大扫描], *Xinhua Online* [新华网], September 16, 2002.

37. Goldstein, *Five Dragons Stirring Up the Sea*, 2.

38. Jiang Huai, Ma Xiaojun, Li Jie, Wang Hanling, and Fan Xiaoju [江淮, 马小军, 李杰, 王翰灵, 樊小菊], "China's Maritime Rights and Interests and the Navy" [中国的海洋权益和海军], *World Knowledge* [世界知识] 1 (2009).

39. "Changing Tack with Sea Strategy," *People's Daily Online*, May 13, 2011.

40. Zhang Bolin and Shi Binxin [张柏林, 石斌欣], "The Yellow-Bohai Coastal Defense Cooperation Zone Is Born" [黄渤首家海防协作区诞生], *China Military Online* [中国军网], July 28, 2009, www.chinamil.com.cn/jfjbmap/content/2010-07/03/content_32315.htm.

41. Li Jie [李杰], "Maritime Law Enforcement Power Calling Out for Efficient Unification" [海上执法力量呼唤高效合一], *China Military Online* [中国军网], July 3, 2010, www.chinamil.com.cn/jfjbmap/content/2010-07/03/content_32316.htm; Jiang et al., "China's Maritime Rights."

42. "Changing Tack."

43. "Office of the State Council Notice Regarding Regulations for the Main Duties, Internal Organization and Staffing of the State Oceanic Administration" [国务院办公厅关于印发国家海洋局主要职责内设机构和人员编制规定的通知], Central Government of the PRC, June 9, 2013, www.gov.cn/zwgk/2013-07/09/content_2443023.htm.

44. "China's Restructured SOA Goes into Official Operation," *Xinhua Online* [新华网], July 22, 2013; "Short Defense Analysis: Five Dragons Disturbing the Sea to End, Chinese Coastguard to be Formed" [防务短评: 五龙闹海结束中国版海岸警卫

队问世], *Phoenix Online* [凤凰网], March 10, 2013, http://news.ifeng.com/mil/forum/detail_2013_03/10/22936298_0.shtml; "China to Restructure Oceanic Administration, Enhance Maritime Law Enforcement," *Xinhua Online* [新华网], March 10, 2013.

45. Office of the State Council Notice, Central Government.

46. "The People's Armed Police Force," China's Ministry of Defense website, http://eng.mod.gov.cn.

47. "China's Restructured SOA Goes into Official Operation"; "Japanese and Chinese Media: 4 Chinese Coast Guard Vessels Patrol the Territorial Waters around the Diaoyu Islands" [日华媒：4艘中国海警船在钓鱼岛连接海域巡航], *China News Online* [中国新闻网], September 13, 2013, www.chinanews.com/gj/2013/09-12/5277693.shtml.

48. "China's Restructured SOA Goes into Official Operation."

49. Author interview with mid-ranking official at SOA, Beijing, June 20, 2013; author's interview with senior researcher at CASS, Shanghai, June 24, 2013.

50. Author interviews with mid-ranking officials at SOA and MPS, Beijing, September 1–4, 2014; Jakobson, *China's Unpredictable Maritime Security Actors.*

51. Author interviews with mid-ranking officials at SOA and MPS, Beijing and Shanghai, September 1–9, 2014.

52. See, for example, "China Marine Surveillance 9010 Vessel Enters Service in Guangzhou" ["中国海监9010" 船在广州入列], October 17, 2014, www.soa.gov.cn/xw/dfdwdt/dfjg/201410/t20141017_33834.html.

53. "China Maritime Police Bureau One Year Review: No Longer Fighting Alone" [中国海警局组建一年观察 执行任务不再单打独斗了], *Southern Weekend* [南方周末], October 9, 2014.

54. Ibid.

55. Zhou Huawei and Zhang Tong [周华伟, 张童], "From the Perspective of the Establishment of the Maritime Police Bureau: Discussions on the Improvement of China's Unified Maritime Enforcement Administration" [以中国海警局的设立为视角，论完善我国海上统一行政执法制度], *Shipping Management* [水运管理], no. 8 (August 2013): 26.

56. Ibid.

57. According to a 2005 document on the Chinese government portal, CMS already had three branches in 2005. See "Subordinate Bodies of the SOA," www.gov.cn/english//2005-09/29/content_73189.htm; "SOA Directs Coast Guard to Establish 3 Coast Guard Sub-Branches" [国家海洋局统一指挥海警 设三海警分局], *Ta Kung Pao* [大公報], July 10, 2013.

58. "China's Restructured SOA Goes into Official Operation"; "Office of the State Council Notice Regarding Regulations for the Main Duties, Internal Organization, and Staffing of the State Oceanic Administration" [国务院办公厅关于印发国家海洋局主要职责内设机构和人员编制规定的通知], Central Government of the PRC.

59. "China Maritime Police Bureau One Year Review."

60. "Restructured China Coast Guard Takes to the High Seas," *Global Times*, July 23, 2013.

61. Ye Xiaonan [叶晓楠], "SOA Restructure: The '5 Dragons Stirring the Sea' Era Comes to an End" [国家海洋局重组: '五龙治海' 时代终结], *People's Daily Overseas Edition* [人民日报海外版], June 26, 2013, 3.

62. Ibid.; Ye Hailin [叶海林], "The State Oceanic Commission Is Going to 'Quietly' Be the Hub of Sea Rights Protection" ['静悄悄' 的国家海洋委员会才是维护海权的坚强中枢], *People's Daily Overseas Edition* [人民日报海外版], March 14, 2013; "Guangzhou Military Region Deputy-Commander: Recommends Each Maritime-Related Department Form Part of the SOC" [广州军区副司令员: 建议各涉海部门组成国家海洋委员会], *Xinhua Online* [新华网], March 8, 2013, http://news.xinhuanet.com/mil/2013–03/08/c_124431874.htm.

63. State Oceanic Administration [国家海洋局], *China's Ocean Development Report 2013* [中国海洋发展报告2013], State Oceanic Administration [国家海洋局], (Beijing: Ocean Press [海洋出版社], 2013), 241. See also Bickford, *Uncertain Waters,* 61–68.

64. Duan Congcong and Wang Anna, "New Department Focuses on Borders," *Global Times*, May 6, 2009; "Foreign Ministry Spokesman Ma Zhaoxu's Regular Press Conference on 5 May 2009," Ministry of Foreign Affairs of the People's Republic of China, May 5, 2009.

65. Jakobson and Knox, *New Foreign Policy Actors in China,* 49.

66. Patrick M. Cronin, "China's Global Quest for Resources and Implications for the United States," testimony submitted to the U.S. Congressional China Security and Economy Review Commission, January 26, 2012, 1.

67. Author interview with senior researcher at Chinese government research institution, Beijing, June 29, 2011. Author interviews with maritime security specialists employed by Chinese government research institutions and Chinese universities in Washington, DC (October 2010), Shanghai and Beijing (June, September 2011, September 2014).

68. Cronin, "China's Global Quest," 2.

69. See *China Security Report 2011* (Tokyo: National Institute for Defense Studies, 2012), 3; Lyle J. Goldstein, "Chinese Fisheries Enforcement: Environmental and Strategic Implications," *Marine Policy* 40 (2013): 189–190; Cronin, "China's Global Quest."

70. "Ministry of National Defense: Chinese Military and Maritime Law Enforcement Forces Combine to Defend National Maritime Rights and Interests" [国防部: 中国军队与海上执法力量共同维护国家海洋权益], *Xinhua Online* [新华网], March 28, 2013.

71. "Vietnam Protests That Chinese Drilling Platform 'Violates Sovereignty,' Large Groups of Chinese and Vietnamese Maritime Police Face off" [越南抗议中国钻井平台 "侵犯主权" 中越大批海警船对峙], *The Observer* [观察者], March 5, 2014.

72. See MSA Weihai Branch Command Center [威海海事局指挥中心], "Weihai Maritime Safety Administration and PLA Troop Unit 91329 Sign 'Agreement on Cooperation and Coordination in Sea-Borne Operations,' Further Deepening Their Cooperation" [威海海事局与中国人民解放军91329部队签署《海上行动协调配合合作协议》,进一步深化合作关系], Weihai MSA [威海海事局], May 27, 2011, www.sdmsa.gov.cn/sdwhmsa/news/%7B7106e498-3031-4e9a-9c02-0c0f53ffc91f%7D.shtml.

73. "CMS Commissars for the First Time Attend Naval Academy to Receive Systematic Training" [海监政委首次走进海军高等学府接受系统培训], *China Ocean News* [中国海洋报], July 27, 2011; "CMS Sets up Training Base at Bengbu Naval Non-commissioned Officer Academy" [中国海监训练基地落户海军蚌埠士官学校], *China Ocean News* [中国海洋报], November 19, 2011.

74. "Training: The Key to Quality Personnel and Cultivating a Good Image" [队伍培训：强素质塑形象的金钥匙], *China Ocean News Online* [中国海洋在线], June 29 2012.

75. "The Training of CMS Commanders" [培养海监指挥员形成常态], *Sina Military* [新浪军事], April 16, 2011.

76. "Training: The Key to Quality Personnel."

77. Ibid.

78. "The Training of CMS Commanders."

79. Author interviews with SOA officials in Beijing, January 18, 2010, March 30, 2011, and September 16, 2011; Author interview with a senior researcher at Chinese government research institution in Beijing, June 29, 2011; Author interview with a senior researcher at Academy of Military Sciences in Beijing, September 15, 2011.

80. "Consultative Committee Member Yin Zhuo Proposes the Formulation of a National Maritime Strategy" [政协委员尹卓提案建议制定国家海洋战略], *Global Times Online* [环球网], March 9, 2010. Yin was interviewed after submitting a paper at the National People's Congress entitled "Formulating a National Maritime Strategy: Preparing a Grand Plan for Maritime Development and Security."

81. The muted criticism came from the head of the oceanic subcommittee of a national high-tech association. He advocated that the SOA be upgraded to a ministry. "Lack of Overall National Plan Allows 'Six Dragons Stirring the Seas' to Each Go Their Own Way in Economic Marine Zones" ["六龙闹海"各自为政海洋经济区缺乏全国统筹], *China Economy Weekly* [中国经济周刊], February 18, 2014.

82. Liu Yiyao [刘轶瑶], "Joint Drill in the East China Sea, by Chinese Navy, China Maritime Surveillance and the Fisheries Law Enforcement Command" [中国海军与海监,渔政在东海举行联合演习], *Phoenix News Online* [凤凰网], October 19, 2012.

83. "Dongguan Leads the Whole Province Developing Joint Military, Police, and Civilian Maritime Drills" [东莞在全省率先开展军警民海上联防演练], *Sina Guangdong* [新浪广东], October 30, 2013.

84. Zhang Yigen and He Peng [张毅根, 何鹏], "Protecting Drilling Platforms: Military-Police-Civilian Surround-and-Destroy Exercise in the South China Sea" [保护钻井平台：军警民南海演练围歼], *China National Defense Daily-Military Special* [中国国防报-军事特刊], August 23, 2014, www.81.cn/jmywyl/2014-08/23/content_6107899.htm.

85. "Vietnam Protests That Chinese Drilling Platform Violates Sovereignty."

86. Author interviews with mid-level officials and senior researchers focused on maritime security issues, Beijing and Shanghai, September 1–9, 2014; Jakobson, *China's Unpredictable Maritime Security Actors*.

87. Minnie Chan, "PLA Reports Maritime Drill near Vietnam Simulating Threat to Oil Rig," *South China Morning Post*, August 24, 2014.

88. Liu Wenping and Li Ding [刘文平, 李丁], "Navy Organizes Combat Study and Training, Air-Sea-Land Integration" [海军组织近海作战研练海陆空融合一体化对抗], *Xinhua Online* [新华网], August 11, 2014.

89. Yu Qizheng and Jiang Feng [虞起正, 姜峰], "China's Navy East Sea Fleet Holds Combat Support Troop Drills 'Haishen-2014'" [中国海军东海舰队举行 "海神一2014" 海上作战支援实兵演练], *Xinhua Online* [新华网], September 14, 2014.

90. "PLA Stages Meteorological, Hydrological Drills," Xinhua, September 28, 2014.

91. Author interview with a senior editor at *Huanqiu Shibao* [环球时报], October 21, 2009.

92. Andrew Chubb, "Propaganda, Not Policy: Explaining the PLA's "Hawkish Faction," pt. 1, *China Brief* 13, issue 15 (July 25, 2013); pt. 2, *China Brief* 13, issue 16, (August 9, 2013).

93. Qian Xiaohu and Mo Xiaoliang [钱晓虎, 莫小亮], "Chinese Navy and Chinese Academy of Engineering Sign Strategic Cooperation Agreement" [海军与中国工程院签署战略合作协议], *Xinhua Onlinet* [新华网], October 23, 2012; Wang Lingshuo and Mo Xiaoliang [王凌硕, 莫小亮], "Chinese Navy and Peking University Sign Agreement for the Innovation and Development of Civil-Military Integration" [海军与北京大学签署军民融合创新发展合作协议], *People's Daily Online* [人民网], April 24, 2013; "East China Sea Fleet Equipment Department Signs a Strategic Cooperation Agreement with College" [学院与海军东海舰队装备部签订战略合作协议], Shanghai Economic Management College website, June 20, 2013, www.semc.edu.cn/xiaoyuannews.asp?NewsID=2395.

94. China's Ministry of National Defense, *The Diversified Employment of China's Armed Forces*.

95. Ibid.

96. Ibid.

97. Wang Peiyun [王佩云], "China's Exploitation of Oil and Gas in the South China Sea and Defense of Its Sovereignty" [中国南海油气开发与主权维护], *China Petroleum Economics* [中国石油经济], no. 10 (December 2012). The journal is sponsored by CNOOC.

98. Ibid.

99. "Deep-water Drilling Begins in S. China Sea," *China.org.cn*, May 9, 2012, www.china.org.cn/business/2012–05/09/content_25339532.htm.

100. Erica Downs, "Business and Politics in the South China Sea: Explaining HYSY891's Foray into Disputed Waters," *China Brief* 14, no. 12 (June 19, 2014).

101. Author interviews with CPC officials in Beijing, September 1–5, 2014; Jakobson, *China's Unpredictable Maritime Security Actors*.

102. Author interviews with CPC officials in Beijing, September 1–5, 2014; Jakobson, *China's Unpredictable Maritime Security Actors*.

103. Li Tang and Gao Yi [李唐, 高毅], "China's Navy Normalizing Patrols to Cover Maritime Borders" [我海军常态化巡逻覆盖万里海疆], *PLA Daily* [解放军报], June 21, 2014.

104. See the chapter by Christopher Yung in this volume. This author did not come across evidence of the PLA's desire to be the lead organization in maritime law enforcement in her interviews.

105. Li, "Maritime Law Enforcement Power Calling Out for Efficient Unification."

106. See Zhou and Zhang, "From the Perspective of the Establishment of the Maritime Police Bureau."

107. For an explanation of the dual command structure, see "Experts Explain PAP Leadership System: The Dual Command of the State Council and the CMC" [专家详解武警领导体制: 国务院和中央军委双重领导], *People's Daily Online* [人民网], August 27, 2009.

108. Michael D. Swaine et al., *China's Military and the U.S.-Japan Alliance in 2030: A Strategic Net Assessment* (Washington, DC: Carnegie Endowment for International Peace, May 2013), 25.

INDEX

About the Contributors

Tai Ming Cheung is the director of the University of California–wide Institute on Global Conflict and Cooperation (IGCC) and the leader of IGCC's Minerva project, "The Evolving Relationship between Technology and National Security in China: Innovation, Defense Transformation, and China's Place in the Global Technology Order." He is also an Associate Professor at the School of International Relations and Pacific Studies, University of California, San Diego. Dr. Cheung is a longtime analyst of Chinese and East Asian defense and national security affairs, especially defense economic, industrial and science, and technological issues. He is author of *Fortifying China: The Struggle to Build a Modern Defense Economy* (Cornell University Press, 2009), and editor of *Forging China's Military Might: A New Framework for Assessing Science, Technology, and the Role of Innovation* (John Hopkins University Press, 2014).

M. Taylor Fravel is an Associate Professor in the Political Science Department and a member of the Security Studies Program at the Massachusetts Institute of Technology. He is the author of *Strong Borders, Secure Nation: Cooperation and Conflict in China's Territorial Disputes* (Princeton University Press, 2008), and *Active Defense: the Evolution of China's Military Strategy* (forthcoming). Dr. Fravel has contributed many book chapters and articles to journals such as *International Security, China Leadership Monitor,* and *Contemporary Southeast Asia.* He has an M.A. in Philosophy, Politics, and Economics from Oxford University, and an M.Sc. in International Relations from the London School of Economics. He received his Ph.D. from Stanford University.

Bonnie S. Glaser is Senior Adviser for Asia in the Freeman Chair in China Studies, where she works on issues related to Chinese foreign and security policy. She is concomitantly a Senior Associate with CSIS Pacific Forum. From 2003 to mid-2008, Ms. Glaser was a Senior Associate in the CSIS International Security Program. Before joining CSIS, she served as a consultant for various U.S. government offices, including the Departments of Defense and State.

Eric Hagt is currently a Ph.D. candidate at the China Studies Center at Johns Hopkins's School for Advanced International Studies. He was formerly the director of the China Program at the World Security Institute in Washington, DC, and chief editor of *China Security*. He has authored articles and book chapters in publications including *Survival, Journal of Strategic Studies, Naval War College Review,* and *China Security,* and the Johns Hopkins University Press book *Forging China's Military Might.*

Linda Jakobson is an independent researcher and Visiting Professor at the United States Studies Centre at the University of Sydney. From 2011 to 2013 she served as the East Asia Program Director of the Lowy Institute for International Policy. Jakobson lived and worked in China for twenty years and has authored six books on Chinese and East Asian society. The Finnish edition of her book, *A Million Truths: A Decade in China* (M. Evans 1998), won the national nonfiction award. Jakobson has published numerous articles and reports on China's foreign and security policy, China's Arctic aspirations, the Taiwan Strait, China's energy security, and science and technology polices. Her last position in Beijing was Director of the China and Global Security Programme at the Stockholm International Peace Research Institute (SIPRI).

Isaac B. Kardon is a Ph.D. candidate in the Department of Government at Cornell University, and is currently on a Fulbright-Hays award in China conducting dissertation research as a Visiting Scholar at the National Institute for South China Sea Studies. He is an Affiliated Scholar at NYU Law's US-Asia Law Institute, where he contributes to its Track 1.5 Law of the Sea Dialogues; Kardon is also an Adjunct Research Fellow with National Defense University (NDU), and was formerly a Research Analyst with NDU's Center for the Study of Chinese Military Affairs. He holds an M.Phil in Modern Chinese Studies from Oxford University, a B.A. in History from Dartmouth College, and studied Mandarin at Peking University, Taiwan Normal University, and Tsinghua University.

Nan Li is an Associate Professor in the Strategic Research Department of the U.S. Naval War College and a member of its China Maritime Studies Institute. He has published extensively on Chinese security and military policy. His publications include *Chinese Civil-Military Relations in the Post-Deng Era: Implications for Crisis Management and Naval Modernization* (U.S. Naval War College Press, 2010); and "China's Evolving Naval Strategy and Capabilities in the Hu Jintao Era," in *Assessing the People's Liberation Army in the Hu Jintao Era* (U.S. Army War College Press, 2014). Nan Li received a Ph.D. in political science from the Johns Hopkins University.

Alice Miller is a research fellow at the Hoover Institution and lecturer in East Asian Studies at Stanford University. She is editor of the *China Leadership Monitor* and author of *Science and Dissent in Post-Mao China: The Politics of Knowledge* (University of Washington Press, 1996) and, with Richard Wich, of *Becoming Asia: Change and Continuity in Asian International Relations since World War II* (Stanford University Press, 2011).

Phillip C. Saunders is Director of the Center for the Study of Chinese Military Affairs and a Distinguished Research Fellow at the Center for Strategic Research, both part of National Defense University's Institute for National Strategic Studies. Dr. Saunders previously worked at the Monterey Institute of International Studies, where he was Director of the East Asia Nonproliferation Program from 1999 to 2003, and served as an officer in the U.S. Air Force from 1989 to 1994. He is coauthor of *The Paradox of Power: Sino-American Strategic Restraint in an Era of Vulnerability* (NDU Press, 2011) and coeditor of books on China-Taiwan relations, the Chinese navy, and the Chinese air force. Dr. Saunders attended Harvard College and received his MPA and Ph.D. in International Relations from the Woodrow Wilson School at Princeton University.

Andrew Scobell is a Senior Political Scientist at the RAND Corporation. He was previously an Associate Professor of international affairs at the George H. W. Bush School of Government and Public Service at Texas A&M University. He is the author of *China's Use of Military Force: Beyond the Great Wall and the Long March* (Cambridge University Press, 2003) and coauthor of *China's Search for Security* (Columbia University Press, 2012). In addition to editing or coediting twelve books, Dr. Scobell has written dozens of reports, monographs, journal articles, and book chapters. He holds a Ph.D. in political science from Columbia University.

Michael D. Swaine is a Senior Associate at the Carnegie Endowment for International Peace. Previously a Senior Policy Analyst at the RAND Corporation, Swaine specializes in Chinese defense and foreign policy, U.S.-China relations, and East Asian international relations. Among the more than a dozen books he has authored or edited is *America's Challenge: Engaging a Rising China in the Twenty-First Century* (Carnegie Endowment, 2011). Dr. Swaine has also written dozens of book chapters and articles, contributing regularly to journals such as *China Leadership Monitor*. He holds a Ph.D. in government from Harvard University, and was a Postdoctoral Fellow at the Center for Chinese Studies at the University of California at Berkeley.

Christopher D. Yung is a Senior Research Fellow at the Center for the Study of Chinese Military Affairs (CSCMA), Institute for National Strategic Studies, National Defense University. Dr. Yung is the lead author of *"Not an Idea We Need to Shun": Chinese Overseas Basing Requirements in the 21st Century* (NDU Press, 2014), *China's Out of Area Naval Operations: Case Studies, Trajectories, Obstacles and Potential Solutions* (NDU Press, 2010), and "Sinica Rules the Waves: The People's Liberation Army Navy's Power Projection and Anti-Access/Area Denial Lessons from the Falklands/Malvinas Conflict," in *Chinese Lessons From Other People's Wars* (U.S. Army War College, 2011). Before entering government service, Dr. Yung was a Senior Research Analyst at the Center for Naval Analyses (CNA). Dr. Yung holds a Ph.D. in international relations and an M.A. in East Asian and China studies from the Paul H. Nitze School of Advanced International Studies at the Johns Hopkins University.

The authorized representative in the EU for product safety and compliance is:
Mare Nostrum Group
B.V Doelen 72
4831 GR Breda
The Netherlands

www.ingramcontent.com/pod-product-compliance
Lightning Source LLC
Chambersburg PA
CBHW020454270326
41926CB00008B/597